AF478051

Reinventing Japan

Other works by Yasuo Takao

Is Japan Really Remilitarising? The Politics of Norm Formation and Change (2007)

National Integration and Local Power in Japan (1999)

Reinventing Japan
From Merchant Nation to Civic Nation

Yasuo Takao

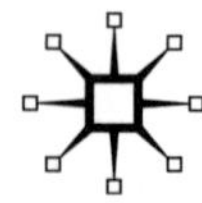

REINVENTING JAPAN
Copyright © Yasuo Takao, 2007.
All rights reserved. No part of this book may be used or reproduced in any manner whatsoever without written permission except in the case of brief quotations embodied in critical articles or reviews.

First published in 2007 by
PALGRAVE MACMILLAN™
175 Fifth Avenue, New York, N.Y. 10010 and
Houndmills, Basingstoke, Hampshire, England RG21 6XS.
Companies and representatives throughout the world.

PALGRAVE MACMILLAN is the global academic imprint of the Palgrave Macmillan division of St. Martin's Press, LLC and of Palgrave Macmillan Ltd. Macmillan® is a registered trademark in the United States, United Kingdom and other countries. Palgrave is a registered trademark in the European Union and other countries.

ISBN-13: 978-1-4039-8414-2
ISBN-10: 1-4039-8414-X

Library of Congress Cataloging-in-Publication Data

Takao, Yasuo.
  Reinventing Japan: from merchant nation to civic nation/Yasuo Takao.
      p. cm.
  Includes bibliographical references and index.
  ISBN 1-4039-8414-X (alk. paper)
  1. Japan—Politics and government—1989– 2. Civil society—Japan. 3. Political participation—Japan. 4. Social capital (Sociology)—Japan. I. Title.

JQ1631.T289 2008
320.952—dc22

                                                                    2007014203

A catalogue record for this book is available from the British Library.

Design by Macmillan India Ltd.

First edition: November 2007

10 9 8 7 6 5 4 3 2 1

Printed in the United States of America.

To the memory of my parents, Misao Takao and Haruo Takao

Contents

List of Figures

List of Tables

Acknowledgments

Japan is experiencing a fundamental transition as part of its modern history. The decade of the 1990s saw the end of the post–World War II era when the Liberal Democratic Party (1955–1993) had brought political stability and economic success to the country and, as a result of which Japan is now in the midst of its greatest social and economic transformation. In the late 1980s, Japanese stock and real estate values skyrocketed and it appeared that the country's state-directed capitalism was eclipsing Western-style capitalism. This time of record-setting prosperity was later identified as the "bubble economy" as Japan's economy suddenly collapsed in 1991. The nation was left economically crippled. The scale of the fall was so startling that there was a "lost decade" of economic stagnation—an image that remains with many Westerners as they recall this developmental state's fall from grace. The October 6, 2005, edition of the *Economist* noted that "Japan [had] mutated from being a giver of lessons to a recipient of lectures." Many observers and scholars have been trying to make sense of the changes within Japan and much has been written recently about the sources of the country's economic stagnation and possible underlying factors including the mistaken macroeconomic policies and the structural decline of the Japanese economy. Also well debated is the structure of the country's economic model. In all this research, it is remarkable that the very positive, sociopolitical consequences of this struggling nation in the lost decade have been largely ignored—until this study. The research embodied in this book commenced in 1997 as part of an attempt to understand the turbulence of Japan in the 1990s, the manner in which it led to a realignment of central-local and state-society power relations, and the very welcome democratization of Japan. As this book will clearly explain, it is this realignment within the relations of power—at national, local government, and grassroots levels—that will determine the face of twenty-first-century Japan.

In writing this book, I have accumulated debts of gratitude to many thoughtful friends and organizations. Many colleagues have given me useful critiques and suggestions in the course of conversations. I would like to mention, in particular, David Edgington, Morris Low, Vera Mackie, Anthony McGrew, John McGuire, and Sandra Wilson. My primary debt is to Hori Masaharu, who has kindly kept me up to date over the past years with the most accurate, reliable information available in Japan. I also especially express my debt to Thomas Schrock, who has wholeheartedly provided me with moral backing.

I would like to thank the Faculty of International Relations at Ritsumeikan University for institutional support, and especially Nakatsuji Keiji for making my research in Japan productive while I was a visiting professor in 2003–2004. I would also like to thank the Department of Social Sciences at Curtin University of Technology in Perth, Western Australia, for a leave of absence that enabled me to continue my research. My special thanks also go to the Australian Research Council (ARC) and Curtin University of Technology for research funding in 2000, 2002, and 2004 that enabled me to conduct research abroad.

The production side of this book would not have proceeded far without the editorial assistance of Sue Summers. Her professional skills at putting complex pieces of my manuscript together contributed to the completion of this book. I am also particularly grateful for the generous support of the Centre for Advanced Studies in Australia, Asia and the Pacific (CASAAP) at Curtin University of Technology.

The first portion of this book draws upon many of my earlier publications including "Participatory Democracy in Japan's Decentralization Drive," *Asian Survey* 38, no. 10 (1998), © The Regents of the University California; "Welfare State Retrenchment–The Case of Japan," *Journal of Public Policy* 19, no. 3 (1999), © Cambridge University Press; "The Rise of the Third Sector in Japan," *Asian Survey* 41, no. 2 (2001), © The Regents of the University California; "Foreigners' Rights in Japan: Beneficiaries to Participants," *Asian Survey* 43, no. 3 (2003), © The Regents of the University California; "Democratic Renewal by 'Digital' Local Government in Japan," *Pacific Affairs* 77, no. 2 (2004), © University of British Columbia; "Co-Governance by Local Government and Civil Society Groups in Japan: Balancing Equity and Efficiency for Trust in Public Institutions," *The Asian Pacific Journal of Public Administration* 28, no. 2 (2006), © University of Hong Kong; and "Japanese Women in Grassroots Politics: Building a Gender Equal Society from the Bottom-Up," *The Pacific Review* 20, no. 2 (2007), © Taylor & Francis.

Finally, my wife, Susan Takao, has played an important part in providing research assistance, critical commentary, and professional editing. For their patience and moral support, I also thank my daughter, Maia, and my son, Makoto.

A Note on Conventions

Japanese personal names throughout the text are presented in Japanese form, that is, with the surname followed by the given name, in reversal of standard Western practice. In making references, I have also referred to Japanese authors in the same manner: surnames first. Newspaper citations refer to morning editions, or else are specifically cited.

Introduction: Civil Society and Local Government

Kenji was born April 7, 1961, in Kurashiki city, Okayama prefecture, a local town about an hour and a half by train from Osaka. His father belonged to the generation that had selflessly supported the state-led economic advances in postwar Japan. Although mentally scarred by the war, Kenji's father continued to work in the same factory, a car parts supplier for Mazda, for some 40 years until his retirement. Given the conventions of the time, he felt compelled to do so and never expressed his thoughts on the matter. However, he provided the encouragement and financial support for his son Kenji to be part of the first generation to gain a university education. When Kenji graduated from a prestigious university in Kyoto, he had the freedom to move away from the monotonous and oppressive convention of "the loyal company worker" that had shaped his father's life.

Today, Kenji works fractional hours as a copywriter, and spends much time with his children. His flexible work hours enable household work sharing with his wife, Sachiko, who is also employed outside the home. Kenji has a personal commitment to buying environment-friendly products. In the area in which he lives, the municipal government has pledged to build and to hand over a playground to the local community group, which, in turn, has promised to maintain it as a safe place for the children. Kenji is an enthusiastic participant in weekly community meetings and has helped to create a self-management plan of the proposed playground. Clearly, Kenji has a love of children and a passion for education. He is not only involved with ongoing Parent Teacher Association (PTA) programs that encourage the success of every child, but also coordinates a project for providing picture books (translated in native languages by volunteers) to children in developing countries. He expressed his broad support of collective needs and issues, when he told me, "Japan has been a peace-loving country in isolation. It is too self-centered to be understood and accepted by others."[1]

In the early twenty-first century, the "local living sphere"—which embraces both the home and its immediate environment—is in transition from a state-centric to a societal space. This book is about the merging forces of civil society in Japan as experienced by ordinary people in their day-to-day lives. Analysis of this important new phenomenon helps shed light on the changing nature of state–civil society relations and the role of local governments in promoting an autonomous civil society. It also reveals the relationship between civil society groups and local government as a key element in Japan's changing structures of governance. To this end, I examine such key issue areas as decentralization, e-democracy, and the manner in which foreign intervention, voluntarism, and the role played by women have converged to form a new national identity and to open the way for the reinvention of Japan in the passage of time from the beginning of World War II (WWII) to the early twenty-first century. The findings strongly indicate that the expansion of associational life in Japan is heading toward a more autonomous civil society.

The shining image of Japan as an "economic miracle" is embedded in the collective narratives of its past successes. Yet Japanese prosperity experienced a long-lasting slump in the 1990s, a decade that was called the "lost decade" by the country's mass media. The findings in this study suggest that to describe this pivotal point in time as "lost" is to miss the crucial accounts of a new nexus of forces in Japan, all poised at the crossroads of fundamental change. Previously, there had been two major turning points in the history of modern Japan: the arrival of Western technology in the late nineteenth century and the Allied Occupation of 1945–1952. It is my view that Japan is now facing a third turning point with the rise of "global" linkages. While these linkages emerge from problems commonly experienced at a global level, it is important to this study to articulate how the consequences of such shared problems are experienced and dealt with at a local level. It is also important to note, in this particular context, that the rapid changes experienced in many Japanese communities are outpacing changes within national policy. To offset the uncertain impact of change, various local communities in Japan have been building up local resources as a means of enhancing their local ability or governance to solve problems and to plan for their future. It is interesting how this merchant nation's fall from grace in recent years has facilitated a major realignment of state-society power relations primarily derived from local initiatives and innovation to bring about democratizing effects. The degree to which this realignment is realized will determine the direction of twenty-first-century Japan.

Historical Survey

It is central to my argument that direct demands for individual control over life choices emerge within the local living sphere. This sphere is more than people's immediate environment; it is also formed by their relationship to the activities they are engaged in, their relationship to production and consumption, their contribution to the continuity and protection of public services, and their degree of self-management and control over the choices that shape their lives. As local living spheres have undergone considerable change within the history of Japan, it is critically important to identify the historical specificity of state-society relations and to empirically examine the applicability of concepts of civil society—primarily founded on the historical experience of the West—to the individuals represented within this study.

In feudal Japan the local lords controlled fiefs and demanded loyalty and feudal dues from the peasants; in exchange, the peasants sought the protection of their agricultural produce. Villagers were more concerned about the immediate environment in which they lived, than about more anonymous and universalistic interests, and formed their own associations, solved their problems locally, and collectively negotiated with local lords over feudal taxes. So while the local living sphere was to a large degree an imposed institution where class mobility was impossible, the villagers were able to develop their own associational way of life as a community group. Most village groups remained beyond the reach of the Tokugawa shogunate, a feudal military dictatorship that ruled from Edo (the *de facto* capital of Japan), and enjoyed a sphere of autonomy.

The urban living sphere of Japan began to emerge in the sixteenth century with the forced resettlement of samurai and the subsequent relocation of their markets around the castles of their lords. In the same time frame these *joka machi* (castle towns) were converted from military outposts into administrative and commercial centers for mobilizing local resources.[2] By the seventeenth century, the castle towns began to secure control over surrounding territories and serve as the hub of market networks that bound surrounding villages together. The feudal dues paid by peasants were part of a network of control that politically bound villages to local lords. However, the peasants retained a measure of autonomy by bartering and trading with each other in their own marketplace. Village officials were mostly peasants rather than members of the governing class and would identify with the interests of their villages when dealing with magistrates and implementing their orders. Village officials would strategically serve the interests of the village by protecting cooperative living among villagers as they protected the interests of the local lords in the feudal domain. This helped the villages to retain ownership of common lands and to provide facilities for mutual aid that enabled the continuity of peasant life within its own immediate circle.[3] In contrast, local lords—along with any help they could provide—remained remote and unaware of the problems of villagers. Although not equivalent to the contemporary notion of voluntarism as such, the villagers had no choice but to rely on self-help and to resort to associations based upon mutual aid.[4]

Feudal Japan did not constitute a spatially unitary hierarchy but comprised parallel hierarchies of various sizes ranging from the family through the village and the feudatory to the shogunate.[5] The Meiji Restoration of 1868 was the point of departure for shaping and molding a different kind of local living sphere while building a modern state and hastening the development of capitalism. Japan was obviously a latecomer in comparison with other nations, yet it showed its own particular pattern of development when Meiji state and business interests joined closely together to catch up with the technologically advanced nations of the West. State interventions in Japan helped to shape the thoughts and attitudes of the general public to ensure the development of a cohesive polity capable of hastening the modernization of the country with minimal opposition. The state and market expanded in an inextricable way and the autonomous space of a civil society that lay outside of state and market forces became very narrow as experienced by people in the local living sphere of their day-to-day lives.

The centrality of each local sphere came to a sudden end in 1871 with the Meiji Restoration, which abolished the feudal domains previously existing as multifarious centers and drew boundaries around their frontier areas. The central Meiji government, being the sole national center, tried to build a single-layered sphere of central-local relations. The first step in its state-building effort was to create a set of institutions to facilitate the central government's intervention into the affairs of local communities. The power to tax was placed completely under central control. For purposes of compulsory conscription, the *koseki* (household register) was established to keep official records of the population. The *buraku* (indigenous natural groups at the grassroots level), who lived in their own strongly cohesive circles in accordance with traditional rules and customs, virtually remained intact in Meiji Japan, but the Meiji government tactically used group cohesiveness to place localities under state control.[6] These efforts to build the Meiji local government system began with the intention to deny local communities independent status and to treat them as purely administrative units.[7] This state activism resulted in the "state-ification" of local communities and undermined the cohesion of voluntary activities that had been flourishing in various communities in feudal Japan. Yet the single-layered sphere imposed in the Meiji Reformation was far from complete as liberal intellectuals resisted this national undertaking[8] and there was strong resistance from village people, who believed the forced amalgamations would impair a historically established zone of "natural" functions.[9] Nonetheless, the local living sphere became a state-centric space that revolved around the implementation of national programs as the state purposefully combined its functions with the private functions of individuals in their communities.[10] For example, a spiritual mobilization, which was sought by national leaders to inspire the local populace for the promotion of imperial nationalism, was instituted to encourage people to increase their savings, to use their goods efficiently, and to work diligently, and it proved to be an effective mode of state-ification for keeping the masses under control. Overall, the Meiji political system was crafted to ensure an effective government for the purposes of building the state with minimal opposition in order to catch up with Western powers. Meiji leaders accordingly took state-building initiatives to assure the survival, security, and prosperity of Japan. In this respect, they were largely successful.

Japan's military defeat in 1945 led to the decline of the political legitimacy of state interventions into the local living sphere. The Allied Occupation of Japan was an unprecedented event in the history of Japan during the course of which Occupation officials attempted to transplant Western ideas and values into this non-Western culture. Basically, the Occupation was an all-American affair in which General Douglas MacArthur was driven by a strong sense of duty, augmented by his sense of idealism, to decentralize Japan's political system and to promote the participation of local communities. As a result, freedom of association was fully guaranteed, tenant farmers became owners of three-quarters of the country, and newly elected local authorities began to act as representatives of localities rather than as agents of the state. Nonetheless, in the midst of this Occupation-led environment, Japanese national bureaucrats were still able to perpetuate state activism and developmentalism under the national goal of industrialization. Local associational life continued primarily with exclusive neighborhood associations as opposed to inclusive, nonresidential voluntary associations with the capacity to bring like-minded individuals together.[11] Neighborhood associations helped to create networks of communal solidarity but tended to confer benefits only to members. This exclusivity would involve risks of undermining the social cohesion of local communities.

Following the Occupation and during the high-growth period of the 1960s, there was broad national consensus in relation to industrialization. Civil society consisted predominantly of producer-led associations such as business, labor, and agricultural associational establishments that had been institutionalized during the late 1950s and 1960s at a national level.[12] This proved to be of considerable help to the fierce determination of Japanese leaders to catch up with Western powers—a determination that had neither died with the end of WWII nor with the introduction of Occupation authority–initiated democratization. Such determination was evident in the goals and strategies pursued by postwar leaders after 1945 when collective briefs in industrialization were widely shared among national elites and local populations. It was visible, for example, within specific patterns of local decision making where democratically elected local administrations strove to meet local priorities at the same time as reflecting the agendas of nationally led regional developments.[13] In the process, local decision making was depoliticized in a cohesive manner and made consistent with the national setting of developmental priorities. Tactically, the national government placated those in the local living sphere by extending to local populations the same material benefits accorded to those on an income tax base within the country's high-growth environment.[14] In tandem, elected local authorities were afforded a measure of local flexibility—a strategic arrangement that was accommodated by national agencies.

By the late 1960s, the results of the country's pro-development priority proved to be unsatisfactory and failed to live up to the expectations of the Japanese people. This was accompanied by growing environmental concerns and issues, and discontented residents pressured their local leaders to place life-oriented needs above the country's developmental needs. Thus, local decision making was politicized—albeit erratically, unsystematically, and often incompletely—as citizens increasingly exhorted elected local authorities to reassess national government policies, particularly its pro-development priority. By the late 1960s, there were sudden increases in local interest group activities with progressive candidates winning more mayoral and gubernatorial elections. In general, local decision making was driven by localized initiatives and policy innovations, yet this decision making was still largely reactive to, and therefore conjoined with, national government inaction and/or the policies and projects arising from national government initiatives.[15] A key dimension of local decision making was that local authorities collaborated with local interest groups to make the national government accountable for national undertakings, or to ensure local needs in the form of vertical central-local relations rather than horizontal arrangements in which local authorities forged partnerships with other local bodies for local governance. Thus, the local living sphere remained state-centric in this regard.

Japan's high economic growth ended in the early 1970s with the 1973 decision to dramatically increase social security benefits having critical implications for the future management of public finances.[16] One of the priorities of government spending was the automatic and incremental expansion of entitlements. A new phase emerged in the 1975 fiscal year when the national government was forced by falling tax revenues for the first time in the years following WWII to issue deficit-covering bonds to finance the government deficit.[17] Once in place, such an expansionary welfare state system was destined to face an additional wave of financial difficulties that would ultimately lead to financial cutbacks. By the 1980s, the governments of nearly all advanced democratic nations were stretched beyond their capacity and were struggling to perform their expanded tasks despite their resort to deficit financing.[18] It was in this decade that the Japanese government shifted its policy objectives from expansion to cutbacks, which was to create a new movement within state-society dynamics. Prior to this point, both civic and voluntary associations in Japan were largely understood to be in opposition to the state. For example, ideology-oriented citizens' movements in the 1960s were often explicitly described as "anti-state" and as "anti-big business." However, the Japanese government of the 1980s began to recognize that the state could benefit from cooperation with voluntary associations that had been pursuing public purposes beyond the reach of the state. This signaled the start of a state-led process to tap societal initiatives and creativity, while pointing to the national government's recognition of its own failure to prevent the worsening of taxpayers' position and its inability to prevent any further erosion.[19] This was also part of a worldwide pattern of governance that was witnessing a continued decline in public trust in government among almost all the advanced industrial democracies.[20] Throughout the 1990s, conservatives in the advanced industrial democracies favored business-enterprise approaches to the provision of public services. In Japan, this economic rationalism, which was intended to bring the national government back into favor, was far from meeting the immediate needs of local communities. This discouraging reality of market-driven reform stimulated further rethinking about the requirements for the role played by civil society between state and market forces. In July 1993, the Liberal Democratic Party (LDP) was thrown out of power after 38 years in office. This event led to continued political realignments and sparked a heated debate over how to reinvent Japan in a politically and socially innovative way. The 1995 Hanshin-Awaji earthquake, which killed over 6,000 people, proved to be a turning point when the rescue operations exposed the inflexibility and incompetence of the state vis-à-vis the versatility and contribution of civil society. The overwhelming response to the catastrophe by community groups was reported widely by the mass media and helped raise public awareness about their importance. As will be discussed in chapter 3, this sociopolitical climate led to a three-year process of negotiations among citizens' groups, government officials, and political parties to introduce new legislation that would enable citizens' groups to obtain corporate status with simple procedures. The Law for the Promotion of Specific Nonprofit Activities (commonly known as the NPO Law) was passed unanimously in March 1998. When this law came into effect in December, the number of volunteers more than quadrupled—from 1.6 million in 1980 to 6.9 million in 1998.[21] The 1990s was a benchmark decade in the rise of civic associations.

One result that holds an especial appeal for the Japanese people has been a newfound interest in the engagement of individual citizens at the grassroots level, a form of governance that has been significantly assisted by local governments.[22] In recent years, Japanese local governments have been seen as separate from the national government, indeed increasingly regarded as an alternative to central authority by those who pursue public purposes unaided by the national government.[23] Independently elected local governments have sought to decentralize and disperse state power, to encourage inclusive participation by local communities, and to ensure the safety and health of individuals in local communities.

The rise of local government in Japan has not been independent of further involvement in the local living sphere. Local residents have increasingly enjoyed social over economic priorities as part of a shift in priorities from production to consumption. Yet this has raised a political problem for local residents, particularly in regard to being able to meet their immediate needs such as education, food safety, garbage disposal, a healthy and clean living environment, and safety. This is a critical point for decision making about what to consume that goes beyond the choices of private, self-interested, and cost-minimizing and wealth-maximizing individuals and entails the increased penetration of private space by public space, such as environmentally responsible consumers and domestic violence awareness. To this extent, political functions are socialized, with the loci of political dynamics residing at the local level with society rather than at the national level of the state.

In Japan, global issues such as cross-border environmental degradation and international migration have also brought a new dimension to local communities. In the field of these global issues, policies are primarily national, but the consequences are dealt with by local communities. Without argument, the impact of globalization is both widespread and particular: its manifestations are multiple, rapid, and concretized in local communities in Japan and elsewhere. It is particularly problematic that the consequences of external forces, such as environmental degradation and labor migration, for example, can outpace the reach of national policies. In Japan, this has propelled a shift in the focus of problem solving from the state to individual citizens unable to escape the consequences of globalization and who have tended to suffer the most. In this context it is believed that independently elected local governments hold the most promise of protecting the rights and welfare of the individual and can act in partnership with civil society groups in the local living sphere. As detailed in chapter 5, there are signs of increasing co-governing by local government and civil society groups in Japan as a means of enhancing the efficacy of local decision making, investments, and collective actions as part of future planning. In this dynamic, the local living sphere is again instrumental in shaping the experience of ever-widening civic participation.

One further development in the 1990s that helps explain the recent surge of civil influence in Japan is the dramatic revolution in information and communication technologies (ICTs). On the one hand, the information-based economy in Japan is driven by economic rationalism that prioritizes private property, private profits, and the market.[24] The use of ICT technologies is clearly directed to commercial benefits and consumer convenience, yet it also compels civil society to adapt to the logic of the globalizing knowledge-based economy. The exclusive nature and scope of national economic policies is such that the national government has remained more accessible to a much wider range of ICT-induced commercial interests. On the other hand, the information society in Japan is inherently more capable than the national government alone of promoting civility, inclusive participation, and social cohesion. Overall, ICTs have many potential roles in the development of social relations as a whole[25] with civil society groups believing that ICTs and knowledge production should enhance knowledge and understandings within the wider society, broaden and deepen individuals' participation in the development of social relations, and lead to a reduction in inequalities and social exclusion. The downside is that ICT access tends to be too personalized for individual interests to be effectively integrated into wider social relations. However, as discussed in chapter 6, in permeating the "local living sphere," ICTs do help to transcend individual differences and integrate them into the wider social domain through their appeal to a common social base.

The Approach

The two key concepts in this book—civil society and the local living sphere—have the capacity to draw a number of observations into the same political dynamics. The conceptualization of civil society offers a distinct and effective lens to examine the manner in which Japanese citizens/people involve themselves in broader political, social, and economic relations. As the concept of civil society is both contested and ambiguous, it is necessary to understand the historical evolution of civil societies in order to define its strict boundaries, and to embrace its wide range of actors, for it to be a consistent and useful tool in a cross-national perspective. It is equally important to distinguish between civil society as an analytical concept and civil society as part of the real life–world phenomena that is inextricably intertwined within and around the experiences of individual citizens. As figure 0.1 illustrates, individual citizens fulfill a multitude of

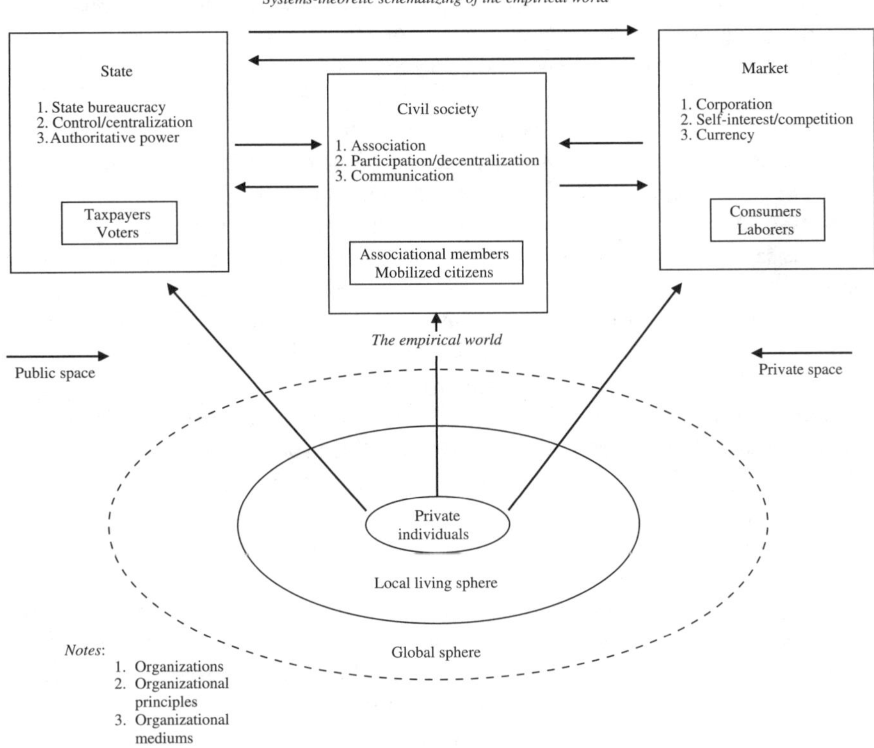

Figure 0.1   Civil society and the local living sphere.

functions, with civil society as just one of those functional spaces. Any individual is likely to be a taxpayer, voter, civil servant, volunteer, consumer, employee, and producer—either simultaneously or at different stages of the life cycle. These multilayered roles are part and parcel of each individual and lend themselves to the development of civic engagement and participation while helping to strengthen civil society and link the state with the market. For this reason, the local living sphere is both a concept and an inclusive and empirical social practice with the capacity to identify and understand immediate issues and problems as they emerge at the grassroots level. It is also a source of local and face-to-face engagement that is the primary driving force for building a trust-based civil society.

Over the past decades, the promise of socialism has been discredited and the efficacy of the modern welfare state has become increasingly unviable. These discouraging realities have continually generated pressures for correcting state failures with antistatist market rationalism widespread among advanced democracies. Yet understandings driven by economic rationalism alone are far from clear in how best to address the failures of the state. Furthermore, state and market failures have opened the way for an upsurge in organized voluntary action in Japan and around the globe.[26] Activists have called for strengthening of civil society and ordinary citizens have helped to take matters into their own hands by pursuing needs and objectives outside the state and market reach.

Such issues and dynamics lend themselves to a working definition of civil society. It is common today for most theorists to use the term "civil society" as a collectively active sphere closely connected to the legal, associational, and public institutions of society independent of the market as well as of the state.[27] As civil society is seen to be autonomous of both state authority and the private actors of corporate firms and families, it can be envisaged as a sphere in which "social actors pursue neither profit within the market nor power within the state."[28] Nonetheless, neoliberals and some neo-Marxists provide a number of arguments and approaches for the market economy to be included within civil society. The first approach tends to see the self-regulating market as a source of social cohesion and to reaffirm the importance of depoliticized society organized apart from the state. In this view, civil society is the sphere of private associations identifying the freedom of civil society with that of the market. It is part of a pervasive historical perspective that a free market is crucial for building civil society apart from the state, yet this intellectual tradition tends to neglect, or even reject, the role of social movements that could lead the state to redistribute economic resources for ensuring social equity.[29] There is the strong possibility that a self-regulating market left to itself in the private sphere is likely to have destructive effects on civil society, such as increased inequalities and weaker solidarity.

The second approach, recognizing these destructive effects, argues that economic activities in civil society are politicized by class relations and modes of production, and proposes some forms of socially steered economy.[30] One of the most influential class theorists, Antonio Gramsci, tended to utilize categories of analysis that viewed the market economy separately from civil society by adopting a tripartite division of state, society, and market. In a similar vein, the Gramscians, utilizing a structuralist analysis of the dominance of the ruling class, argue the tripartite division to be based upon coercive state power that reinforces a class-based civil society and structures the market economy. The Gramscians claim there is no such thing as civil society independent of the state and corporate power. They see civil society to be largely co-opted by the state and believe that corporate power ultimately dominates state policymaking.

The studies presented in this book do not support these sweeping arguments. Rather, this book focuses precisely on the pluralist discourse of civil society, that is, the non-class-based forms of collective action related to associational and public institutions of society that are formed outside the state and the market. To examine the flowering of civil society activism, it is not useful, and even misleading, to conceive civil society as the entirety of sociocultural life outside the state and the market economy. It is necessary to this argument that civil society can be identified either with "sustained, organized social activity that occurs in groups"[31] or with "the extent that these (the structures of socialization, association, and organized forms of communication of the lifeworld) are institutionalized or in the process of being institutionalized."[32] In line with the argument of Alexis de Tocqueville that the essence of democracy is founded on active participation,[33] this book argues that modern civil society is based on the structure of egalitarian and politically relevant associations rather than the civic culture of apathetic and apolitical individualism. Civic engagement and participation are politically relevant to the extent that ordinary citizens are capable of influencing the central state system through the articulation of their personal interests within the public arena. In this respect, political parties and parliamentarians are required to aggregate and represent a wide range of interests in political processes and, in doing so, become mediators between civil society and the central state. It is a dynamic concept in which internal change emerges as a key issue for reinvigorating and defending the autonomy of civil society. Particularly important are the social movements that continually enliven and rejuvenate civic culture.[34] Nonetheless, our conception of civil society does not embrace the view that social movements will replace representative democracy but instead sees civic engagement as a means of changing existing civil society structures and complementing the institutional arrangements of representative democracy. Today, most theorists agree that in pursuing both private and public goals and objectives, civil society organizations are politically relevant to the interests of the state. To help explain the interface between civil society and state, Tocqueville proposed "political society" as an overarching political sphere that mediates between the sphere of civil society and the sphere of the state. However, his conception of civil society was too narrow to recognize the possibility of a public sphere within civil society.[35] When broader, yet clearly defined boundaries between the sphere of civil society and the sphere of the state are drawn, the notion of "political society" appears more as an unnecessary category of public sphere. In an advanced democracy, publicly elected representatives, political parties, and elections all help to aggregate and foreground certain social interests and, in the process, mediate politically between civil society and state authority. To this end, they typically reside and compete to assume power within the realm of the state. In contrast, other politically influential actors such as public interest groups, the mass media, and public opinion do not generally seek to seize state power or to replace existing state agents with their own agents. Although such actors may create a shift of emphasis toward institutionalization and a movement-oriented civil society, they still remain within the sphere of civil society rather than the realm of the state. There are exceptions, but it is important to see civil society as a functional sphere in which some actors may cross the boundary into another sphere in order to pursue multiple and shifting organizational goals.[36] There are also actors who will be active within a number of functional spaces as local governments remain a part of the state apparatus, operate within a structure of political constraints and opportunities, and are a potential partner of civil society groups. This is evident with advocacy-oriented civil society groups that often depend vertically upon the resource mobilization and political opportunities that local governments can provide through their connection to the national government. Here is an example of how local governments mediate the relations of civil society groups with the central state. Yet, at the same time, independently elected local governments have the capacity to work horizontally and to share responsibilities for local governance with civil society groups when they are not co-opted by the state. In this respect, they exist apart from the central state and can be considered an actor within the realm of civil society. This understanding, which will be empirically assessed in the following chapters, suggests that the inclusion of local governments in civil society serves to enhance opportunities for civic engagement and participation.

The merit of including local governments in civil society can also be presumed on the basis of a number of theoretical understandings:

1. There is no a priori reasoning why local governments established by the state might not be included as actors in civil society if offered the opportunity to work with civil society groups. It is true that local government is normally seen as part of the state apparatus and that the majority of scholars consider it to lie outside of civil society. Yet, as the state takes responsibility for an increasing range of provisions, its organization becomes more complex and the fragmentation of its apparatus becomes more visible. There is no single and cohesive state interest that can monitor all aspects of policy including its implementation by state agents. Even in the most hierarchical areas of the state system, the delegation of decision-making power to lower levels of government is inevitable.[37] Thus, there is some separation between local governments and the central state. Jonah Levy also argues for the inclusion of independently elected local authorities within the realm of civil society. He points to the decentralization reforms in France in the early 1980s where local governments—widely seen as an alternative to the state—were designed explicitly to bolster civil society by bringing power within the reach of ordinary citizens.[38]

2. There are local governments that do not have a predominance of coercive power over residents, yet they retain the potential to horizontally organize all social networks, associations, and community solidarity, and thereby reduce nationally imposed administrative relations, by societal steering at a local level. This capacity for societalization by local governments merits their inclusion in civil society. Furthermore, the concept of a state that can monopolize the use of coercive power[39] is unrealistic, for state power is dispersed throughout increasingly complex subsystems including local governments. Assertive local governments collaborating with community groups have less incentive to wield power over individual residents or to maintain general obedience to national commands. Given the historical specificity of Japan's centralized state power that disorganized voluntary social networks and associations in the past, I would argue that the societalization of local governments is one of the most potentially fertile ways of promoting the proliferation of civic engagement.

3. Local government is not an exclusive service provider, but can deliver better services by engaging voluntary organizations and community groups

in trust-based partnership arrangements. The attributes of service providers of local administration and the recipients as citizens appear to be mutually exclusive. In the historical past, there is no doubt that public administration was an exclusive organization that attempted to monopolize the provision of certain services such as education and public health. Citizens, in turn, demanded not only improved services but also that their voices be heard. In totality, government and citizens can, and do, share responsibilities for pursuing public purposes particularly given the fact that it is citizens who provide local administration with information, who oversee the provision of services, and who participate in the delivery of services. In this clear dimension of the societalization of local government, it can be seen that local government does not exclusively monopolize the resources of a specific authority or its finances and does not compete to assume power within the state.

A stronger civil society does not necessarily ensure democracy. Democracy building in civil society is not automatic. Even in mature democracies, some observers argue that the multiplication of special interests has undermined the workings of representative democracy and has continually influenced and distorted decision making in favor of better-organized interests. In the Japanese context, the possible source of cohesion amid this undue distortion lies in the peculiar role of local government in the local living sphere where the three functional spaces of the state, civil society, and the market are intricately interconnected. First, because independently elected local governments, through their connections to the national government, are empowered to disperse some degree of political power among ordinary citizens as opposed to special interest groups. This is another indication of the manner in which local governments mediate between civil society groups and the central state. Second, local governments are able to raise public awareness of the civic duty of individuals to participate in community decision making in a responsible manner. Thus, local residents are not mere recipients of public services, but are expected to pursue public purposes and to share a number of responsibilities with local authorities in community affairs. In this respect, local governments facilitate civic participation and can also be seen as actors in civil society. Third, in order to meet the immediate need of consumption requirements as opposed to production priorities in the local population,[40] local governments tend to attribute social responsibility for creating higher standards of living in the community to the marketplace. To this end, they encourage investors, consumers, and employees to demand corporate transparency and accountability as part of its social responsibility.

State, civil society, and market each consists of a body of private persons who will function in each of these spheres. Most will be consumers who, given information about price and quality, will make purchasing decisions and consume goods and services in the marketplace. Some may also belong to a self-help service provider in civil society, such as Oxfam, that will boycott sweatshop goods, and may buy "no sweat" goods. Others may belong to a civil society advocacy group mobilized to lobby for information disclosure legislation concerning consumer goods and services, and thus may wish to be informed consumers. In the above-mentioned examples, the local living sphere is the realm of citizens' involvement in both the market and civil society; these two dimensions of private persons' behavior are inextricable to the extent that private persons are motivated by ethics and values as well as material benefits. Citizens' involvement in the local living sphere also concerns the public world of the state. When citizens vote for representatives, their voting behavior will be influenced by a number of interests other than those as consumers and associational members. For example, in relation to production, they may elect a person who will represent the interests of laborers within the realm of the state. They are then in a better position to sell labor power and bargain—individually or collectively—through the unions for better wages and working conditions in the marketplace. They may also participate in labor strikes, which need to be guaranteed by the state and accepted by others in civil society. Therefore, the local living sphere is a reflection of private persons' involvement overlapping and interconnected with the spheres of state, civil society, and market.

Nonetheless, neither state nor market forces currently working in public interest in the areas of health, safety, and welfare appear to be actively engaged with the concerns and objectives of the local living sphere. Over the past two decades or so, the mechanism of state protection for public safety and welfare that had been established by the 1950s in major industrialized countries no longer seems to be effectively functioning. During the late 1980s and 1990s, a search for new ways to ensure public safety and welfare helped lead to the formation of economic rationalism in those countries. Yet the consequences of state policies that subordinate all social needs to the market have come at the expense of social equity. The existing structural frameworks of state power and market forces underpinning public safety and welfare have become less relevant in solving day-to-day problems of the day in the local living sphere. Without denying the fundamental necessity of state power and market forces, it is nevertheless important to recognize that organizations in civil society compensate for those areas in which the state and the market have failed to meet societal needs. It is the inclusive and participatory approaches in civil society that are proving to be more viable. The protection of the environment, for example, is being met more by civil society and less by the market price mechanism and the system of state policies. At an early stage of industrial pollution, the interests and obligations of the polluters (manufacturers) and victims (local residents) appear to be causally distinctive and mutually exclusive. However, when taking into account that pollution is a byproduct of both production and mass consumption, the distinction between offender and victim begins to blur. At a fundamental level, citizens within a civil society must act together to change their consumption patterns so as not to pollute the local living sphere. Irrespective of what is happening within the market and state policies, there is still the need to exercise responsibility at a community level. This ethic, and subsequent practice, is just as necessary in an aging society where the long-term care of the elderly will require community-based voluntary services to be able to give personalized attention to those in need. This is a crucial part of aged-care services that neither standardized government programs nor private for-profit organizations are able to provide. In these important policy areas, local government may act, not as an exclusive service provider, but as a partner of civil society groups for sharing public responsibilities. This lends itself to a trust-based partnership between local government and civil society groups where decisions are optimally made in accord with the various needs of individual citizens and action taken at a community level.

Such participatory approaches focus on the fulfillment of public interests, needs, and purposes, yet public and private interests are not necessarily mutually exclusive in civil society. Nevertheless, Hannah Arendt, a German political theorist, highlights the importance of separation of the public sphere (political life) from the private sphere (family) by arguing that "society," as a sphere of mediation between public and private, disturbs the integrity and autonomy of the public and private spheres.[41] She fails to recognize that the normative ideas of the public sphere are compatible with the actual interpenetration of the public and private spheres as a product of modernity.[42] To have a better understanding of the historical evolution of the public sphere, Jürgen Habermas, one of the most influential scholars of critical theory, has proposed a societal notion of the public sphere, as contrasted with the state-centric public sphere.[43] In his view, the public sphere is best seen as the place of private persons who join together through public discourse and articulate interests for the betterment of civil society. He believes the public sphere to be degraded when public opinion is constrained by the increasing influence of the state and the market. Habermas does not present a methodology for institutions within advanced societies to unify the deliberative exchange of communication and to ensure democracy building as an integral part of debate among private persons. As I will discuss in chapter 6, the use of ICTs has a potential for unifying communicative actions and strengthening democracy. ICT-based technological mediation is already constructing new forms of participatory democracy in the public sphere and it is local governments that are best equipped to accommodate this participation as part of civil society. Finally, the interpenetration of the public and private spheres has been strongly evident in a socially mobilized society. Gendered approaches to civil society see the public sphere to be male dominated, and clearly the nature and scope of both public and private spheres, and the divide within and across these spheres, will need to be reevaluated within civil society to ensure fair obligations and rewards for both women and men. The feminist movements of the past did affect change within the social opportunities open to women as they strove to make changes within their domestic and private lives and their interactions with the public sphere. At this point, it is the fluidity of women's interactions between private and public spheres that needs to be further enabled and articulated within civil society.

The Main Text of This Book

As a researcher and social scientist, I am primarily interested in potential sources of social cohesion and prosperity that derive from decision-making processes within the reach of ordinary citizens. This book focuses on societal and local institutions, and, more especially, independently elected local governments. The value of this focused study is to elucidate the manner in which the extended role of Japanese local governments intersects with many issues at the heart of state-society relations. This focus, while valuable in studying the broad perspective, also delves into the dynamics of the developmental processes in civil society. The vitality of Japan's civil society is emerging at the grassroots level where local populations are neither effectively co-opted by the state nor sweepingly swallowed up by business enterprises in the era of globalization.

The first part of the book, chapters 1–5, provides a structural survey of the circumstances under which the forces of civil society are emerging at the grassroots level in Japan. The second part of the book, chapters 6–8, explores the patterns and direction of civil society in Japan by examining selected key areas at the local level.

Chapter 1 illuminates the influence of cultural dispositions or widely shared briefs, not reducible to individuals alone, on the formation of civil society. This chapter examines the formation of norms, amid changes within national security, which have been constructed and reconstructed under the umbrella of pacifism, the key symbol of Japan's collective identity. Central to this chapter is a major shift in understandings of shared values and identity that paved the way toward proactive pacifism in the 1990s, an identity that became embodied at the grassroots level, and has since been associated with specific civic values such as participation and voluntarism.

By the 1980s Japan, like nearly all Organisation for Economic Co-operation and Development (OECD) member countries, had no choice but to resort to deficit financing given stagnant tax revenues combined with public demand for additional and improved public services. Faced with the fiscal crisis, the Japanese government fully committed itself to fiscal reconstruction through spending cutbacks. Chapter 2 examines the impact of welfare state retrenchment on local communities in Japan. The Japanese national government has not been successful in setting limits on local financial discretion and it has been found that consumption interests are most effectively organized at the local level as it is far easier for consumers of public services to press their demands on the closest agency responsible for providing them.

This book raises pressing questions. How can local communities ensure the sustainability of community development and service provision? How can local authorities perform effectively and be accountable for consumption-oriented community needs? In the chapters that follow, I will provide a detailed description of Japan's pathways to enhance local ability or governance to solve community problems and plan for the future.

This social renewal is not only about localities affirming their right to decide how they should be governed and financed, but is also about promoting individual residents' rights to benefits and their obligations to civic participation. Chapter 3 first describes the circumstances under which citizens' voluntary associations have arisen in Japan. It then examines the nature of these voluntary organizations and the role they expect to fill, and finally, assesses their potential impact on political processes and social life. This grassroots activism represents not just a major institutional wisdom produced by welfare state retrenchment but also an inevitable development evolving out of the failures of the existing sectors.

Today, the loss of efficacy within the old strategies of national unity and centralization is apparent in decentralization drives. Chapter 4 focuses upon decentralization from the perspective of the local living sphere and assesses the institutional capacity of local governments and groups to meet the preferences of local populations through civic engagement and participation. It also looks at how local institutions and groups have taken matters into their own hands through local initiatives to help counter central government inaction. Efforts at the local level have been particularly concerned with gaining a measure of autonomy for local residents. In practice, once decision-making authority is delegated to localities, local residents are expected to play a key role and to take responsibility for local political processes.

Chapter 5 focuses on local governance, examining the ways in which voluntary organizations and community groups can contribute to the formation of local resources and governing ability by working with local government in trust-based partnerships. This illustrates a particular phenomenon: the cases of local governance developing through local government and nonprofit organization (NPO) partnerships that have been rapidly spreading across the nation and are now a relatively common form of local governance in Japan.

In recent years, an alternative public space in local governance seems to have been developing due to ICT-based technological mediation. Chapter 6 examines the public use of ICTs as tools of democratic renewal, with special reference to the political engagement and participation of citizens. It explores how Japanese local communities have managed to mobilize ICTs for wider citizens' participation. ICT-based technological mediation is helping to construct new forms of participatory democracy that may complement the representative system of government.

Reinventing Japan requires alternative actors as well as alternative spaces. In order to revitalize the shrinking size of the working-age population, Japan would need millions of women and immigrants in the workplace. Chapters 7 and 8 address the new roles of women and foreigners respectively. Chapter 7 examines the gendered nature of local resources and gender differences in the salience of Japanese local politics, with special reference to the growth in numbers of women candidates in Japanese local elections. It assesses the potential of increased women's voices in Japan, which can be seen as an alternative way of problem-solving in Japanese society.

Chapter 8 examines the impact of Japanese local government initiatives for promoting the protection of foreigners' rights and thus facilitating the integration of foreign residents into the host community. Immigration policymaking normally takes place at the national level, yet the concrete consequences of international migration are mostly felt at the local level. Evident in this chapter is the premise that local government is the most important factor for promoting foreigners' rights in Japan and the driving force for determining the pathways that Japan has adopted for the integration of immigrants. In Conclusion, findings acknowledge that the developmental state's fall from grace in recent years is facilitating a shift of power to within state-society relations with some welcome democratic benefits.

CHAPTER 1

National Identity and Democracy:
Reactive Pacifism
to Proactive Pacifism

"It is citizens' autonomy that does not blindly follow leaders."[1] Nonetheless, "the unsolved problem is that many individual Japanese felt [in the war's aftermath] that the responsibility of war and aggression had already been settled, and that they had been the victims of [Japan's] militarism."[2] "Although harboring resentment, distrust and ill-feeling against the militarism that had mobilized the nation into the aggressive war, the [Japanese] people neither held themselves accountable for the war, nor took action to indict and punish those deemed responsible."[3] In the 1990s, it was argued that Japan should not confine itself to "inward-looking pacifism" but move "towards a stance of peace building beyond the mere scope of peace keeping."[4]

This chapter explores the influence of cultural dispositions on civil society by examining the construction and reconstruction of pacifism, which the Japanese people increasingly embraced as part of their national identity in the aftermath of World War II (WWII). Pacifism as a national construct did not come from the country's leadership, but from ordinary people, who were guarding against the revival of militarism in Japan.

By the end of the Pacific War in August 1945, large areas of major Japanese cities had been reduced to ashes, and the majority of city people survived on no more than a bowl of sweet potato leaf soup a day. Everyone was equally poor. They were angry and bitter about their experience of war, the excesses of the Japanese military, and the militarist regime that had taken over the country in the 1930s. The majority of citizens believed Japan to be a genuine "peace-loving country" and they saw themselves as *heiwashugisha* (pacifists), a very special term that is well ingrained in the collective consciousness of the Japanese people. It is important to distinguish between the emergence of liberal democracy in postwar Japan and the grassroots struggles of the Japanese people toward pacifism and collective peace, but the two are actually overlapping movements in postwar

Japan's experience. The misery caused by war and subsequent defeat had left the Japanese people with very little to hold on to or to believe in. What was important was that militarism never be revived. To this end, "peace and democracy" was adopted as the mantra of ordinary citizens who were collectively seeking to democratize Japan in order to steer the country away from its militarist past. Pacifism was widely accepted as a distinctive value of the Japanese nation and as an integral part of *kunigara* (national character), and is now acknowledged as one of the key components that shaped Japan's national identity in the aftermath of war.

In the initial stages of belief and identity formation, the attention of the people was primarily focused upon their immediate wartime experiences, the misery of early postwar Japan, and the subsequent search for internal stability and national security. The widespread antimilitarist ethic served as a key guide for national survival and integration, and although it did not provide a viable framework for the rebuilding of civil society, it did help to counter the overbearing influence of the state.

It was soon after the adoption of the new Japanese Constitution in 1947 that the Japanese people began to identify pacifism as part of democracy. Prior to this time, freedom and democracy were abstract concepts that held little appeal, for they were too remote from the context of everyday life. However, when pacifism became aligned with democracy and was set against the possible rekindling of militarism, it was seen as far more than a concept, as it lay at the heart of the individual rights of the Japanese people. In other words, the Japanese people, who had felt victimized by their militarist government,[5] had found their own democratic pathway through pacifism, which they saw as the antithesis of militarism. Initially, Japan's pacifism was more inward looking than externally oriented; the aim was to secure individual rights by countering any possible revival of militarism rather than to feel remorse or to directly confront and apprehend their wartime history or the excesses of their own military. The important issue at this point in time was to consolidate the antimilitarist ethic through democracy as a means to domestic peace and prosperity.

As an important aspect of Japanese identity, pacifism is a dynamic concept that has been shaped by different circumstances and historical periods. Once many Japanese people began to feel prosperous in the early 1960s, understandings of pacifism were increasingly depoliticized and, as I will discuss later in this chapter, linked with popular affluence. The 1990s presented a number of challenges and crises that impacted upon the prosperity of the country and the perceptions of national security. A new variant of pacifism emerged specially in the 1990s that was widely adopted by people at the grassroots level and that looked beyond national borders to seek the recognition of other countries in the post–Cold War environment. To achieve this recognition, the majority of Japanese voters thought it necessary to revise the so-called peace clause, Article 9 of the constitution, so that Japan could assume a proactive pacifism beyond the borders of the country and take on a role in international society. Interestingly, this emergent proactive pacifism was closely associated with significant changes in the public consciousness, including an increasing public awareness of civic values such as participation and voluntarism that pursued public purposes rather than the interests of individuals or special groups.

The manner in which collective understandings of pacifism emerged and became a standard of legitimate behavior in post-WWII Japan is remarkable given that the effectiveness of social and legal norms is not simply derived from the military and political power of nation-states or from the financial power of business interests. Just as interesting is the manner in which collective understandings of pacifism changed in the mid-1990s. To address this phenomenon, I trace the evolution of Japan's social and legal norms regarding national security and the Japanese people's collective self-understandings of pacifism by analyzing changes in components of public opinion, which have been surveyed by the Japanese government and mass media over many years.[6] Particularly important is the manner in which public opinion surveys have reflected new norms of public discourse about national security and how these norms have responded to changing structural factors, such as threats to Japan's security within its immediate environment and its dependence on the U.S. military for its security. Public opinion surveys reveal a shift in the existing norms of national security toward an externally oriented stance, that is, an increasing concern with foreign affairs and emphasis on the importance of Japan's contributions to the world, as a result of changing structural factors.

Norm Formation and Reactive Pacifism

In post-WWII Japan, the first election of 1946 was a chaotic event that served as a *de facto* national referendum on Japan's new constitution. The famous Article 9, which had been inserted into this U.S.-drafted constitution, obligated Japan to "forever renounce war . . . and the threat or use of force as a means of settling international disputes" and committed it not to maintain military forces. In short, Article 9 was an expression of the initial expectation of the Allied Powers to prevent Japan from becoming an aggressor again in Asia. The great majority of Japanese people endorsed the renouncement of war, and polls show that immediately after the election, 70 percent of voters considered the peace clause to be a necessary part of the constitution.[7] Yet the people's perception of Article 9 was quite different from what the Allies had expected. The immediate lesson they had learned from war was that they were victims of their own military; they were less concerned about the atrocities committed by the military in the Pacific and other areas. Thus, the civilian thrust into the peace clause was prompted less by Japan's wartime atrocities and aggressions against others than by their own wartime sacrifice, suffering, and hardship.[8]

The outbreak of the Korean War in 1950 threatened the security of the region and had a dramatic impact on the public perception of national security. In a public opinion poll conducted in Japan in November 1950, 54 percent of respondents considered the country's armed forces to be necessary to defend the nation; as of December 1950, 48 percent did not believe that Japan would be able to maintain its neutrality in armed conflicts.[9] Less than a year later, 76 percent were in favor of Japan's rearmament.[10] Although the Socialist Party and its affiliated labor unions and left-wing intellectuals continued to promote Japan's neutrality in international affairs, the debate sparked little enthusiasm among the general public. Threats to the region had effected a distinct change in the perception of national security.

In 1952 Japan became independent of the Allied Occupation, although U.S. forces remained on Japanese soil under the terms of the U.S.-Japan Security Treaty signed in September 1951. The conservatives were divided over the country's postoccupation policy. Prime Minister Yoshida Shigeru wanted to adhere to the terms of the American alliance through an incremental buildup of armed forces but was challenged by Hatoyama Ichiro in his party. Hatoyama hoped to revise the new constitution and then to rearm the country with independent military capabilities. Yoshida failed to establish a stable party structure, and Hatoyama became prime minister in 1954. The national government then began to recentralize its control over education and police, whose functions had been mobilized by Japan's wartime governments in the 1930s to create a totalitarian regime. While this had caused a great deal of political unrest, the public was just as suspicious of the recentralization drive and attempted rearmament. It was at this time, in the mid-1950s, that the Korean War ended and the public perception of national security changed once again. In the 1955 general election and the 1956 upper house election, the Hatoyama-led conservative forces failed to win two-thirds of the National Diet (the Japanese parliament) seats, which was constitutionally required to initiate amendments to the constitution. Public opinion polls in 1955 showed that the number of people who were opposed to the revision of Article 9, and thus to rearmament, continued to increase and exceeded the number of respondents who favored it.[11] Nonetheless, it is very important to note that more than half of the voters supported the 1954 government's decision to establish the Self-Defense Forces (SDF) and only 30 percent were opposed to it. This is consistent with the results of opinion polls held in 1956 and 1959, where 58 percent and 65 percent, respectively, wished to maintain the existing SDF.[12] So while the public strongly resisted Hatoyama's initiatives for constitutional change and rearmament, they did not necessarily reject the development of defense capabilities. Perhaps the most important aspect of the domestic debate was whether to revise or maintain the constitutional status quo. Any increase in support for Article 9 in its existing form did not stem from a literal interpretation of unarmed pacifism, but rather from protests against a return to Japan's militarist past. Editorials in major newspapers reflected public sentiment by arguing that the ultimate goal of Japan's democratization was not a return to the militarist takeover of the 1930s.[13] Thus, the debates surrounding Article 9 were part of an inward-looking process, restricted to the national level and without any particular concern for external relations with other states. This was the mid-1950s, when pacifism in Japan was focused on national integration and stability rather than peace-keeping efforts in the Asia-Pacific region.

A massive public campaign against the renewal of the U.S.-Japan Security Treaty ended in July 1960 when Prime Minister Kishi Nobusuke conceded leadership of the ruling Liberal Democratic Party (LDP) to Finance Minister Ikeda Hayato. Ikeda then shifted away from a politics of confrontation by replacing Kishi's open advocacy of constitutional revision with a "growth-first" stance, which considered economic growth to be the highest priority for national policy. By the early 1960s, the Japanese people were beginning to feel prosperous and confident for the first time in their lives. Japan's economic achievements had brought higher living standards and expectations and had an impact upon the people's perception of pacifism. Overall, they believed that economic prosperity would be the best way of deterring Japan from returning to its militarist past.

After the 1960 Security Treaty crisis, which had led to Prime Minister Kishi's fall from power, those who favored the constitutional status quo increased rapidly in number.[14] In the 1963 general election, Prime Minister Ikeda declared, "I will never revise the constitution during my term of office." A major strategy of the LDP leaders was to reinterpret the constitution in a manner acceptable to the public and, in the process, clarify the role of the SDF and the stationing of U.S. troops in Japan.[15]

Widespread affluence and security made it easier for people to reflect on shared understandings of pacifism, and it was during this time that the public began an active inquiry into the circumstances and conditions of WWII and those who had died in the war. In 1963, for the first time in postwar Japan, the national government held the National Memorial Prayer Services for the War Dead. The affluent middle class began to recognize the atomic bombings of Hiroshima and Nagasaki as a collective, rather than individual, experience, and editorials in major newspapers increasingly portrayed the Japanese people as unprecedented victims of overpowering forces and Japan as the sole atomic-bombed nation in war.[16] This augmented a sense of collective distinctiveness that contributed to the growth of a Japanese national identity. Importantly, this was not a strategic construction by national leaders, but a social construction arising from the views, perceptions, and experiences of the Japanese people as a whole. It was a unique identity informed by two separate yet interacting dynamics: a "pragmatic" pacifism supported by economic affluence and a "passive" pacifism driven by a sense of victimization.

This emerging identity was sensitive to changes in Japan's strategic environment, particularly in 1969, when the United States was failing in its war in Vietnam and President Nixon declared that Asian allies should do more to defend themselves rather than seek the help of American troops. For the first time in post-WWII Japan, there was a lively debate about the role of Japan's pacifism in the context of international relations. In the early 1970s, editorials in major newspapers consistently construed pacifism as indispensable to Japan's security policy,[17] and intellectuals and opinion leaders began to discuss a desirable form of pacifism at the policy level. By the late 1970s, as I will describe in more detail later in this chapter, the majority of the Japanese people collectively identified themselves with a pragmatic and passive form of pacifism that was then established as a norm for Japan's national security policy.

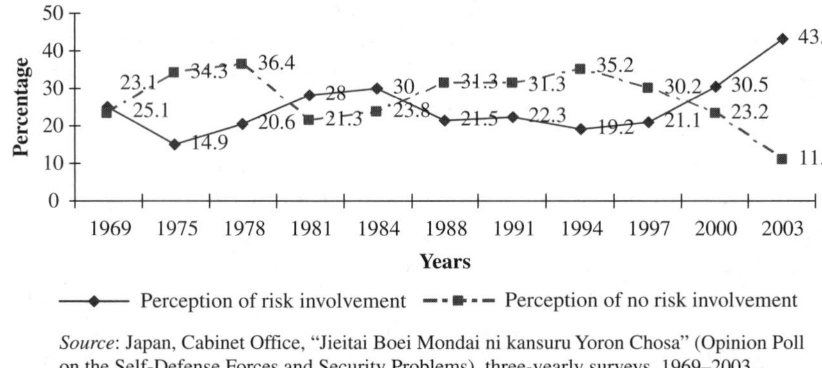

Source: Japan, Cabinet Office, "Jieitai Boei Mondai ni kansuru Yoron Chosa" (Opinion Poll on the Self-Defense Forces and Security Problems), three-yearly surveys, 1969–2003.

Figure 1.1 Japanese perception of armed conflict involvement, 1969–2003.

Since 1969, the Cabinet Public Relations Office has conducted triennial surveys to gauge public sentiment on national security and on the likelihood of Japan's involvement in war. It has asked the Japanese people, "Considering the present state of world affairs, do you think there is a danger that Japan will become, or will be forced to become, involved in armed conflicts?" Responses indicating that "there is a danger" or "there is no danger" have fluctuated in line with changes in the strategic environment. As figure 1.1 indicates, there were cyclical swings in the ratio of those who recognized the likelihood of Japan's involvement in war. It can also be seen that the imminent prospect of war declined toward the end of the Vietnam War and then bounced back during the Soviet military buildup in the Far East from the mid-1970s to the early 1980s. It then dropped in the post–Cold War environment of 1988–1997 and peaked in 2003 after the 1998 test firing by Pyongyang of a suspected Taepodong-1 missile that flew over Japan's main island of Honshu.

The "Taepodong shock" reminded Japanese people of their vulnerability and lack of preparedness for war and/or interventions from outside its borders. This fear was further intensified when North Korea decided to restart its frozen plutonium-based nuclear program in December 2002 and then admitted to possessing nuclear weapons in April 2003. The conundrum for the Japanese people was that in taking a pacifist stance, and pursuing freedom, they were left vulnerable to the possibility of external threats. The Cabinet Public Relations Office surveyed the Japanese by asking, "What sorts of national security arrangements should we use to protect Japan?"

As detailed in figure 1.2, the majority of people, by the late 1970s, endorsed the protection of Japan through the existing SDF and Japan-U.S. security regime. They implicitly reiterated their opposition to an unarmed, neutral Japan, endorsing the maintenance of the *status quo* in which Japan would

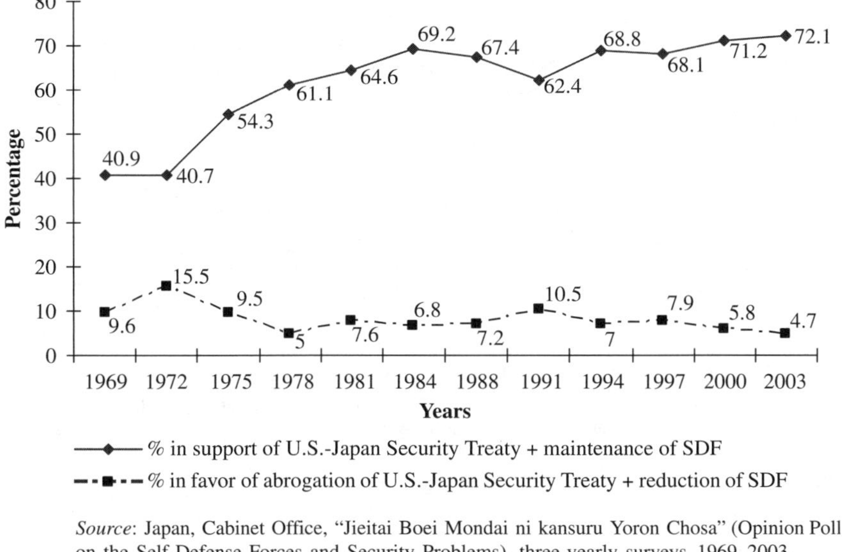

Source: Japan, Cabinet Office, "Jieitai Boei Mondai ni kansuru Yoron Chosa" (Opinion Poll on the Self-Defense Forces and Security Problems), three-yearly surveys, 1969–2003.

Figure 1.2 Japanese perception of national security, 1969–2003.

continue to rely on the existing SDF and Japan-U.S. security arrangement. Those who wanted to repeal the U.S.-Japan Security Treaty and to reduce or abolish the influence of the SDF, or those who took a pacifist stance based on Japan's unarmed neutrality, accounted for a marginal proportion of the respondents. Throughout the 1960s, after the treaty crisis ended, the Japanese were concerned about the possibility that U.S. bases stationed in Japan could drag the country into an American war. During this period, just over 35 percent of respondents believed that the U.S.-Japan Security Treaty was "useful" in maintaining Japan's peace and security.[18] Meanwhile, the Japanese government morally supported the U.S. engagement in the Vietnam War but did not send Japanese forces into the area. In 1970, over 65 percent of Japanese people believed the U.S.-Japan Security Treaty was "useful" as they saw no alternative but to accept the existing level of SDF capabilities.

The perception of security threats and measures tends to reflect the level of defense spending in most countries. The survey conducted by the Cabinet Public Relations Office asked the Japanese people whether the government should "spend more," "spend less," or whether it was "about the right amount." As figure 1.3 shows, the "spend more" and "spend less" answers were the opinions of the minority and showed a significant correlation to perceived threats from the external environment. In contrast, the "about the right amount" responses constituted the majority opinion and indicated the gradual acceptance or legitimization of the existing SDF and U.S.-Japan security arrangements.

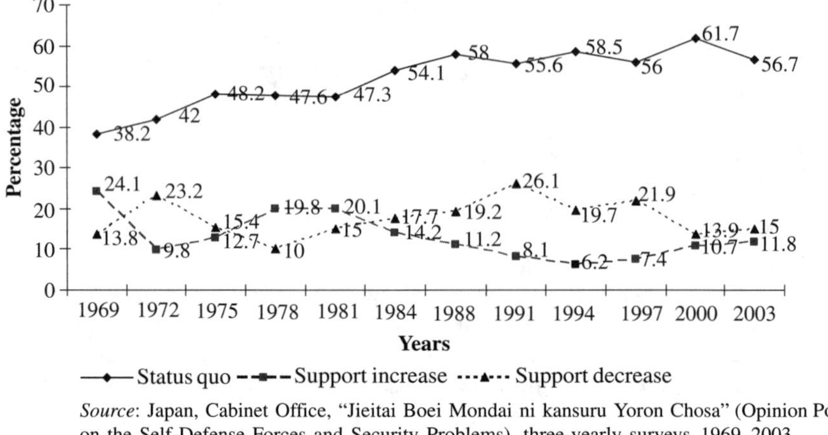

Source: Japan, Cabinet Office, "Jieitai Boei Mondai ni kansuru Yoron Chosa" (Opinion Pol on the Self-Defense Forces and Security Problems), three-yearly surveys, 1969–2003.

Figure 1.3   Japanese perception of defense spending levels, 1969–2003.

Changes in citizen support for defense spending are conventionally measured by "net support for defense spending," which represents the percentage of those supporting increases in spending minus the percentage of those calling for spending reductions; the neutral responses are excluded. The net support assumes that the "increase" and "decrease" responses can be seen as strong attitudes calling for change rather than continuity, and that "about the right amount" of defense spending response is closely associated with a lack of opinion or neutral attitude.[19] The net support for defense spending in Japan, the United States, France, and Germany suggests a correlation between public opinion and threats from the external environment.[20] While this general observation failed to identify specific responses by the Japanese people to defense spending, the responses to the category of "about the right amount" in Japan are too disproportionately large to ignore. An overwhelming majority of the Japanese people have continued to support the existing level of defense spending, while opinion polls continue to show that the Americans, British, and French have never overwhelmingly favored any of the three categories for defense spending.[21] In these countries, the responses to the increase, decrease, and neutral categories are proportionally equal and therefore compete with each other. Yet, as I am about to explain, the high proportion of the neutral responses in Japan is not necessarily a reflection of a lack of opinion or low information levels among the respondents. In the United States and Western Europe, public support for defense spending is largely responsive to changes in the relative growth of defense and social spending.[22] Increases in defense spending, for example, will heighten negative public reaction when there are concurrent decreases in the funding of civilian programs. Thus, defense spending presents a challenge to public priorities when it exceeds the rate of social spending. However, when there is growth in social spending, there is also an expectation and acceptance that defense spending will grow at a similar rate. In the Japanese context, public opinion does not appear to be responsive to the relative growth of defense and social spending priorities. In Japan, social security transfer payments as a percentage of GDP rose steadily from 4 percent in 1969 to 18 percent in 2002,[23] but despite this, the majority of the Japanese have supported existing levels of defense spending rather than an increase in defense spending. This is not to suggest that Japanese citizens are not responsive to budgetary priorities, but rather that their neutral responses present a significant indication of their collective expectation of pragmatic pacifism. During the late 1970s and the early 1980s, the collective expectation of national security based on specific forms of pacifism was widely accepted by the Japanese public. As mentioned earlier, the Japanese pacifist sentiment had two dominant aspects: first was the pragmatic aspect, in that the Japanese people preferred low-cost defense and nonmilitary means to high-cost and risk-involving defense capabilities for serving their economic prosperity; second was the passive aspect, in that the Japanese people had no desire to return to the country's militarist past and were reluctant to change the constitutional status quo of the post-WWII order. There was also the influence of the historical era. In early postwar Japan, there was a highly politicized locus of ideology-oriented groups, each with competing visions for Japan's security arrangements, ranging from unarmed neutrality to independent military capability. In the economic prosperity of the 1960s, pacifist sentiment was depoliticized and the collective beliefs of pacifism became tied directly to the daily lives of the Japanese people to protect their increasing level of material affluence.

Norm Changes and Proactive Pacifism

Norms or collective expectations are not static and fixed products but are always in a process of construction and reconstruction. Very often it is external threats and crises that weaken commitments to existing norms as citizens begin to adopt new ideas to solve collective problems. As new physical and psychosocial environments arise from the impact of external threats and crises, normative consensus may begin to break down. As will be discussed below, social interaction may lead to new collective understandings, such as those surrounding Japan's public safety and security in the 1990s. Political change is more likely when collective understandings are successfully implemented and consolidated within political processes. The strength of new collective beliefs depends on the extent to which they become institutionalized and subsequently become the complete source of influence for regulating or constraining state policies without coercive pressure.

In the 1990s, the debate surrounding Japan's pacifism entered a new phase as a result of the post–Cold War environment. During this time, Japan's good reputation for public safety deteriorated dramatically owing to a series of unexpected crises and events such as the decade-long economic recession; the Korean Nuclear crisis (1993–1994); the Great Hanshin earthquake (1995), which demonstrated the failure of the state to secure public safety and health; the

Aum Shinrikyo's Sarin gas attack (1995); the "Taepodong shock" (1998); and the nuclear accident at the Tokai Nuclear Plant (1999). Social unease spread dramatically throughout the general public following a combination of market and state failures, external threats, and the absence of reliable governance in Japan. All these factors pushed the general public to a new understanding of national identity.

The Gulf Crisis of 1990–1991 led to an increased regional tension that ignited much debate in Japan on its security capabilities. A pivotal part of this debate was the survival of Japan's self-imposed inward-looking pacifism set against the remaking of Japan as a nation willing to take part in international security measures. The passive and pragmatic elements of pacifism began to unravel in the early 1990s, with major newspaper editorials reflecting divisions within the community. *Yomiuri Shinbun* ridiculed Article 9–based security as a "one-country pacifism" and proposed that Japan become a "normal nation" with an active security policy. In contrast, *Asahi Shinbun* sought to preserve the spirit of Article 9 as an "essential attribute" to Japan's nationhood.[24] *Mainichi Shinbun* also emphasized the importance of Japan's peace-oriented security policy, while suggesting that it move away from an "inward-looking pacifism" by looking beyond national borders and becoming part of the international community.[25] In the 1990s, there was no argument among major national newspapers that the Japanese had been victimized by the atomic bombings and by their military. *Asahi Shinbun* and *Mainichi Shinbun* overwhelmingly acknowledged Japan's earlier role as an aggressor against foreigners and foreign countries during WWII while recognizing the steady rise of peace consciousness beyond the limits of a self-centered, "one-country" ideology.[26]

In the early 1990s, the general public in Japan began to think that the country should broaden its contribution to solving global problems and realized that the legal and constitutional constraints under Article 9 were rigidly limiting the capacity of such a contribution. This generated a sense of contradiction and incongruity among the Japanese people, who increasingly expected Japan to take strides toward assuming the responsibilities expected by the international society.

From 1995 to early 1996, Japan's peace consciousness—which had been largely expressed through opposition to the revision of the existing "peace" constitution—began to waver. Data provided by major national newspapers from public opinion polls in the mid-1990s showed that, for the first time since the early 1950s, the number of people wanting the constitution to be revised exceeded those who opposed its revision.[27] Between 2000 and 2004, over 20 such opinion surveys were conducted by major national newspapers and the Japan Broadcasting Corporation (NHK). According to the results of these surveys, 46–65 percent of respondents endorsed the revision of Article 9, while only 14–36 percent opposed it.[28] The primary reason underpinning the support for revision was the need for Japan to assume a role in international society.[29] However, it is very important to note here that the prorevision respondents did not necessarily wish to revise the entire Article 9. Some 30–36 percent of respondents wanted to eliminate just Clause 1, the renunciation of war; and in 2005 some 70 percent sought revision of Clause 2, the prohibition on the maintenance of armed forces.[30] In 2006, there was still clear aversion to military involvement, which was expressed through the support of Clause 1 together with considerable apprehension about the need to explicitly recognize the existing SDF, which presented a contradiction of Clause 2. At present, the majority of people acknowledge this contradiction between the existence of armed forces and Clause 2 by calling for the revision of Article 9. However, they prefer to see the SDF's constitutionally recognized position only in terms of the defense of Japanese soil and its participation in the UN's non-combatant peacekeeping operations.[31] In short, the majority of Japanese people appear to seek a proactive form of pacifism that will be recognized by other countries, but retain a profound aversion to militarism.

The Gulf Crisis of 1990–1991 presented a challenge to both the Japanese government and to the Japanese people. Japan's massive financial contributions to shoulder part of its international responsibility were described by foreign observers as "too little, too late" in the passage of the Gulf War, and it was heavily criticized for its "checkbook diplomacy." This was to become a turning point for Japan with a notable rise in the number of nongovernmental organizations (NGOs) involved in international exchange and cooperation activities. The number of global NGOs in which Japanese groups participated increased from about 400 in 1960 to nearly 2,000 in 1995, with more than 50 percent established in the first half of the 1990s.[32] These groups participated in a variety of fields, including education, development aid, environmental conservation, medical care, and refugee relief, and were engaged in activities such as advocacy, financial aid, humanitarian relief, and the provision of information, expertise and technical training.[33] This upsurge of voluntarism and participation was closely associated with significant changes in the public consciousness of social responsibility. According to Japan's Economic Planning Agency (EPA), the number of people surveyed who wanted to contribute to society in some way increased from 45 percent in 1977 to 75 percent in 2000.[34] Indeed, the opinion survey on private non-profit organizations (NPOs) conducted by the Cabinet Office in August 2005 indicated that nearly 80 percent of those surveyed thought it "important to take [social problems and issues] into their own hands."[35] This swing in public opinion encouraged the government's effort to create an active defense policy. In 2001, the former prime minister Nakasone Yasuhiro stated: "As things are, every survey is in favor [of revision]. After all, we politicians must keep in mind this big change in the national view."[36] The revision of the constitution was more feasible given this dramatic change in current public opinion. Other senior LDP politicians sent a strong message to Prime Minister Koizumi Jun'ichiro by asking: "Prime Minister, now will you address this change in national consciousness?"[37] Prime Minister Koizumi admitted: "I see [Japan's] Self-Defense Force essentially as military forces. It is not natural that we aren't allowed to admit it."[38] The prime minister thus directly emphasized the necessity of revising Article 9 of the constitution. However, the National Diet members' perception of national security was different from the changing collective expectations of the general public. In 2004, 66 percent of the lower-house members believed that Japan should be able to invoke the right to defend itself.[39] At the same time, 96 percent of the LDP Diet members thought it necessary to revise the constitution, with 84 percent members in favor of invoking the right of collective self-defense.[40] Over one-third of the National Diet members understood "collective self-defense" as participation in UN noncombatant peacekeeping operations and in UN combatant peace-enforcement operations, with only 8 percent supporting joint military operations with allies.[41] At present, only a handful of cabinet members and some hawkish LDP politicians argue that Japan should lift its prohibition against collective self-defense in order to promote U.S.-Japan joint military operations on an extended scale.

By 2000, when the so-called Armitage Report was released, the United States clearly expected Japan to share not only financial costs, but also the risks incurred from military emergencies. This was also part of Joint Vision 2020, the blueprint of the U.S. military to "establish the ability of operating alone or with allies to defeat any adversary." The release of this document placed an onus on Japan to engage in military action directly and to contribute the SDF in international disputes. Joint Vision 2020 concluded that Japan's prohibition against collective self-defense was a constraint on alliance cooperation and that the lifting of this prohibition would allow for closer and more efficient security cooperation.[42] In essence, the willingness of the United States to tolerate Japan's so-called "free ride" was at a crossroads, with the U.S. deputy secretary of defense, Paul Wolfowitz, calling for Japan to provide "boots on the ground" in Iraq.[43] It then offered the U.S.-UK security partnership as a model for a new U.S.-Japan alliance. This was a difficult moment for a country aligned with pacifism, and the focus of how to measure the public good of the U.S.-Japan alliance then moved toward military risk sharing as opposed to providing money for strategic aid and the stationing of U.S. forces in Japan. The Japanese government found itself under increasing U.S. pressure to undertake actions diametrically opposed to Japanese public opinion.

There were a number of potential factors that may have facilitated significant shifts in Japan's national security policy. First, Japan's changing peace consciousness gave politicians the green light for pursuing a proactive security policy. Second, new single-seat constituencies with 300 seats, which were introduced along with 180 seats in proportional representation into the 1994 voting system for the lower house, have created the "winner-takes-all" nature of LDP's election contests. Third, emergency defense bills, which were passed in June 2003, have equipped Japan with a domestic guideline for dealing with military emergencies.[44] Fourth, as U.S.-Japan security ties were overhauled, the focus turned away from U.S. commitment to the defense of Japan to the pressure from the United States for Japan to support its involvement in a major conflict in Asia.[45] Yet, given the assessment of the public and politicians' perceptions described earlier in this chapter, Japan is still far from seeing the realization of its collective self-defense capabilities, which will explicitly allow joint military operations with U.S. forces. To date, the Japanese government has only provided "rearguard support" for the war on terrorism by dispatching an SDF Aegis Destroyer to the Indian Ocean, an exercise that in real terms had little to do with the defense of Japan.[46] Japan, however, is seeking some form of continuity within its policy change where SDF activities are not construed as the use of armed forces. The U.S.-UK security partnership does not present a viable model for a new U.S.-Japan alliance. At least, Japan is a long way from growing into the "Britain of East Asia."

In the nationwide election of the lower house in September 2005, the LDP won only 48 percent of the total votes but gained the largest share of seats (296) in postwar politics. This landslide win may indeed be attributed to the switch in the electoral system from multimember to single-member constituencies. As a result, the governing coalition now commands a two-thirds majority in the lower house, which enables them to initiate constitutional amendments before submitting them to the upper house, and potentially to a national referendum for ratification. The LDP, together with its coalition partner, the New Komeito Party, and the largest opposition, Democratic Party, has agreed to discuss the necessary legislation for holding a national referendum on constitutional revision. While this agreement will take the LDP one step closer to constitutional revision, there is little to suggest that the Japanese political mainstream will contemplate the constitutional endorsement of Japan's military participation in the United States' global strategies. The widespread belief that Japan should assume a greater responsibility in international society lends itself to constitutional revision of Article 9 but only within the parameters of a strong aversion to military involvement. Surveys conducted by the Cabinet Public Relations Office indicate the popular endorsement of a proactive security policy, with the number of respondents supporting Japan's participation in UN noncombatant peacekeeping operations increasing from 46 percent in 1991 to 80 percent in 2000.[47] In contrast, only some 23–24 percent of respondents felt that Japan should also participate in UN combatant peace-enforcement operations.[48]

The new collective expectations of international responsibility have not lessened widespread aversion in Japan to military involvement. LDP politicians cannot afford to operate outside of normative structures in political action. In amending the constitution, politicians are constrained by collective expectations and political structures that require endorsement by the majority at a national referendum. Since less than one-third of the Japanese people currently think that Japan should lift its prohibition against collective self-defense,[49] it is highly unlikely that a proposal for lifting the constitutional prohibition of collective self-defense with allies would be submitted to the voters for ratification. At present, it appears that the public would accept changes in the constitution that would explicitly recognize Japan's right to self-defense, that would legitimize the role of the SDF within existing levels of defense spending, and that would enable the use of the SDF in UN-backed peacekeeping operations and humanitarian aid. If the constitution is revised, it is more likely that it would provide the Japanese government with an opportunity only for covert remilitarization to meet the demands of the Unites States for power sharing. There have already been efforts to meet U.S. pressure in, for example, the introduction of the 2001

Anti-Terrorism Special Measure Law, which covertly stipulates that the SDF can use their weapons not only to protect themselves, but also to protect "those who are with them on the scene and have come under their control while conducting their duties" (Article 12-1). In this way, the Japanese government may be able to modify the national security policy, yet these will only be changes around the edges of the policy rather than a fundamental shift in policy. Of course, it is possible that dramatic exogenous shocks such as a new regional threat or a debilitation of the U.S.-Japan alliance could significantly change the nature and scope of existing legal and social norms.

Conclusion

The Japanese state is probably less autonomous from civil society in national security issues than are major Western and industrialized Asian states. Conversely, Japan's pervasive culture of antimilitarism has mattered greatly in the autonomy of civil society, albeit in a direct and specific way. The collective understandings of pacifism have not only set parameters for the direction of Japan's national security, but have also directly affected important civil society values such as participation and voluntarism. In post-WWII Japan, national security has remained the one policy area where national leaders and the general public have clearly differed in their belief systems. Social norms became embedded in formal structures—notably the peace clause of Article 9—as the collective expectations of voters were articulated through political processes. The collective call for a passive, pragmatic pacifism successfully constrained conservative politicians in the 1970s and 1980s. In the 1990s, Japan's pacifism entered a new phase as a result of dramatic shocks and crises in the nation. The general public began to search for a new and appropriate form of pacifism that impacted upon perceptions of the national identity. By the mid-1990s, collective expectations and beliefs helped shape a more proactive form of pacifism. Nonetheless, the development of a proactive pacifism as part of changing expectations within civil society has remained within the widespread ethic of antimilitarism. By placing a constraint on the limits of proactive pacifism, Japanese voters have exercised a degree of autonomy over the state and on the formation of state policies to the advantage of civil society groups. Furthermore, the emergence of a proactive form of pacifism has been closely connected with changes in the public consciousness and social responsibility and has proved to be a driving force for participation and voluntarism of civil society groups in Japan.[50]

National identity in Japan was reconstructed during the 1990s, a time of crisis and impending threat when it was no longer tenable to maintain Japan's inward-looking pacifist ethic. In the post–Cold War environment it was crucial to the Japanese people that their stance on pacifism, and the national identity that this had created, be recognized by the international community. By the mid-1990s, a new externally oriented pacifism in relation to other countries was steadily established in the collective identity of the Japanese people.

CHAPTER 2

A Local Focus of the Nation-State: Production to Consumption Priorities

It is important not just to consider the abstract notion of the "nation-state," but to explore the concrete manifestations of public policies as they are felt and dealt with at the local level. The career choice to be a public servant used to be driven by the assurance of life-time employment [in Japan's government sector]; yet, today the youth are taking such chosen careers more seriously. Even after finishing their work, they [junior local government employees] get together to help plan the future of their town. These gatherings are spreading across the nation, becoming linked with local residents.[1]

The first priority of central government is and always has been to maintain private sector profitability, whereas that of local authorities has been to provide for the consumption requirements of various groups in the local population.[2]

The purpose of this chapter is to examine the impact of welfare state retrenchment on local communities in Japan. I argue that, while being forced to shift its policy focus toward retrenchment, Japanese national government has hardly been successful in setting limits on local financial discretion. Central government's policies targeting local governments for cutbacks require special considerations geared to particular circumstances at the local level. Consumption interests are most effectively organized at the local level, because the consumers of public services find it easier to press their demands on the closest agency responsible for providing them. In Japan, publicly elected local authorities have strongly confronted the central government in order to protect the interests of local communities against welfare state retrenchment.

Taxpayers are somewhat contradictory in their outlook; they neither wish to accept tax increases nor to see benefit cuts in a fiscal crisis of government. Yet municipalities and prefectures have always acted as *de facto* primary service providers in the history of modern Japan. This raises a number of questions: How can local communities ensure the sustainability of community development and service provision? How can local authorities perform effectively and be accountable for the consumption-oriented community needs? How can local residents be held responsible for the consequences of their collective and individual demands? In the chapters that follow, I will provide details of Japan's renewal as a civic nation: a social reimagination that is not only about a matter of institutional innovations aimed at how to govern localities, but also about affirming the rights and obligations of citizens to benefits.

Background of Welfare State Retrenchment

In the postwar period, welfare state expansion was a dominant theme in advanced industrial democracies. By the 1980s, however, nearly all Organisation for Economic Co-operation and Development (OECD) member countries had resorted to deficit financing as stagnant tax revenues combined with political pressure for increased public services. Faced with the urgent necessity of fiscal reconstruction, conservatives in advanced industrial democracies have favored cutting public services throughout the 1990s. As always in times of retrenchment, elected officials have needed to win the goodwill of voters and interest groups for these unpopular cutbacks. There is no doubt that the politics of retrenchment is distinctively different from that of growth. I will examine this new stage in the development of the welfare state by analyzing the impact of retrenchment politics on Japanese local communities in the context of Japan's recent fiscal reconstruction.

From the mid-1950s to 1970, Japan enjoyed a high economic growth, yet it managed to stabilize the size of national and local government expenditure at slightly less than 20 percent of gross domestic product (GDP). However, the patterns of public spending changed over time with the ratio of government expenditure to GDP rising steadily from 21 percent in 1971 to a high of 30 percent in 1983. This fundamental change was primarily due to the rapid growth of social security expenditures caused by major changes in social policy in the early 1970s.[3] The Japanese government therefore followed the "zero-ceiling" policy from 1983 to 1987, which amounted to a freeze on government spending. In fact, from 1984 to 1989, the ratio of national and local government expenditure to GDP held steady once again, remaining under 30 percent.[4]

Despite this seemingly successful use of austerity measures, the ratio of social security expenditures to GDP continued to increase with no sign of a downturn. Indeed, it is evident that the government austerity campaign in Japan was not necessarily related to social program cutbacks. Social security expenditures as a percentage of GDP rose from 12 percent in 1980 to 13 percent in 1985, to 15 percent in 1993, and to 17 percent in 2000. This would seem to signal the difficulties faced by government enterprises in relation to welfare state retrenchment.

There are two main reasons why one would expect Japan to have an effective retrenchment policy. The first is derived from a salient feature of local government spending in Japan. In relative terms, Japan spends more on local government than any other major OECD member country; however, its local authorities are also among the most regulated in the world. In the Fiscal Year (FY) 2003, for example, national government spending accounted for only 4.3 percent of GDP while local government spending was 12.4 percent of GDP, representing three times the spending by national government.[5] According to the 1997 National Accounts of OECD, local government spending in Japan accounted for a high of nearly 80 percent of the entire government sector (excluding social security funds), as compared with Britain's 30 percent, France's 34 percent, and Italy's 51 percent. The Japanese ratio was even comparable to those in federal systems, including the United States (66 percent), Canada (81 percent), and Germany (83 percent). Despite high spending, Japan's local government collects a disproportionately small percentage of total tax receipts. This is mainly due to the state-mandated local tax rates and assessment methods. In FY 2003, for example, the local government collected only one-third of such revenue, relying on national funds and local loans for 49 percent of its total revenue. This unusually high yet heavily regulated level of local government spending would seem to make it relatively easy for the central government to have cuts in spending and programs.

The second reason for Japan to have an effective retrenchment policy is related to national government spending, but in some senses is more critical for the Japanese people as it concerns an ideological consensus that values self-reliance. According to the *Revenue Statistics* of OECD member countries for 2002, for example, Japan's taxes as a share of GDP were slightly over 25 percent, comparable to the United States' nearly 30 percent, but much lower than Britain and Germany (both about 35 percent), Italy (40 percent), and France (nearly 45 percent). This reflects a deeply held tradition of self-help in Japanese society that sees external assistance as a form of interference or even personal defeat. These values are reflected in the framing of Japan's social legislation. Under the Livelihood Protection Law, for example, the welfare minister determines the minimum standard of living as an incentive to "self-sufficiency." The law implicitly assumes that too much direct relief may create disincentives to personal achievement.[6] These values are also reflected in high savings rates in Japanese households. Despite a sluggish growth in income and a hike in taxes, the proportion of disposable income saved in Japanese households was 14 percent in 1997, well above the G-7 average of 10 percent, according to the OECD *Economic Outlook* of June 1998. Primary motives for household savings remain precautionary ones to provide for accidents, illness, and unemployment.[7] Given this emphasis on traditional values of self-sufficiency, Japan continues to hold a weak ideological consensus on the legitimacy of government help.

For both of these reasons, one would expect Japan to have developed a strong retrenchment policy in a bid to scale back the government's commitments to social programs. But do such expectations really hold up under close examination? We need to remember that retrenchment takes place in the specific context of politics,[8] and is inevitably carried out within an organizational framework that is distinctively different from that of welfare state expansion.[9] In a bid to formulate a comparative theory of retrenchment that takes account of such factors, the present chapter will examine the underlying political framework in which retrenchment is carried out in contemporary Japan, with particular emphasis on the salience of local finance.

Retrenchment in Central-Local Government Relations

In this chapter, retrenchment also signals a reordering of priorities in national policy that moves toward economic rationalism. This policy orientation derives from fiscal conservatism, which argues that a high level of public expenditure for social welfare will reduce capital investment and employment while promoting inflation. Fiscal conservatism emphasizes the direct connection between greater social spending and government deficits. In welfare state retrenchment, the utmost priority of fiscal policy in many OECD countries has indeed been deficit reduction.

Borrowing should not exceed the net investment of the public sector if future generations of taxpayers are to be spared higher taxes for debt-servicing costs. But do politicians heed this rationale? There is little reason to expect them to, especially if it entails unpopular policies, such as tax increases and program cuts. In a democratic sense, government should spend as its population desires. Yet most voters wish to reduce their taxation and social security contributions, while resisting spending and program cuts.[10] How can central government bring policy closer to economic rationalism? Deficit reduction can be achieved either by tax increases or program cutbacks, including retrenchment. Yet neither measure is politically feasible.

The financial institution of central-local government relations may help the central government to ease this dilemma. At the structural level, salient features of fiscal rules between levels of government provide the central government with potential for maneuvering beyond the limits of these political difficulties; manipulating or even changing the institution of public finance is one way to "sell" the policy in order to win the goodwill of government organizations and to restrict the ability of voters to scrutinize program cutbacks. According to retrenchment patterns observed by Paul Pierson, this dimension may be called systemic retrenchment.[11] In such a way, there is an avoidance of blame, not by directly targeting specific programs for spending cutbacks (which Pierson defines as programmatic retrenchment), but rather by changing fiscal rules between the levels of government.

A related component of economic rationalism is the belief that the central government should coordinate local government finances in a bid to balance the general government budget and to stabilize the economy. Patterns of central-local government relations are thus more likely to be affected by systemic fiscal constraints and incentives than ever before. Variations in central-local government relations may be accounted for by contextual differences, ranging from the political entrepreneurship of a particular leader to the particularities of historical traditions. At a time of massive retrenchment attempts, however, it is argued that systemic fiscal constraints will narrow the range of these differences, creating a new political landscape.

In what forms do central-local financial relations facilitate retrenchment? Under what circumstances? With what effects? This chapter attempts to answer these questions by examining a recent reshuffling of financial relations between central and local government in Japan.

Manipulation of Central-Local Financial Arrangements

The political difficulty of programmatic retrenchment makes the manipulation of central-local financial arrangements an attractive measure for spending cutbacks, particularly as this can help to "hide" cutbacks and their implications from the scrutiny of individual taxpayers and interest groups. In short, financing programs through local governments may remove or restrict taxpayers' ability to see a relationship between their contribution and public service offering, while insulating elected officials from political accountability. Such manipulation also makes it increasingly difficult for ordinary taxpayers to trace responsibility for retrenchment effects.

Cutbacks in financial resources do not necessarily entail a significant loss of political power as other resources may be mobilized to reach an agreement between different interests for reducing expenditures. A case in point is the turf wars among central bureaucracies that transfer funds to local governments so as to maintain the volume of approval and permission by bureaucrats and to hush up any losses sustained by cutbacks. Despite fiscal constraints, bureaucrats retain the power to allocate national funds to local governments within the diminished limit. As part of its retrenchment strategies, the central government may seek to limit the total expenditure of all local governments to help stabilize the economy. As government deficits increase, the public sector becomes a net demander of funds in markets. For economic stabilization, government deficits must be financed by savings within the private sector. Yet managing such deficits without driving up interest rates is nearly impossible in the absence of high saving rates in the private sector. The need to prevent public deficits from adversely affecting the economy may induce the central government to coordinate with local governments in order to control their spending levels. In welfare state expansion, by contrast, the central authority tends to regulate both spending patterns and the amount spent on specific items. As a rule, the central authority is concerned mainly with the allocation of resources rather than their total size—as long as increased resources can meet public demand.

It is rare for retrenchment politics to be an exercise of local autonomy in which decisions made by local government are accountable to local residents. It is more likely that such politics, and subsequent power struggles, are dominated by a limited range of interests and entail manipulation behind closed doors. At the administrative level, policymakers, such as National Diet members, bureaucrats, big business, labor unions, and local authorities, reconcile conflicting interests within the retrenchment "bandwagon."

Targeting local governments for spending cutbacks has proved to be an ineffective means of addressing the problem of rising costs associated with the advanced welfare state. While it seems that the distinctive institution of local finance has enabled the central government to maneuver beyond the limits of welfare state retrenchment without facing the scrutiny of taxpayers or voters, this strategy has failed to produce radical changes in social welfare systems.

Programmatic Retrenchment and New Taxes

In Japan, a 1973 policy decision to dramatically increase social security benefits had critical implications for the current and future management of fiscal policy. In that year, public pension benefits for employees were raised from 20 percent of the average salary to 43 percent; free medical care for the elderly and subsidies for expensive treatments were introduced, and the government's health insurance coverage for the self-employed increased from 50 percent to 70 percent. The driving force behind welfare spending, including this sudden surge of social benefits, was the automatic incremental expansion of already broad and relatively generous entitlements. At the same time, general income levels continued to grow, welfare pensions were indexed to keep pace with inflation, and Japanese society was aging faster than any other advanced industrialized society. The radical reform of 1973, compounded by these factors, created a fast-growing vested interest in the welfare sector. Outlays of public pension programs rose from ¥177 billion in 1969 to ¥2,331 billion in 1975. Social welfare expenditures for the elderly increased from ¥21 billion in 1969 to ¥429 billion in 1976. Once in place, such expansionary systems were destined to face cutbacks in one form or another. In the mid-1970s, the need to rethink existing welfare programs began to be widely acknowledged among conservative forces, such as the Ministry of Finance, Liberal Democratic Party (LDP) politicians, and business leaders, who were concerned about the long-term growth of state welfare expenditures and higher taxes. But their attempts to radically restructure these programs failed. In the end, only two significant changes were implemented: the replacement in 1983 of free medical care for the elderly with a patient co-payment system, and the establishment in 1985 of the National Pension, which unified two major pension systems into a single fund.

Despite these reforms, since 1973, the growth of social security expenditures as a percentage of GDP has roughly correlated with the growth in the number of elderly persons over 65 as a percentage of population. The GDP ratio for social security expenditures rose from 8.8 percent in 1975 to 12.4 percent in 1990, keeping pace with the growth in elderly population from 7.9 percent to 12.1 percent over the same period. In Japan, tax burden to national income has been correlated with social security expenditures since the mid-1970s, reflecting the close relationship between welfare state expansion and tax increases. From the mid-1960s to the mid-1970s, the ratio of taxes to national income remained almost intact with a low of about 18 percent. The ratio then exceeded 20 percent in 1979 and continued to rise to a high of 28.1 percent in 1990. Yet the increase in tax revenue proved to be unhelpful in managing the expansion of social benefits. As a result, outstanding national and local government debt as a percentage of nominal GDP has continued to mount and has shown no sign of leveling off. Japan's public debt, according to OECD sources, reached 155 percent of nominal GDP in 2003, by far the worst among OECD countries.

By 1980, intense pressure by the Ministry of Finance successfully persuaded a reluctant Ministry of Health and Welfare to pursue a patient co-payment system in place of the free medical care program for the elderly. After a series of negotiations within the LDP government, the Health Care for the Aged Law was passed in the National Diet in August 1982, requiring people aged 70 or over to pay ¥400 on their first visit to the doctor each month and ¥300 a day for hospital stays for a maximum of two months. Although LDP Diet members endorsed the principle of co-payment, these nominal adjustments resulting from the political process were hardly a solution to the shortage of resources for medical care.[12] Retrenchment of free medical care paralleled that of pension systems. At the time of the 1982 budget process, with the media publicizing a "zero ceiling" on budget growth, the Provisional Commission on Administrative Reform (attached to the Prime Minister's Office or PMO), successfully pressed the LDP to agree to a consolidation of government pension systems.[13] In a 1984 cabinet decision, existing pensions were unified to create the new National Pension. Yet the 1985 pension reform failed to raise the eligible age and thereby failed to provide a real resolution to the expansion of subsidies to public pension programs. It did, however, slightly increase the contribution rate of individuals to the pension fund.

Despite the rhetoric of "small government" during the 1980s, popular entitlement programs remained largely intact. The Ministry of Finance was desperately concerned with the resulting budget deficit, attempting to introduce a new consumption tax (value added tax, VAT) in 1977. Following a recommendation from the Tax Council, Prime Minister Ohira Masayoshi announced that his administration would start collecting a consumption tax in FY 1980. In the general election of 1979, however, the LDP failed to secure a stable majority in the National Diet and the proposal quickly disappeared from sight. Ohira was not alone. Prime Minister Nakasone Yasuhiro also failed in his 1987 drive for the introduction of a VAT, facing intense opposition from small-sized business groups who had been long-term supporters of the LDP. The Ministry of Finance had learned from these earlier attempts and finally succeeded, through the Takeshita Noboru government, in introducing VAT in April 1989. This legislation was passed at the end of 1988, when public opinion was overwhelmed by the headline grabbing inside stories of the Recruit bribery scandal.[14] Exemptions and reduced rates for small businesses made the VAT more acceptable to this particular interest group, yet the new tax with an identical rate for the wealthy and the poor was deemed to be unfair and aroused the indignation of the average taxpayer.[15] According to a 1988 Japan Broadcasting Association (NHK) survey, 83 percent of respondents believed that the central government needed to be more accountable for the tax reform. In the election of July 1989, the LDP lost its upper house majority for the first time in the party's history, a devastating loss that was said to result from resentment against the new tax.

Since then, the issues surrounding the 1989 consumption tax have continued to undergo scrutiny by politicians and interest groups. However, the end of the

LDP's 38-year rule in 1993 did not necessarily provide easier access to fiscal reconstruction. The Ministry of Finance successfully persuaded Prime Minister Hosokawa Morihiro to propose an increase in the consumption tax rate, but without consensus within the non-LDP coalition Hosokawa was forced to abandon the proposal. In summer 1994, the LDP came back to office by forming a coalition government with the Social Democratic Party of Japan (SDPJ) and the Shinto Sakigake (New Party Harbinger).[16] By this time, Japan's economic slump had created increased political pressure for tax cuts and the Ministry of Finance used this as an opportunity for fiscal conservatism while conceding the necessity of income tax cuts, so long as they were offset by consumption tax increases. The LDP saw this approach as politically feasible, since the proposed tax cut package would precede, by some three years, the three to five percent VAT increase mooted for 1997.[17] After pushing through this controversial consumption tax increase, the Ministry of Health and Welfare introduced a publicly subsidized home care scheme for the elderly, which passed into law in December 1997. This scheme had public support, since it was seen as necessary in an aging society. Yet the new program has been added to the social security apparatus in a piecemeal fashion, so that no one can ascertain the level of government expenditure or the extent of taxpayers' contribution. There is public consensus on just one issue: the consumption tax increase will not eliminate the outstanding debt of central and local government.

Local Government and Systemic Retrenchment

In postwar Japan, national ministries vied with one another to create new grant programs and to increase supervisory power in the form of approvals and permissions. This turf war contributed to divided national control over local government spending through the uncoordinated growth of national funds transferred as specific grants from national ministries to local governments. The grant system, which was perceived as favoring coalitions of ministries, politicians, and interest groups,[18] sparked fears that total local expenditure could get out of control.[19] In the early 1980s, Japan's central bureaucracy came under attack by Prime Minister Nakasone Yasuhiro who was determined to implement neoliberal reforms as manifested in small government, deregulation, and privatization. One of the most important goals in this campaign was to target uncoordinated specific grants for massive reductions in national government spending. Since then, the political climate has forced the central government to impose tight controls on ministerial spending. Even the most politicized line ministries, such as agriculture, construction, and transportation, have had to accept that they are not exempt from these fiscal constraints.

An understanding of such organizational struggles requires knowledge of the sources of local revenue. The revenue of Japanese local government can be divided broadly into four categories: direct local tax (covering 34 percent of total local government revenue in 2003); general grants (21 percent); specific grants (14 percent), and local public loans (15 percent). National law prescribes the legal basis, objectives, and other details for local tax items; the revenue source of direct local tax is thus heavily regulated.[20] Yet national grants are relatively versatile, although their reshaping is subject to political pressure. More efficient steering of national grant programs has become a central strategy of the central government to reduce the high level of its deficit. An equally important target for manipulation is the heavily regulated system of local loans. The central government sets an annual limit on total local loans and issues permission within that limit; however, in 2006, according to the 1999 Collective Decentralization Law, the raising of local loans could be organized through consultation with, rather than by permission of, the central government. Therefore, changes in the amount and nature of the transfer payments and local loans could be seen as a reflection of the reordering of policy priorities for fiscal reconstruction.

Political Strategies

The Japanese local government system provides the central government with three key maneuvers for spending cutbacks. The first is the flotation of local loans for which the central government issues permission. The financial imbalance between central and local government requires the central government to guarantee financial resources to local government. Yet increases in local loans discharge the central government from the burden of covering the shortage of local government revenue. In this way, the central government is able to increase national fiscal elasticity by substituting local loans for national taxes. It is a strategy that makes it very difficult for taxpayers to trace responsibility. The second maneuver is a policy of across-the-board cutbacks for specific grants in an attempt to avoid the issuance of additional national bonds. Furthermore, across-the-board reductions may allow elected officials to evade the scrutiny of interest groups, help bureaucrats to save face, and prevent voters from assessing the actual impact on different programs. The third central government maneuver for spending cutbacks is the transfer of national funds to local governments in the form of general grants. The provision of general grants comes with no strings attached, yet it has operated an effective means of controlling total local government expenditure. As a significant part of local government services are financed by the centrally fixed grants, local authorities with a higher ratio of general grants are likely to contribute to national fiscal policy by limiting their total expenditure. This large ratio of general grants to local government revenue tends to obscure the relationship between the level of local taxes and the level of local services.

National transfers to local governments (as a percentage of national tax revenue) dropped from 67 percent in 1980, to 53 percent in 1985, to 44 percent in 1990 as national government debt-servicing costs (as a percentage of national government expenditure) continued to rise during this period from 11 percent in 1980 to about 20 percent in 1990. Between 1991 and 1993, the central government managed to avoid issuing deficit-covering bonds, as the bubble economy had created a large income tax base. By 1993, the ratio of those transfers bounced back to over 50 percent. Since 1996, just as national government debt-servicing costs remained stable at slightly over 20 percent, national transfers stabilized with a slight fluctuation around 60 percent. The inverse relationship between debt-servicing costs and national transfers between 1980 and 1993 was very strong, with national fiscal elasticity and transfer payments powerfully aligned during this period.[21] In other words, as debt-servicing costs increased, the transfer of national funds to local government decreased.

To examine this trend, it is necessary to analyze two key items of national transfers: local allocation tax (general grants) and national treasury disbursements (specific grants). During the period from 1980 to 1990, local government revenue and general grants rose in parallel, increasing 1.72 times and 1.77 times respectively. By contrast, specific grants expanded more slowly, rising only 1.01 times over the same period. The fiscal squeeze of the central government exerted strong pressure on specific grants. There are two major categories of specific grants: national treasury share (or partial subsidies), which pays the legally promised share of the central government in the costs of functions, and national subsidies (or promotional subsidies), which encourage local governments to improve the quality of their services. Partial subsidies as a percentage of local government revenue declined rapidly from 20 percent in 1980 to 11 percent in 1996, while promotional subsidies fluctuated between 4.3 percent and 4.7 percent during the same time frame. This implies that the central government depended heavily on the obligatory shares for the implementation of spending cutbacks. Thus the LDP successfully avoided a much-needed reform of promotional subsidies programs that had been criticized as sources of LDP patronage politics.

Under the slogan of "fiscal reconstruction without tax increases," the LDP national government hammered out an across-the-board policy of "zero ceilings" that excluded both general grants and bond expenditures. In 1982 the Ministry of Finance began to impose the principle of zero growth on budget requests and in 1983 that of minus growth. It also suggested a predetermined budget size for individual national ministries. Although subject to negotiations, these guidelines set a framework for each ministry's budget request. In order to maintain the scale and scope of their turf, national ministries had no choice but to reduce their contribution ratios of partial subsidies, thus transferring the financial burden to local governments.

The decline of partial subsidies resulted from a variety of cutback tactics: reduction of share ratios, incorporation of those subsidies into general grants, and increases in local projects without national aid. LDP leaders feared that a priority ranking for grant cuts would threaten their power base by cutting material benefits to their political support groups.[22] Instead, the central government in 1985 implemented an across-the-board 10 percent reduction of share ratios in all partial subsidies that covered more than 50 percent of expenses. Nonetheless, the grant cuts heavily influenced the single policy sector of welfare where pressure groups were neither strongly organized nor supportive of the LDP. The cuts targeted 19 welfare sector grant programs, representing 46 percent of the total of designated programs and about 80 percent of the total value of spending cuts.

Until 1988, the central government continued to reduce various share ratios. Between 1985 and 1994, the total reduction amounted to ¥9.3 trillion. In FY 1988 alone it reached a high of ¥1.8 trillion, representing three percent of total local government revenue.

To achieve the targeted ceilings, the Ministry of Finance mobilized a variety of "special account manipulations." As a result, budgeting techniques and detailed data became so complex that only finance bureaucrats in the finance and home affairs ministries could fully understand them. The new techniques and gimmicks presented taxpayers with a black box. Equally important, the purpose of the share ratio cuts was never made explicit; consequently the redistribution of functions between central and local government remained conveniently unclear. In reality, of course, the grant reduction heavily influenced national contributions to social benefits, dispersing obligations between levels of government.

But why did line ministries accept grant cuts without any serious opposition? In fact, specific grants (partial and promotional subsidies) reached a high of 3,515 programs in 1981 and gradually fell to 2,250 programs in 1995. As of 2002, these subsidies have stagnated at the 1999 level of 2,480 programs. However, the massive number of approval, permission, and report duties remained almost unchanged from the early 1980s to 2002; in 1999 and 2002 that number was 11,581 and 10,621 respectively. Despite changes in the sources of funding, the ministries were able to preserve the network of grants-in-aid through which to direct the administration of specific local government departments.[23] The grant programs, whose administration entailed a large number of approvals and permissions, assured line ministries that they would retain effective control over local authorities. In 1996 the most politicized ministry, agriculture, handled an astonishing 486 purpose-specific grant programs; however, the total value of these grant programs at ¥3,000 billion was disproportionately low. Indeed, in absolute terms, purpose-specific grants by the Ministry of Agriculture dropped by 25 percent between 1983 and 1988. During this period, purpose-specific grants by the Ministry of Health and Welfare increased by 15 percent (¥14,000 billion in 1996)—a striking contrast suggesting that the needs of Japan's aging society were prohibiting a fiscal squeeze on social benefits. It is hardly surprising that purpose-specific grants for these benefits were at the heart of the problem of financial reform.

Unlike line ministries, the Ministry of Home Affairs sought to reform the grants-in-aid system by itself. In response to the across-the-board 10 percent share ratio cut—a measure that would impose an estimated financial burden of ¥580 billion on local governments—the Ministry of Home Affairs proposed boosting local financial discretion through the incorporation of specific grants into general grants. This would have dealt a fatal blow both to the line ministries and to the locally elected LDP Diet members. In the end, the chairperson of the Policy Affairs Research Council of the LDP intervened with a compromise—granting ¥100 billion in "special" general grants and by giving approval for local construction loans totaling ¥480 billion. Because both the finance and the home affairs ministers confirmed the temporary nature of share ratio cuts, extensive incorporation was not deemed acceptable. However, line ministries admitted that a limited incorporation was needed. The budget ceiling set by the Ministry of Finance was contributing to the pressure on ministerial expenses. These ministries consequently began to transfer some specific grants to general grants, in order to make up for the shortfall between available resources and their obligations. In December 1992, for example, the incorporation into general grants of partial subsidies for public day care was proposed abruptly by the Ministry of Health and Welfare to meet the ceiling for the following fiscal year. Between 1985 and 1996, the number of specific grants incorporated in this scheme was only 83, but between 1997 and 2002, that number reached 214, amounting to 9 percent of total specific grants. Despite this effort to incorporate specific grants into general grants with no strings attached, the central government was yet to transfer part of its taxation power to local governments as of 2007. Therefore, national transfer payments to local governments remained intact at about 45 percent of national general expenditure (for example, 45.1 percent in 1980 and 45.5 percent in 2002).

Retrenchment Impact on Local Consumption Requirements

The impact of grant cuts and reforms on overall social security expenditures merits discussion. In Japan, local government finance rapidly became an important tool for organizing retrenchment policy at the national level. It is important to inquire if a reshuffling of central-local financial relations could provide a real solution to a host of fiscal problems in the welfare state.

In Japan, welfare state retrenchment has dramatically changed the nature of national aid to local governments. National grants remain important, but ever-increasing social benefits have opened the grants-in-aid system to the scrutiny of fiscal conservative forces in Japan. The ability of bureaucrats to strengthen themselves by preserving national grant programs has had an increasingly dysfunctional impact on welfare state retrenchment. Fiscal conservatism has thus targeted national grant programs for spending cutbacks. Across-the-board grant cuts have been particularly effective in persuading various political interests to focus on retrenchment policy. While the Japanese government has indeed reduced the number of grant programs and made some structural changes in national transfers to local governments, the growth in social security expenditures has been more resilient than first anticipated. The grant program cuts have not made significant changes in the local spending level of social benefits. These cuts, as table 2.1 indicates, have certainly hit welfare expenditures hard, with the ratio of specific grant contributions to local governments' public welfare dropping rapidly from 45 percent in 1980 to 27 percent in 1995. As overall public welfare expenditures by local governments have increased incrementally over the same period, it appears that local governments have been able to preserve and strengthen the spending levels of social programs by bearing the brunt of the extra financial burden.

Why should they take on this additional burden? The central government often failed to live up to its legal commitments to local governments[24] by contributing

Table 2.1 Retrenchment impact on public welfare by local government, 1980–2003

	Expenditure		Revenue (%)		
	In billion (Yen)	*% of GDP*	*General revenue*	*Specific grants*	*Others*
1980	5,028	2.0	44.9	44.7	10.4
1985	6,252	1.9	54.6	35.0	10.4
1990	8,228	1.9	61.0	27.9	11.1
1995	11,980	2.4	59.7	27.1	13.2
2002	14,303	2.9	63.3	27.1	9.6
2003	14,540	2.9	63.5	28.6	7.9

Source: Figures are calculated from Japan, Ministry of Internal Affairs and Communications (MIAC) (known as the Ministry of Home Affairs until 2000), *Chiho Zaisei Hakusho* (White Paper of Local Public Finance), various issues, 1982–2005.

Note: Public Welfare Expenditure = Public Aid + Children's Welfare + Welfare for the Aged + Social Welfare + Disaster Relief.

a reduced percentage of a legally standardized cost—not the actual cost—for each spending item of public welfare. This was often referred to as "overburdening" in the media and local government reports. Nonetheless, local governments tended to provide essential welfare services in accordance with actual needs. Take, for example, the construction of day-care centers. The central government set national standards for the construction of day-care centers (e.g., 5m^2 per child and ¥32,100 per m^2), but local government municipalities continually established much higher standards than those of the central government. This was a result of the failure of the central government to provide adequate payment for proper conditions to meet public demand.[25] These activities may be significantly related to differences in budgeting practices between central and local government, which play a crucial role in undermining the implementation of spending cutbacks. For local governments, the total budget figure is likely to reflect the weight of changes in public demand.[26] At the national level, however, it is likely to reflect projections of how fiscal policy affects economic conditions in the next financial year (although each decision is subject to various political pressures).[27]

A broader perspective can be ascertained by exploring the patterns of overall social security expenditures, while drawing on sources of the Social Security Advisory Council (attached to PMO until 2000). National fund contributions (primarily from tax revenues) as a percentage of social security net expenditure were about 40 percent in 1980, falling to under 25 percent by 1997. In the same year, local governments' contributions reached 16 percent of social security net expenditure. Therefore, the remainder was covered by the contributions of individual employees and employers. In 2002, reflecting the progress of Japan's aging society, the payments of benefits related to the elderly accounted for 60 percent of all social security benefits. It was the central government that contributed the substantial share of social insurance expenses such as health and pension insurance. With this in mind, it is clear that cuts to grant programs alone are unlikely to lead to a radical solution to "uncontrollable" social security expenditures.

It is important to note that in Japan the role of local governments in restructuring the social security system has become more important than ever before.

The Golden Plan, a ten-year strategy to promote health care and welfare for the elderly, was established in 1989. In the following year, the welfare service administration was transferred to municipalities, and the establishment of the Local Health and Welfare Plan for the Elderly was made mandatory by the state. Later, in a bid to meet expanded needs, the finance, home affairs, and welfare ministers agreed to establish a New Golden Plan, starting in 1995, with a five-year budget of ¥9,000 billion. Equally important to changing needs and conditions was publicly subsidized home care scheme for the elderly that began to be implemented by municipal governments in the year 2000.

Local Financial Burden

The effect of these changes on individual local governments has been a source of irritation to local authorities. As part of specific grant allocation, Japanese public policy on aid is concentrated on rural prefectures, such as the financially poor Shimane and Tottori, which are categorized, according to their financial health (or financial strength index) as Group E. As a result, per capita specific grants in rural prefectures (e.g., Shimane's ¥211,652 in 2000) are much higher than those in urban prefectures (e.g., Aichi's ¥46,333 in 2000). In 2000 each resident of Group E was paid nearly five times as much as residents of Group A, which includes the rich, urban prefectures of Osaka and Aichi. The gap between Group E and Group A, of course, does not directly reflect differentials of service provision among prefectures. Rural prefectures need more money per capita to provide the same service level as urban areas, particularly given the need for improvements in their living infrastructure. Nonetheless, the structure of selective regional aid has provided a breeding ground for LDP patronage politics.[28]

By 2010, it would appear that the weight of changes in public demand will inevitably influence the grants-in-aid system. In the early 2000s, however, as the population aged 65 and over has been growing, individualized social services, such as visiting nurse, home care, and other social aid programs for the elderly, have also expanded dramatically. Unlike infrastructural public works, which are relatively independent of population size, individualized service delivery in urban areas is more expensive than it is in depopulated areas. Urban prefectures, such as Tokyo and Osaka, have become quite vocal about the lack of funds in the form of specific grants for such services.

Despite the across-the-board ratio cut, the 1985 grant reduction hit social benefit expenditure particularly hard. This was especially the case for individualized social services, which represented 92 percent of the affected services. Urban prefectures were not happy; at a September 1994 general meeting of the National Association of Governors, members called for national funding cutbacks to be withdrawn. As Tokyo Governor Suzuki Shun'ichi observed, "Even in times of fiscal difficulty, the national government should not take measures its own way."[29] Even worse, financially rigid cities, such as those in Fukuoka and Hokkaido prefectures (including the closed coal mining region, which had spent extensively on direct relief), bore the greatest financial burden. Municipal assemblies in

Fukuoka and Hokkaido, which were to assume extra financial responsibility of ¥20 billion and ¥17 billion respectively, petitioned the cabinet to alleviate the burden.

Interestingly, however, while the small towns and villages wanted more aid money and less-complicated allocation procedures, they initially did not wish to see this system abolished.[30] In particular, conservative assembly members, who organized local support for LDP Diet members, had no desire to lose this channel for voter mobilization. In larger municipalities, by contrast, chief executives tended to support the incorporation of specific grants into general grants to enable fiscal coordination among city departments. From the point of view of the departments themselves, however, the proposal had few advantages for their interests were accommodated by the corresponding line ministries and they were dependent on the grants-in-aid system for expertise and information. In addition, specific grants allowed city departments to avoid political turf wars for budgetary shares.[31]

The grant cutbacks also heavily affected the financing of public works. Between 1980 and 2000, the operation costs of grant-supported local projects fluctuated between ¥8 trillion and ¥12 trillion. By contrast, the operation costs of projects that had not attracted grant support rose sharply from ¥5 trillion in 1980 to a high of ¥18 trillion in 1993. By the mid-1980s, grant support was being squeezed and local governments were encouraged to carry out projects alone. This resulted in project delays. Equally important, between 1992 and 1994 the Ministry of Finance further promoted non–grant-supported projects by granting permission for sharply increased levels of local loans in order to stimulate the "post-bubble" economy. Local loans as a percentage of GDP jumped from 1.6 percent in 1991 to 3.5 percent in 1995. The servicing costs of these loans were included in the calculation of general grants, thus providing an incentive to local governments to set up their projects without national grants. In FY 1996, while national public works represented only ¥10 trillion, local public works without national grants amounted to ¥17 trillion. In this way, the Ministry of Finance was able to maintain the existing scale of public works, while attempting to reduce the financial burden of the central government and, at the same time, boost the drop in domestic demand created by public works throughout the country.

By 1997, however, local tax revenue began to drop significantly and the limit ratio of 20 percent for the flotation of local bonds—that is, the three-year average of the ratio of the general revenue that was allotted to the sum of the debt payments to the sum of the standard financial scale of local governments—hit many local governments. Accordingly, local public works without national grants declined to ¥15 trillion in 1997 and then fell to ¥12 trillion in 2000.

Between 1985 and 1996, partial subsidies as a percentage of local government revenue declined by 32 percent. To compensate, general grants were expected to rise. However, the shortage of revenue sources for general grants had been apparent since 1975. The shortage as a percentage of local government revenue averaged 6 percent between 1975 and 1987, dropping to 1.6 percent between 1988 and 1991 (the period of the "bubble economy"), and rising again to 7 percent between 1992 and 1996. The revenue sources of general grants were drawn from three national taxes (income tax, corporation tax that provisionally was 35.8 percent in 2000, and liquor tax), with 32 percent of these taxes transferred as general grants to local governments. Although the declining fiscal capacity of local governments increased the necessity for general grants, the parallel decline of national tax revenue resulted in a fall of general grants revenue. Despite the continuous shortage, the 32 percent formula of main revenue sources has remained intact—although supplementary sources of consumption tax, ranging from 24 to 29.5 percent in 1994, and 25 percent of tobacco tax were added to general grants revenue in 1989. The Ministry of Finance thus forced the need to resort to borrowing, with local loans, particularly those between 1975 and 1995, covering 53 percent of shortages.

Macroeconomic Implications

In practice, the amount of local allocation tax for general grants is determined through negotiations between the internal affairs and finance officials. Local authorities spend the money but they cannot directly participate in negotiations. Instead, they have to entrust internal affairs officials to represent their interests. With the shortage of revenue for general grants in 1975, the then Ministry of Home Affairs assumed the role of adjuster, obtaining comprehensive information on local finances.[32] Meanwhile, as national fiscal capacity became more rigid, the benefits of general grants in which the Ministry of Home Affairs had a predominant interest began to spill over to the Ministry of Finance and line ministries. Line ministries, which were responsible for implementing government programs, tried to meet reduction targets by incorporating parts of specific grants into general grants, while the Ministry of Finance issued special permission for local loans to cover the shortage of revenue sources for general grants. In this way, general grants failed to fulfill a stabilizing function for local financial resources.

In the early 1980s, when national bond expenditures increased dramatically, the Ministry of Finance had already expressed concern about the limits of its fiscal strategy particularly as the financial burden had been transferred from the central to local governments, with the total amount of spending unchanged. The problem of high bond dependence had also been transferred from the central to local governments. Since 1991, the Ministry of Finance has recognized the necessity of reducing overall central and local spending.[33] Coordination between central and local governments over expenditures was now seen as crucial to the achievement of macroeconomic goals. The attitude of the home affairs officials also changed with the admission that a reduction of general grants was necessary.[34] To maintain home affairs' jurisdiction, however, they argued that the existing allocation ratio of the three national taxes for general grants (that had been fixed at 32 percent in 1966) had to be retained. To achieve this, the home affairs officials maintained the allocation ratio while reducing the total amount of spending on general grants.

This reduction amounted to ¥450 billion in 1991, ¥850 billion in 1992, and ¥400 billion in 1993, thus contributing to the stagnant growth of general grants. Between 1989 and 1995, general grants as a percentage of GDP fluctuated between 3.2 percent and 3.3 percent. (Cf. They rose continually from 2.8 percent in 1984 to 3.3 percent in 1989.) This fluctuation was primarily due to a mixture of plus growth factors, including the incorporation of specific grants into general grants and the addition of local debt-servicing costs in the calculation of general grants, together with minus growth factors, notably the reductions in grants already discussed. In the process, the Ministry of Finance shifted its policy focus from the transfer of financial burden to the total control of local government expenditure.

To control total local government expenditure for macroeconomic purposes, the Ministry of Finance largely organizes the distribution of general grants, which are less politicized than specific grants. This interest by the Ministry of Finance has had important implications for individual local governments. Since general grants are allocated according to the fiscal need of individual local governments, a number of Japan's 3,000 local governments, including the Tokyo Metropolitan government and 104 municipalities in 2002, were not eligible to receive any money at all. The number of nonallocation municipalities averaged about 150 in the 1990s, after reaching a low of 48 in 1978 and climbing to a high of 180 in 1986. If specific grant programs had been completely integrated into a general grant program, then some local governments may have been forced to depend solely on their own direct resources for revenue. They have continued to depend solely on their own direct resources for revenue given the painfully slow progress of grant reorganization. On the whole, local governments were not vocal about the management of general grant allocation until the late 1990s when finance and home affairs officials agreed to provide them with sufficient local loans to redress funding shortages.[35] From the standpoint of maintaining local autonomy, direct local tax yields also needed to be increased to solve the problem of loan dependence. But this solution was not practical, either. Nearly 50 percent of municipalities, towns, and villages had a financial strength index (the total value of basic financial revenue/basic financial demand value) of only 0.3 or under. No matter how they increased local taxes, the effect on the fiscal capacity remained negligible and, as result, they had to depend on national transfer payments. Even local politicians in rich municipalities were hesitant to increase their local tax yields, as they might face the scrutiny of local voters.[36] They preferred to receive national funds the exchanges of which were less visible to local residents.

In essence, general grants function as a common source of tax revenue for local governments. In practice, this has enabled the Ministry of Finance to inject some elasticity into the fiscal structure of the central government. The major concern with local finance measures has focused on the Ministry of Finance's ability to mobilize general grants. On the positive side, the common nature of general grants enables their allocation to be relatively objective and politically neutral, with the decision making based on the computation of the complex fiscal needs of individual local governments, rather than on simple criteria such as area and population. On the negative side, the allocational procedures and practices are so complex that, in practice, professional finance bureaucrats tend to make technical decisions behind closed doors. Information on the itemized fiscal need of individual local governments is available to the public, yet only the bureaucrats in charge can figure it out.[37] In other words, the system has become a means for national fiscal control.

Despite the enhanced control of the bureaucracy, increases in central and local bond expenditure and debt-servicing costs have exceeded reductions in general government spending and will continue to grow faster than national income. Deficit reduction has become one of the most important goals of economic policy. As yet, budget deficits in general government have not dealt a serious blow to the Japanese macroeconomy. The high saving rate of Japanese households sustained a high level of private investment in high-growth periods (e.g., 1988 to 1991) that helped to finance government deficits during periods of fiscal squeeze.

Between 1983 and 1987, as government deficits were restrained, the high saving rate of Japanese households turned Japan into a leading world lender by expanding capital outflow with no corresponding increase in interest rates. The phenomenon of "crowding-out," in which a bond pushes up interest rates to a high level and restricts private investment, has yet to occur in Japan. These indications suggest a stable macroeconomy.

However, it is important to note that household savings as a percentage of disposal income dropped continuously from 16.5 percent in 1985, to 11.9 percent in 1995 and to 5.8 percent in 2004. Should the aging of the population continue to impact on the rate of saving in Japanese households, it is likely that the decline in capital formation will eventually lead to serious economic problems throughout the country. Perhaps the worst-case scenario is that without fundamental fiscal reforms, all assets of Japanese citizens could be absorbed by government bonds. As a countermeasure, deficit reduction must be carried out prior to other objectives in economic policy, doubly so since the Japanese government has frozen its campaign to cut budget deficits while drastically increasing the deficits for economic stimulus packages. To this end, the government clearly needs to reform taxes and to restructure social benefit programs. The urgent necessity of deficit reduction may facilitate significant structural reform and cutbacks despite political pressure. Indeed, it could render major cutbacks acceptable to the population at large and therefore politically legitimate.

In 2003 the Koizumi cabinet was finally ready to design and implement fiscal decentralization by adopting the slogan *sanmi ittai* (trinity or three-in-one) that aimed to reduce or abolish specific grants, simultaneously transfer a part of national taxes to local taxes, and change the structure of general grants. This slogan opened up opportunities for various actors to represent their interests in the reform processes. Finance officials were mainly concerned about stabilizing the level of total spending on general grants, while internal affairs officials wished to reduce specific grants (through which line ministries had controlled counterpart local departments in the past) by devolving part of the national tax base to local governments. Big business claimed that the mechanism of general grants, which had supported the weak fiscal capacity of a local government, should be either downsized or abolished to take self-supporting business enterprise approaches to the provision of local public services. By the end of 2003, local governments, including small villages and towns that had not wished to see the grants-in-aid system abolished, concertedly proposed the abolition of designated promotional and partial subsidies with a compensating devolution of the national tax base. In 2005 the central government and the six national associations of local authorities agreed on the transfer of ¥3 trillion in sources of tax revenue to local governments and a reduction in national transfer payments to local governments of the order of ¥4 trillion. Fiscal decentralization is now finally under way but the agreement is far from resolving the problems of public finance in Japan.

Conclusion

Over the past three decades, demographic and economic changes have forced the Japanese government to shift its policy focus toward retrenchment. This shift indicates the obvious tightening of fiscal constraints on government, a reality that has not been easy for political players and interest groups to accept. A better understanding of welfare state retrenchment can be achieved by examining the following relationships: welfare state expansion and the administrative difficulties that social policy expansion raises; macroeconomic problems and welfare state expansion that can produce adverse effects on the economic structure; and welfare state retrenchment and political pressures that make it difficult to carry out unpopular retrenchments as part of social policy.

This chapter has focused on the impact of retrenchment on the Japanese local government system. In a comparative perspective, Japanese local finance is more regulated than that of other OECD countries. Furthermore, Japanese local government is more integrated into central government (in both financial and functional terms) than is the case in other OECD countries. Thus, it is likely that institutional environment will affect the role of local government in the process of welfare state retrenchment. In other words, the Japanese national government is well positioned to target local governments for retrenchment initiatives. A major finding of this study is that despite this close integration, the retrenchment policy of the central government has been curtailed by its need to conceal its activities from voters and specific interest groups that have brought it to power.

Manipulation of Public Finance

In tandem with the manipulation of public finances, the growth of the welfare state has been limited by its own struggles to restore balance to the budget. Pivotal to such struggles is programmatic retrenchment that targets specific programs because spending cutbacks typically impose material losses on specific groups of voters. It is up to pro-retrenchment coalitions to provide proposals that are acceptable to both politicians and the electorate. Yet it is electorally inexpedient for politicians to target specific programs for spending cutbacks, as this may cause material losses for specific groups within their own constituencies. The coalitions thus seek to maneuver in ways other than programmatic retrenchment in order to avoid the scrutiny of voters. The present analysis shows that the distinctive institution of central-local finance in Japan has allowed the central government more latitude for retrenchment practices. Targeting national transfer payments that indirectly finance programs has lowered the visibility of program cutbacks and obscured the trail of responsibility, as implied by Pierson's theory of the "visibility" and "traceability" of negative consequences.[38] In the 1990s, local governments in Japan collectively spent about 75 percent of public expenditure, while receiving about 35 percent of local government revenue in the form of national transfer payments. In the case of Japan, therefore, this type of financial manipulation has had a significant effect on retrenchment.

Manipulation of Nonfinancial Resources

Even when program cutbacks are disguised in such a way, reductions in transfers to local government may still affect the interests of specific branches of the state apparatus. Advocates of retrenchment need to persuade affected officials to transcend their special interests for the good of common goals. In this study, the central government protected line ministries' interests by substituting administrative control measures for financial ones. The central government effectively dropped promotional subsidies, which had bred LDP patronage politics. Instead, it primarily targeted legally promised shares transferred from national ministries to local governments. The implementation of this target required the manipulation of incentives to affected bureaucrats. Maintaining the volume of approvals and permissions issued by these bureaucrats was one way of ensuring compliance between different bureaucratic interests for reducing expenditures. The politics of retrenchment, although revolving around financial losses, acknowledged that financial resources were only one among a variety of possible power resources.

Institutional Change in Public Finance

As an increasing range of social benefits can lead to government deficits, the necessity to control government spending becomes urgent. The systemic constraints in the administration of public finance tend to emphasize questions relating to the amount of expenditure as opposed to the process of expenditure. There is a need for a strong shift in political leadership toward financial burden sharing rather than financial credit sharing. In the 1980s, the LDP government altered the institutional rules of budgeting by introducing the principles of "zero ceilings" and "minus ceilings." In the early 1990s, the Ministry of Finance acknowledged the necessity of controlling overall central and local spending for macroeconomic purposes. Alliances of top LDP politicians and finance bureaucrats joined forces with big business leaders to attack the line ministries for "mindless growth" in specific grant programs. The interest of the Ministry of Finance did not lie in its ability to allocate specific grants to line ministries, but rather in its ability to determine levels of general grants that are less politicized by politicians and their interest groups. In recent years, the abolition of specific grants has been firmly placed on Japan's political agenda but political leadership in this respect has yet to be tested. In postwar Japan, the national grants system lay at the heart of public finance. In the 1990s, its foundation began to crumble under conditions of budgetary crisis. Government deficit financing inevitably involved attempts at institutional change, particularly the reshuffling of transfers of national funds to local governments.

Political Accountability

The major political challenge of retrenchment policy is to disguise or hide the actual effects of spending cutbacks on specific groups of voters. The present findings demonstrate that changes in central-local financial arrangements can allow a central government to maneuver beyond the limits of political difficulties. This study suggests that retrenchment politics are not a matter of participatory autonomy in which decisions made by local government are accountable to local residents, but rather that of manipulation behind closed doors. In the case study presented, it was increasingly difficult for ordinary voters to trace responsibility for retrenchment effects. Retrenchment strategies, such as the use of budgetary technicalities and the mobilization of national transfer payments not tied to specific programs, have undermined taxpayers' ability to see a relationship between their contribution and the public service offering and have helped to insulate central and local officials from political accountability. Equally important, rather than creating incentives for local tax-collecting efforts, the inherent incentives of national transfer payments created dependency traps for local governments. Local chief executives were less responsive to the extent to which national transfer payments determined levels of local government spending.

Nondecision Making

The task of restructuring a social welfare system for retrenchment purposes is a hazardous political activity that may be derailed by any one of a multitude of factors. Perhaps the most influential factor of these involves a voter mobilization strategy for electoral success or a turf war within the state apparatus. This has proved to be true in Japan's attempt to restructure the social welfare system in a radical way. The central government has been able to make only peripheral headway in programmatic retrenchment. Furthermore, its attempts to restructure the social welfare system have not been represented in any strong ruling body; instead policy elites have tended to maintain their vested interests against new proposals of retrenchment. Irrespective, the central government has continued to attempt some forms of systemic retrenchment, although the effort has been far from easy. In this chapter, we have seen that Japan's public finance underwent significant institutional change, placing local authorities and other organizations under tighter constraints. However, we have also seen that the central government has been able to contain local government spending only to the extent that it has minimized retrenchment politics. Targeting local government for retrenchment may have enabled the central government to avoid political difficulties, yet such a strategy has failed to solve the problem of rising costs associated with expanding social benefits.

Perhaps the most fundamental condition for effective retrenchment is change in basic social values—in particular, views on the limits of welfare state expansion. There are as yet no studies in the literature that focus on these particular changes of values in Japanese society. Nonetheless, an ideological consensus on the legitimacy of retrenchment to facilitate welfare reforms seems, at least intuitively, to be a necessary condition for solving the problems of welfare state retrenchment. It is likely that the frequent mass media coverage of who should shoulder the burden and responsibility for a rapidly aging society will help shape public opinion on necessary reforms. Ongoing government campaigns for deficit reduction may make the impending crisis in government spending and management more visible to the public and thereby set the political stage for further retrenchment.

Finally, another fundamental condition for solving the problems of public finance in Japan is the attempt to reconnect citizens with government institutions and decision-making processes. As government becomes more decentralized, the problems of public finance require more active participation at the local level by informed citizens who need to work together to find solutions. Over the last decade, there has been rapid growth in the number of nonprofit organizations throughout Japan as citizens work together to overcome the inability of the public sector to cover some of the specialized needs of the population. This will be explored more fully in the following chapter.

CHAPTER 3

The Rise of Voluntary Associations: Exclusive Chien-Ketsuen to Inclusive Voluntarism[1]

In Japanese society, there has been a clear shift to individualism, to the "me" and "myself" sort of code of behavior in the daily life of community members. By this token, religious and labor union membership and voter turnout have declined considerably in recent years. Does this mean that Japanese people are "bowling alone?"[2] Many active members in Japan's various communities believe otherwise. "I think that membership has been migrating to other types of civic organizations and engagements."[3]

"*Chien* [neighborhood ties], *ketsuen* [kinship ties] and *kaishaen* [company ties] were ways of cooperative life in traditional Japan but also sources of favoritism and exclusiveness in postwar Japan. Today I need to go out and gather with friends to participate in wider communities."[4]

Perhaps one of the most important changes to have arisen around the globe in the post–Cold War era is that which has occurred in the relationship between the state and citizens. While acknowledging the limits to welfare state expansion, it must also be recognized that the welfare state has been under siege for some time owing to government policies that have targeted social services for spending cutbacks. But there has been a remarkable upsurge in the third, or nonprofit, sector, which Lester Salamon has defined as comprising "a massive array of self-governing private organizations, not dedicated to distributing profits to shareholders or directors, pursuing public purposes outside the formal apparatus of the state."[5] He claims that this has arisen from an associational revolution in which third-sector organizations are paving the way for alternative governance that is more accountable in its efforts to meet human needs.

Despite the diverse ways in which people organize social life, it has been possible to distinguish two broad complexes of organizations in modern society: the market or the private sector and the state or the public sector. Beginning in the twentieth century and extending well into the present, the state has provided an ever-increasing number of services in advanced industrial democracies. The emergence of the welfare state has produced a great variety of ways in which the private and public sectors relate to one another as well as myriad ideologies and associated political activities ranging from antistate liberalism to totalitarianism. By the early 1980s, however, many observers began to speak of the welfare state in terms of its limitations. Concurrently, observers increasingly recognized that a third sector, possessing its own unique organizational features, was on the rise.[6] There seem to be many reasons for the emergence of this sector. One of the most compelling is that organizations in this new sector compensate for those areas in which the private and public sectors have failed to meet societal needs.[7] Thus, the third sector represents not just a major institutional innovation produced by the retrenchment of the welfare state but also an inevitable development evolving out of the failures of the existing sectors.

Yet, these arguments do not provide a fully adequate explanation for this significant development. For one thing, civil society needs to have reached a certain level of maturity to produce the private, nonprofit organizations (NPOs) or nongovernmental organizations (NGOs) found in the third sector. Independent citizens and the great diversity of society are absolutely critical for such a sector to develop.[8] More importantly, it must be remembered that the range of experiences associated with this development in different countries represent considerable variation in cultural traditions, developmental paths, and social norms.

In Japan, the debate over alternative governance in civil society has heated up in recent years. The mass media began to recognize the importance of third-sector-oriented organizations when nearly 1.3 million people voluntarily participated in the relief operations following the 1995 Kobe earthquake. The number of NPO-related articles that appeared in the three main national newspapers— the *Asahi Shinbun, Yomiuri Shinbun,* and *Mainichi Shinbun*—increased continuously from 178 in 1990, 850 in 1992, 1,455 in 1994, 2,151 in 1995, to 2,868 in 1997.[9] Is Japan in the midst of its own associational revolution, or are current developments a sign that the country is taking part in a revolution that is global in scale? To answer this question, one must first consider some important aspects of the market and the state in modern Japan. First, it must be borne in mind that the developmental paths of the market-state relationship in Japan stem from the country's historical tradition and its status as a late-developing state, as shall be explored below. Second, and equally important, the type and direction of change in the ties between the state and societal groups represent an alternative to existing political ideologies. Third, citizens' groups are motivated by neo-radical desires to take matters of governance into their own hands by means of grassroots initiatives. Finally, the demands of a now-prevalent economic rationalism have led to the promotion of a small government philosophy that has resulted in the delegating of some governmental functions to the emergent third sector. The political debate over these matters led the National Diet (national legislature) to pass the Law for the Promotion of Specific Nonprofit Activities (NPO Law) in March 1998.

The emergence, dimensions, and activities of the third sector in Japan merit closer attention. Accordingly, this chapter first seeks to describe the circumstances under which third-sector-oriented NPOs have arisen in Japan. It then examines the nature of these organizations and the role they expect to fill, and finally, assesses their potential impact on political processes and social life. As discussed in this chapter, NPOs are seen as a collective body of autonomous private organizations whose primary concern is neither to achieve gains for an individual or group with respect to the distribution of income in the market nor to influence a government's decision-making process in narrowly specific areas; rather, NPOs advocate policies and collective self-help actions that constitute steps taken toward producing alternative governance.

The available evidence regarding third sector organizations in Japan supports a number of claims. An economic rationalist point of view considers the role of third sector organizations from the perspective of cost effectiveness. Despite the wish to implement cost-effective administration as part of the welfare state retrenchment process, Japan's traditionally strong yet divided bureaucracy has had little success in efficiently delegating governmental responsibilities to the third sector as an integrated part of national policy. The bureaucracy's efforts have been moderated owing to the challenges of numerous parliamentarians to bureaucratic control over the third sector. But the unpopularity of such regulated delegation has made it likely that Japan will see an ongoing upsurge of neo-radicalism. The individuals and groups already participating in organized activities stand ready to exploit opportunities to take local initiative and voluntary action outside state control. Even though they may operate independently and be transparently accountable in their activities, such organizations must undertake projects that correspond with and satisfy the specific interests and concerns of those institutions and others who provide them with funds. Thus, it seems certain that the increasing availability of official funding will have a significant impact on the roles played by third sector organizations.

NPO Expansion

The appearance of third sector organizations in Japan corresponds with the increase over time in the number and influence of social groups in Japanese society. Prewar Japanese society saw the presence of powerful private groups such as big conglomerates and powerful political associations that supported and sought to benefit from state domination. The postwar Allied Occupation attempted to transform the relations between state and society. Accordingly, trade unions and economic associations, which had been suppressed or otherwise controlled in the prewar period, were now encouraged to participate and take a larger stake in society as part of the Occupation's democratization process. The developmental priorities of the 1950s and early 1960s failed to live up to the expectations of the citizens, and industrial pollution and its effects became a major problem. By 1970, there were as many as 3,000 local citizen groups dedicated to protesting pollution problems. Their protests represented not only a new form of political participation but also the emergence of a new political culture. Since the late 1980s, Japan has caught up with the West and the country's society has entered the postindustrial phase. Since then, there has been much talk of a new role for citizens' voluntary groups in a strong society. In such a society, the state cannot transform private practices or resist private demands and is constantly under pressure by the public for fulfilling its demands. Under these conditions, such citizens' groups are expected to advocate policies and propose alternative projects as part of the overall process of restructuring state and society.

The 1990s have seen a remarkable and rapid expansion of two new types of NPOs in Japan that are different in nature from the more traditional trade unions, neighborhood associations, schools, and religious organizations. The first, the voluntary NPO, is regarded by local activists and journalists as an NPO in a narrow sense: an organization that essentially is based on voluntary activities undertaken at the grassroots level. The second type, which some financial bureaucrats and conservative politicians wish to promote, is described as being a *gyosei itaku* (administrative consignment) organization, the term referring to the act of the state administration consigning specific functions to private organizations.

Japan was reported to have some 500,000 NPOs in the late 1990s. The nonprofit sector includes some 85,000 citizens' voluntary organizations, approximately 26,000 *koeki hojin* (public benefit organizations), over 12,000 *shakaifukushi hojin* (social welfare corporations), nearly 70,000 trade unions, about 73,000 political associations, and some 184,000 religious organizations.[10] A 1997 Economic Planning Agency (EPA) survey of 1,159 citizens' voluntary organizations found that 86.4 percent were not registered that had no legal recognition.[11] Public benefit organizations are a narrowly defined category of NPO. There are two types of public benefit organizations: the *zaidan hojin* (foundational organization) and the *shadan hojin* (corporational organization). Authorization for organizations of these types to be established must come from the national ministry in charge in accordance with Article 34 of the Civil Law. Approximately 4,000 of all public benefit organizations are administrative consignment organizations.[12] As for social welfare corporations, they are sectorally defined nonprofit organizations covered by the Social Welfare Service Law. Permission for such organizations to be established must come from either the prefectural governor concerned or the Ministry of Health and Welfare (which merged with the former Ministry of Labor to become the Ministry of Health, Labor and Welfare in 2001).

In 1996 the output of nonprofit activities as defined by the EPA was worth ¥27 trillion (US$250 billion).[13] This is a striking figure. One would expect Japan to have only limited nonprofit activity given the country's pattern of bureaucracy-initiated community developments. But according to the Johns Hopkins Comparative Nonprofit Sector Project, Japan's nonprofit sector is one of the world's largest in terms of the number of people involved, with its 1.4 million workers (1.2 percent of the population) being second only to the 7.1 million (2.6 percent) in the United States and ahead of France (800,000, or 1.5 percent), Britain (900,000, or 1.6 percent), and Germany (1 million, or 1.3 percent). The project's findings also indicated that Japan's operating expenditures in the nonprofit sector account for 3.2 percent of the gross domestic product (GDP), a level comparable to France's 3.3 percent and Germany's 3.6 percent.[14] It is also worth noting in this regard that 3.2 percent of Japan's GDP—the second largest in the world—represents an even more significant quantity of resources than is available in France or Germany. More recent data shows that the production output of the nonprofit sector rose from 1.6 percent in 1970 to 3.7 percent in 1997 as a percent of GDP, with the two new types of NPOs contributing greatly to this growth.[15] Yet the percentage of production output of the nonprofit sector in 2001 remained the same as the percentage in 1997. That more traditional NPOs played a role in contributing to the sluggish growth of production output is perhaps indicated by the stagnation in their numbers. The number of labor unions declined from 70,821 in 1997 to 62,805 in 2004; private schools decreased from 17,384 in 1997 to 15,652 in 2005; and religious organizations dropped from 227,558 in 1997 to 182,634 in 2002.[16]

However, Japan's voluntary organizations in the nonprofit sector experienced rapid growth from the late 1980s. A 1996 EPA survey of 10,000 citizens' voluntary organizations illustrates the trend, with 12.7 percent of the 4,152 organizations that responded having been established between 1966 and 1975, 23.9 percent between 1976 and 1985, and 43.6 percent between 1986 and 1996.[17] Citizens' voluntary organizations are engaged in a variety of activities. According to the EPA survey, their focus areas include social welfare (37.4 percent of all organizations), community planning (16.9 percent), education and sports (16.8 percent), environmental issues (10.0 percent), health and medical care (4.7 percent), and international exchange and cooperation (4.6 percent).[18] In December 1997, the passage into law of a publicly subsidized home care scheme for the elderly sparked an increase in the number of registrations of NPOs involved in social welfare activities as organizations sought to become designated as service providers. The growth pattern in this area more generally seems to be a reflection of globalization and welfare state retrenchment. There has been a notable upsurge in the number of NPOs involved in international exchange and cooperation activities and environment issues as well. The number of globally organized NGOs in which Japanese groups participate increased from 412 in 1960 to 1,863 in 1994, and the number of NGOs (whose main office is in Japan) accredited by the United Nations Economic & Social Council (ECOSOC), rose from 8 in 1987, 15 in 1999, to 28 in 2005. As for environmental organizations, by 2004 there were 3,914 registered with the Japan Environment Association.[19]

It should be noted in passing here that the reason why private organizations for the promotion of international cooperation or the protection of the environment are often called NGOs rather than NPOs is that this is the term adopted by the United Nations (UN) and specialized UN agencies in invitations to participate in their conferences (i.e., Article 71 of the UN Charter). In Japan, the term "NGO" is often used in a general way to indicate international or domestic nongovernmental and nonprofit citizens' organizations that address such global issues as development concerns, human rights, environment, and peace. Some scholars argue that NPOs are primarily self-help-oriented membership organizations, while NGOs are service organizations that deal directly with clients or beneficiaries.[20] Although it is analytically useful to make a distinction between NPOs and NGOs, they overlap in their activities and practices.

The emergence of citizens' voluntary organizations parallels that of administrative consignment organizations. The continuous increase in the government budget deficit since the Fiscal Year (FY) 1975 has prioritized deficit reduction as one of the most urgent objectives of national policy. To this end, all government activities have been under review and made targets of administrative reform. In the early 1980s, this was accompanied by Japan's conservative government's move toward economic rationalism. To promote small government, the Second Provisional Commission on Administrative Reform (*Dai-ni Rincho*) was formed in 1981. The commission's final report of March 1983 called for the government to clearly stipulate and delegate the various activities, duties, and responsibilities of government to private organizations. The conservative government of Prime Minister Nakasone Yasuhiro thus began to see such organizations as having integral roles to play in public administration. In parallel with this shift, the government also privatized some state-operated enterprises, particularly those in deficit such as the National Railways. Both developments were part of the small government initiative. Administrative consignment cases have increased dramatically since the late 1970s, as may be inferred by the growth in the number of legal provisions enacted in this area (59 from 1966 to 1975, 124 from 1976 to 1985, 238 from 1986 to 1997, and 330 from 1998 to 2003).[21] In FY 2002, 683 organizations received consignment payments from the central government totaling ¥170 billion (US$1.5 billion), while 3,053 organizations received some ¥502 billion (US$4.6 billion) from prefectural governments.[22]

The development of nonprofit activities has been an ongoing process. This continuity makes it difficult to separate the two new types of NPOs from traditional NPOs. Consider, for example, environmental groups. In the earlier stages of growth in environmental movements, such groups were concerned mainly with the visible impact of industrial pollution on local communities. They operated primarily as pressure groups that worked to remove the immediate and identifiable causes of industrial pollution by urging the state not to pursue growth-first policies and by seeking to recover through litigation the damages caused by industrial pollution. They quickly identified the direct sources of environmental problems (that is, industrial pollution) and those responsible for it, and displayed a sense of community solidarity. In the mid-1970s, however, this pressure group activity began to weaken and collapse as their interests became diffused. They turned their interest toward more localized pollution problems and, as a result, the connections and communications among groups across the nation faded or were severed. Furthermore, they failed to transfer their earlier concern for environmental protection in local communities to wider environmental issues. Nature conservation activists—who were gradually organizing themselves in the same time frame—promoted the general interests of conservation by advocating more general policies and taking collective self-help action rather than taking action against specific government policies. The development of a national trust movement was a reflection of these changes, with organizations arising in the mid-1980s that used private contributions to purchase and manage the "irreplaceable"—notably historic buildings, neighborhoods, and natural landscapes.[23] As a broad category, environmental organizations have been shifting from focused pressure groups to self-help-oriented groups with a more direct participatory orientation. Supporting this growth of nonprofit activities is a 1985 law that permits individuals and corporations to deduct charitable contributions to these national trust organizations.

Social welfare groups represent more than one-third of citizens' voluntary organizations. They have changed in line with the aging of Japanese society. Social welfare corporations, which were created and audited under the Social Welfare Service Law of 1951, dominated the field of welfare NPOs in the postwar era. These corporations were greatly dependent on public funds—relying on them for 80–90 percent of their total income—and were heavily regulated by the government. With the beginning of the twenty-first century, the percentage of Japan's population aged 65 and over is continuing to rise. This has put considerable pressure on existing welfare organizations, which are unable to cope with the increasing demand for individualized social services such as visiting nurse, home care, and other social aid. As a result, citizens' voluntary organizations oriented toward self-help for the elderly have been organized in increasing numbers since the mid-1980s to meet these needs.[24]

The new social welfare organizations are essentially service providers, in contrast to the advocacy groups that preceded them. The distinctions between the service areas these organizations cover and the scope of public welfare services are not clear. It is clear, however, that government bureaucrats tend to expect such organizations to function as an extension of the government in the provision of services. To this end, organizations operating in this area receive more public subsidies than any other type of voluntary group.[25] This has not dampened the dramatic growth in voluntary welfare activity, although the exact nature of the partnership between these groups and the public sector has yet to be specified.

Historical Tradition to Economic Rationalism

In prewar Japan, there were no NPOs as such, but there did exist self-governing natural groups at the level of *buraku* (indigenous natural groups at the grassroots level) that served the villagers' interests by protecting their communal lifestyle that had developed from the need to improve agricultural production during the Tokugawa period. Born of necessity, the communities existed outside the formal apparatus of the political system. With the Meiji era came the development of a new local government system, and the national government began to make tactical use of *buraku* cohesiveness to place localities under more centralized control.[26] The central authority's ongoing effort to incorporate grassroots groups into state administration reached its peak in 1940 when the home ministry officially reorganized 199,000 community-based organizations into a nationwide network of 1.2 million *tonarigumi* (neighborhood associations). The wartime mobilization effort made participation in these associations compulsory and imposed uniformity in their organization. The associations were then made collectively responsible for rationing consumer goods, providing civil defense training, and managing public health and fire-fighting activities. They eventually occupied a strategic position in the government's effort to keep the masses under control throughout the wartime mobilization.

The associations were abolished after the war in 1947 by order of the Occupation authority. As the legacy of the associations made the public wary of the potential for community groups to be used as a means of state control, the central government handled its relations with social groups with extreme caution in the early postwar period. It was the rising tide of administrative reform in the 1980s that saw the revival of the historical tradition of close ties between the state and social groups through the new administrative consignment approach. The remaining vestiges of bureaucratic domination tenaciously adapted to the rhetoric of small government by being promoted under the banner of economic rationalism. Conservative forces, including Liberal Democratic Party (LDP) politicians, bureaucrats, and leaders of big business, clearly acknowledged the importance of the nonprofit sector, but they tended to see it as playing a complementary, yet nonofficial, government role. The influential LDP politician Kato Koichi observed, "The national bureaucracy began to wonder in recent years if it would be necessary to have [private voluntary organizations] compensate for those areas where our administration cannot easily manage."[27] Okawara Yoshio, an adviser to the Ministry of Foreign Affairs, went even further in commenting, "I would be most pleased if, . . . we could see [organizations] engaged in assistance activities that are truly hands-on, that can be directed where they are needed most [*kidoteki*] and offered with care and precision [*kimekomakai*]. This would help the national government in those areas where it is not good at providing assistance."[28]

More importantly, as described below, bureaucrats essentially have made every effort to preserve the network of regulatory controls over the nonprofit sector. Apart from administrative consignment organizations, it has been extremely difficult for NPOs to obtain their legal status and was even more so before the enactment of the NPO Law. In accordance with Article 34 of the Civil Law, applicants for public benefit organizations must satisfy certain financial qualifications: foundational institutions must have more than ¥300 million in funds and an annual activities budget of at least ¥30 million. Even more difficult, NPOs must obtain authorization from a prefectural department or a national ministry in order to operate legally. The criteria for such authorization are not statutorily defined. Furthermore, once an organization has been authorized, it is often subject to prefectural or ministerial supervision.[29] A large number of NPOs thus choose to go unregistered. These unregistered organizations have no choice but to operate with the legal status of a private individual rather than a public benefit organization, which affects, for example, how they manage their income and assets, how they file their tax reports, and forces them to lease office space without the tax-deduction benefits for such an organization.

Perhaps the greatest threat to eroding the self-governance of authorized NPOs lies in their personnel links with and financial dependence on specific national ministries or prefectural departments. In the past, ex-bureaucrats have been invited onto the board, or offered a directorship or senior positions in the authorized NPOs they had monitored during their government career in the classic *amakudari* (descent from heaven) arrangement. In 1998, 2,441 out of 6,869 (35.5 percent) public benefit organizations under the jurisdiction of national ministries had ex-bureaucrats as directors, while 5,563 out of 19,606 (28.4 percent) such organizations under prefectural department jurisdiction had such individuals in key posts. As of 2003, the practice of *amakudari* remains strong, with 2,325 out of 7,009 (33.2 percent) under national jurisdiction and 5,095 out of 18,987 (26.8 percent) under prefectural jurisdiction.[30]

There are two dominant features linked with the incorporation of ex-bureaucrats as key personnel. First, the successful implementation of the small-government approach is largely dependent upon the use of public benefit organizations. Second, these organizations are dependent on national or prefectural governments for a significant proportion of their revenues. In FY 2002, 533 of the 7,086 public benefit organizations under the jurisdiction of the central government received national grants of ¥413 billion (US$3.8 billion), and 4,459 out of the 19,132 public benefit organizations under prefectural government jurisdiction received prefectural grants of ¥377 billion (US$3.4 billion).[31] These national and prefectural grants accounted for about 10 percent of the total revenues of public benefit organizations. In this mutually reliant relationship, *amakudari* essentially satisfies two aims: (1) it allows the government ministries and departments to protect the scope of their turf, and (2) it allows public benefit organizations to continue to receive government funds. While bureaucrats will tolerate a certain degree of autonomy on the part of these organizations, the latter cannot afford to undermine the interests of the ministries or prefectural departments concerned. However, the bureaucratic tendency to treat the authorized NPOs as an outpost of their departments was reduced somewhat in September 1996 when the cabinet, responding to pressure from the general public as well as the LDP's coalition partners, the Social Democratic Party of Japan (SDPJ) and Shinto Sakigake (New Party Harbinger), finally acknowledged that NPOs had been major destinations for *amakudari*. To redress the imbalance that resulted, the government decided to reduce the number of ex-bureaucrat directors in the authorized NPOs by over 60 percent. As a consequence, the number of public benefit organizations with ex-bureaucrats dropped from 1,017 in 1997 to 451 in 2003.[32] However, this reduction, when implemented, amounted to only 44 percent.

Economic Rationalism to Alternative Governance?

The political foundation for grassroots nonprofit activities in Japan was laid in the late 1980s. The LDP lost its majority in the National Diet's upper house in the 1989 national election, which produced a major power shift of domestic forces. Splinter groups broke away from the LDP and the party's 38-year-long rule came to an end in the 1993 lower house election, bringing to a close its position as one of the most dominant forces shaping the legitimate political economy of the developmental state.

At the same time, the strong yen brought more cash to Japan. The competitive export sector shifted its focus from foreign trading to direct investment and Japanese companies learned new modes of operation. They learned, for example, that they could more easily be accepted as part of a local economy by forming partnerships with local NPOs in host countries. The companies then brought what they learned back to Japan. November 1990 saw the formation of the One Percent Club of the Keidanren (Federation of Economic Organizations) by 176 economic organizations that committed themselves to contribute more than 1 percent of their net profits to corporative philanthropy.

Following the collapse of the bubble economy in 1991, it became apparent that the legacy of heavily regulated markets was counterproductive for the recovery of Japan's ailing economy. Furthermore, the long-held dominant but neutral reputation of bureaucrats was tarnished by the involvement of a number of civil servants in a variety of scandals, such as those involving HIV-infected blood products, the bailout of bankrupt mortgage companies, and the alleged cover-up of mishaps at a nuclear power plant.[33] While the dominance of the central bureaucracy helped to block its accountability to the general public, the traditional views of the bureaucracy as being prestigious, neutral, and reliable were steadily changing. The government's inability to cope with the crisis of the Kobe earthquake and the market's failure to revitalize the Japanese economy left many with the sense that neither was capable any longer of fulfilling social needs.

The situation changed once the proposed institutionalization of the nonprofit sector was put on the agenda in the National Diet, eventually culminating in the passage of the NPO Law. Two months before the Kobe disaster, a nationwide liaison organization called the Association for Institutionalizing Citizens' Activity (C's [*sic*] *Shimin Katsudo o Sasaeru Seido o Tsukuru Kai*) was established to promote the legislation of a law on NPOs. The association had wide support throughout the nonprofit sector and sought to achieve its goal of shaping the government's agenda for nonprofit organizations by working with certain political parties, specifically, Shinto Sakigake, SDPJ, and Shinshinto (New Frontier Party).

Immediately after the January 1995 earthquake, the national government finally organized an 18-ministry liaison council that was charged with drafting legislation concerning voluntary organizations. The council produced a draft that was rejected by NPO leaders on the grounds that NPOs were too narrowly defined, which would diminish their self-governing status. This was followed in February and March by the creation of NPO project teams by the government coalition (LDP, Shinto Sakigake, and Japan Social Democratic Party) and Shinshinto. These teams were created with the intention of drafting NPO legislation, the goal being to produce a law created by National Diet members rather than bureaucrats. Around the same time, a coalition of groups in the nonprofit sector including C's, the NPO Promotion Forum, and the NGO Activity Promotion Center launched the Liaison Council for the Institutionalization of Citizens' Activities. The council began forging links between NPO leaders and National Diet members as a means of attracting the attention of the mass media to the NPO law issue. These activities led to a three-year-long process of negotiations over the law that put NPO leaders in a position to play a direct role in the law-making process. The political parties then opposed the bill proposed by bureaucrats, as some National Diet members were determined to exclude the influence of the national bureaucracy from the negotiation process.[34] The NPO Law that the National Diet members had drafted was passed unanimously in March 1998 with the support of all political parties.

This unanimous passage was the product of efforts to reconcile conflicting interests among political forces. Such senior LDP leaders as Nakasone Yasuhiro and Miyazawa Kiichi, although recognizing the rise of private NPOs and NGOs, had failed to plan for how their existence would affect the relationship between the state and its citizens. Some new LDP leaders, such as Kato Koichi, tended to see the activities and objectives of NPOs not as being an alternative but as being complementary to those of the state; accordingly, in the view of these new leaders, bureaucrats would have to accept the presence and participation of NPOs given that they were unavoidably increasing in number. The Democratic Party of Japan (DPJ) went further and sought to encourage NPO initiatives in civil society. The party's leader, Hatoyama Yukio, was determined to help establish an alternative approach to governance oriented toward citizen participation, a call matched by proposals from the party that Japanese society was shifting away from being centered on the state and was revolving more around its citizens.[35] Finally and interestingly, traditional leftists and younger LDP politicians took the view that citizen activities were not necessarily opposed to society's institutions of power and pragmatically supported NPO participation in policy formation. On August 5, 1999, 204 National Diet members from five political parties (including the LDP) acted independently of their parties to create the NPO Diet Members League. On November 25, such young LDP Diet members as Aichi Kazuo and Kumashiro Akihiko—who had issued strong calls that private individuals be allowed to deduct charitable contributions from their taxes—established the LDP Special Committee on NPOs.

The Legal Framework and Recent Trends

The legal status of a citizens' voluntary organization can be defined under either the Civil Law (Article 34) or the NPO Law. But legal provisions are imprecise, so it is not clear how organizations based on the NPO Law will be legally differentiated from those established under the provisions of the Civil Code. There are as yet no legal precedents associated with this dual structure. Equally important, the NPO Law dictates that central and local governments are obliged to authorize the official status of a *tokutei hieiri katsudo hojin* (specified nonprofit activity organizations), but those who drafted the law did not include a detailed description of the nature of statutory constraints that would be applicable to the thousands of diverse service organizations.

To be authorized under the NPO Law, an organization must meet certain conditions. It cannot distribute profits to its members (Article 2-2-1). Less than a third of its employees are to be paid (Article 2-2-1). The organization may develop, modify, or promote a specific policy but is prohibited from supporting any particular political or religious belief (Article 2-2-2). It must promote public purposes (Articles 1 and 2-1), the interpretation of which allows considerable scope for administrative discretion. A survey of prefectural officials in charge of NPO applications found that 22 of the 47 prefectures consulted with the EPA about how the NPO Law should be applied, with many respondents pointing out that "application samples supplied by the Agency were more useful than the law itself."[36] The survey also found that 80.9 percent of the respondents thought the scope of activities designated under the law was quite vague.

Immediately after its 1998 enactment, the NPO Law did not bring immediate and tangible benefits to the authorized organizations. NPO income from for-profit activities as defined under the Corporation Tax Law was still taxed. At the local level, most municipalities had already applied or planned to give exemptions to, or reductions of, some local taxes for activities defined as nonprofit under the NPO Law. All 47 prefectures had already taken this action. Of equal importance to NPOs was Finance Minister Miyazawa Kiichi's reluctant announcement of February 4, 1999, that the government would move toward granting extensive tax-preferential treatment for charitable contributions.[37] This was expected to change the funding landscape for NPOs. Prior to this, the 1990 tax law permitted business corporations to make deductions for a wide range of charitable contributions and the 1988 revision of the tax system had enabled private individuals to claim deductions for charitable contributions made to *tokutei koeki zoshin hojin* (special public interest–promoting organizations). As of 1998, 3.5 percent of all public benefit organizations fell into this narrowly defined category. As a consequence of this, only 1 percent of the total revenue raised by the nonprofit sector came from private charitable contributions. The EPA's 1996 survey of citizens' voluntary organizations showed that such organizations received only 4.8 percent of their total revenue from charitable contributions; and corroborating this finding, the Cabinet Office 2001 survey of NPOs, which was incorporated under the NPO Law, indicated that these organizations also received 5.5 percent from contributions.[38] As for corporate giving, in FY 1996 corporations donated ¥490 billion, or about 9 percent of the nonprofit sector's total revenue.[39] In contrast, contributions were the largest revenue source for NGOs, accounting for 43.9 percent of their total revenue for 1996.[40]

From August 1999, the nonpartisan NPO Diet Members League examined proposals for tax deductibility for donations to NPOs. The members worked with NPO leaders to hold open forums across the nation. Certain progressive measures exempting NPOs from taxation were finally introduced in March 2001 when the National Diet passed the Law Amending in Part the Special Tax Measures Law. This was the first legislation to loosen the bureaucratic grip over tax privileges for NPOs, asking eligible NPOs to receive tax-deductible donations. Although the legislation represented a major gain by NPOs, to gain the tax privilege NPOs had to satisfy strict conditions, especially the requirement that donations and grants must constitute more than one-third of total revenues. According to C's survey, only 10 percent of NPOs were expected to receive tax-deductible contributions.[41] Even worse than expected, after one year, only

10 NPOs (or 0.1 percent of NPOs) had been approved to receive the tax status.[42] In April 2003, further revisions of the Special Tax Measures Law came into effect to ease the rising criticism of the restrictive system. Under the revised law, the conditions that NPOs must satisfy to gain the tax privilege were somewhat relaxed; for example, the one-third minimum requirement of total revenues from donations and grants was reduced to one-fifth for a trial period of three years. The impact of these amendments on NPOs has yet to be observed.

NPOs expect that acquiring official status may help them to increase their membership and collect more charitable contributions. According to a survey partially conducted by C's, 86.3 percent of 402 respondents saw the expected official designation as an opportunity to increase their organizations' reputation and 56.5 percent applied for the status in order to receive government subsidies or collect dues from their members.[43] Not surprisingly, the survey also found that 86.3 percent of respondents wanted to see charitable contributions exempted from taxation and that 62.7 percent expected to see a further lowering of taxes on those activities specified as for-profit in the Corporation Tax Law.

Most of the citizens' voluntary organizations that file applications for official designation have been established during the 1990s and are financially better off than the average unregistered organization. Between December 1998 and January 2000, there were 1,834 NPO applications (1,698 at the prefectural level and 136 at the national level) of which 1,317 (1,220 at the prefectural level and 97 at the national level) were eventually approved. It is important to note that government officials asked for revisions and resubmission on 80.6 percent of all applications, often instructing the applicants to alter the type of nonprofit enterprise they sought to create or change the scope of nonprofit activities they would undertake.[44] According to C's 1999 survey, the responses of nearly three-quarters of the applicants were local in their focus. The Kobe earthquake experience clearly had a major impact on the formation of NPOs, with 56.7 percent of the organizations applying for authorization being established after 1995. Overall, most of the organizations were quite new, with 75.4 percent established after 1990. The survey also found that 64.4 percent of all applying organizations were involved in activities related to health, medical care, and social welfare, as opposed to 21.2 percent focusing on the environment, 18.9 percent involved in international cooperation activities, and 12.4 percent addressing human rights issues (though it should be noted that some organizations indicated activities in more than one category). This concentration in health, medical care, and social welfare activities is probably due to the inauguration of a publicly subsidized home care scheme for the elderly in April 2000—according to the survey's results, 31.1 percent of the organizations applied in anticipation of becoming designated care providers under this program.[45]

As noted above, the organizations that applied for authorization seemed to be financially well off compared to unregistered citizens' voluntary organizations in general. Slightly more than half (53.5 percent) had paid employees, while only 23 percent of the 4,152 unregistered organizations could afford paid employees. Nearly one-third of the applicants had an annual budget in the ¥10 to ¥50 million range while more than two-thirds had budgets over ¥1 million. In contrast, almost half of the unregistered voluntary organizations in Tokyo had annual budgets under ¥500,000. More than 80 percent of the unregistered organizations emphasized that receiving government aid was an urgent necessity. The NPOs applying for recognition were of a similar view, with 82.8 percent of those that applied in anticipation of receiving more tax-preferential treatments in the future time indicating their desire for increases and improvements in financial aid from the government.[46]

Despite a desire for government aid, most citizens' organizations can also be seen as a spontaneous manifestation at a grassroots level of people's need to participate in shaping some aspect of society. They undertake their activities with the goal of helping themselves, rather than to make up for deficiencies in state administration.[47] In this respect, an increasingly important concern is NPO accountability, as NPOs need to be accountable to nonmembers as well as members in order to fulfill their roles as responsible service providers. Some NGOs, such as those dealing with human rights issues and abuses, and environmental deterioration, have attracted massive numbers of nonmember beneficiaries all around the world. Though they may benefit from the NGOs services, these NGO beneficiaries nonetheless have found it extremely difficult to hold the organizations accountable for their activities.[48] Perhaps the most important is information disclosure. The NPO Law (Articles 28-2 and 29-2) requires both the authorized NPOs and the government departments concerned to release certain information, upon request, about an individual organization's activities. The types of information to be released include reports on an organization's business activities encompassing its balance sheets, data on assets and liabilities, and a list of its directors. Since NPOs receive preferential treatment in terms of their tax status and the kinds and amounts of government aid they are eligible for, the general view is that these organizations should disclose information about their activities to validate that they are indeed operating in the pursuit of public purposes.

While the 1997 EPA survey on 1,159 registered and unregistered citizens' voluntary organizations found that 81.1 percent acknowledged the necessity of providing the information, only 19.1 percent felt that the information they were able to release provided sufficient information to satisfy public needs owing to inadequate workforce, financial resources, and know-how. The survey also showed that welfare service providers (92, or 62.6 percent, of 147 organizations) were less likely to believe that disclosing information was more of a necessity than policy advocacy groups (35, or 89.7 percent, of 39 organizations). Most critically, 40.3 percent of 940 citizens' voluntary organizations felt that the information released to their own members was inadequate. Grassroots organizations lack not only financial resources but also sufficient numbers of workers with the right expertise.[49] While better technology is becoming more accessible and affordable, NPOs need to recruit capable staff members and accumulate know-how so that they can make better use of the available technology to collect more data; create better reports; build networks with partners, supporters, and beneficiaries; and generate public interest in their operations.

The key reason underlying the difficulty of NPOs to be fully accountable to their stakeholders is more fundamental and concerns the self-defining orientation of these organizations. There are no uniform criteria accepted by the wider community for evaluating the performance of NPOs. While criteria for evaluation are often formulated for nonprofit organizations receiving government consignment payments or grants as a means of ensuring their accountability, there are no simple, uniform measures that can be applied to NPOs as there are for assessing the performance of for-profit business firms.

The degree to which NPOs are fulfilling their responsibilities cannot be determined in the absence of universally externally accepted criteria. Furthermore, NPOs are expected to fulfill missions that do not necessarily make it possible for them to operate with total economic efficiency. As part of their operation, they may place value on activities or missions that are economically inefficient, such as providing charity or engaging in volunteer activities. It is the fundamental diversity of NPOs that is the challenge, for any criteria to evaluate how well such organizations meet their obligations would have to be equally diverse.

A 1998 EPA survey of the general public found that approximately 20 percent of respondents were already involved in citizens' voluntary activities and about 80 percent of nonactivists were willing to participate in future.[50] Nonetheless, NPOs will need to overcome the obstacles outlined above and adopt criteria acceptable to the public if these organizations hope to gain the trust and confidence of the wider community. Doing so will make NPOs more accountable and thus facilitate a good reputation as service providers. Japan's grassroots nonprofit organizations have the potential to expand the basis of their membership and nurture future NPO leaders, but in order to do so these organizations will have to make some adjustments as to how they address the issues surrounding their accountability to members, the wider community, and governments.

The 2003 amendment of the NPO Law involved several changes in order to expand the authorized fields of nonprofit activities and, as a result, NPOs can now be incorporated relatively easily under this law. As table 3.1 shows, there were 15,578 NPO organizations incorporated as of February 2004; and the number is still increasing rapidly. In December 2004, the Koizumi cabinet announced a plan for reform of the public interest corporation system, but its official guidelines for reform of Japan's nonprofit sector as a whole remained untouched. In 2006 there were no clear government guidelines for providing incentives for nonprofit activities. Authorization for NPO incorporation offers little in the way of promoting nonprofit activities and NPO leaders are closely monitoring the development of forthcoming bills that might include concrete measures to promote their activities.

Table 3.1 NPOs incorporated under the NPO Law, 1999–2004

	1999	*2000*	*2001*	*2002*	*2004* *(as of February)*
National authorization	135	323	587	997	1,418
Local authorization	1,589	3,477	6,009	9,667	14,160

Source: Calculated from materials provided by Japan, Council for the Promotion of Decentralization, April 9, 2004.

Conclusion

In Japan, citizen-initiated organizations traditionally were seen as antiestablishment or antigovernment in orientation. Far from being a major source of private initiative, civil society organizations established during World War II functioned as an arm of government. The Japanese government, like that of Britain, has seen the nonprofit sector as being an integral part of state administration and has sought to cosign the delivery of some services to specific NPOs. In Britain, the promotion of the nonprofit sector's activities has come as part of a coordinated social policy intended to reduce government spending on social services. However, while Japan's ministries and local governments have promoted the use of NPOs to provide ministry-specific services, they have done so only in a piecemeal fashion rather than through a coherent and coordinated effort.

Over the past decade, Japan has seen extraordinary growth in the nonprofit sector that essentially stems from spontaneous grassroots initiatives. The organizations that have arisen are a result of concerned individuals identifying specific social needs in their immediate environment and taking matters into their own hands to meet those needs. It seems certain that NPOs will play an even greater role in satisfying public purposes while remaining independent of formal government organizations. NPOs, however, do need to be institutionalized further—a process that includes improving accountability, acquiring greater manpower and know-how, and establishing statutory measures designed to promote and protect NPO activities—to gain the trust and confidence of the public. Most NPOs recognize the limits of total self-management and hope to establish cooperative relationships with central and local governments as well as commercial enterprises. Financial support has not kept pace with organizational growth in the nonprofit sector and NPOs will have to rely on government aid as their primary financial resource. In fact, the 1996 EPA survey indicated that central and local government aid already represented nearly one-quarter of total revenues for citizens' voluntary organizations—second only to membership fees. That said, while NPOs wish to receive more and better government aid, they also seek to minimize or even eliminate any government regulation of their activities. This desire to remain independent is expressed in the manner in which their organizations are formed, arising as they do from the initiatives of private citizens rather than from social groups or households that have typified traditional grassroots organizations as *buraku*. Most of Japan's NPOs have operated as service organizations, while few as yet have acted as advocacy groups. For example, even the country's largest environmental organization, the Wild Birds Association (49,000 members), is in no way structured to take on the duties generally expected of an advocacy group. NPOs, regardless of the activities they undertake, will need to be innovative if they are to make maximum use of the scarce resources available to them and to operate in a transparent way to ensure accountability. By so doing, NPOs will be able to persuade both the public and government officials that they offer viable alternatives to government agencies as a means of satisfying public needs.

CHAPTER 4

Democratic Decentralization: Participation in Local Community Decision Making

Delegation of decision-making power to the primary competent body (or subsidiary) is suitable for meeting the varied needs and circumstances of citizens. This arrangement can help to facilitate close democratic interactions and promote transparency in government decision-making processes. The Maastricht Treaty prescribes the European Union as a public place "in which decisions are taken as closely as possible to the wishes of citizens."

"In Japan, with the one exception of bureaucrats, big businessmen, politicians, local authorities, journalists and academics are calling, in chorus, for decentralization. However, they are singing in multiple voices, rather than one voice."[1]

National unity and centralization have proved to be an effective strategy for Japan's modernization since the early years of the Meiji period (1868–1912). These approaches are no longer fitting or relevant to twenty-first-century Japan for they require excessive centralization of government decision-making authority and an overconcentration of major business headquarters in the city of Tokyo. The limitations of the earlier strategies for modernization are also reflected in recent decentralization drives based upon the Fourth National Comprehensive Development Plan of 1987 that calls for multipolar and dispersed patterns of development. It has taken some ten years for the changes initiated in the second half of 1997 to move to the implementation stage.

The impetus toward decentralization, however, has been increasingly overshadowed by economic stimulus policy and deregulation. Frustrated by lack of firm action, local residents working at the grassroots level, have taken matters into their own hands through local initiatives, such as freedom of information lawsuits initiated by individuals, locally mooted referenda, and ombuds (OMBs) activities. This chapter assesses the capacity of individuals working as a collective to introduce policy in Japan in spite of the central government's painfully slow action.

Japan's decentralization movement has focused on delegating decision-making authority to local government in an effort to meet the diversified preferences of citizens in an advanced economy. Activity at the administrative level has involved the consolidation of municipalities (regionalization), a redistribution of tasks between levels of government, and a reshuffling of their financial relations. Struggles over the different responsibilities of central and local government have been dominated by a number of specific interests including those of the National Diet legislative members, bureaucrats, big business associations, labor unions, and local authorities. By June 1993, both houses of the National Diet had unanimously agreed to promote the decentralization drive. Then, in 1999 Japan's clear-cut turn toward functional decentralization resulted in the Collective Decentralization Law that abolished the system of the agency-assigned functions that had been in operation ever since the 1889 Meiji Constitution.[2] From 2000, the decentralization movement progressively shifted its almost exclusive focus on functional decentralization toward a focus on fiscal decentralization, which is ultimately expected to provide local authorities with the necessary financial resources for functional decentralization.[3] As part of this process, agency-assigned functions were specifically abolished to make national ministries' circulars and notifications automatically null and void. Thus, local government officials no longer had to rely on the directions of national ministries and were able to work autonomously as policymakers and planners for public management. While this amplified the scope of policy areas that local assemblies could deal with on an independent basis, local politicians were now held accountable for much greater areas of local governance and ordinance making.

With decision-making authority delegated to localities, local residents were expected to play a greater role and assume some responsibility for local political processes. They have proved to be well prepared for this challenge, for they had already initiated freedom of information lawsuits, local referenda, and paved the way for an ombuds representative.

Decentralization from Above

The process of decentralization—far from being a monolithic administrative movement—can be best appraised through three ideological perspectives. The first is political reformism, which aims to root out the various sources of "money politics." In June 1993 both houses of the National Diet acknowledged that centralized transfer payments such as the grants-in-aid system constituted one source of "money politics" and they passed a resolution calling for the promotion of decentralization. The second perspective focuses upon economic rationalism. When an alliance between top Liberal Democratic Party (LDP) politicians and business leaders (with LDP strongman Nakasone Yasuhiro in the vanguard) sought to promote "small government" along with political reform, Japanese industry and some financial institutions were dissatisfied with the slow progress of administrative reform. To help rectify the situation, the Third Council for the Promotion of Administrative Reform, an advisory body to

Prime Minister Hosokawa Morihiro, strongly urged deregulation and decentralization in its final report of October 1993. The last perspective of "liberal autonomism" can be seen as a set of ideas favored by the associations of local authorities. These associations sought to establish a basis for self-government that would leave local government free to provide a range of specific services. In September 1994 the six national associations of local authorities collectively submitted a recommendation advocating this view to both the National Diet and the Murayama Tomiichi cabinet.

In an attempt to reconcile conflicting interests, the Murayama cabinet, in December 1994, finalized a set of guidelines for decentralization. Six months later the Decentralization Promotion Law was passed in the National Diet, and that July the Committee for the Promotion of Decentralization was established in accordance with the legislation. Although the decentralization advocates affirmed the general significance of decentralization, a rift remained over detailed implementation. The most controversial issue centered on a lively political debate about *ukezara* (saucer), a term describing how the decision-making authority of the central government "spilt" over into the "saucer" of local government's capacity. As part of the *ukezara* debate, the local authorities' competence to act as decision-making authorities was questioned. If they were not competent, then existing levels of municipalities and prefectures would need to be reshuffled or amalgamated to facilitate the desired levels of decision-making capacity. The public debate also probed the need to redraw financial and functional responsibilities between all levels of government.

Prefectural governors and big city mayors perceived their local governments as competent to carry out the responsibilities demanded by decentralization. However, chief executives at the town and village levels were less sure. According to a survey of local chief executive perceptions conducted by the business daily *Sankei Shinbun* in December 1995, 49.6 percent of 1,905 respondents saw local government as incompetent to carry out the responsibilities demanded by decentralization. But the confidence of prefectures (100 percent) and municipalities (70.2 percent)—compared with that of towns and villages (39.1 percent)—was sufficiently large to call the findings of this survey into question. There were also inconsistencies in the evaluations of local government competence, making it unlikely that the amalgamation of municipalities in cities, towns, and villages would ever be legislatively enforced. Instead, there was a call for voluntary amalgamation that relied on the 1995 revision of the Law Concerning Special Measures on the Merger of Municipalities. However, prefectural governors remained uneasy about central government policies that aimed to increase the responsibilities of municipalities. They generally opposed the abolition of prefectures and any form of prefecture merger,[4] yet business organizations were calling for prefectures to be abolished and replaced by larger regional units.[5] There were also a handful of influential politicians including Ozawa Ichiro who suggested doing away with prefectures and consolidating municipalities as part of a larger structure.[6] In short, the political debate on territorial reorganization has been highly controversial.

The *ukezara* debate provided the Ministry of Home Affairs (MOHA) and other bureaucratic authorities with a pretext for delaying the delegation of decision-making authority to local government. The recommendation submitted by the six national associations of local authorities recognized the likely politicization of territorial reorganization. They then affirmed the goal of decentralization while delaying any decision on changes within the existing two territorial levels of government. The business community came to support this position. In December 1994 the Murayama cabinet subsequently announced that a motion for territorial reorganization would be tabled for the present time, a move perhaps calculated to defuse the *ukezara* debate that had served national bureaucrats as a pretext for delaying decentralization.

In March 1996 the Committee for the Promotion of Decentralization submitted to Prime Minister Hashimoto Ryutaro an interim report in which it bluntly proposed the complete abolition of agency-assigned functions. Unfortunately, the relevant national ministries had not been consulted, an action that was considered to be a radical departure from traditional practices. Two months later, the economic organization federation, Keidanren, and the Rengo trade union council hailed the report but also appealed for further decentralization.

When preparing its December 1996 First Recommendation Report, the committee was forced to include only those recommendations on which relevant national ministries agreed.[7] The LDP then regained a lower house majority in September 1997 and this new political climate lent support to the resistance of national ministries to the proposal. Then, economic problems surfaced. In November a number of established financial institutions including the Hokkaido Takushoku Bank and Yamaichi Securities collapsed in rapid succession. The Hashimoto cabinet feared that the diminishing credibility of the Japanese financial system might cause a panic. Market stability now became an overriding priority, with decentralization and deregulation presenting themselves as mutually exclusive forces. The prime minister was apprehensive that decentralization might lead to reckless organizational growth of the public sector at the local level.[8] Some business leaders agreed, arguing that local government regulations would undermine deregulation efforts such as those for the Large-Scale Retail Stores Law,[9] which has functioned to protect local merchants against big business. Thus, liberal autonomist ideas lost ground, while economic rationalism gained ascendancy.

By October 1997 the Committee for the Promotion of Decentralization, headed by Moroi Ken, a deputy chair of the Nikkeiren (Japan Federation of Employers' Associations), submitted the Fourth Recommendation Report to the prime minister. The committee recommended that out of 530 agency-assigned tasks, about 60 percent should be replaced by the *jichi jimu* (independent local functions) and about 40 percent by the *hotei jutaku jimu* (assigned functions that must be explicitly defined in legislation).[10] In May 1998, despite resistance from line ministries, the cabinet adopted the Decentralization Promotion Plan, which reflected a strategic element of economic rationalism rather than the liberal autonomy associated with a grassroots democracy. Business leaders proposed a smaller government with lower corporate taxation rates to meet the challenges of globalization and to stop the "mindless" budgetary expansion of national subsidies. Siding with this business interest, the Ministry of Finance favored subsidy cuts to local governments by abolishing agency-assigned functions, while later shifting the tax base to local government as a form of compensation. In April 2000 the Collective Decentralization Law took effect by abolishing agency-assigned functions but without compensating devolution of part of the national tax base to local authorities.

The 2001 Final Report of the Committee for the Promotion of Decentralization suggested fiscal decentralization to be the next step in the overall process of decentralization. In 2003 the Council on Economic and Fiscal Policy, run by Takenaka Heizo, minister of state for economic and fiscal policy and for financial services, came up with the reform package of the *sanmi ittai* (trinity): elimination or reduction of national subsidies, review of the Local Allocation Tax (block grant to local governments), and transfer of tax revenue resources to local governments. Four years later, this fiscal decentralization, which would enable local governments to make their own decisions, has yet to be realized.

Decentralization from Below

Localities call for the national government to decentralize decision-making power so that policies can be geared to the needs and circumstances of those local communities that bear the brunt of major issues and problems. The main benefit of decentralization, as experienced from below, is the meeting of the preferences of local residents through their political participation.

Freedom of Information

To be able to effectively participate in political processes, local residents must be informed of matters of concern to all stakeholders. In Japan, information disclosure has come to be recognized as a right of all residents. Since the early 1980s, local authorities have guaranteed this right in the form of local government ordinances, and residents have been increasingly able to utilize these ordinances in a participatory manner through their own initiatives and through the use of the OMBs system in subsequent years.

The necessity for information disclosure first emerged as a focus of debate during a 1976 political crisis in which senior executives of the U.S. aircraft manufacturer Lockheed gave testimony before a U.S. Senate panel about the firm's lobbying activities in Japan aimed at selling their aircraft to All-Nippon Airways. Japanese prosecutors arrested ex-Prime Minister Tanaka Kakuei on bribery charges concerning these lobbying activities on the strength of crucial information obtained under the U.S. Freedom of Information Act. In May 1980 the Ohira cabinet, noting the importance of freedom of information, announced temporary administrative measures aimed at information disclosure. Unfortunately, an ex-Self-Defense official was revealed to be a Soviet spy in 1980, while an ex-KGB member exposed an espionage network operating throughout Japan. During the same time frame, the LDP was attempting to pass a law to define and limit access to state secrets, and pressure for the legislation of information disclosure waned.

Local government, however, was not distracted by "high politics." In March 1982 the town of Kanayama in Yamagata prefecture became the first to adopt an information disclosure ordinance.[11] At the prefectural level, Kanagawa prefecture led the way with an information disclosure ordinance that came into effect in April 1983. Perhaps the most important move came in 1985 with the enactment of an information disclosure ordinance by the Tokyo Metropolitan government, an initiative that succeeded in spreading the notion of freedom of information to many localities. In the mid-1980s, local authorities followed Tokyo's lead with the number of local government disclosure ordinances enacted rising rapidly from 56 in 1985 to 178 in 1990.[12] As table 4.1 shows, as of April 2005, 97 percent of all 2,465 local governments in Japan were providing such services at some level.

It is important to ask if local citizens seized the opportunity to seek information from their local level officials. A 1984 survey of the Tokyo Metropolitan government's 2,024 employees found that 87.5 percent had never received a request of any sort from any local residents to inspect administrative documents. In practice though, local citizens elicited information informally as it was a well-established and common practice for local politicians to gain support within their electorates by providing assistance through an informal disclosure of information about government activities. However, once Tokyo's information disclosure ordinance was enacted, the number of requests for disclosure expanded rapidly (see table 4.2) and, since the spring of 1995, increasing calls for disclosure of entertainment and travel expenses by local officials have shown even more possibilities for use of data. In its rulings of the lawsuits of June 20 and August 29, 1996, the Tokyo District Court accepted the claims of residents by ordering the Tokyo Metropolitan government to release documents related to local- and national-level civil servant business entertainment expenses that the government had initially declined to release. Equally important were the three events—the HIV-infected blood products scandal, the mortgage company (*jusen*) bailout,

Table 4.1   Growth of information disclosure ordinances, 1996–2005

	1996	*1997*	*1998*	*1999*	*2000*	*2001*	*2002*	*2003*	*2004*	*2005**
Ordinances	336	395	580	908	1,426	2,178	2,669	2,937	2,950	2,380
Ordinances/ Total local governments	10.2%	12.0%	17.6%	27.5%	43.2%	60.1%	81.2%	90.1%	93.1%	96.6%

Source: Adopted from material provided by Japan, Ministry of Home Affairs (MOHA) (1996–2000) and Japan, Ministry of Internal Affairs and Communications (MIAC) (2000–2005).
Note: *The figures for 2005 reflect the mass amalgamations of towns and villages. The number of local governments dropped from 3,170 in 2004 to 2,465 in 2005.

Table 4.2 Information disclosure requests to the Tokyo Metropolitan government, 1985–2004

	1985–89	1990–94	1995–99	2000–04
Requests	935	2,655	10,969	13,402
Release	411	813	2,539	5,944
Partial release	280	850	6,393	4,992
No release	122	281	461	287
Information not available	122	711	1,576	2,179
Release ratio (%)	85.0	85.5	95.1	97.4

Source: Data provided by Tokyo Metropolitan Government, Policy Information Office.
Note: Release Ratio = (Release + Partial Release)/(Cases Claimed − No Existence) × 100.

and the alleged cover-up of mishaps at a nuclear power plant—that had a substantial impact on the climate of public opinion in relation to freedom of information and compelled the government to release relevant data to its citizens.[13]

Japanese local government spent most of its time carrying out agency-assigned functions until the 2000 abolishment of this system. If provisions for local information disclosure had not applied to these functions, a large proportion of data would have been excluded from public access. Following a lengthy 1982 National Diet debate, the MOHA and the Legislative Bureau jointly concluded that the management of and access to information, even that concerning agency-assigned functions, was a matter of local discretion.[14] However, those functions that pertained to the management of information (such as census registration) would remain under the supervision of the relevant minister and would not be affected by the 1982 decision. As of 2007, no detailed descriptions of the nature of statutorily defined obligations regarding disclosure have been produced. Thus, the impact of information disclosure on agency-assigned functions remained unclear until the 2000 abolishment of agency-assigned functions.

In contrast with agency-assigned functions, it has been clearly established that personal and private information is exempt from disclosure procedures. For example, personal information grounds were cited as the reason for the denials of disclosure requests on about 80 percent of the unreleased documents in Saitama prefecture in the early 1980s[15] and on about 50 percent of those in Kawasaki city in the late 1980s.[16] Japanese local government has taken broad measures to protect personal privacy and has enacted separate ordinances rather than include special provisions within ordinances that pertain to information disclosure. Local authorities were also under popular pressure to institutionalize the protection of personal information given that the number of personal information protection ordinances enacted by local governments increased dramatically from 227 in 1985 to 1,129 in 1995.[17]

As of 1995, 33.3 percent or 1,085 of Japan's villages, towns, and cities enacted some form of ordinance for privacy protection, with 29.9 percent of these ordinances extending protection of personal information not only to individuals but also to corporate bodies. Correspondingly, 35 of 36 prefectural ordinances on information disclosure designated information about corporate bodies' activity

Table 4.3 Growth of personal information protection ordinances, 1996–2005

	1996	1997	1998	1999	2000	2001	2002	2003	2004	2005*
Ordinances	1,195	1,304	1,399	1,521	1,738	1,982	2,161	2,413	2,612	2,417
Ordinances/ Total local governments	36.2%	39.5%	42.4%	46.1%	52.7%	60.1%	65.7%	74.0%	82.4%	98.1%

Source: Japan, Ministry of Internal Affairs and Communications (MIAC), *Hodo Shiryo* (News Releases), September 12, 2005.

Note: *The figures for 2005 reflect the mass amalgamations of towns and villages. The number of local governments dropped from 3,170 in 2004 to 2,465 in 2005.

as an item that local authorities might decide to withhold to protect their commercial interests. Many information disclosure ordinances specified two conditions for the release of commercial activity information: first, where withholding such information might harm the life, health, and safety of residents and; second, when information relates to unfair or illegal activities that might affect the interests of consumers. As table 4.3 indicates, by 2005, 98 percent of all local governments in Japan were implementing such advanced protection measures of personal information at some level.

Necessary Participatory Institutions

When the central government delegates authority to local government, the responsibility of local assemblies to represent residents' interests becomes more important than ever. Innovative policymaking by assembly members is expected. However, a review of assembly member–initiated ordinances compiled by the National Association of Prefectural Assembly Chairpersons shows that between 1980 and 1994, only 317 bills were initiated by prefectural assembly members, and of these bills more than two-thirds related to the internal rules of assembly committees or elected assembly members.[18] Similarly, the National Association of Municipal Assembly Chairpersons found as few as 95 assembly member–initiated bills passed in municipal assemblies between 1989 and 1993.[19] The drafting of policy thus remained largely located within the local administration.

Despite the expected importance of local assemblies, 46.7 percent of the respondents to the 1995 *Sankei* survey considered local assemblies' checks against the local administration to be insufficient or weak. To understand this result, there is one fundamental point of reference for the system of party coalitions at the local level. For some time in post-WWII Japan, the public perceived the invisible presence of "an alliance of local politicians" that cut across almost all existing political parties and their assembly representatives. To be reelected, local politicians must display to their constituents their constant desire to defend and enhance the specific position of localities over and above the ideology and policies of their own national party. This is important, as Japanese local governments raise only one-third of their revenue through local taxes, with the remaining revenue provided by national government's funds (and perhaps local loans). It is these competing ties and allegiances between local and national party interests that form a key characteristic of this centralized fiscal system. This was well illustrated in the unified local election of spring 1995 in which a number of political parties supported a joint candidate for prefectural governor or municipal mayor so that all parties concerned would be assured of being part of the ruling coalition.[20] As a result, almost all parties shared power without opposition, thus seriously limiting the democratic functioning of local assemblies to hold their chief executive accountable for local residents.[21]

Increasing conflict between the priorities of local assembly members and the concerns of residents is another important issue in the devolution of authority by the central government to local government. A 1995 survey of urban areas conducted by Kato Tomiko, for example, showed that the majority of municipal assembly members (about 60 percent) were self-employed, while the self-employed among the total population represented only about 10 percent.[22] The majority of residents in urban areas were company workers who might not have shared the views of the self-employed about commercial activities in local communities and whose concerns tended to center on the improvement of livelihood infrastructure. For example, in the mid-1990s, there were a number of instances in which local assemblies attempted to carry out "expensive" or "harmful" projects against the wishes of the majority of residents. One such example was the International City Exposition scheduled to be held in Tokyo in March 1996. In the gubernatorial election of spring 1995, candidate Aoshima Yukio (who did not have the support of any political party) stated that he would cancel the exposition if elected. His stand proved to be popular and when elected he followed through on his pledge. Another example was the scaling-back of a project to build an elaborate new city hall in Ota city, Gunma prefecture. In Ota's May 1995 mayoral election, an independent candidate who ran on a platform of opposition to the project defeated the incumbent who had been elected for five consecutive four-year terms. The new mayor followed through on his promise and proceeded to halt the construction. In these and other cases from 1995 and 1996,[23] it was not until local elections were held that the preferences of local residents became visible.

The 2000 enforcement of the Collective Decentralization Law was accompanied by the expansion of local ordinance-making power with local assembly members responding positively with proactive policies over a number of years. The general principle that local assemblies should be able to make ordinances regarding both the *jichi jimu* and the *hotei jutaku jimu* (providing that they are not contradictory to national laws) has certainly enhanced the capacity for local policymaking.[24] The National Association of Municipal Assembly Chairpersons and the National Association of Prefectural Assembly Chairpersons have also helped to initiate improvements in policymaking mechanisms, such as committee hearings and investigation/research for accumulating expertise, standing committees for policy studies, information sharing, and field investigations. The number of assembly member–initiated ordinances at 47 prefectural assemblies increased significantly from only 74 cases in 2000 to 179 cases in 2002 and, with the exception of Tokyo, these new policy-oriented ordinances at municipal assemblies rose from 51 cases in 1998 to 136 cases in 2002.[25] As of 2003, 43 out of the 47 prefectural assemblies provided a full-text database system for their minutes and 381 out of the 698 cities (including special wards in Tokyo) also followed suit. As of the same year, assembly sessions at 27 of the 47 prefectural assemblies and at 583 of the 698 cities had been televised.[26]

Audits provide one of the most important forms of accountability in Japanese local government. However, under the existing audit system it is often an assembly member or former local government employee who is appointed auditor. The standards for the four-person prefectural level audit committees are set by individuals who are assembly members and others who are recognized as "people of exalted ideas." A November 1995 survey conducted by a House of Councilors subsection showed that only 19 out of 180 prefectural auditors were external appointments.[27] Often, assembly members rotate the auditor post among former local officials[28] who have proved to be reluctant to expose any illegality of practices by their former coworkers. Thus, the appointment of former local officials as auditors has worked to move the process away from strict auditing to protection. When fraud by his audit secretariat came to light in April 1996, Tokyo Governor Aoshima announced that the Metropolitan government would, for the first time, appoint external persons to the audit commission. On the same day, the national government's 24th Local System Investigation Council proposed the establishment of a system of external auditors.

The problem of auditing arrangements, however, exceeded the appropriate procedures for the appointment of auditors as it was alleged that over 90 percent of audit requests by residents across the country had been refused.[29] In general, the audit commission was expected to manage local finances efficiently rather than to detect or prevent illegal practices. This practice was effectively illustrated in a circular issued to all local governments by the MOHA stating that it was not appropriate to inspect the contents of the social expenses of local chief executives.[30]

Clearly, it has been necessary for local government to increase the transparency of its administration. Perhaps the single measure with the greatest potential to promote this transparency is freedom of information. Access to information is essential if local residents are to pursue participatory autonomy. To this end, participatory institutions such as initiatives for legislative proposals and OMBs systems may serve to ensure effective use of available information.

The OMBs System

Nakasone Yasuhiro, chief of the Administrative Management Agency in the late 1970s, made the astute observation that it was not necessarily useful to copy the OMBs system of foreign countries.[31] So, in 1979 an advisory body to Prime Minister Ohira proposed an extensive, long-term study to identify an OMBs system that would be suitable for Japan.[32] Six years later in 1985, an Ombuds Study Group announced the need for OMBs-like functions to be introduced in

Japan. Yet, by 2007 no major initiatives had been undertaken at the national level. Although the role of the MOHA was to represent the interests of local government within the national bureaucracy, the ministry remained very reluctant to introduce an OMBs system. In its support of national bureaucracy, the MOHA effectively blocked the local government's effort to introduce a third party to oversee public bidding for government contracts by issuing a notice calling on local governments to "be exhaustive in their inspections of bidding and contract procedures undertaken by auditors."[33]

Embedded within the drive of conservative politicians to identify an OMBs system suitable for Japan is a long-standing cultural aversion to confrontational decision-making practices in Japanese society. The LDP itself has strongly adhered to conciliatory and less-conflictual methods in their parliamentary negotiations. Politicians believe that all parties concerned should talk directly and settle by mutual concession to win the goodwill of the other party in their subsequent relationships. Thus, the involvement of the third party, in this instance an ombudsperson who would delve into the rights and wrongs of a case, would undermine the existing aspirations and strategies that work toward consensus within Japanese culture. Some observers echo these politicians' view by arguing that the OMBs systems should be regarded as more a source of dialogue and agreement than as an organ of surveillance over administrative practices.

These cultural arguments were subsequently embraced and expanded upon by bureaucrats, many of whom argued that the Japanese parliamentary system was already effectively monitoring and policing bureaucratic agents in the absence of an OMBs system. In their view, *kokusei chosaken* (the constitutional right to conduct investigations in relation to government) has a particularly important role in the parliamentary monitoring system. Chino Torao, former director of the Board of Audit, has argued that National Diet members take on an OMBs role by exercising this right, which also allows them to call upon witnesses.[34] Consequently, many bureaucrats believe that monitoring difficulties should be solved not by introducing a new OMBs system, but rather by revitalizing the functions of the existing monitoring system.

Although it is argued that local politicians have already played an OMBs role in local affairs, many have attracted a reputation for *dobuita seiji,* which translates as "sewer cover politics." In this respect, a constituent requiring a sewer cover would only need to make a single call to the local politician and the whole neighborhood would get one as well. In principle, all residents should be given right of access to these OMBs-like services, but in practice, such a service, as in the case of the sewer cover, is usually extended to the special interests of a network of voters who owe loyalty to the individual candidate.

In the groundswell of a push toward a more transparent system, citizen's groups are now investigating the *shokuryohi* (food and entertainment expenditures) of local officials by resorting to information disclosure ordinances. In an early case won in 1989 in the Osaka District Court, a prefectural-level OMBs group asked for the release of information about the governor's social expenditures. That same year, the former deputy mayor of Kawasaki won the city's mayoral election on a campaign that promised the creation of an OMBs system that would be based—unlike residents' OMBs organizations—on an ordinance. The drive to get such a system established was also part of growing concerns over the graying of Japanese society and the quality of public services that the elderly could expect. Thus, in 1986 a local group petitioned the city assembly to introduce an OMBs system to oversee these services and to establish a method for complaints about such services to be directed to the local government's Citizen's Counseling Service. The number of complaints received by the service rose significantly in the late 1980s, but many of the problems went unresolved as the extent of the service's authority remained ambiguous.[35] As the demand for an OMBs system was high, the former deputy mayor, when elected in 1989, immediately dealt with the matter.

Other local governments that followed this new initiative included Isahaya city, Nagasaki prefecture, in 1992; Niigata city, Niigata prefecture, in 1993; Konosu city, Saitama prefecture, in 1993; and Okinawa prefecture in 1995. Still others established similar governmental, purpose-specific OMBs programs. For example, a welfare OMBs program to protect the needy was created by Nakano ward, Tokyo, in 1990 and another in Yokohama city in 1995. Information disclosure OMBs officers to resolve complaints about local authorities' disclosure decisions were appointed by Saitama prefecture in 1983 and Zushi city, Kanagawa prefecture, in 1989.

Between 1991 and 1994 in Kawasaki, for example, 656 complaints were made, of which 234 were ruled in the complainants' favor. Many of these complaints had to deal with such quality-of-life issues as road conditions, day care, care of the elderly and physically and mentally challenged persons, state pensions, and education.[36] Educational problems such as bullying and "unofficial" report cards have also been presented as major issues that Kawasaki's OMBs officials have had to address, as none of the municipal government departments that oversee education had been able to handle and help resolve such problems.

Such monitoring initiatives exist at the local level in Japan today; however, they have limits and are costly. It is quite clear that, independent of the administration, OMBs officials should be attached to local assemblies in order to fairly investigate administrative practices. The national Local Autonomy Law, however, does not give local authorities legal power to attach OMBs bodies to local assemblies. In fact, there are no assembly OMBs systems in Japan; the existing OMBs bodies are attached either to the administration or to local chief executives.[37] Although these bodies are neither independent nor empowered to force parties concerned to observe their decisions, in practice municipal authorities are strongly inclined to follow them. Equally important, the presence of OMBs officers in and of itself seems to have given a serious impetus to local government employees. The OMBs programs may serve as internal grievance machineries; moreover, OMBs officers, appointed by local chief executives, are easily able to persuade city departments to implement their recommendations promptly.

Another aspect of the limits of the local initiatives is the question of increasing purpose-specific OMBs programs. It is important to recognize that political forces involved in the creation of such programs tend to build a close network of specific social groups or organizations. As a result, the purpose-specific programs may be responsive to certain designated interests but not necessarily to interests outside of these networks. As yet there are no reports of such negative outcomes. Although this aspect needs to be examined, some observers emphasize the promising role of purpose-specific OMBs officers in local affairs. Former Shimane governor Tsunematsu Seiji, for example, has pointed out that local residents now expect the OMBs system to play a preventive role as well as serve local residents as a watchperson.[38]

Local Referenda

The 1976 report of the Local System Investigation Council called for the establishment of local referenda. The council recognized that Japan's local government system was based on representative democracy, while pointing out that there were certain issues that needed the endorsement of the total resident body through referendum.[39] In 1987 an advisory body to the MOHA also emphasized the necessity of local referenda.[40] The 1996 interim report of the Committee for the Promotion of Decentralization, although not specific about the roles of residents and their responsibilities for participation, suggested that the holding of local referenda be examined further. Despite these reports and recommendations, the central government has not yet institutionalized a local referendum system through national legislation.

There are, however, some forms of local direct participation in Japan that have developed over time. Article 95 of the Constitution states, "A special law, applicable only to one local public entity, cannot be enacted by the Diet without the consent of the majority of the voters of the local public entity concerned, obtained in accordance with law." A redrawing of the prefectural boundaries of territorial units, for example, cannot be legislated without this consent. The Local Autonomy Law prescribes three types of dismissal by popular vote: the dissolution of the assembly (Article 76), the dismissal of an assembly member (Article 80), and the dismissal of the chief executive (Article 81). It also provides two types of initiative: first, the enactment, amendment, or abolition of a local ordinance (Article 74) in which the assembly is free to accept or reject residents' initiatives; and second, the inspection of the administration of local affairs (Article 75) the result of which the auditors must release to the public. In recent years, the number of cases of these two types of initiative has continued to climb, while numbers for the three types of dismissal have dropped significantly.[41] Perhaps the most important moves have been in the direction of issue-oriented initiatives and referenda for which local residents have demanded the enactment of relevant ordinances. A number of examples are discussed below.

The impetus for local referenda drives has again come from the grassroots level. In the 1980s, tensions and conflicts between residents and their assemblies were increasingly evident, and elected local authorities (chief executives and assembly members) became more divided with respect to issues ranging from the construction of nuclear power plants to garbage disposal facilities and the housing of U.S. armed forces. In 1982 Kubokawa town, Kochi prefecture, enacted an ordinance to hold a referendum regarding the establishment of a nuclear power plant. The vote was never actually taken because the nuclear power plant project was put on hold. In other instances, specific issues drew attention to the necessity for referendum to be held but elected local authorities rejected the need. In 1984, for example, a group of residents campaigning against the construction of housing for the U.S. armed forces in Zushi city, Kanagawa prefecture, obtained the signatures of two-fifths of the eligible voters on a petition demanding the enactment of an ordinance requiring the city to hold a referendum for any important municipal problems. The majority party in the assembly then rejected the demand, with the city's conservative mayor explaining that a local referendum " would obstruct the smooth and proper performance of municipal management in representative democracy which is the basis of local autonomy."[42]

The two landmark referenda, held in Maki town, Niigata prefecture, and Okinawa prefecture, in August and September 1996 respectively, demonstrate how local referenda should be institutionalized. Five local governments, including that of Maki, had enacted ordinances for referenda about the construction of nuclear power plants. Maki, once subject to strong pressure for communal conformity sometimes at the expense of individual independence, gradually moved toward participatory autonomy over the issue of nuclear power. In 1994 the pronuclear town head was reelected with only 45.9 percent of the total vote. Antinuclear residents became increasingly vocal, arguing that the pronuclear attitude of the town's government did not reflect the wishes of the townspeople.[43] When antinuclear candidates gained the majority in the 1995 town assembly election they were able to enact a nuclear referendum ordinance, and the town head was eventually forced to resign from office the following year. His successor was the leader of a group calling for a referendum on the power plant question, which he then scheduled for voting in August 1996. Large numbers of handbills were distributed and community meetings were held by both sides leading to a high voter turnout of 88 percent, with more than 60 percent of votes cast against the construction of the power plant.

The Maki referendum was an advisory one, the results of which bound neither the town's head nor its assembly. Nevertheless, the weight of popular pressure and opinion made its rejection politically risky. As the new town head commented, "Given full information, our townspeople decided not to live with the nuclear power plant. Whether a new town head takes office or a new assembly is elected, we must absolutely pay attention to their decision."[44] The chief result of the Maki referendum was not the resolution of the nuclear question but rather the revelation of problems underlying the referenda system. As the construction permits of nuclear power plants were subject to uniform statutory conditions, the referendum in Maki clarified the limitations on local decision making. Immediately after the referendum, the director general of the National Resource and Energy Agency vowed that he would continue to promote the Maki nuclear power plant in accordance with the national energy policy.[45] In November 1996

Home Affairs Minister Shirakawa Katsuhiko further underlined the limitations when he emphasized that the referendum's results "would not be binding on the national government or other local entities except for the authority concerned."[46] Decentralization at the administrative level, more specifically further delegation of decision-making authority to local government, was required for the referendum process to work in the interests of local residents and to safeguard the will of the local community.

In general, a local referendum is held in response to a failure in representative democracy. However, the reasons for holding the September 1996 prefectural referendum in Okinawa were different. Unlike the Maki case, there was already broad consensus over the subject of the referendum—a reduction of U.S. military bases located in Okinawa—and prefectural authorities had been responsive to the preference of residents in this matter. The underlying purpose of the referendum was to influence political processes at a national level relating to the issue of Okinawa base reductions.[47] This method, without legal binding force, addressed problems of political autonomy—in particular, the extent to which local authorities were able to influence national policymaking. When the Okinawa prefectural assembly passed the referendum ordinance on readjustment and reduction of the U.S. bases in June 1996, Prime Minister Hashimoto predicted, "No doubt, it'll get tough. The influence is inestimable. I think that this will make it more problematic."[48] Two days later, Hashimoto met with Okinawa governor Ota Masahide to announce a ¥5 billion package to help revitalize the island's economy. In response, Governor Ota agreed to cooperate with the central government in its effort to forcibly renew the leases of privately held lands for U.S. military use. Ota's decision to cooperate after months of refusing to act as a proxy for landowners disappointed some members of this latter group. Moreover, despite initial expectations, the Okinawa issue ultimately failed to become the focus of the October 1996 House of Representatives election campaign.

Hashimoto's statement after the vote was an acknowledgment of 90 percent of Okinawans who had voted in favor of a reduction of the American presence and had used the referendum as an opportunity to assert their rights vis-à-vis the central government. If the ultimate goal of the local referendum is to prevent local assemblies from ignoring the wishes of the electorate, then the Okinawa case was far from ideal for the issue at hand was not a local affair that could be best left to individual localities to decide. By contrast, what the Maki case did illustrate well was the effort required for the referenda to work effectively within the context of Japanese local government. The ever-increasing number of local-level attempts to implement single-issue-oriented referenda in Japan, such as that in Maki, also implies that residents feel that their representatives have failed to represent them adequately. Perhaps the best aspect of the Maki referendum was that it insulated the "people's vote" from the strong pressure of traditional special interests in the community. Yet, in summary, the usefulness of local referendum will depend upon the chosen topic and the need for appropriate procedures.

The local referendum—whereby the residents of a particular locality can vote for a special national law applicable only to that locality—is but one mechanism under Japan's legal system that offers direct democracy. There are also the "recall" and the "initiative" mechanisms by which voters can remove an elected official from office and propose an ordinance respectively. When voters believe that their local assembly or chief executive no longer accurately represents them on a particular subject, they will usually resort to the recall rather than the initiative mechanism. This is largely because an embattled assembly or chief executive is likely to reject any initiative aimed at the enactment, amendment, or abolition of a local ordinance. Thus, pushing for a recall has offered a strategic way of preventing the implementation of unwanted measures and, as a result, opposing factions and single-issue groups have been able to abuse it. In Maki, a recall campaign was used as a tool in the political struggle and it eventually forced the pronuclear town head to resign. Given the problems that can arise with the recall and initiative mechanisms, local residents clearly need some form of local referendum to make this expression of local opinion more orderly. Recent local initiatives for referendum have responded to this need.

In 2002 local and permanent foreign residents in Maihara town, Shiga prefecture, voted in a referendum on town merger with neighboring localities. Since then, the execution of local referenda has increased dramatically: 7 cases in 2002, 84 cases in 2003, 174 cases in 2004, and 85 cases as of March 2005. As table 4.4 shows, during the same period, 959 local ordinance proposals for referenda (more than half of which were initiated by residents) were made at local assemblies, and 452 were adopted. Over 90 percent of those proposals were related to the issues of merger with neighboring localities. This was primarily due to the 1999-revised Municipality Merger Promotion Law, which set the deadline of March 31, 2005, for merger applications.[49]

In Japan, none of the results of local referenda under the existing arrangements, except for those provided for in the Constitution's Article 95, are binding. Their purpose is to advise the government on the views of voters on a particular issue. Although advisory, this form of referendum can significantly improve the responsibility and accountability of local government. As the Maki case demonstrated, local assemblies and chief executives tend to take more notice of local residents' views once expressed in a referendum. However, should they ignore the preferences of the local residents, a legally binding referendum may

Table 4.4 Growth of local referendum ordinances, 1996–2005

	1996	1997	1998	1999	2000	2001	2002	2003	2004	2005*
Proposals	10	12	23	23	18	25	95	271	477	116
Enactments	2	4	4	1	4	7	45	145	219	43

Source: Adapted from Ueda Michiaki, "Jumin Tohyo no Kako Genzai Mirai" (The Past, Present, and Future of Local Referenda), *Information Services,* no. 51, May 31, 2005, http://www.jilg.jp/iservice/info51_1.html (accessed August 2005).
Note: *The figures for 2005 are as of April 1, 2005.

be necessary to stop any unwanted measures. Nevertheless, some academics argue that such a form of local referendum would be unconstitutional.[50] Moreover, the nature of the choices allowed for provides no middle ground, polarizing an issue into "yes" and "no." This is why advisory referenda can be seen as offering a means of encouraging two opposing camps to consult with one another and work toward compromise. If legally binding local referenda are institutionalized in Japan, then they should be implemented only when all other methods have failed.

Institutionalizing local referenda in Japan needs to be accompanied by a fundamental reform in the relationship between the central and local governments. The delegation of decision-making authority to local governments is required to implement local referenda more effectively. However, as the welfare state expands, the central government will inevitably delegate greater responsibilities to local governments. Prior to the enforcement of the Collective Decentralization Law, this delegation was characteristically based on the straightforward implementation of a national policy as a system of agency-assigned functions. The disregard of the referendum process, as illustrated by the Agency of Natural Resources and Energy when it reiterated its intention to develop the Maki nuclear power plant in spite of the townspeople's wishes, demonstrated the need for further delegation of decision-making power to local governments. But first, it is necessary to identify those matters where resolution would be best left in the hands of local government. It is also important for local citizens to choose what is appropriate for consideration under a referendum in a responsible and intelligent manner. Ideally, the resolution of some basic questions with community-wide implications, such as a veto on the construction permits of nuclear power plants, should be delegated to the local community level and may also provide an appropriate subject for referendum. Other basic questions, such as the introduction of new public services that could potentially be expensive, however, seem unsuitable for decision by such means.

Conclusion

The establishment of a participatory autonomy under which local residents must be given the capacity to take active part in local political processes can be seen as another *ukezara* of decentralization. There is a specific character to the ways in which citizens participate in such processes in Japan. The sense of immediacy and reality that the citizenry experiences in local politics has driven them to act in a united manner. The concept of freedom of information has achieved sufficient stature as a result of recent scandals to catch the public's eye. It follows from this that the OMBs system and referendum procedures allow scope for positive action. At the same time, the limitations of such action must be recognized. In practice, local discretion has been widely circumvented by nationally defined regulations, rules, and guidelines, and the aforementioned positive action measures cannot be effectively integrated into a problem-solving mechanism without further decentralization at the administrative level.

The Committee for the Promotion of Decentralization challenged centralized bureaucratic control over local government activities with its blunt proposal for the abolition of agency-assigned functions. The national government followed through on this proposal in 2000. To implement autonomous local functions, however, the national government must guarantee sufficient independent financial sources. The Council on Economic and Fiscal Policy has been involved in a reshuffling of financial relations between levels of government. At the time of writing in early 2007, the Abe Shinzo cabinet is seeking to come up with a comprehensive plan for fiscal decentralization, and the issue of political leadership has yet to be tested. Local communities expect the Abe administration to cope with fiscal challenges in an equitable way. They wish to see the promotion of devolution in areas that contribute to the autonomy and vitality of local communities, and a shifting of the tax base to the local level so that more of decision making is given in the hands of local residents. In meeting this demand, fiscal decentralization is confronted by two key obstacles: difficulties in eliminating subsidies for public works that preserve the jurisdiction of line ministries and breed LDP's entrenched pork-barrel politics; and difficulties in reducing the massive national debt for which the Ministry of Finance is primarily interested in spending cutbacks rather than devolving the tax base.

CHAPTER 5

Co-Governance by Local Government and Civil Society Groups: Balancing Equity and Efficiency for Trust in Public Institutions

We cannot leave everything to governments and markets. Assuming that the government meets its role and the market functions efficiently, is that sufficient? I don't think it is. The role of civil society remains extremely important to ensure social cohesion. I'm working with my colleagues to participate in building our community, and we take this mission very seriously. We do have a feeling of our own shared responsibility.[1]

Governance at the local level increases the visibility of individuals affected in decision-making. It is easy to identity pro-active individuals within the community as they are more a participant and less an observer in the decision-making process.[2]

This chapter highlights the manner in which local governments have developed a range of participatory partnership models to work with voluntary organizations and community groups in trust-based partnerships of institutional building. In exploring the experience of Japan, I show how local governments have made considerable progress toward the reconciliation of equity principles with economic efficiency, and how strong leadership, innovation in policy, and inclusion of civil society groups enhance the level of local government's performance by fostering a sense of participation in community decision making, by encouraging cooperation rather than mistrust, and by contributing to the stock of social capital within a relatively short time frame. It is also been proven that effective mayoral leadership can play a critical role in creating networks between local authorities and community groups resulting in a high growth of social capital within a relatively short time frame.

At a local government level inclusive policies are necessary given the rising levels of mistrust and skepticism toward public institutions in advanced democracies. At present, we are witnessing two emerging worldwide patterns of government reform to address the apprehensions of community members. The first approach aims to promote greater equity throughout the community and the second approach strives for economically efficient governance. Typically, there is a trade off between equity and economic efficiency. However, my research findings strongly indicate that local governments will make considerable progress toward democratic benefits-oriented partnership models of conciliation with economic efficiency by engaging civil society groups in co-governing partnership arrangements that accrue positive outcomes in the rebuilding of social capital and trust. Also discussed in this chapter is the upsurge in the number of voluntary associations/nonprofit organizations (NPOs) in Japan. These associations and organizations have proved to be critical to government renewal as they are directly associated with increased levels of accountability, participation, and transparency in local governments.

Citizens in advanced democracies hold less trust in governments than a decade ago. This is a disturbing trend that appears to be accelerating. In major European countries such as Britain, Germany, and France, surveys indicate that only one-third of eligible voters trust their governments while public trust in nongovernmental organizations appears to be on the rise. This trend is also evident in Japan.[3] In exploring how the credibility of governments can be restored in the eyes of constituents, this study uncovered two major patterns of government renewal in advanced democracies. First, the promotion of economic efficiency and consumer convenience within the provision of public services; and second, the securing of democratic benefits, such as participation and equity, within institutional building including the institutionalization of temporary or habitually practiced procedures between the state and civil society. It is clear that local governments, which administer less populated and smaller areas, are inherently more capable of accommodating direct democracy than national governments. To date, local governments have directed their attention to meeting the demands of residents, yet it appears they have achieved this at the expense of economic efficiency given that fiscal deficits of Japanese local governments have dramatically increased in recent years.[4] The present challenge for local governments is to sustain the delivery of democratic benefits while upholding their mandated task of maintaining economic efficiency. By building participatory frameworks with civil society groups, local governments are better positioned to reconcile equity principles with economic efficiency that, in turn, has advanced the growth of social capital and trust. In other words, when local governments unleash the cooperative potential of local communities, they also help raise public awareness of political issues, promote political participation, and enhance trust in public institutions. It is clear that effective leadership and innovative policy at a local government level has the capacity to further the development of social capital in a relatively short time frame but *only* when taking into account the traditions of regional culture that set the parameters of social capital formation over a longer period of time. It is the institutionalized participation of citizens in local governance in the form of agenda setting, policymaking, administrative evaluation, information disclosure, and ombuds (OMBs) and referenda systems that provide a medium for the physical materialization of social capital at a local level.

Social Capital and Local Governance

The conceptualization of social capital in the field of political studies was pioneered by Robert Putnam and expanded and refined by others, such as John Helliwell, Alejandro Portes, and Stephen Knack. Putnam defines social capital as the feature of social networks that enables citizens to act together more effectively to achieve shared objectives, and equates social capital to what he calls "civic trust."[5] Putnam and others suggest a direct relationship between social capital and the performance of public institutions.[6] A number of contributors to the literature on social capital have also sought to define the sources or antecedents of social capital formation as social capital is generated in civil society. Francis Fukuyama and Putnam see the origins of social capital in centuries of cultural evolution, both arguing that government policies have had little impact on its formation.[7] As discussed below, others argue that social capital can be produced and accumulated in a rather short period of time to help solve the problems of political and economic development.[8] Peter Hall specifically emphasizes the importance of government policies in influencing prevailing levels of social capital.[9] He argues that government policies introduced in Britain following World War II (WWII) helped to maintain the existing levels of social capital by emphasizing an egalitarian social and educational framework. Similarly, in some instances of community development in Japan, it is reported that strategic mayoral leadership helped initiate and/or further the development of social capital.[10] While the norms and values underpinning social networks are primarily developed by cultural and historical forces, social capital is not necessarily culturally determined. Most academics and social scientists feel that there are other elements than macro factors that influence the origin, continuity, and change of social capital in a given community. I argue that it is the specific capacity of local government for effective leadership and policy innovation, together with its ability to include citizens and communities within decision-making processes, and to provide future payoffs for their participation and cooperation, that will increase available resources of social capital.

The capacity for both physical capital ("nonhuman" resources such as machines) and human capital (human resources such as skills) is inherent in an individual, but social capital is produced in social relationships between individuals.[11] Social capital is primarily measured by linkages and networks between individuals and viewed as a property of collectivities in society. Social capital cannot be directly used by individuals in marketplaces and political processes while both physical capital and human capital can be traded in markets and directly mobilized by individuals to pursue objectives. The key components of social capital, such as "social trust" and "norms of reciprocity," then help to determine the ability of individuals to associate with one another.[12] Norms of trust shared among people can promote cooperative behavior in society. In this respect, Putnam makes a distinction between "bridging" (or inclusive) social capital that brings people together across different social divides and "bonding" (or exclusive) social capital that deepens ties among members of a network who share a similar social identity such as race and ethnicity.[13] If social capital is about the norms and values of social networks that "bond" similar people and "bridge" diverse people,[14] then the accumulation of social capital needs to be maintained, invested, and converted into physical outcomes of governance.[15] It is this process through which social capital is transformed into concrete outcomes that is necessary for enhancing the performance of public institutions.

A key factor in local government capacity, one that would help to explain the considerable variation in resources of social capital across localities and countries, is the relative degree of social and political equality among citizens.[16] In theory, the dissatisfaction of the poor with the existing allocation of resources, together with the concern of the rich with the possible redistribution of resources, will work against collaborative efforts for inclusion and equity. There are, however, two factors in Japan that help overcome this barrier and promote the growth of social capital. The first one lies in the relatively egalitarian nature of Japanese society, especially in respect to income distribution. Second, local governments in Japan have proved to be a driving force of progressive policies although they vary considerably in their capacity for political, fiscal, and functional autonomy/ discretion that provide incentives for citizens and communities to undertake collective action. The 1999 Collective Decentralization Law has largely expanded the scope of discretionary local functions by abolishing the system of the agency-assigned functions in which service provisions were assigned by national government to local governments. In 2003 the national government proposed a reform package to provide local authorities with adequate financial resources for functional decentralization.[17] This would help to facilitate the strength of policy innovation and executive leadership in local governments, which has depended upon the degree of functional and fiscal decentralization within Japan's recent decentralization movement.

Japanese Specificities and Local Governance

A key challenge of governments throughout the world is to counter the loss of public confidence in the ability of public institutions to meet their needs. In comparison to other advanced democracies, there is, in Japan, far less mistrust in local governments. On the one hand, a position as a local civil servant is deemed to be one of the most desirable jobs among university graduates.[18] On the other hand, local government services and responsibilities have greatly contributed to maintaining social cohesion by covering a broad range of functions such as education, public health, and social welfare on a daily basis. However, the expenditures of local governments are extremely high for a unitary system and comparable to major federal systems. In the Fiscal Year (FY) 1997, subnational government expenditures in Japan accounted for a high of nearly 80 percent of the entire government sector (excluding social security funds), compared with 34 percent in France, 30 percent in Britain, and 51 percent in Italy (all unitary systems), and 66 percent in the United States, 81 percent in Canada, and 83 percent in Germany (all federal systems).[19] These comparative figures show that Japanese local governments are one of the busiest and most active public institutions in the world. A survey conducted in 2001 by Nippon Telegraph and Telephone (NTT) Data on perception of residents in the capital region shows that 47 percent of respondents felt their views to be adequately represented at the municipal level in contrast to just 8 percent at the national level.[20] Taking all factors into account, local authorities in Japan have been relatively successful in demonstrating the ability to mediate conflict, to respond to citizens' demands, and to allow for representation of community interests.

Given the stereotyped image of Japan's bureaucracy-led state building, it would be expected for Japan to have a large government. But this is far from accurate. The size of public spending remained just under 20 percent of gross domestic product (GDP) from the mid-1950s until the early 1970s, while other industrialized countries, with the exception of the United States, embarked on a welfare state commitment to big government. Although most industrialized countries experienced a comparative expansion of the public sector, Japan and the United States took a different path along with their low tax burden policies. In 2005, Japan and the United States still had comparatively small public sectors at 37.4 and 36.6 percent of GDP respectively, compared with Britain at 44.9 percent, Germany at 46.8 percent, France at 53.9 percent, and Sweden at 57.2 percent in the same year.[21] The size of government employment also demonstrates how small the public sector is in Japan. The number of government employees per 1,000 population in Japan is exceptionally small: 35.1 (2004), contrasting sharply to 58.5 in Germany (2001), 73.0 in Britain (2001), 80.6 in the United States (2001), and 96.3 in France (2001).[22]

Despite the small size of the Japanese government, its public debt is the highest in the world, especially considering its future liabilities resulting from the country's aging population. Since FY 1975, Japan has relied on government bond issues to make up for falling tax revenues. The ratio of national and local government debt to GDP in Japan rose from 68.6 percent in 1992 to 158.9 percent in 2005, while other G-7 countries were able to stabilize their ratios during this period.[23] Local public finance is now near crisis levels. The ratio of local government debt to GDP increased rapidly from 14.7 percent in 1991 to 40.7 percent in 2004; and the burden ratio of local public debt service (to the total value of ordinary financial resources) surged correspondingly from 10.9 percent in 1990 to 19.4 percent in 2003.[24] The increased debt service costs are squeezing discretionary spending with the ratio of recurring expenses reaching a high of 90.3 percent in 2002.[25]

These Japanese specificities have significant implications for government renewal, including the promotion of economic efficiency and consumer convenience and ensuring democratic benefits and social equity. The 1999 Collective Decentralization Law directed attention to functional decentralization.[26] Since 2000, the decentralization movement has also moved toward fiscal decentralization, which is expected to allow local authorities to raise adequate financial resources for functional decentralization.[27] This decentralization drive has inevitably led to the delegation of decision-making power, and has been accompanied by more responsibilities for local authorities. Such additional responsibilities have put local authorities on the spot to acquire and manage key resources such as funds, information, and expertise by themselves instead of relying on transferred national resources. At the same time, local governments have to quickly learn to use these self-acquired resources efficiently in order to gain public confidence in its democracy-building processes.

As mentioned earlier, Japanese local governments are a relatively trusted institution that effectively provide nationally uniform services.[28] However, they are now facing the challenge of meeting the diversified demands of residents and need to collaborate with various providers of resources, such as residents themselves, NPOs, and the corporate sector, to maintain and strengthen public trust in their institutions. Local governments will increasingly need to cooperate with these nongovernment actors to realize the potential of their useful resources. In other words, local governments must go beyond being a mere service provider to establish and coordinate additional private-public partnerships and to develop social capital.[29] To this end, local governments must enhance their capabilities by reinvigorating their institutions and by becoming a policymaker rather than just implementing nationally defined policies. In Japan, local government is expected to play a critical policymaker's role in integrating two aspects of local governance: managerialization (or a manifestation of efficiency) and politicization (or a consequence of equity). The first aspect involves business enterprise approaches (New Public Management [NPM] paradigm) to the provision of public services, which are taken to promote cost cutting and consumers' convenience. Residents are likely to support NPM measures to improve the efficiency of local government enterprises currently operating at a massive deficit, although they might also question their trust in the local government given rapid outsourcing and privatization of administrative responsibilities. In the second aspect, politicization, local governments are expected to take advantage of participatory democracy to develop networks of new resources acquisition by reestablishing relationships with citizens (partnership paradigm). Local government in general can be seen as the first stop for assistance to meet consumption requirements in the local population rather than production priorities.[30] As I will soon describe in more detail, Japanese local governments are initially likely to adopt partnership-oriented approaches and explore the possibility of simultaneously implementing both partnership and business paradigms, depending on the fiscal situation of each local government.

Efficiency/Convenience and Local Governance

In Japan, before the fiscal crisis began to exert pressure on local authorities in the 1990s to search for efficiency improvements, local governments did not shy away from a considerable scale of the old-type outsourcing of their activities. They had simply been contracting with the private sector to take over parts of their public functions for which they remained accountable. The lowest share of employment in the Japanese public sector was already too small to keep all public functions in-house. Pressures from local government employees' unions to retain in-house provision were negligible due to the employment practice of retaining the employees for as long as they were able to work.[31] In recent years, major growth in a new type of outsourcing funded by private finance, the Private Finance Initiative (PFI), has come about in industrialized countries to improve efficiency in the public sector. Nonetheless, many Japanese local governments are very reluctant to initiate PFI projects while in some countries such as Britain and Australia, the development of the PFI has rapidly increased the volume of outsourcing in recent years. As described below, there are several disincentives for Japanese local governments to use private finance for service delivery. Perhaps the most important implication for local governance lies in the fact that PFI projects are designed to develop a method primarily aimed at improving the efficiency of public functions, while focusing less on democratic benefits. Responsibility for service delivery of the PFI projects still remains with the public sector, but often without the participatory mechanisms centered on service recipients. To this extent, these projects are less likely to gain public trust for elected local governments.

In October 2003 the (national) Action Plan for the Promotion of Regulatory Reform increased the number of public service areas to be open to the private sector. A cabinet decision was then immediately made with the greatest emphasis being given to the promotion of outsourcing local government services. Interestingly enough, without waiting for this prime ministerial initiative, Japan already was not far behind other major OECD countries in outsourcing local government services. According to a nation-wide survey of 579 municipalities across the nation and 23 special wards in Tokyo on *gyomu itaku* (outsourcing) conducted by Nikkei Research Institute of Industry and Markets in 2001, municipal governments (579 municipalities and 23 special wards in Tokyo) had extensively outsourced certain services, such as janitorial and security services for public facilities and garbage collection. The survey indicated that 97 percent of the municipal governments had already, totally or partially, outsourced janitorial services (87 percent for complete outsourcing), 83 percent totally or partial outsourced security services (69 percent for complete outsourcing), and 76 percent totally or partially outsourced garbage collection (45 percent for complete outsourcing).[32] In April 2003 the Ministry of Internal Affairs and Communications (MIAC) conducted a complete survey on the status of services outsourced in all municipalities. As table 5.1 indicates, a major share of general office work and facility administrative services has been outsourced, although percentages are low for some services such as those related to education. In Japan, unlike in Britain and the United States, for example, it is very rare for local government employees to repair traffic lights or government vehicles. The number of local government employees who provided technical assistance steadily declined from 317,000 in 1993 to 236,000 in 2002, indicating a gradual progress of outsourcing in the areas of technical services.[33] Perhaps, one reason why NPM approaches prevailed in Britain and the United States is that government employees had engaged directly in providing too many kinds of services in a rigid, statutory way.[34] Nonetheless, as mentioned earlier, the size of government employment in Japan is already too small to scale down in a radical fashion. At the local government

Table 5.1 Status of services outsourced by municipal governments in Japan, 2003

General office work outsourced to the private sector

Types of office work	*Partial/complete outsourcing as % of all municipalities*
At-home food distribution services	96
Dispatch of home helpers	91
Cleaning the main building of government offices	86
General garbage collection	84
Reading the water meter	82
Maintenance of information processing and systems	82
Collection of human waste	78
Security of main building of government offices	71
Maintenance, repair, and cleaning of roads	67
Creation and operation of websites	49
School lunch	44
Salary calculation	36
Telephone exchange	33
Driving public vehicles	29
Information desk and reception	20
School custodians	20

Facility administrative services outsourced to the private sector

Types of facilities	*Partial/complete outsourcing as % of all municipalities*	*Complete outsourcing as % of all municipalities*
Sewage disposal facilities	92	36
Urban parks	91	22
Hospitals	90	4
Community centers	90	59
Hot springs and health centers	88	58
City halls	88	41
Car parking lots	79	46
Swimming pool	76	34
Gymnasiums	75	24
Track and field stadiums	75	30
Garbage disposal facilities	74	17
Libraries	74	3
Public halls	73	14
Recreation centers for children	71	30
Nursing homes	70	29
Medical clinics	63	18
Day-care centers	60	6

Source: Adapted from Japan, Ministry of Internal Affairs and Communications (MIAC), *Status of Implementation of Outsourcing of Services in Municipalities,* March 2004.

level, such radical personnel reduction is unfeasible unless specific service areas, such as compulsory education, are entrusted largely to the private sector.

In 1999 the PFI Law was initiated and passed by the National Diet. The PFI Promotion Committee, which was created under this law in the Cabinet Office, reviewed the existing statutory system of presupposing government investments in capital projects and recommended some guidelines to acquire private financing. In June 2001, for the first time, the Japanese government officially recognized the necessity of applying NPM approaches to administrative reforms in the Basic Policy for Economic and Fiscal Policy Management and Structural Reform (so-called *Honebuto Hoshin*).[35] Despite state-led PFI initiatives, only 20 percent of local governments in Japan are actively working on institutional building for the utilization of private financing. According to a 2004 government survey, only 22 percent of local governments have institutionalized a set of PFI-related policies and rules to some degree, and 78 percent have not undertaken anything yet or have no interest in encouraging private financing for capital projects.[36] As of June 2006, the national government has completed or is undertaking 31 projects and local governments 177 projects under PFI guidelines.[37]

Japanese local governments acknowledge the existence of serious barriers to the introduction of PFI. The 2004 nationwide survey conducted by the Cabinet Office, indicates that nearly 30 percent of local governments identify a lack of adequate private investors as one of the key impediments, followed by 24 percent who regard an insufficient understanding of PFI by residents to be a barrier. There are four basic limits on the introduction of PFI at Japan's local level. First, in Japan, there are no institutionalized mechanisms that allow local authorities to dismiss or transfer their employees who are affected by a PFI contract to the status of the contracted private company. Personnel reduction is thus less likely to occur in the delivery of existing services. As a result, PFI initiatives at the local level concentrate primarily on new projects that will not affect the existing personnel arrangements. Second, general trading companies or general building contractors at the national level seem to be the only private investors who are able to achieve the merits of cost cutting for Value-for-Money (VFM). Although a PFI method seeks to achieve the best cost-effective performance by focusing on the delivery of services rather than the acquisition of an asset, there is scope at the beginning for a PFI project to fund the construction of public infrastructure. In Japan, most PFI contracts have required relatively big capital costs of construction at an early stage as well as management and maintenance. As of November 2003, 91 percent of the successful bid prices exceed ¥1 billion and 33 percent are over ¥10 billion.[38] The required capital costs tend to restrict bidding to competition among only big business groups. Third, despite these predominant bidders, local governments tend to protect and nurture local companies for vitalizing local business. According to a survey conducted by Japan's Fair Trading Commission in 1999, nearly 90 percent of local governments had preferential policies for local business, such as placing an order to give priority to local companies or preferential use of local materials and products. Some local governments were forced to cancel their PFI pilot projects under pressure from their local assemblies, which expressed concern over the negative impact of dominant general contractors on local business.[39] Finally, in nationally defined cost-cutting PFI guidelines, there is a significant problem of lack of emphasis on institutional building for participatory planning, implementation, management, and monitoring of PFI projects.[40] The next section will examine the development of local governments' initiatives for establishing participatory mechanism centered on residents in local governance.

Democratic Benefits and Local Governance

The Japanese government seems to be gradually drawn to NPM approaches. Despite this convergence, there has been wide criticism of NPM, which tends to neglect virtues rooted in the public sector, such as ethical standards, social equity, justice and representation, and to depoliticize the public sector by keeping policy formation, implementation, and evaluation in the hands of the professional administration.[41] In Japan, local governments have been very reluctant to apply business enterprise approaches directly to their public administration. They have instead been using participatory approaches to narrow the gaps between their fiscal capacity and public demand. This requires that they must win the goodwill of residents for cooperation in and understanding of the fiscal crisis they face. These approaches are expected to allow residents to share the responsibility of community development and fiscal health with local authorities, and thus to promote the cohesion of local governance by understanding the local governments' capacity. To adequately provide public goods in the midst of local fiscal crises, local governments in Japan have also been increasingly developing their networks with voluntary organizations and community groups in the form of horizontal partnerships rather than NPM-led clientele relationships.

As table 5.2 shows, indicators for implementing NPM measures taken by local governments are relatively low, while those for promoting citizens' participation are quite high. One of the indicators, administrative evaluation, is usually regarded as a component of NPM, but it is included as an indicator of participation promotion in this table. Japan has an evaluation system in place for the performance of the national bureaucracy, but the system lacks participatory or third-party evaluation measures and primarily serves the purpose of self-evaluation. By contrast, administrative evaluation methods have been widely used by local governments to increase the participation of local communities and to support the formation of accountable policy and the implementation of responsive enterprises.[42] The role of citizens, as conceived in NPM, is recognized as consumers rather than participants in local governance. It is evident that there is an increasing concern among Japan's local authorities about the limited focus of NPM to deal with local governments' obligations. According to a data analysis based on measurement indexes of both NPM and partnership models, only 6 percent of municipalities represent a pattern of managerialism-oriented governance, with 35 percent accounting for a pattern of weak commitments to both the models; on the other hand, 35 percent demonstrate a pattern of

Table 5.2 Patterns of local administrative reforms in Japan

NPM indicators as a percentage of municipalities			
Balance sheet		Statement of administrative cost calculation	PFI
Partially or fully created	Fully created	Already created	Already introduced or under consideration
47.6	5.8	20.7	6.7

Sources: Japan, Ministry of Internal Affairs and Communications (MIAC), *Chiho Kokyo Dantai no Baransushito-to no Sakusei Jokyo* (Status of Creation of Balance Sheets in Local Government), August 5, 2003; Japan, Cabinet Office, *PFI ni kansuru Zenkoku Jichitai Anketo* (Questionnaire on PFI for Local Governments), March 23, 2004.
Notes: As of March 2003, 1,541 of 3,235 municipalities partially or fully created their balance sheets and only 189 municipalities fully created their balance sheets. In the same survey, 670 municipalities had created their statement of administrative cost calculation. As of February 2004, 142 of 2,121 municipalities answered that PFI projects were under consideration or had already been introduced.

Participatory indicators as a percentage of municipalities		
Information disclosure ordinances	Privacy protection ordinances	Administrative evaluation
Enacted	Enacted	Already introduced or under consideration
93.0	98.0	87.4

Sources: Japan, Ministry of Internal Affairs and Communications (MIAC), *Hodo Shiryo* (Press Release), July 30, 2004 and April 1, 2005; Japan, Ministry of Internal Affairs and Communications (MIAC), *Chiho Kokyo Dantai ni okeru Gyosei Hyoka no Torikumi Jokyo* (Status of Implementation of Administrative Evaluation in Local Governments), April 7, 2006.
Notes: As of April 2004, 2,903 of 3,123 municipalities had enacted information disclosure ordinances; and as of April 2005, 2,370 of 2,418 municipalities had enacted privacy protection ordinances. As of January 2006, 1,813 of 2,075 municipalities had already introduced or were developing some forms of monitoring and administrative evaluation for their performance.

partnership-oriented governance, with 24 percent exploring both the models in an eclectic way.[43] This study found that a pattern of managerialism-orientation was primarily influenced by the conditions of local government finance (the more squeezed local finance becomes, the more local authorities adopt NPM measures) and that a pattern of partnership-orientation was affected by neither financial nor demographic factors.[44]

Local Government's Role in Social Capital Formation

The 1990s in Japan have seen a remarkable and rapid expansion of voluntary organizations that pursue public purposes at the grassroots level on the basis of voluntary activities. These organizations are referred to as NPOs in this study. The number of NPOs in Japan dramatically increased 6.4 times over two decades.[45] In recent years, case studies on Japan have demonstrated the positive relationships between voluntary associations and social capital formation.[46] Some found that these voluntary associations are less likely to form a strong network of "bonding social capital" for exclusive groups, but would rather promote a formation of "bridging social capital," which reaches beyond their own groups and networks to other diverse groups.[47] Others demonstrated that a network of "bridging social capital" is likely to enhance citizens' political participation.[48] In these findings, it is very important to note that local governments in Japan have significantly contributed to social capital formation by engaging NPOs in local communities. Local governments have helped NPOs to remove and prevent barriers, such as lack of information, expertise, and financial resources, and helped the NPOs to develop horizontal partnership arrangements with local governments. As described below, in this process a network of social capital in NPOs has been accumulated in a rather short period of time.

The Law for the Promotion of Specific Nonprofit Activities (NPO Law), which was enacted in December 1998, dictates that prefectural governments are obliged to authorize the status of NPO Legal Persons—NPOs incorporated under the NPO Law—whose activity base is located within their localities. After its 1998 enactment, the NPO Law did not immediately bring about tangible benefits to the authorized organizations. Not surprisingly, over 81 percent of voluntary organizations surveyed thought it necessary to receive support from local administration, with 76.4 percent of the respondents wanting financial support, 49.2 percent wanting venues for activities and information exchange, 47.9 percent wanting activity-related equipment and goods, and 44.5 percent wanting expertise support.[49] All 47 prefectural governments enacted local ordinances to implement the authorization of NPOs under the NPO Law and, as table 5.3 indicates, many of those governments, such as Aomori, Iwate, Miyagi, Hyogo, and Kochi, simultaneously enacted their own NPO collaboration/support ordinances. Although the precise figures are not available, an increasing number of municipal governments, such as Ichikawa, Mino, Sendai, and Suginami (Tokyo ward), are actively supporting voluntary organizations by enacting their own municipal ordinances. While NPO income from for-profit activities as defined under the National Corporation Tax Law was still taxed at the national level, most municipalities and all 47 prefectures had already applied for or planned to give exemptions to or reductions of some local taxes for activities defined as nonprofit under the NPO Law.[50]

As shown in table 5.3, the institutional capacity of NPO support enhances the ability of prefectural governments to play a key role in social coordination with NPOs. Besides this institutional capacity, another important capacity of local governments is a political one, which refers to the ability to provide voluntary activities with opportunities for effective political participation. The weaker the public confidence in government, the less likely citizens will participate in governance processes.

The study in this chapter found that mayoral leadership is a critical ingredient in transforming social coordination into a network between local authorities and community groups and in promoting citizens' political participation. Mitaka city in Tokyo and Shiki city in Saimama are two examples. In recent years, Mitaka city, hampered by a fiscal squeeze, has been leaning on the private sector for assuming

Table 5.3   Prefectural support for voluntary nonprofit activities in Japan, 2004

(% of all prefectural governments)				
NPO policies[1]	Support ordinances[2]	Research on NPOs[3]	Support facilities[4]	Financial support[5]
95.7	42.6	72.3	80.9	27.7

Source: Calculated from material provided as of May 31, 2004, by Japan NPO Center.
Notes:
[1]Those prefectures that formulated basic guidelines for the promotion of NPO activities and/or established a set of rules for partnerships with NPOs are counted in this column.
[2]A few prefectures included NPO support articles in their implementation ordinances of the national NPO Law while others enacted their NPO support ordinances separately.
[3]Those prefectures that conducted investigations and surveys on the actual situation of NPO activities account for the percentage.
[4]Most prefectures provide permanent venues, which are usually called support "Plaza" or "Center," for information exchange, meetings, office space, and access to office equipments.
[5]Nearly a third of prefectures created NPO trust funds or incorporated foundations for NPO funding support.

many of its responsibilities, shifting beyond one-sided outsourcing toward equal partnerships with the private sector. One such example was the establishment of the Ghibli Museum in 2001. A construction site was offered by the Tokyo Metropolitan authority to Mitaka city as a potential spot for a new cultural facility, but the city was unable to find the finances to build it. In 1998 Mitaka city found that Studio Ghibli, the world-renowned animation studio, was planning to build a museum. After negotiations the Ghibli Museum was built on the site and financed by Studio Ghibli, which then donated this facility to the city. In return, Studio Ghibli was able to permanently display its work under municipal management.[51] Despite this newly developed NPM approach, the heart of Mitaka innovation lies in the collaboration of the municipal government and its residents. The values that distinguish Mitaka communities—including devotion to "resident-first policy"—are a heritage from Mitaka Mayor Suzuki Heizaburo's leadership (1955–1975) to advocate and represent the residents. In 1956, for the first time in Japan, the city opened a day-care center for under-one-year-old infants, and by 1974 it became the first municipality in Japan that had expanded the treated sewage system to cover the entire population. In 1974 Mitaka city opened the first multipurpose community center in Japan, which was managed by a resident council representing diverse community groups. The successors of Mayor Suzuki embraced and expanded this participatory stance by setting up a resident council centered on community planning, an information-disclosure mechanism, and administrative efficiency–enhancement measures.[52] By 1998, a Nikkei survey ranked Mitaka city as the best city in Japan for being an "efficient and open" public institution.[53] Around this time, many voluntary organizations and community groups came forward to take initiative for community building. In 1998 the Mitaka City Town-Making Research Institute, which was established by academics, municipal employees, and other residents in 1988, urged the mayor to adopt citizens' participation at the beginning of drafting a city plan.

This resulted in a "Partnership Agreement" in 1999 between the city and the Mitaka Citizens Plan 21 Council, which consisted of 375 local residents from diverse groups, for drafting a citizens' city plan. Ten issue-focused committees in the council held over 770 meetings, collected information, accumulated expertise, and consulted with city departments, and, in 2001 the council submitted the completed plan to the city. In this process, local residents began to understand the gaps that existed between functions and capacity of the municipal government, and several voluntary groups within the council emerged as NPOs for taking the next step to realize the citizens' city plan.[54]

Another example is Shiki city's innovation to reconcile the gaps between social equity and economic efficiency, which was led by Mayor Hosaka Kunio. In 2001 he was elected with his campaign slogan of "Shiki City of citizens, created by citizens." It was estimated that the fiscal need of Shiki would begin to substantially exceed its fiscal capacity by FY 2006 and that the population would begin to decline in 2008. Mayor Hosaka held meetings with city officials regarding residents' perception of citizen involvement in community affairs and found that nearly 90 percent of residents believed that "citizens should do what citizens can do" and 80 percent agreed that "[they] would help to provide public services with their expertise, experience and time to spare."[55] The city assessed all 1,648 categories of its public services and concluded that nearly half of those services, except for those involving the exercise of public authority and the protection of privacy, could be delivered by community groups.[56] In 2003 Shiki introduced an Administrative Partnership System, in which the city would entrust designated tasks to Citizens Public Interests Activity Groups (NPO Legal Persons, voluntary organizations, and other community groups). In this respect, the administrative partner is not a mere subcontractor of the public administration but rather is expected to share local governance with local authority. These groups must be registered with the city to participate in these activities and to share such responsibilities. To enable the collaboration, the Administrative Partnership System ensures due process: the third-party evaluation committee of six members, including five publicly recruited citizens, specifies the nature, scope, and responsibilities of collaborative tasks. Upon specification, the city presents a collaborative enterprise for which the registered groups competitively bid. The successful groups must enter into a partnership agreement with the city and implement their tasks and responsibilities according to the agreement. In FY 2003 the evaluation committee designated seven enterprises for collaboration with residents' groups, and the municipal government began to introduce three of these enterprises.[57]

A common aspect of these joint enterprises, and indeed other similar enterprises throughout Japan, is mayoral leadership, which provides local residents with new network loci. This stems from Mitaka's public forum for policymaking and Shiki's information exchange for co-governing, aimed at building local stocks of social capital on already accumulated social trust. The network provides local residents with an enhanced sense of responsible participation rather than a sense of mere receipt of public services. It would seem that government policies could do much to influence the accumulation of social capital. Of course, it is important to note that the degree of influence varies in comparative perspective according to barriers and resources of the political system, in which local authorities can provide incentives for associational engagement to "bridge" diverse groups or to undertake collective action.

Local Government Institutions as a Medium for Converting Social Capital into Public Institution Performance

The influence of social capital on local government performance is a distinctive process; the key source feeding this process is found in the peculiar role of participatory institutions as a medium for social capital. In other words, social capital does not contribute directly to government performance, but serves it indirectly through a medium. The operation of institutions that promote active participation in community associations and that monitor the performance of elected political elites drives local governments to improve the welfare of residents and govern more effectively.[58]

A 2003 nationwide survey on social capital, conducted by the Cabinet Office, suggests that the upsurge of voluntary organizations is creating a new form of relations based on social trust, which is different from earlier neighborhood-based exclusive relations.[59] The new form is described by the survey team as repeated interaction in "horizontal and open" networks, which corresponds with Putnam's concept of bridging social capital. These voluntary organizations are typically considered to be service providers that deliver services that corporate and public sectors have failed to provide, although recent studies show that they have extensively transformed the status of service delivery through their partnership with local governments and their input into government policy.[60] Other researchers argue that a shift from social to political participation in voluntary associations is inevitable.[61] Indeed, a 2003 survey on the relationships between NPOs and political participation in Aichi prefecture indicates that nearly 51 percent of those who participate in NPO activities consider "influencing local government policy" as an NPO's role, which would act as a constraint against opportunistic free-rider behavior within the voluntary sector.[62] Another survey explaining these causal chains, conducted across the nation by NTT Data in December 2001, shows that those who have participated in municipality-sponsored community action or wish to do so in the future also express a wish to engage twice as much as the average respondent in two-way relationships with municipal administration.[63]

A pioneering work on local policymaking in Japan, conducted by the Local Autonomy Studies Resource Center in 1978, demonstrated that the weight of influence by citizens' groups and public opinion on local policymaking had become stronger, while that of local assemblies and their members had been declining in urban areas.[64] A 1998 study on municipalities in Tokyo and Kanagawa prefectures also confirmed this trend in relation to the enactment of local ordinances for recycling. In this study, local government officials were asked to identify the most influential actor; 36 percent identified the national government,

28 percent chief executives, and 12 percent citizens' groups (cf. 8 percent with prefectural governments and 4 percent with assembly/their members) in relation to this specific area of governance.[65] Equally important to the findings of this study is that 54 percent of local government officials believed citizen-initiated contacts with officials had "deepened relations of trust" between local government and citizens' groups.[66]

How can voluntary associations become directly influential in the decision-making processes of local governments? Informal activities such as joining football clubs and choral societies do not directly account for the level of influence. Instead, citizens' groups or NPOs mobilized by the community to cooperate with local governments need to be well informed, monitor the performance of government, hold elected officials accountable, participate in policymaking, evaluate the performance of government, and remove under-performing elected officials. To this end, there is a need for an articulation of the institutionalized participatory mechanism by which mobilized citizens' groups affect the performance of public institutions. There are a set of participatory institutions at the local level in Japan that include administrative evaluation, freedom of information, local referenda, residents' councils/forums, and OMBs.

The mechanism of local ordinances for freedom of information illustrates the links between NPOs and government performance. Public trust in governments arising from social capital may promote local government's effectiveness through its effects on the behavior of decision-making elites. But this requires institutional arrangements that, in this case, include information disclosure systems in order to structure the relations of public trust. The effective operation of information disclosure systems is assumed to allow NPO activities to be well informed and to hold elected elites accountable for government performance. The 2003 Cabinet Office survey on social capital found that nearly 70 percent of those who participate in NPO activities identify their ability to "connect with diverse people in local community" as one of the most valuable rewards of participation.[67] On the other hand, only 23 percent of those who do not participate in NPO activities answered they could trust most people, with one-third of these 23 percent respondents wishing to begin participating in NPO activities.[68] In fact, unlike neighborhood association activities, in which nearly 70 percent of the participants take part as a matter of customary practice, more than half of NPO participants do so out of self-motivation.[69] NPO participants are more likely to resort to the use of information disclosure and positively involve larger issues for the welfare of the community by "bridging" diverse groups with a stronger sense of social trust.

Figure 5.1 shows the pattern of association over time in four major prefectures (Tokyo, Osaka, Kanagawa, and Hyogo) between the number of NPO Legal Persons and the number of information disclosure requests for public documents. These four prefectures had enacted local government information disclosure ordinances: Tokyo in 1985, Osaka in 1984, Kanagawa in 1982, and Hyogo in 1986. Despite the enactment of these ordinances in the mid-1980s, the number of requests in these prefectures only began to surge in the spring of 1995, when

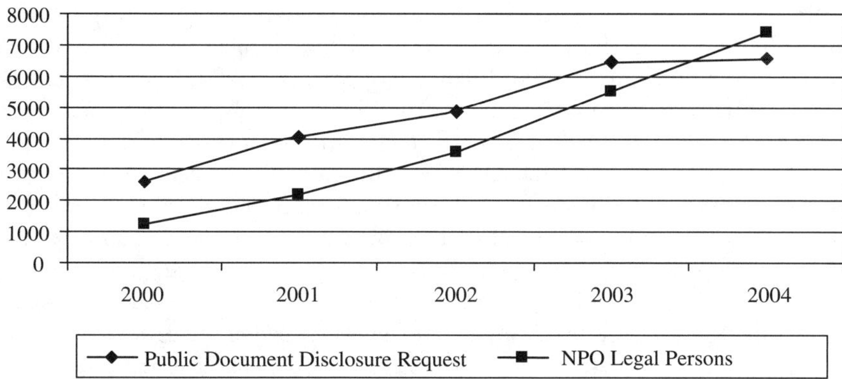

Sources: Bureau of Citizens and Cultural Affairs, Tokyo, *Tokyo-to no Jiho Kokai* (Information Disclosure by Tokyo Metropolitan Government), 2004 edition; Public Relations Office, Osaka, *Osaka-fu no Joho Kokai* (Information Disclosure by Osaka Prefectural Government), various years; Prefectural Residents Bureau, Kanagawa, *Joho Kokai Seido Unyo Jokyo* (Implementation of the Information Disclosure System), various years; Planning and Management Department, Hoygo, *Hyogo-ken no Jiho Kokai/Kojin Joho Hogo* (Information Disclosure and Personal Information Protection by Hyogo Prefectural Government), 2004 edition; Japan, Cabinet Office, "NPO Hojin no Ruikei Ninsho Dantaisu no Suii" (Trends in Authorized NPO Legal Persons), available at: http://www.npo-homepage.go.jp/data/pref.html; last accessed June 2006.

Note: Tokyo, Osaka, Kanagawa and Hyogo are counted as Major Prefectures in this figure.

Figure 5.1   NPOs and public document disclosure requests in major prefectures, 2000–2004.

disclosure of entertainment and travel expenses by local officials demonstrated the possibilities for the use of such data to prevent abuses in public spending. Since the late 1990s, the number of information requests would seem to be closely associated with increases in the number of NPO Legal Persons. From 2000 to 2004, although fluctuating over the years in those prefectures, education (20 percent on average), abuses in public spending (15 percent on average), land use (15 percent on average), food-related business permits (15 percent on average), and industrial pollution (10 percent on average) were among the top fields of requested public documents. Except for some cases of land use and business permits requested for commercial purposes, an overwhelming number of requests were for noncommercial purposes or for pursuing public purposes. Most information requests were made by individual citizens and citizens' groups, yet the ratio of information requests by groups and individuals representing organizations increased by 47 percent from the late 1990s to 2004. This trend corresponds to both the upsurge of voluntary associations in the late 1990s and the increased number of NPO Legal Persons between 2000 and 2004.[70]

Another institutionalized participatory mechanism is "direct demand" (initiative). Article 74 of the Local Autonomy Law empowers eligible voters with the ability of direct demand. The signatures of one-fiftieth or more of the electorate are required to demand the approval, amendment, or abolition of local ordinances, which then obligates chief executives to call a special meeting of the assembly, and to submit the proposed ordinances together with their opinions on the matter. Perhaps the most common type of direct demand in recent years was the one calling for the enactment of local referendum ordinances. There are three types of proposals for local referendum ordinances: direct demands (555 cases between 1979 and 2005 across the nation), assembly-members' proposals (244 cases during the same period), and chief executives' initiatives (326 cases during the same period). However, the final decision rests with the local assembly, which is not bound to adopt the proposal. Only 16 percent of direct demands successfully led to the implementation of local referenda, in comparison to 39 percent of the assembly-members' proposals and 91 percent of the chief executives' initiatives.[71] Therefore, local residents were quite active in the mobilization of direct demands, although less successful than elected officials in holding local referenda.

Between January 2003 and March 2005, 343 cases of holding local referenda in Japan were reported and, with the exception of just 1 case, were related to the merger or consolidation of local governments.[72] The ongoing merger process of municipalities derived from the promotion of voluntary amalgamation—relying on the 1999 revised municipality merger promotion law, which set the deadline of March 31, 2005, for merger applications. The 1999 Collective Decentralization Law accelerated this process, and the Local Administration Bureau in the MIAC worked on designing measures to speed up municipal mergers. Accordingly, the number of municipalities dropped significantly from 3,232 in 1998 to 1,820 in 2006.[73] The ongoing merger process triggered a burst of public criticism and dissatisfaction and obviously provided residents, who had been proactive in voluntary associations, with opportunities to organize the action of direct demands, as indicated in figure 5.2. The study of various assembly minutes suggests further that neighborhood-based associations also were very active in signature campaigns necessary for making direct demands to chief executives, although the statistics regarding the degrees of involvement by both voluntary and neighborhood-based associations are not available.

In these cases, 67 percent of local referenda were held owing to a failure of the chief executive and/or the assembly to represent the broad interests of residents, with 15 percent being held over divided views among residents and 18 percent being used for the confirmation of already existing consensus. Of course, this is based on overall patterns of residents-executive-assembly relations over a specific issue or problem, and thus these patterns are not mutually exclusive. An investigation of the motives of direct demands, which were submitted in 2003 in the Kanto region, including Tokyo, found three key reasons: correcting an "unjust" decision and enhancing accountability (19 cases), as a tool of political disputes (no detailed reasons were provided for not representing the wishes of residents) (10 cases), and neutral inquiry (2 cases).[74] Most citizens' groups that organized the signature campaigns for direct demand were prompted to mobilize and to

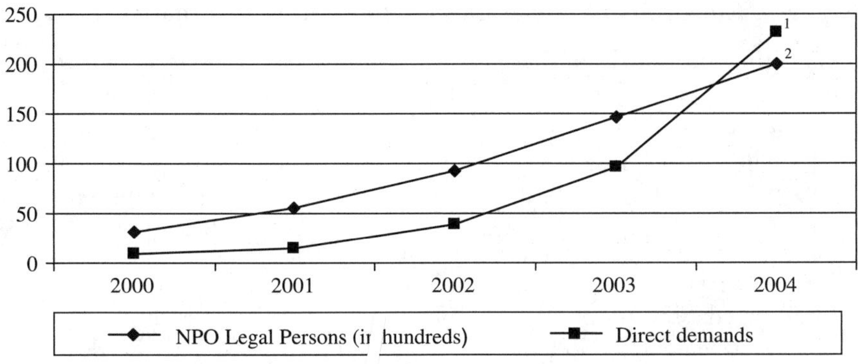

Source: *JILG: Information Service*, Vol. 51 (May 2005), p.4; Japan, Cabinet Office, "NPO Hojin no Ruikei Ninsho Dantaisu no Suii" (Trends in Authorized NPO Legal Persons), available at: http://www.npo-homepage.go.jp/data/pref.html; last accessed June 2006.

Notes:
[1] With reference to citizens' direct demand for the enactment of local referendum ordinance, under the Local Autonomy Law, the signatures of a minimum one fiftieth of the electorate must accompany a demand to the mayor or governor.
[2] Total number of NPO Legal Persons authorized in all 47 prefectures.

Figure 5.2   NPOs and direct demands for local referenda in Japan, 2000–2004.

make the government aware of the wishes of the community. The system of direct demands provided opportunities for residents and communities to influence the outcomes of local issues and decisions.

The benefits of the participatory institutions, in pursuit of a balance between equity and efficiency for building public trust in local governments, became notable when specifying these new processes, conditions, or methods. There are several positive contributory factors to this end. First, community support through the participatory process is a key condition for gaining the democratic legitimacy of local government's performance. Second, civil society groups are expected to share responsibilities derived from public functions. This is consistent with the expectation from inside and outside civil society groups that function sharing should evolve into responsibility sharing. Third, the sharing of responsibilities has led to significant scope for using the participatory institutions to develop reciprocal accountability between local government and residents. Fourth, the participatory approach is likely to reflect locally specific priorities as it is based upon the local government's principle of working with local populations to identify and act on the priorities of the community. Fifth, participation can therefore lead to better resource management for it is likely to tap into the innovation and resources of local communities and increase coordination and flexibility among local populations.

The Limits of Social Capital and Local Governance

In evaluating local stocks of social capital, it seems reasonable to note that some forms of social capital contribute little to social cohesion. The forms of social capital that are provided by membership of certain exclusive groups, such as ethnic and religious groups, may impose harmful consequences on the larger community should members reinforce existing social divisions by seeking to further their interests only. In general, bonding or an exclusive organization tends to confer benefits to members only.[75] In a similar vein, the 2003 Cabinet Office's report on social capital points out that human relationships based on old neighborhood-based associations would involve risks of developing exclusive networks of civic engagement.[76] Nonetheless, these arguments seem to overlook that bridging social capital may also impose negative externalities and exclusiveness on the community. As mentioned previously, it is in an egalitarian society that voluntary activities are more likely to contribute to social cohesion. On the other hand, these activities may cause the accumulation of social capital to be biased in a more divided society. This can happen in two basic ways. First, a divided society fails to guarantee equal access to NPO and other voluntary activities. Well-to-do people have the time and money to participate in voluntary activities and may end up forging connections among these people. Second, those who are excluded tend to accumulate their own stocks of bonding social capital or exclusive social trust in order to represent their interests and identity.

Prominent among the phenomena related to the bias in question is the "volunteer divide" or social gaps in access to voluntary activities. Despite the image of an egalitarian nation, one of the country's pioneering studies indicates that this divide is still quite visible in contemporary Japan.[77] This 2000 study found that nearly 45 percent of the respondents in high-income households (with annual income more than ¥10 million) had participated in volunteer activities, in comparison to slightly over 20 percent of respondents in low-income households (with annual income less than ¥2 million). It also indicated that volunteer participants were more concerned about public health and safety (allocation of resources) than economic equality (redistribution of resources).[78]

Given their good track record in the policy area dealing with social problems and issues, Japanese local governments also have much to offer in overcoming the limitations of social capital as a property of society as a whole. In post-WWII Japan, local governments' social policies were quite innovative, so much so that they were referred to as the *sakidori fukushi* (front-running welfare) or *uwanose fukushi* (add-on welfare). Local governments were able to put a range of social issues onto the national agenda by implementing innovative policies, such as the initiation of free medical care for the elderly and the participation of foreign residents in local referenda. They continued to add an extra benefit to the nationally defined standards of social services, such as the introduction of day-care centers for under-one-year-old infants and add-on services for the public including mandatory long-term care insurance (LTCI). In the 1980s, fiscal conservatism in Japan began to target national transfer payments to local governments for spending cutbacks. Despite the significant reduction of these payments, the growth in social welfare expenditures at the local level was more resilient than first anticipated. Indeed, social welfare spending at the local level as a percentage of GNP increased from 2.0 percent in 1980 to 2.4 percent in 1995.[79]

As fiscal decentralization progresses in Japan, local authorities will not only gain control over local finances, but also assume responsibility for fiscal management. In this context, participatory institutions, as described before, are expected to play a key role. Local government is now providing opportunities for effective political participation whereby diverse groups in the community are being invited to solve the problem of closing the gaps that exist between local needs and capacities. The accumulated experience and expertise of local government in social policy can be utilized in this inclusive manner. The impact of inclusive participation on negative externalities has yet to be seen, but the extensive use of participatory institutions by local governments in Japan remains encouraging.

Conclusion

To renew public confidence in government processes, local governments—as an immediate public institution—have worked more to secure the demands of the public than the pursuit of economic efficiency. The findings of this study indicate that local governments might be inherently more capable of accommodating participatory partnership models than taking business enterprise NPM approaches. Yet the fiscal crisis of local governments in Japan has increased their responsibilities for improving the economic efficiency of their performance. To solve this added burden, local governments have worked toward the reconciliation of democratic participatory models with economic efficiency. This study has demonstrated trust-generating co-governance between local government and civil society groups to be a key component of the reconciliation process. The findings also demonstrate that Japanese local governments, especially mayoral leadership, have played a critical role in transforming social coordination into a network linking local authorities and community groups and have thus been able to make a positive contribution to the formation of social capital formation in a rather short period of time. In the process, local governments have provided local residents with new horizontal network loci for promoting relations based upon social trust. Community networking has helped to enhance a sense of responsible participation among the members as opposed to their being mere recipients of public services. Those well informed about the principles of local governance and those who have participated in its processes understand the gaps between public demand and fiscal capacity and are more likely to become responsible partners of local government in the reconciliation process of equity and efficiency.

Stocks of social capital, as evident in the cooperative capacity of the local community, do not directly affect the performance of local government. This cooperative capacity needs to be organized and mobilized by citizens to develop into well informed groups (NPOs in this study) who monitor, consult with, work with, and, if necessary, punish elected public officials through the channels of participatory institutions. The findings of this study also confirm the relationship between an upsurge of voluntary associations/NPOs in Japan and increased levels of accountability, participation, and transparency in local government procedures.

These are significant findings that are yet to be analysed in cross-national variation. By drawing attention to the need for an explanation of leadership/policy-led social capital formation and the indirect linkages between social capital and government performance, this study contributes to constructive theory building of local governance.

CHAPTER 6

"Digital" Local Communities:
Disengagement to Participation

As I spend the majority of my day working in Tokyo and commuting, I often felt an outsider in the town in which I live. But now, at any hour of the day, I can talk through an online forum to the people and officials in the city of Yamato and I'm now developing a sense of belonging, for the first time, within my own community.[1]

Sakaiya Taichi, Director of the Economic Planning Agency (1998–2001), once warned that Japan would turn "from an advanced into a mediocre country," given its dispassionate approach toward information technologies. Indeed, Japan lagged far behind the United States in the IT revolution and e-government constructions of the 1990s. In 2003 the Japanese government admitted that the country was finally able to move on from a catch-up to frontrunner phase.[2]

Voting is a fundamental act where citizens are seeking informed others to represent their interests. Ideally, citizens should be able to participate more fully in political processes by providing their ideas, feedback, information, and knowledge between elections. Currently, the use of information and communication technologies (ICTs) appears to be providing the democratizing potential for improving public participation in decision-making processes and for producing desirable social outcomes. The commuter quoted above often spent an evening or a weekend participating in an online forum where over 2,300 registered people, including the mayor, municipal government employees, community activists, journalists, and others, were able to engage in discussion. If they so wished, they could communicate on a daily basis on topics ranging from street lighting to municipal budgeting, often covered by the local media and circulated through city departments and neighborhood meetings. The major benefit of the online forum is that it has helped to frame debates, move issues onto the political agenda, and engage members of the local community within the process.

This chapter examines the Japanese government's use of ICTs as tools of democratic renewal, with special reference to the political engagement of citizens. It illustrates how Japanese local governments are able to integrate ICTs to further citizens' participation in political processes and, as such, makes a contribution to the general argument that it is local governments rather than national governments that are inherently more capable of accommodating the engagement of the community. A prominent corollary of this claim is the assumption that ICT-based technological mediation is now facilitating new forms of participatory democracy that may complement the representative system of government.

The chapter is presented in five sections. The first section provides the key definitions, identifies the important factors, and highlights the characteristic qualities that are likely to explain the impact of ICTs on democratic renewal in political processes. The second section introduces background figures that demonstrate the degree of preparedness of the Japanese government to develop the use of ICTs, and its capacity to sustain e-government development. The third section highlights the national bureaucracy's tendency to delay the adaptation of ICTs and to preserve its own turf. The fourth section emphasizes how political fragmentation within the Liberal Democratic Party (LDP) has prevented Japan from pursuing IT policies. Finally, as part of this chapter, I assess the capacity of local authorities to solicit public inputs and to disseminate information as part of the policymaking.

Democratic Benefits of an e-Based Government

Public disengagement from political processes has become a serious issue in advanced democracies where citizens are increasingly skeptical of political leadership. In this respect, the application of ICTs to the public sector is seen as an exciting new potential for democratic renewal. Over the 1990s, advanced democratic nations, such as the United States and Britain, have been engaging in a momentous technology-based struggle for political relevancy. It is not yet clear whether new ICT-based political procedures will facilitate, broaden, and deepen citizens' political participation, and thus strengthen democratic processes. Many observers emphasize the capacity of ICTs to enhance citizens' direct participation in the political process.[3] Others, however, argue that, in practice, it will prove more difficult to articulate and aggregate citizens' interests via personalized ICT access to government bodies, and that the technology is more likely to cause fragmentation and individualization.[4] In contrast, there are other critics who argue that increased use of ICTs will provide ruling elites with yet another medium for state control[5] and that the gap between those who have access to ICTs and those who do not may exacerbate inequality and social exclusion within the community.[6]

Indeed, it is important to examine whether the ICT revolution might create a shift in power in the relationships between the state and its citizens. Is it feasible that the inclusion of ICTs in government structures would help to reengage citizens in political processes? It is possible that greater integration of ICTs in citizen-state relationships is both inevitable and irreversible. But if so, is it potentially desirable? Are there hidden difficulties or drawbacks? This study is an attempt to answer these issues by examining Japan's adaptation to the call for e-government.

ICTs have been widely used for e-commerce and online entertainment for some time, but the use of ICT technologies by government is still in an early stage of development. The application of ICTs to the government sector is by no means straightforward—in terms of capacity to pursue political relevancy or to handle information in the political processes. It is expected that ICTs will improve the quality of participation in, and the transparency of, policymaking by promoting dialogue and deliberation on policy issues and problems. Nevertheless, even advanced e-based governments, such as those found in Singapore, the United States, and Canada, continue to focus predominantly on the commercial benefits and efficiency of service delivery through ICT application, and far less on any democratic outcomes. The pressures presented by the call for e-government are experienced differently among countries, depending on the range of different experiences associated with their adaptation to ICT development. These differences also illustrate the considerable variation in preexisting institutional arrangements and organizational cultures within each country.

Two major patterns of development among advanced ICT-driven governments are emerging. In countries where New Public Management (NPM) business enterprise approaches to the provision of public services prevail, ICTs are used primarily to cut costs and to promote consumers' convenience. In other countries where strong political leadership takes advantage of centralized Web-based initiatives, government ICT use aims to further international competitiveness and market liberalization. The U.S. government's official portal to all government information services and transactions, called FirstGov.gov (which officially changed its name to USA.gov in January 2007), represents an example of this NPM-oriented pattern.[7] The introduction of this portal was designated as a priority policy in 2002 by Vice President Dick Cheney to enable citizens to "get it done online." In contrast, Infocomm 21, an ICT blueprint of the Singapore government, is an example of a centralized Web-based pattern introduced by strong political leadership. Guided by this blueprint, the Infocomm Development Agency of the Singapore government specifically coordinates the use of ICTs by both the public and private sectors to increase the country's competitive advantage in the global market.[8]

As illustrated in this chapter, the application of ICTs to government in Japan has not yet been championed by either NPM-educated public officials or by a concerted political leadership. E-government in Japan continues to lag years behind e-commerce and online entertainment, partly because the fragmentation of power in the government party (LDP) has hampered its progress.

Analytical Frameworks

To further the analytical strength of this study, I deal with the term "e-government" in a specific way. Although e-government is partly an outcome of the application of cost-effective ICTs and infrastructures to the machinery of government, I see its ultimate strength and goal as making government more accountable, responsive, and equitable in the wider community. To examine the impact of ICTs on these particular aspects of democratic processes, this study focuses on the policy impact of e-government in two fundamental ways: first, public input into policymaking that may increase the extent of citizens' participation and the responsiveness of the government; and second, the dissemination of information by government to enhance its own accountability and transparency.

A number of key actors such as politicians, political parties, bureaucrats, interest groups, the media, and the general public are involved in policymaking and policy implementation. Their activities converge in government policy initiatives that have been put forth by decision makers or advisers including ministers, their senior officials, and other high-ranking bureaucrats at the national level; and chief executives and their senior officials at the local level. ICTs influence these actors in the policymaking process. As e-government resources and programs in most countries reside predominantly with the administrative side of government, there is the need to explore the manner in which government policymakers are adapting ICTs for policymaking purposes and how they are interacting with key actors—especially legislators and the general public—within the context of policymaking and in terms of representative democracy. To this end, I assess the impact of e-government at a local and national level, and analyze the effect of ICTs on multilevel government functions. The central claim of this study is that local government in general is far better positioned than the national government to develop institutional arrangements in which ICTs can be applied to democratic gains and objectives, and to engage citizens in wider political processes. This central claim is supported by four basic dimensions of how ICTs are integrated into political processes. First, the general public is more likely to play a participatory role in the more mundane activities of government.[9] Second, the application of personalized ICTs to political processes tends to work better in a political community with a smaller population. Third, cross-sectoral IT policy is better coordinated in the less-fragmented apparatus of government.[10] Fourth, political leadership, which is capable of coordinated action, is a necessary condition for an integrated government approach to ICT development. It is important to note that the potential of ICTs is not inherently democratic. To achieve ICT-driven democratic objectives, political leadership would have to provide integrative solutions for the previously compartmentalized government structures.

The application of ICTs to local government for democratic renewal has very important implications when placed in a broader theoretical perspective, especially when looking at the impact of this application on representative democracy. While the representative system of government is the core of any advanced democracy, there exist, in every Western democracy, some forms of direct participation that have developed over time to compensate for the inherent weaknesses of the system. These are more apparent at the local level where there are a wide range of direct mechanisms, such as local referenda, recalls, petitions, citizen panels, participatory planning, public hearings, neighborhood associations, and so forth. These newly emerging technological mediation tools are causing a transformation in the complementary arrangements of the representative and direct systems, and addressing different phases of the democratic process including agenda setting, planning, budgeting, decision making, implementation, and evaluation, all within the context of Japan. The potential impact of ICTs at each of these phases will be analyzed within this chapter from two distinct viewpoints of information management: public input and information dissemination. I will also examine how ICT mediation helps to create innovative and new forms of direct democracy at each phase, and how this works to complement representative systems.

Finally, it is important to note that there is a certain condition that is necessary for my central claim to be valid and reliable. Local government in different countries is extremely diverse in financial, functional, and political terms, ranging from self-government to an outpost of central government, and featuring both unitary and federal systems. Local authorities depend heavily on their political autonomy and financial capacity for the successful use of ICTs to improve citizens' political engagement. This chapter addresses these factors within the context of a local government system in transition in Japan.

Japan's Readiness for E-Government

One would expect that technologically advanced Japan would be at the vanguard of e-government application. Interestingly enough, according to a global survey of national e-governments in 2004 as shown in table 6.1, 17 countries were ahead of Japan, offering complete transactions online.[11] Japanese households are also slower than those in other major "wired" countries in their readiness to utilize and leverage ICTs for e-government. The ratio of Internet users to total population can be constructed as a crude index of individual readiness. As table 6.2 indicates, the ratio of Japanese Internet users has barely reached advanced international standards. Several years ago, Japan's foundations for IT human resources were comparable to some major Organisation for Economic Co-operation and Development (OECD) countries, but as of 2007 these countries far exceed Japan in terms of Internet users as a percentage of the total population.

Another global survey based on the Networked Readiness Index (NRI), which is calculated from 2003 figures, shows that the Japanese government still needs to catch up with leading ICT-enabled governments. The Japanese government's capability to use ICTs is only seventeenth out of 102 countries (Government Readiness Index [GRI] = 4.92, rank = 17). It is helpful to contrast this to Singapore (GRI 6.17, rank 1) and the United States (GRI 5.62, rank 3), and importantly to Malaysia (GRI 5.46, rank 5) and South Korea (GRI 5.25, rank 9).[12] The entry of the latter two countries reflects the political leadership and actions taken by government officials in Malaysia and South Korea to promote IT policies. In line with its lack of readiness, the Japanese government's usage of ICTs is also relatively low (Government Usage Index [GUI] 4.36, rank 14) in contrast with Singapore (GUI 6.45, rank 1) and the United States (GUI 5.51, rank 2).[13]

Table 6.1   UN e-government readiness index of major OECD countries, 2004

Country	E-Gov. Index	Country	E-Gov. Index
USA	0.9132	Singapore	0.8340
UK	0.8852	Germany	0.7873
Sweden	0.8741	Japan	0.7260
South Korea	0.8575	France	0.6687
Australia	0.8377		
Canada	0.8369		

Source: United Nations Online Network in Public Administration, "United Nations Global E-Government Readiness Report 2004," http://www.unpan.org/egovernment4.asp (accessed August 2005).
Note: "E-Government Readiness Index" presents a composite index for the requisite conditions, including Web measure, telecommunication infrastructure, and the human capital necessary to ensure that citizens have free access to information and services. The higher the index, the more advanced the e-government.

Table 6.2   Changes in the ratio of Internet users to total population, 1997–2002

	1997	1998	1999	2000	2001	2002
Sweden	21.3	33.0	44.3	56.4	63.6	64.7
US	20.1	29.0	39.4	59.9	59.8	59.1
UK	2.0	18.0	23.7	33.6	55.3	56.9
Australia	6.7	24.2	36.4	43.9	52.5	54.4
Canada	n/a	29.6	42.8	n/a	45.7	53.4
Singapore	14.7	n/a	n/a	44.6	49.3	51.8
S. Korea	1.5	3.9	32.3	34.6	46.4	n/a
Japan	7.9	11.1	15.4	37.2	n/a	39.2

Source: Data from NUA Ltd., *NUA Internet Survey* (2002), http://www.nua.ie./surveys/howmanyonline/index.html (accessed July 2004).
Note: For each year, the NUA has chosen the highest ratio of Internet users among the available monthly ratios.

The popular Economic Planning Agency director Sakaiya Taichi, who had been appointed from the private sector, took this backwardness in IT policies in Japan seriously. He used the slogan "IT National Movement," and proposed a Voucher Scheme for IT Workshops, in order to enhance Japan's human capital capacity. This government scheme was intended to subsidize the costs of ICT training for 30 million people aged 20 and over, with its budget of ¥300 billion in fiscal year (FY) 2000. The scheme was central to a plan to build foundations for the successful implementation of e-government, namely, increasing access to ICT equipment and skills for those people who did not have either the resources or the trust in their own skills and abilities to go online. While there was an expectation that this scheme would make e-government inclusive and participatory, there were major newspapers such as *Asahi Shinbun* that cynically reported the voucher scheme as little more than "merchandise coupons." Finance ministry officials immediately attacked Sakaiya's idea as *baramaki* (mindless spending), and conservative LDP lawmakers joined in by saying that the government should spend more for direct economic stimulus.[14] The idea quickly dropped and the national government officially accepted the proposal as premature.

After his abortive attempt, Sakaiya reemphasized that it was important for Japan to join a group of advanced IT countries through the promotion of Internet access and literacy. Indeed, the 2001 White Paper on Information and Telecommunications found that three-quarters of non-Internet users in Japan wished to be taught to use the Internet.[15] The "e-Japan Strategy," which was adopted in 2001 by the IT Strategy Headquarters (a joint committee of government and private sectors chaired by Prime Minister Koizumi Jun'ichi), set a five-year goal to make Japan the world's most advanced IT nation. More than five years have passed since the announcement of the e-Japan Strategy. This period has shown that many serious obstacles must be overcome in order for Japan to advance to such a level of e-government.

Ability of Bureaucrats to Delay Implementation

In the most advanced examples of countries that have adopted e-government such as Australia, Britain, Canada, and the United States, the dramatic developments in terms of ICT application are closely associated with a continuation of NPM reforms that have displaced the principles of traditional public administration by introducing a neoliberal and business enterprise approach to the provision of public services. The utilization of ICTs is aimed at cutting costs for public services and reducing personnel in public agencies, with expanded management information flows. In contrast, Japan's public administration is not fully adhering to the principles of the NPM paradigm.[16] In a 2001 cabinet meeting, the Japanese government officially acknowledged, for the first time, the necessity of applying NPM approaches to administrative reforms. In practice, however, administrative reforms have proved to be a far cry from "business-like" NPM principles.

In Japan, bureaucrats are still able to maintain their professional status and privileges, despite administrative reforms. Their tenacious ability to delay administrative reforms can be found in three well-known cases: the *dokuritsu gyosei hojin* (independent administrative institutions), the *gyosei hyoka* (administrative performance evaluation system), and the *kan-min koryu* (corporate partnership with the state administration). In 1997 the idea of independent administrative institutions, which would be legally independent of the state administration, was adopted by the Japanese government to facilitate reductions in the number of government employees. Nonetheless, the 1999 Management Law (which is applied to these institutions) prescribes that the operation of the "independent" institutions is not to be based on a self-supporting accounting system, but must rely upon transfers from national funds whose cost-effective use is to be closely monitored by the national bureaucracy. The bureaucracy's power to preserve itself can also be seen in the administrative performance evaluation that the national government began to implement in 2001. An evaluation commission, which is attached to the Ministry of Internal Affairs and Communications (MIAC, formerly known as the Ministry of Home Affairs), has only been able to facilitate the one process—that of self-evaluation for the performance of bureaucrats. There is clearly a lack of participatory or third-party evaluation measures.

Equally important, the 2000 Law for Personnel Cooperation between the National Government and the Private Sector, which promotes corporate partnership, was expected to develop a horizontal personnel exchange between the two sectors. Yet the existing personnel links remain dominantly vertical in the sense that ex-bureaucrats often take top positions in those corporate firms they monitored during their government career. In practice, these administrative reforms are far removed from the implementation of a neoliberal and business enterprise approach.

Japan's Ministry of Finance has never officially made specific reference to IT investment as a key measure in alternative service delivery for cost reductions, which contrasts sharply to the dialogue that has taken place in advanced e-government countries. The US Treasury Department has worked closely with NPM principles and has been the main driving force behind IT investment; the Treasury Board of Canada Secretariat has been leveraging ICTs to rationalize administrative functions, and the Treasury in Britain has committed itself to a multibillion-pound IT investment. In Japan's efforts toward administrative rationalization, problems are arising from a number of ministries including the Ministry of Finance. Not surprisingly, IT initiatives are cutting across the boundaries of ministerial jurisdiction and this had led to a number of "turf wars."

Prime Minister Obuchi Keizo created a special budget of US$5 billion for the Millennium Project of the year 2000. The funding supported ministerial activities, including IT initiatives, yet it soon became clear to ministries that their IT developments and technologies would not be operational without the construction of a centralized public authentication system. Thus, the Ministry of Public Management was co-opted as a core agency and as a "bridge certificate authority" to help authenticate data exchanges such as the supply and registration of information and the submission of applications, and to act as a point of transfer of such data to "ministry certificate authorities" within each of the nation's ministries. In order to ensure the successful implementation of digital signatures and authentication systems, individual ministries' authentication systems had to be compatible with the bridge authentication system. Subject to this centralized system, each ministry applied to the Ministry of Finance to obtain its own IT-related budget, while still developing its own authentication system with the aid of the private sector and through government procurement. This led to individual initiatives with the strong possibility that IT funds were being wasted through the duplication of efforts. More disturbingly, the companies submitting tenders, such as Japan IBM, NTT Data, and Japan UNISYS, created the phenomenon called by Japanese journalists as the "one yen bid." From 1999 to 2000, the successful bids were, on an average, 60 percent of estimated costs, with nine of these bids never reaching 5 percent of estimated costs.[17] The reason why these companies accepted extremely low profit margins or significant losses was self-evident. They were competing to win the goodwill of the ministry concerned in order to establish subsequent relationships, with the hope of being retained by the ministry for ongoing IT investment. This rationale is a reflection of traditional practices in Japanese public administration where, with respect to government procurement, interested groups were always informally consulted before the bidding opened.

In this public bidding process, the national bureaucracy single-mindedly sought to install internal communication networks rather than any other ICT applications. In 1997 the Wide Area Network (WAN), an interministerial communication system among national ministries, came into operation. In August 2000 the MIAC, which had been charged with monitoring local affairs, developed a wide range of guidelines for local government IT policies. The guidelines were intended to promote "administrative simplification, efficiency and transparency," and to this end, they pledged to establish an online link from national ministries to all local governments.[18] In October 2001 the Local Government Wide Area Network (LGWAN), which was to be jointly operated by multiple local governments, was put into operation on a trial basis. When the WAN was connected with the LGWAN in April 2002, the engagement of the national government in the development of a common system infrastructure between levels of government to meet national policy objectives placed local governments under pressure to implement nationally defined IT strategies.

In 2002 the National Diet (national legislature) passed three related bills for administrative procedures for online projects, with the objective of implementing online delivery of all national administrative procedures by 2003. While the complete data is not available at the time of writing, it is doubtful that these changes have taken place unconditionally. The leading party, the LDP, clearly acknowledged the difficulty in completing such a task on time and successfully persuaded the cabinet to adopt the three bills as general rules to be applied to over 600 national laws (without these laws having to be amended). This was because some LDP Diet members had been concerned about hundreds of amendment processes that could provide individual ministries with opportunities to delay the implementation.

The MIAC,[19] which was acting as coordinator for the online projects of all ministries, identified 253 administrative procedures that were not suitable for online delivery or that could be performed online but required more time beyond the 2003 deadline in order to become fully operational, and estimated that ministries would be able to make only 59 percent of planned online procedures "unconditionally" available via the Internet by 2003.[20] According to partially available data, as of March 2004, the advanced e-based MIAC managed to offer 576 out of about 1,000 possible applications/notifications that citizens could get online.[21]

All national ministries in Japan have websites, which offer access to home pages with information on various topics. The number of home pages within each website varies greatly, reflecting the nature and type of functions carried out by specific ministries. Government branches that have to deal with highly politicized issues, such as the Defense Agency, tend to be risk averse and disseminate less information on their sites. Some branches, such as the Ministry of Justice, which require established and stable functions, are under less pressure to disseminate new information. In contrast, other ministries, such as the Ministry of Health, Labor and Welfare, which directly deal with the day-to-day concerns of citizens, need to be accessible by the general public and, to this end, actively disseminate information. The majority of those home pages, however, are neutral factual sites featuring descriptions of organizational history, structure, functions, press releases, speeches of staff members, lists of publications, and basic statistical figures.

The home pages of national ministries' websites in Japan are still used primarily to disseminate information rather than to solicit public inputs. One exception is the introduction of "public comments," a feature introduced by the cabinet in 1999. Each ministry was instructed by the cabinet to make it possible for the public to express its views on the ministry's policy initiatives. In 2003 the actual number of policy items that were put forth by each ministry for "public comments" were still relatively small: Health, Labor, and Welfare (43), Economy, Trade and Industry (31), Agriculture (27), Internal Affairs and Communications (18), Transportation (13), Education (9), Justice (4), and Finance (1); Foreign Affairs and Defense had none.[22]

The Defense Agency, the policies of which require a greater degree of secrecy than that of other ministries, did not adopt a public comments system. The wider use of public input may be seen by some bureaucrats as a threat to the security of sensitive information pertaining to other countries, and to the demands of military intelligence. In the case of the Ministry of Foreign Affairs, the policymaking situation is more complex. The ministry actively disseminates information on its website, catering both to foreign observers and Japanese citizens, perhaps because it wishes to establish an influential presence in diplomatic circles. On the other hand, it has barely utilized a public comments system for public inputs. In general, foreign policy remains stable as frequent shifts of policy may confuse other countries. However, as foreign policy also demands immediate reactions to external events and requires little legislation, it is highly unlikely that the ministry would invite public comments.

Line ministries, such as Health, Labor, and Welfare; Economy, Trade and Industry; and Agriculture, that are responsible for initiating and implementing specific government programs, have been more active in inviting public comments than staff ministries such as Justice and Finance that provide planning, budgetary, and organizational support for line ministries. Line ministries' solicitation of first-hand information from the general public has not only been a symbolic solution to legitimizing their initiatives, but has the capacity to provide useful policy advice at a working level. Nonetheless, as described below, all line ministries, while actively soliciting public comments, have carefully avoided a political backlash from special interest groups.

Obviously, bureaucrats who manage a public comments system fear they could be swamped by the increasing volume and fast transmission of public comments. Less than half of all policy items made available for public comments provide specific departmental e-mail addresses for submission, with most requiring and/or recommending submission of hard copies.[23] It is also doubtful whether public comments have been treated seriously in deliberations. In general, there is an acknowledgment of receipt rather than a response to individual comments. In most policy items open to public comment, ministries put up a short summary of all submitted comments on their home pages at the end of solicitation periods, but have provided no substantive discussion of how these comments were treated in the policy process.

Failure of Political Leadership to Deal with Legislators and Bureaucrats

Strong political leadership is considered to be one of the most important assets for a government in its adaptation of ICTs. The rise of wired countries such as Singapore, South Korea, and Malaysia to the top ranks in terms of government readiness to employ ICTs is a reflection of policies and actions taken by national leaders. They are both willing and sufficiently able to persuade citizens to use the Internet and thus create a link between private practices and the centralized Web-based initiative for enhancing competitiveness in global markets. In this context, it is expected that politicians are more likely to perceive IT investment as a key tool in restructuring government.

The fiscal crisis of the Japanese government, which started issuing deficit-covering bonds in 1975, led to a new type of political leadership. This was evident in the 1981–1985 campaign for cutting ministerial spending, which was just one initiative arising from the strongest top-down political leadership in the modern history of Japan. Led by Prime Minister Nakasone Yasuhiro (1982–1987), it targeted the bureaucracy for imposing controls on ministerial spending and sought a smaller government base. To assist the process of retrenchment, the Nakasone leadership privatized some government enterprises, particularly those like the National Railways that had been operating at a massive deficit. It appeared that Nakasone's initiatives followed in the footsteps of Margaret Thatcher's ideological success of the early 1980s. But his main intention was to control the bureaucracy rather than to implement economic rationalism for cost-cutting purposes.[24] He explicitly called for a more "presidential" style of government in Japan, which was evident when he incorporated the Administrative Management Agency into one section of the Prime Minister's Office in an effort to create a mechanism for control over the bureaucracy. He also decided not to let the bureaucracy reform itself, but rather entrusted such initiatives to the Second Provisional Commission on Administrative Reform (1981–1983) and nonstatutory advisory bodies.

Unlike Nakasone's top-down leadership, Prime Minister Koizumi (2001–2006) demonstrated his strong desire to prioritize "structural reforms" including administrative changes at the systemic level and to promote his popularity within the country.[25] Yet the LDP politicians, acting as champions for special interests in government decisions, posed considerable challenge to Koizumi's reforms. Their resistance to reform reflected LDP politician's predilection for expensive and often useless public works that would, they claimed, stimulate the economy. That their claims were also targeting votes from rural Japan remained unstated.

The key to Koizumi's strategy in combating pork-barrel politics was the 2001 creation of the Council on Economic and Fiscal Policy, attached to the Cabinet Office. At council meetings, "policy intellectuals" were assigned from members of the private sector to initiate and draft virtually all important ideas and issues concerning national agenda setting and budgets. Importantly, they were not expected to adhere to narrow political pressures. Koizumi's cabinet members then responded to their initiatives, and council memorandums that, in effect, acted as blueprints for decisions made within the cabinet. Many of their initial ideas had been strategically placed in the hands of the council's neoliberalists including the ex-academic Takenaka Heizo, minister of state for economic and fiscal policy and for financial services, and Honma Masaaki from Osaka University. Council members from big businesses willingly gave full support to these initiatives.

One of the major initiatives taken by the council has been Japan's social security reform. It is expected that the Individual Account System of Social Security proposed in 2001, if finally adopted, will have an across-the-board effect on welfare policy. It was designed to build an e-government in the field of health and social welfare. The introduction of social security numbers will allow the setting up of an ICT mechanism in which the taxpayer can access information regarding the levels of social security contributions and benefits at the individual level. While some government agencies need to be amalgamated in order to operate such an integral system, both the Tax Administration Agency and the Social Insurance Agency have strongly rejected the idea of merging their agencies for this purpose.[26] Social welfare bureaucrats have also argued that this highly individualistic approach can be counterproductive to maintaining a socially equitable welfare system.

Even more critical, anti-Koizumi LDP leaders were increasingly hostile to council-led reforms. The LDP leader in the lower house, Aoki Mikio, once publicly stated that he was discontented with the fact that opinions of key people from the private sector had been praised highly and were thus shaping the prevailing trend of politics and economies.[27] Kamei Shizuka, LDP faction leader, appealed to the public by pointing out that the reforms would neither construct roads nor build factories. "How will the market ever pick up," he asked, "while they are destroying localities?"[28] By November 2002, the anti-Koizumi LDP leaders were becoming strident, and Nakasone called for the replacement of the prime minister. In effect, Koizumi's reforms have been constrained by the old guard of anti-Koizumi forces.

Despite this Koizumi bashing, LDP politicians seem to have clearly acknowledged Koizumi's reformist impact on the LDP victory in the 2001 upper house election and in securing another win in the 2003 lower house election. After all, it is electoral benefits rather than policy or reform initiatives that concern politicians the most and both sides of the political divide have taken the opportunity to prioritize ICT use for electoral purposes.

As of February 2003, 81 percent (587 out of 723 members, with four vacancies) of all National Diet members in Japan had their own home pages, essentially for electoral purposes. The break down of this figure indicates that 83 percent (394 out of 477 members, with three vacancies) of all members of the lower house and 79 percent (194 out of 246 members, with one vacancy) of all members of the upper house had home pages.[29] For the most part, these home pages have been used to provide biographies of the members, to recruit and organize supporters, to disseminate information regarding their activities in the National Diet, and to neutralize their opposition candidates.

In Japan, the Public Office Election Law controls all electoral activities from the size and placement of campaign posters to the number of postcards a candidate can send to supporters. The MIAC has officially interpreted the law so that the use of words and pictures on home pages for electoral purposes is prohibited during the legally defined period of election campaigns. While there are indications that this particular ban will be lifted,[30] the MIAC has no intention of removing the ban on soliciting votes by e-mail, which may be uninvited yet reach a large number of voters.[31] During this period, candidates will be unable to defend themselves on the Web or by e-mail against any defamation or slander. Most National Diet members favor the open use of home pages, and some strongly argue for lifting the ban on both home pages and e-mail during the campaign period.[32] Unfortunately, there is little evidence that ICTs are being utilized to promote public debate and participation for national agenda setting and in the legislative process.

E-Participation in Japanese Local Government

In his influential article, "Bowling Alone: America's Declining Social Capital," Robert Putnam has drawn attention to the fact that Americans no longer actively participate in politics or trust their government's ability to have the answers to economic and social problems.[33] In 1995, when he published this article, Japan's voter turnouts were the lowest in its electoral history and participation in electoral politics was at near-crisis levels. The voter turnouts for local elections dropped to 55 percent in the mid-1990s, which was the lowest level in postwar Japan.[34] The phenomenon of *o-ru yotoka* (all parties ruling together) in local assemblies, where almost all parties share power without political opposition, has undermined the healthy functioning of those bodies. In 1995, 43 percent of mayoral candidates ran on *both* government and opposition tickets.[35] After the 1995 unified local election, there were no opposition forces in 30 out of the 47 prefectural assemblies.[36] Thus, the capacity of local assemblies to keep their chief executives in check was seriously constrained.

In Japan, the public disengagement from formal political processes has certainly attracted considerable attention. While voting is an essential component of political participation, there are other ways of connecting citizens in political processes. By 1970, for example, up to 3,000 local citizens groups had been formed in Japan to protest against industrial pollution. As a result, Japanese local governments successfully coordinated this form of political action and developed one of the most effective systems in the world for pollution control, which was subsequently adopted by the national government. This unprecedented degree of political autonomy in Japanese local government is recorded in the literature,[37] with some scholars arguing that political pressures were brought to bear on the national government from the local level;[38] and others claiming that the national government depended on local governments for the successful implementation of national policy.[39] Building on this progressiveness at the local level, the development of a Web-enabled government, through which information becomes a power resource for local innovation, may further encourage citizens' participation in community development and enhance the exercise of local autonomy.

Indeed, some studies show that the phenomenon of disengagement from voting does not necessarily signal a decline, but rather a change in political processes.[40] As illustrated in this chapter, newer forms of political participation are emerging, as Japanese local governments go through a period of transition. The 1999 Collective Decentralization Law has allowed local governments to carry out their functions independently in order to meet the needs of individual local sectors. Furthermore, this law has laid the foundation for participatory renewal in political processes, with the possibility that ICT functionality may provide a key tool for local residents to exert real influence on local issues.

The e-Japan Strategy aims at providing cost-effective and convenient public services to citizens.[41] However, citizens' participation is not included in the list of priorities. A series of recent national laws, such as the 1993 Administrative Procedural Law, the 1999 Freedom of Information Act, and the 1999 Collective Decentralization Law, require that administrative relations with citizens should be altered to provide the foundation for citizens' participation. But the Japanese national government has so far failed to commit to realizing this assignment through the employment of IT policies.

Despite the national government's lack of action on the matter, the Collective Decentralization Law itself gives local authorities a window of opportunity to promote the engagement of citizens through IT policies. Before the enforcement of this law, national ministries retained legal forms of control through the practice of agency delegation, in which each national ministry assigned specific functions to the related departments of prefectural governments and, through prefectural governments, to related municipal departments. To preserve their jurisdiction, national ministries competed against one another and directed the related departments primarily through the use of circulars and manuals. These circulars and manuals were regarded as the official interpretation of national laws by the related departments. As the number of assignments increased, the number of circulars and manuals ballooned to tens of thousands. The Collective Decentralization Law, which came into effect in 2000, then abolished the agency delegation system and, as a consequence, the circulars and manuals became void. This gave local governments greater space for information sharing and coordination among the different departments, creating the infrastructure for IT policies.

Perhaps the most fundamental condition for effective promotion of political engagement is to assess citizens' potential for participating in community action.

In December 2001 NTT Data conducted a nationwide survey on municipality-sponsored community action among those aged 20 and over across Japan. The results found that 11 percent of respondents had participated, and continued to participate, and that some 30 percent of respondents had never participated yet expressed a wish to do so at a future time. Furthermore, the potential participants indicated that they would engage twice as much as the average respondent in two-way online relations with municipal administration.[42] Compared with the latest voter turnouts at local elections in 2003, the percentage of potentially active participants proved to be surprisingly high.

In response to expressions of interest in participatory politics, local governments have initiated most of the promised administrative reforms; the national government either followed suit or expressed indications that they would do so in the future. In the early 1980s, Japanese local authorities began to guarantee information disclosure as part of residents' right to be informed, and thus provided the basis for political participation. As of 2002, 81 percent of local governments in Japan have adopted information disclosure ordinances, simultaneously exempting personal and private information from disclosure procedures.[43] During this time frame, 80 percent of Japanese local governments enacted some forms of ordinance or internal administrative rule for privacy protection.[44] They have also experimented with some participatory institutions, such as ombuds and referenda systems, to ensure the effective use of available information. In Japan, the national authority argues that the parliamentary system has worked effectively to monitor bureaucratic agents, yet local authorities have given residents right to ombuds-like services at the local level. Similarly, as discussed in the last chapter, Japanese local governments often hold local referenda due to a failure of representative democracy or because of local assemblies' inability to hold their chief executives accountable for major local issues such as the construction of nuclear power plants. According to *Asahi Shinbun*'s Digital News Archives, the number of articles in which the word "ombuds" was used rose from about 500 in 1984–1992, to nearly 4,900 in 1997–1999; references to the phrase "local referendum" also increased from about 400 in 1984–1992, to nearly 4,400 in 1997–1999. This dramatic increase in media coverage coincided with local initiatives for participatory institutionalization.

In Japan, as table 6.3 indicates, many progressive localities have been building momentum for the use of ICTs as they develop in the direction of participatory democracy. A survey of local governments in 2002 by the MIAC shows that 66 percent of prefectures and 15 percent of municipalities have created a new department for specializing in IT projects; furthermore, all prefectures and 96 percent of municipalities have a home page, with 94 percent of prefectures and 68 percent of municipalities providing some form of online two-way communication with constituents.[45] Japan's spending on local e-government lent continued to increase from US$5.7 billion in 1989 to US$14.4 billion in 2001.[46]

As of 2002, all prefectures and 90 percent of municipalities had put in place their own Local Area Network (LAN), and 40 percent of prefectures and 6 percent of municipalities were connected through the WAN with national ministries.[47]

Table 6.3 ICT development by Japanese local governments in 2002 (%)

	Prefectures (47)	*Municipalities (3,241)*
Local interdepartmental networks	100	90.3
Networks with national ministries	40.4	5.9
Special departments for IT	66.0	15.4
Home pages	100	95.6
Online two-way communications	93.6	68.1

Source: Japan, Ministry of Internal Affairs and Communications (MIAC), *Hodo Shiryo* (News Releases), October 17, 2002.

Local governments have thus been heavily involved in the process of installing internal communication networks for purely administrative purposes. Nonetheless, the findings of this study indicate that a significant number of local governments have taken initiatives to create a system necessary for the enhancement of information network contents and applications. Given the need to solve a wide range of community-specific issues, such a system has been built around forms of participation and consultation with the intention of reflecting the will of constituents as primary content creators.

It appears that many local government initiatives have arisen from the expectations that citizens have of local authorities. Another NTT Data survey, conducted in August 2001, on the perceptions of residents aged 20 and over in the capital region, indicated that 47 percent of the respondents felt their views were represented at the municipal level whereas only 8 percent felt their views were recognized at the national level.[48] This survey also indicated that 23 percent of respondents had accessed their municipal government home pages, with 10 percent having visited the cabinet home page, 10 percent the ministries' home pages, and only 3 percent having sought out the National Diet members' home pages.[49] The respondents had much more confidence and trust in mayors (54 percent) and city departments (51 percent) than in National Diet members (12 percent) and the national bureaucracy (12 percent).[50] These results imply that it is more likely that the local government rather than the national government would develop an immediate safeguard to meet citizens' needs and would successfully operate a "G2C" (Government to Citizens) mechanism for democratic renewal.

Citizens' Engagement in Policy Consultation and Debate

In June 2002, for the first time in Japan, Niimi city in Okayama prefecture held online voting for mayoral and city council-members' elections. This experiment certainly made the electoral administration more effective. All votes were counted in 25 minutes with the exception of absentee ballots that took two hours to count manually.[51] Although online voting enhanced administrative efficiency, it did not necessarily make the government more responsive to local needs. Progressive local governments in Japan have been less eager to use online voting, pursuing instead online discussions on community issues that enable local residents to participate in areas of governance beyond electoral politics.

According to a 2002 investigation conducted by NTT Data, there were 733 *denshi shimin kaigishitsu* (e-citizens council rooms) hosted by municipal governments in Japan.[52] These essentially operate as online forums designed to connect local residents to the administrative policy side of government. Before ICTs, there were many non-IT-based public forums for citizen input into policy consultation at the local level. In 1996 Fujisawa city in Kanagawa prefecture recognized that participants were limited by time and space at public forums and began, for the first time in Japan, to develop an online forum. By 2001 a steering committee was publicly recruited by the city to set up specific rules, roles, and tools to keep online discussions focused on key community issues in a responsible manner; over 1,400 (and the number continues to increase) registered citizens have participated in the online forum, ensuring a grassroots agenda-setting impact in their community.[53]

Another local innovation can be seen in the Ichikawa Information Plaza, which began to operate in 2002 as a key information provider for community development. This facility was provided by Ichikawa city in Chiba prefecture and is managed by a nonprofit organization, the Ichikawa Life-Network Club (i-LNC). The i-LNC coordinated 400 IT support volunteers who, in turn, have been encouraging more people to create information contents. This process assisted in gathering the online input necessary for identifying the various areas that required community action. At the same time, the Information System Department of the city office, along with its accumulated information and resources, moved to a section of the Ichikawa Information Plaza. It sought to build a local database holding resource-related information and community needs. The digital delivery of such data would be expected to revitalize community participation by matching specific needs with available resources.[54]

Some local communities face structural difficulties in facilitating community development. Yamato city in Kanagawa prefecture, a residential town where the daytime population falls drastically as residents commute to their workplaces in Tokyo, has found it difficult to build a strong sense of community. In 2000 the city started an online forum of "any place community" where 900 registered residents and 1,400 registered city employees shared information regarding the successful implementation of municipal services, ranging from road repairs to education.[55] This online forum helped connect residents and the city office and made dialogue on specific issues and events possible at any hour of the day.

Transparency in Decision Making

In Japan, local budgeting works are assigned to finance departments by local chief executives, and these chief executives in turn revise the budget by prioritizing, or ranking, the requested enterprises. The drafts are sent to local assemblies for passage. Politicians then make the most of the close connection between spending and votes. In FY 2003, Yokohama city, in connection with municipal budgeting, disclosed the budgeting process for all city enterprises, including the outlines, the requested and assessed amount, and the assessment reports for about 2,500 enterprises on its home page.[56] It had been customary for mayors of Yokohama to informally negotiate with various assembly groups in a bid to assure passage of the budget. With this new practice, informal and clandestine contacts between the mayor and politicians were minimized and open debates in the assembly were made more visible.[57] Iwate and Nagano prefectures have provided a similar online disclosure of their budgeting, and Aomori and Kochi prefectures are also planning budgeting transparency.

Once funds have been allocated to specific projects, the budget enters the implementation stage. Kawasaki city in Kanagawa prefecture has provided an online check sheet of project progress to allow residents to monitor the implementation process. This check sheet, available on its home page, is intended to provide accountability to residents in terms of objectives, spending levels, necessity of projects, progress evaluations, and further planning, and to receive the residents' feedback.[58] At the implementation stage, government projects in Japan are notorious for indulging in *dango* (bid-rigging), which is the widespread collusive practice of pre-bidding for public works. In FY 1999, without offering an on-the-spot meeting, Yokosuka city in Kanagawa prefecture started inviting tenders on its home page, thus preventing bidders from contacting one another or influencing city officials. It was found that the average number of bidders per project rose rapidly from 9 in previous years to 22 in 1999; that local business as a percentage of successful bidders increased from 68 percent in 1998 to 80 percent in 1999; and that the average of the successful bid prices as a percentage of the city-estimated prices was 86 percent, a savings of ¥3.2 billion.[59] Gifu and Okayama prefectures have also been experimenting with an online bidding system for public works. In 2001 the Tokyo Metropolitan government began to use a procurement database for public notices, with vendor qualifications and delivery of goods for approximately 24,000 vendors and, in the latter half of 2003, it started an online bidding process for public works on a large scale.

Participatory Performance Measures

Japan has an evaluation system for the performance of national ministries, but the system lacks participatory or third-party evaluation measures and primarily serves the purpose of self-evaluation, thus protecting the interests of national bureaucrats. In contrast, evaluation methods have widely been used by local governments to increase the participation of local communities and to support the formation of accountable policy and the implementation of responsive enterprises. As of 2002, 98 percent of prefectures and 100 percent of government-designated municipalities have introduced a performance evaluation system. Sixteen percent of municipalities have adopted such a system, and forty-nine percent of municipalities planned to adopt one in the near future.[60]

In 1995 Mie prefecture, for the first time in Japan's public sector history, used a performance measure, and currently uses it not only to assess its performance but also to decide what the government should and should not provide to citizens, businesses, and special interest groups. In a more comprehensive way, Aomori prefecture has developed a policy marketing method that is designed to allow residents to participate in the entire administrative cycle of planning, implementation, and evaluation. The case of Miyagi prefecture is the latest local innovation. Since 2002 the prefecture has conducted an annual survey of 4,000 residents to judge "prefectural citizens satisfaction," and has linked this data to its performance evaluation system to prioritize prefectural projects and even to cancel projects that have already commenced. A significant number of local governments, such as Nagano prefecture, and Kushiro, Odawara, Oota, Shiogama, and Yokosuka cities, have adopted this Miyagi policy.

This growth in participatory performance measures reflects the widespread use of "public comment" systems in which local authorities invite residents to comment on and evaluate specific agenda items in order to receive citizen input on decision making. In April 2000 Fukui prefecture became the first local government in Japan to operate a public comment system. As of 2001, 68 percent of prefectures and 18 percent of municipalities had set up a public comment system on their home pages.[61] The number of public comment systems has increased dramatically in the last several years. Although this data is not included in government statistics, almost all local governments that provide home pages operate such a system for their residents who are usually able to participate by post, telephone, facsimile, and more typically by e-mail.[62]

Unlike national ministries' responses, local authorities' responses to public comments are extraordinarily open and forthcoming.[63] The most vigorous implementation of public comments can be found in Iwate prefecture where every single comment that is relevant to a policy item is shown and given a specific response on the system's home page. Each of the policy issues opened up to public comment is finalized with a report on the home page giving details on how the comments have been or will be used for policymaking and implementation. In Iwate, the number of comment contributors for an issue has reached up to 200, especially in contentious policy areas such as community development and education.[64] The system is manageable and functional in responding to and reflecting the citizens' comments. In contrast, the labor-intensive nature of feedback to a large number of nationally solicited comments makes this type of system less feasible at the national level.

Barriers to E-Participation

Japanese local governments acknowledge the existence of serious barriers to the development of e-participation. In two nationwide surveys on sources of barriers to the progress of infrastructure building for the electronic delivery of administrative information, over 60 percent of local governments identified a lack of available funds as the key impediment, followed by nearly 60 percent of local governments regarding an insufficient number of computer-literate staff as a secondary impediment.[65] Public forums for e-participation, such as "e-citizens council rooms" and "public comments," provided by local governments, do not necessarily ensure citizens' engagement. Participation alone is also no guarantee for desirable community development. As existing case studies of Japanese local governments suggest, there are three fundamental impediments to the successful implementation of public inputs to the policy process: lack of public awareness, digital divide, and weak privacy protection.

The first problem, lack of public awareness, is seen clearly even in the most successful case of e-participation in Fujisawa city where only 1 percent of the city's total households were registered as participants in the online forums. At least one-third of eligible voters who are willing to participate, according to the NTT Data survey, need to be made aware that the opportunity exists. The cases of Fujisawa, Ichikawa, and Yamato suggest that guidelines and rules need to be publicized to encourage participation, to emphasize participants' personal responsibility, and to build online trust with residents. This is essential in order to accommodate the new forms of political participation that online participation requires.

The digital divide is the second problem. A survey on the use of the Internet by elderly and physically challenged people conducted by the Postal Administration Research Centre in 2000, indicated that none of the 465 elderly respondents and only 8 percent of 1,416 physically challenged respondents were Internet users.[66] Although ICT development is claimed to have improved the living infrastructure of socially disadvantaged groups, these figures would indicate otherwise. It is important to note that the use of ICTs does not replace existing political processes, but rather offers an alternative. There also needs to be other means of participation available to those who choose not to use ICTs. At the same time, ICT use needs to become more accessible. Niimi city, as just one example, has made it possible for visually impaired people to vote online.[67]

The last barrier is privacy, which is a key element of liberal democracy. Security measures are technically difficult to implement for e-participation. According to a survey on the information security of local governments conducted in 2002 by the Information-Technology Promotion Agency, 65 percent of respondents suggested that their staff lacked the capability to complete a security measure, and only 37 percent appropriated a budget for the implementation of security measures.[68] As of 2002, 47 percent of prefectures and 20 percent of municipalities had introduced a computer security policy for protecting any personal information provided to them, with 26 percent of prefectures and 12 percent of municipalities periodically checking up on the security of their computer systems.[69] Despite the importance of privacy in data gathering, the level of local governments' keenness to address this issue is quite low. It is likely that securing privacy will become a key issue for gaining widespread trust in e-participation activities in the future.

Political Leadership

Gubernatorial or mayoral leadership is a crucial ingredient in local governments' ability to promote information dissemination and solicit public inputs in the policy process. Some Japanese local areas are similar to one another across such variables as geographical setting, population size, public fiscal need and capacity, and industrial structure. However, some local governments are very active in e-democracy development, while others are not. This study has found that a wide range of e-participation innovation comes from resource-poor prefectures such as Aomori, Iwate, and Nagano, and small cities such as Fujisawa and Yamato. After reviewing the cases of e-participation success in Japan, most observers have come to the conclusion that capable chief executives make the critical difference.[70]

Investments in IT infrastructure by local governments in Japan have been costly. By 2000 over 60 percent of local governments exceeded their debt service ratio by 15 percent or more (interest and repayment/financial resources) and their outstanding debt was equivalent to 37 percent of the gross domestic product (GDP). Although 75 percent of prefectural authorities and 68 percent of municipal authorities have difficulties in allocating funds for IT investment, the gap in terms of ICT used for internal administration among local governments seems to be negligible.[71] Most local authorities have been using ICTs to restructure their government internally and have developed substantial infrastructures for further ICT application. But there are some variations in the ways in which local authorities attempt to transform government in terms of their external interface with citizens. Since they developed their e-government initiatives on the basis of existing IT infrastructures, local governments such as Yamato, Kawasaki, and others have not depended on financial resources so much, but rather have relied on ideas and leadership to ensure the innovative implementation of increasing public inputs into policy discussions.

In Japan, policy coordination by the prime minister and his cabinet at the national level is seriously constrained by the pluralistic structure that disperses power among national ministries and lends itself to political fragmentation due to the factionalism within the leading party, the LDP. In contrast, mayors and governors are better positioned for policy coordination. They are directly elected on the presidential model, and have greater power to exercise control and direction over budgeting and over the personnel of their entire government. Most importantly, in 2000 the agency delegation that had undermined local chief executives in favor of national ministries was legally abolished so as to allow local leaders greater discretion in promoting their own administrative program. As far as IT policies were concerned, local departments were brought together to work with an IT section of the Planning or General Affairs Office, which was not associated with any national ministry but which the mayor or governor had exclusive control over.

Conclusion

E-participation in Japanese local government is still at an early stage and most of the expected participation outcomes that e-local government has promised have yet to be seen. Nonetheless, the findings in this study of Japan would support the argument that ICTs have the potential to enhance local democracy by providing residents with a new opportunity to participate in the policymaking processes. On the other hand, the Japanese national government seems to be pushing the delivery of online services over and above the delivery of democratic practices. At present, online delivery of services is geared toward administrative efficiency and citizens' convenience although it is likely that the government will eventually offer all-important procedures online for everyone's benefit. It seems that the trend of ICT technology mediation is moving toward decentralization and participation at the local level, and toward economic rationalism and managerialism at the national level.

This preliminary investigation leaves room for a more comprehensive contribution to a comparative theory of e-government. It does, however, suggest some plausible hypotheses about ICT-driven democratic transformation. Having examined Japan's adaptation to ICTs at different levels of government, this study also proposes that local government in general is far better positioned than the national government to integrate the use of ICTs for public input and information dissemination in policymaking processes. The findings support this claim through a set of tentative hypotheses that lend themselves to further examination in a comparative perspective. One of the most intriguing hypotheses deals with how governments are changing the ways in which they handle information in the policymaking process. Perhaps the strongest tendency about information management is the government's use of ICTs for disseminating its information rather than for initiating public input into the policymaking process. This is based on the tendency of policymakers to avoid the scrutiny of the general public while at the same time attempting to maintain wide-based support. It is understandable that policymakers in general operate from a "blame avoidance" perspective in getting their ideas accepted. As this study shows, Japanese line ministries operating at the national level have been less reluctant to solicit public comments than Japanese staff ministries, but it is not reasonable to hold the line ministries accountable for the use of public comments in the policy process. National ministries, which dealt with national security or sensitive information regarding other countries, did not solicit public comments at all. Another hypothesis involves dissemination procedures only. Even if policymakers give priority solely to information dissemination, access to information is less likely to be guaranteed in politically sensitive areas such as national security, confidential negotiations, and the identification of the key people who influence decisions. The scope of information disseminated by policymakers through ICTs tends to be closely associated with political considerations; the more policymakers see political disadvantages, the less likely they are to disseminate information. In this study, Japanese national ministries, which were under less pressure to disseminate new information, seemed to have little information on their websites, while active disseminators of information in Japanese national ministries appeared to control the contents in order to avoid a hostile reaction from special interests groups.

From the viewpoint of Japanese local governments observed in this study, public input and information dissemination is likely to be facilitated when the government is not concerned with protecting national security and does not have to deal with organized special interest groups. A case in point, local government tends to engage in the more mundane activity of local communities, while national government handles issues of "high politics" such as defense and taxation. The political community at the local level consists of a smaller population with less-divided community interests, influenced less by ideologies or class-based needs and more by specific local needs; this gives the mayor or the governor an opportunity to more readily identify interests aggregated by and articulated through e-participation. Local government is thus more likely to solicit public input and to disseminate information. As described in this study, some local governments not only actively solicit public input, but are also more actively transparent and accountable in the use of public input into the policy process.

Equally important to information management is the technical nature of ICTs as mediation tools. However, personalized ICT access may also lead to problems in the promotion of better decisions through public input given the notion that easy and immediate access to policymakers through the use of ICTs will produce massive amounts of public comments, including off-topic junk mail and hate literature, which governments would be unable to manage. Soliciting the input of outsiders through the use of ICTs tends to be time consuming and probably costly, thereby complicating and slowing the progress of policymaking. As a result, policymakers continue to be reluctant to use public input gained from the use of ICTs.

There seems to be a tendency among Japanese national ministries included in this study to constrain the free flow of public comments, thus preventing a flood of public comments. On the other hand, Japanese local governments, which operate as the smallest administrative units of government, adapt better to the personalization of ICTs in the policymaking process. Some local governments in this study demonstrated that while they have not only been able to handle the input, they have spent substantial time responding to individual comments.

Given the more constrained predictions, as stated above, strong and capable political leadership may remain an essential contributory factor to directing information management toward democratic benefits. The direction of ICT development needs to be further integrated to allow for a "joined-up government" approach to policy information acquisition and utilization, rather than the traditionally compartmentalized means of information management. The use of ICTs needs to be coordinated between government departments, rather than spanning the boundaries of bureaucratic jurisdictions and causing turf wars among coalitions of departments, legislators, and special interests groups. To win the goodwill and ensure the cooperation of all the actors concerned, political leadership must be adept at accumulating political resources beyond formal authority, and must learn to use them in an effectively purposeful way.

At the national level, the state apparatus in general is much more fragmented, operating as different branches. The apparatus is less able to coordinate IT policies even for straightforward administrative cost cutting, particularly given the resistance of national bureaucrats and LDP politicians demonstrated in this study. To the extent that they are less fragmented, local authorities are better able to coordinate IT policies by using information shared among local government departments and citizens. In this sense, cross-sectoral IT policy is better coordinated in the less-fragmented apparatus of government.

This hypothesis needs to meet a fundamental condition in order to be feasible, that is, local authorities must have discretionary power and political autonomy vis-à-vis national government. Political leadership by chief executives at the local government level has proved able to integrate ICTs to the extent that there is available room for the exercise of political autonomy vis-à-vis national government. Currently, new decentralization measures in Japan allow considerable scope for local interpretation of national laws, far less administrative constraints on local authorities in the provision of public services, and far more information sharing for ICT-enabled political participation. Equally important, Japanese local governments, unlike the national government, have a presidential system that allows for strong political leadership by directly elected chief executives. Thus, mayors and governors in Japan exercise greater control over budgeting, personnel, and organization than does the prime minister.

In Japan, as in all other developed industrial nations, most ICT-driven resources reside in the executive branches of government where there is an obvious concern about the long-term implications of state-citizen relationships and executive-legislature relationships. E-participation, which is institutionalized by the administrative side of government, provides a way of reaching out to citizens who are currently opting out of wider political processes. This does not necessarily reflect a decline of representative democracy; rather, it suggests the necessity of adapting to newly emerging realities. In this sense, both executives and representatives are required to discover new roles and forms that characterize political participation in the early twenty-first century. ICTs could prove to be an essential tool for reconnecting citizens and the state, but they will not replace representative democracy with direct e-democracy. Instead, ICTs provide an opportunity to rediscover the necessity of representation. Thus, e-participation is a way of complementing and enhancing the existing representative structures.

CHAPTER 7

Women in Grassroots Politics: From Voters to Politicians

I think that we need to elect female representatives to national assemblies to address women's issues and into local assemblies to help solve community problems surrounding children and the family.[1]

Increasing the number of female representatives alone will neither change politics nor increase the autonomy of the local community. Women who belong to existing parties and organizations that pursue vested interests have been unable to change the political system. It is broadly citizen-based independent female representatives who are given a free hand . . . who can make a difference.[2]

The 1979 United Nations (UN) Convention on the Elimination of All Forms of Discrimination against Women highlights the importance of equal participation of women in public life. Since the early 1960s, women in Japan have voted in elections at a significantly higher rate than men. However, Japanese women's participation in policy formulation and decision-making processes lags far behind the participation of women in other major democracies. The principles of gender equality are endorsed by the Japanese constitution, yet their incorporation into social practice is yet to be fully realized. While there are no legal constraints on the rights of Japanese women to stand for public office, they are proportionally underrepresented in local and national elected assemblies. In 1999 there was a landmark law that substantially contributed to gender equality when the Japanese government, for the first time, prescribed men and women to be equal partners and denounced discrimination against women on the basis of stereotypical gender norms and roles. This was followed by the introduction of an unprecedented number of policy changes and legislative and organizational reforms at the national level. In the same year, women's groups operating at the grassroots level led policy, organizational, and legal changes by successfully conducting a major nationwide campaign, "More

Women to Assemblies!" This led to an unprecedented increase in the number of women elected as representatives at the local level.

The purpose of this chapter is to assess women's expanding political role in Japan, and to explore the potential of female representatives to provide alternative viewpoints and frameworks for solving the problems of wider political disengagement in this male-dominated representative democracy. In making their voices heard, women are highlighting the need for egalitarian institutions, in tandem with creating new associations and promoting public discussion in civil society. In my discussion, I will highlight the watershed events of 1999 that helped pave the way toward a gender-equal society in Japan, with special emphasis placed on the importance of grassroots missions in eliminating barriers to the participation of Japanese women in political institutions and processes.

Representative democracy in post–World War II (WWII) Japan is now at a crossroads: Japan's voter turnout has been alarmingly low and floating voters, who drift from party to party, or who abstain from voting, are continuing to rise. While this could be a sign of widespread political apathy, it is more likely to be a reaction to the old pork-barrel politics that has long favored special interest groups. In this respect, it is political alienation rather than apathy that may appropriately explain the degree and nature of political disengagement in Japan. Currently, there is an exceptionally high demand for an alternative way of politics in Japan, which is unparalleled in the recent history of the country. This has provided an opportunity for reformists and new political groups to work toward democracy building. Already, forward-looking women's groups in Japan are proposing alternative forms of political renewal.

In December 1945 the Japanese government, guided by General Douglas MacArthur, revised an election law for the House of Representatives granting Japanese women, 20 or over, the right to suffrage and those 25 or over, the right to candidacy. Articles 14, 24, and 44 of the 1947 constitution, drafted by the Allied Occupation authority, declared equality for all men and women. Yet the commitment to democracy was rhetorical rather than substantive as the opportunity provided for the exercise of legal equality failed to achieve tangible outcomes. Some 40 years later, Liberal Democratic Party (LDP) politicians were still extremely reluctant to compromise strongly entrenched patriarchal beliefs that women should remain at home.

Women's rights first became an issue for the UN following the World Conference of the International Year of the Woman in 1975. This led to the articulation of an international standard of women's rights that differed from the social and legal norms experienced and understood in the Japanese context. By the mid-1990s, the UN increasingly strengthened its mechanisms on the protection of women's rights, which were then ratified by member states including Japan. The Beijing Women's Conference of 1995 also helped stimulate a political climate for genuine gender reform, and domestic actors in Japan, particularly women's groups and female political leaders, increasingly incorporated compliance to international norms on national agendas and policymaking processes.

The national government enacted the Basic Law for a Gender-Equal Society in 1999, which was the first time that a paradigm of gender-equal society had been articulated by Japanese authorities. This law required the state to create institutional mechanisms promoting equal gender participation and gender equality. Sweeping changes in women's rights within just a few years had a strong impact on a country that was notorious for the absence of legal reforms. There were changes at the level of law and policies as well as changes at the grassroots level. However, many leaders of women's organizations believed that genuine gender reform could be only achieved through raising the awareness of Japanese women. By the late 1990s, key women's organizations were increasingly participatory and action-oriented toward the actualization of equal rewards for women. They were responding to UN calls for increasing the number of female assembly representatives to at least one-third of seats, so that women would have an influence in the wider society. As a result of their efforts, there were a record number of women challenging men for assembly seats in the 1999 unified local elections. The number of female candidates in these elections had increased from 2,144 in the 1995 unified local elections to 3,065 in the 1999 unified local elections, an increase of 43 percent. However, women's share of seats in local assemblies in 1999 was just 6.2 percent, which was a very low figure in a cross-national perspective.[3] Those who played a key part in the movements working to increase women's presence in politics were, in the main, citizen-based independent candidates.

At this point I have mainly examined the top-down nature of state-led gender reform and explained the circumstances under which the conservative party in power came to address gender equality as part of reforms in Japanese politics. Equally important is an examination of the bottom-up activities of grassroots organizations at the forefront of campaigns organized to raise women's awareness and to change policy agendas for gender reform by increasing the number of women representatives in politics and decision-making processes. My lens for these changes is 1999, the year in which two watershed events took place simultaneously. First, there was a radical change of direction toward a gender-equal society that began with the 1999 enactment of the Basic Law for a Gender-Equal Society at the national level. The second was the unprecedented success of grassroots campaigns to increase women's share of seats in the 1999 unified local elections. My examination of these campaigns centers on independent female candidates, not affiliated with any political party, who are supported by voluntary groups whose goal has been to attract nonorganizational voters irrespective of their gender. There are notable gender-based differences in the manner in which Japanese women are becoming more active in politics and in gaining political backing with the support of government policies and private initiatives as part of their political participation and advances.

Women as Independent Candidates at Local Elections

Most studies of Japanese politics are dominated by two contrasting approaches. First, a traditional legal-formal approach is widely adopted by Japanese scholars who see the activities of the elite as particularly conspicuous and important in Japanese politics. The second is the behaviorist approach introduced by American scholars, such as Scott Flanagan and Bradley Richardson, whose studies are dominated by broad characterizations of mass political behavior. Both approaches pay remarkably little attention to Japanese women. On the one hand, in the male-dominated power elite in Japan, the existence of Japanese women is treated as an irrelevant consideration, hardly mentioned in major textbooks of Japanese politics.[4] On the other hand, studies of Japanese political behavior tend to construct generalized characterizations at the expense of concrete observations, which also contributes to significant gender biases.[5] While there is a growing body of English-language studies on Japanese women, little attention is given to ordinary Japanese women in political life. The pioneering work of Susan Pharr on the political socialization of women activists at the grassroots level has helped pave the way for the next generation of systematic studies of women in Japanese politics.[6] Anne Imamura is one of the first scholars to comprehensively examine particular patterns of community participation among Japanese housewives.[7] While providing a new insight into narrowly focused area studies on Japan, Imamura's assumption of the culturally constrained Japanese woman with little reference to wider social processes is not particularly relevant to a comparative theory of women in politics. Some scholars raise questions about the reliability of cultural constraints imposed by Japanese traditions.[8] In recent years, new empirical studies on Japanese women have emerged, and comparative theorists have drawn attention to this new development within academic scholarship. Studies indicate significant gains in the socioeconomic status of Japanese women accompanied by their increasing participation in local politics. Dennis Patterson and Nishikawa Misa found that nonpartisan/independent Japanese women are more knowledgeable of and more purposive in politics than previously thought.[9] This lends itself to the argument that the overarching trend of political disengagement in Japan is reflecting the alienation, rather than the apathy or apolitical nature, of the Japanese electorate.[10] Robin LeBlanc embraces and expands upon the interpretation of this larger trend by pointing out that Japanese men and women are equally alienated without any clear gender difference.[11] So what is it that underpins the gender difference in the distribution of political attitudes? Some scholars argue that resources, such as increased access to education and jobs, do little to explain gender differences in Japan.[12] Perhaps the latest and most important findings on Japanese women in political life lie in the fact that Japanese women overwhelmingly perceive barriers to political participation as gender specific.[13] Existing studies to date also recognize Japanese women as neither more nor less willing than men to voice their views in political processes although they do see women to be more constrained than men in political participation. At the same time, the findings of my research clearly indicate that Japanese women are becoming more engaged in politics and that they are overcoming gender-specific barriers to stand for election. I illustrate this increased participation by focusing on independent female candidates at local elections while pointing out that the increase in numbers of female representatives is not necessarily a direct reflection of the inclusion of their voices in political processes.

In the initial stages of agenda setting, the majority of female representatives tend to work together on a nonpartisan basis to support women's issues such as day care, maternity leave, and sexual harassment policies. When it comes to decision-making processes however, the same women are subject to a variety of political constraints. Those women affiliated with a political party may be influenced by party ideology and the special interests of party support organizations, while women linked with more personalized neighborhood/kinship-based support groups may be influenced by the special interests of those groups. Although the increase in the number of female representatives has made it easier to retain women's issues on the political agenda, and to occasionally introduce gender-related policies beyond the scope of partisan politics, it is largely citizen-based female independents who have spearheaded the demand for gender reform at the local level. Literature findings indicate that there are more citizen-based independent female representatives than male representatives in Japan and that, in respect to patterns of their constituency, there are clear differences between assembly-men and -women. Arguably, there are three distinct types of local assembly members: neighborhood/kinship-based representatives, progressive party-supported representatives, and citizen-based independent representatives.[14] Neighborhood/kinship-based representatives often run as independents even though they may be affiliated to the conservative LDP. Progressive party-supported representatives are likely to be a member of one of the progressive parties: Japan Communist Party, Democratic Party, Clean Government Party, and Social Democratic Party. Citizen-based independent representatives typically get support for election campaigns from voluntary groups in order to attract nonorganizational and floating votes. These three types of local assembly members are not mutually exclusive. Party-affiliated representatives, for example, may partly depend on the support of neighborhood associations for collecting votes. In 2002 the three types of representatives by gender were broken down into the following categories: assembly-men—the neighborhood/kinship type (67.1 percent), the progressive party-affiliated type (14.8 percent), the broad-citizen-based type (18.1 percent); and assembly-women—the neighborhood/kinship type (25.9 percent), the progressive party-affiliated type (44.4 percent), the broad-citizen-based type (29.7 percent).[15] Thus, there are far more female than male party-affiliated representatives; far less female than male neighborhood/kinship representatives, and more female than male broad-citizen-based representatives, a number that is on the increase for women. On the whole, as my research findings indicate, the lowering of barriers to women's political participation has proved to be especially difficult in Japan; however, grassroots organizations have played a crucial role in assisting women to overcome barriers in order to stand as independents at local elections.

Japan's Readiness for Gender Equality

Given high adult literacy rates and educational levels in Japan, it would be expected that there would be little difficulty in raising women's consciousness and capabilities to actively participate in economic and political activities and to take part in decision-making processes. Interestingly enough, according to an international survey, *Human Development Report 2005,* Japan ranks 11th (among 177 countries) with 0.943 of the Human Development Index (HDI), and 14th (among 140 countries) with 0.937 of the Gender-Related Development Index (GDI). However, Japan drops to 43rd place (among 80 countries) with just 0.534 of the Gender Empowerment Measure (GEM).[16]

Even more critical, according to the February 2006 data compiled by the Inter-Parliamentary Union (IPU), Japan sank to 105th place on women's share of seats in a lower or single house (9 percent). Today, many developing countries such as Rwanda (48.8 percent), Pakistan (21.3 percent), and the Philippines (15.7 percent) far exceed Japan in terms of women's share of seats in a lower or single house.[17]

"Japan's Vision of Gender Equality: Creating New Values for the Twenty-First Century," a public policy paper submitted by the Council for Gender Equality on July 30, 1996, argued that improving the status of women alone was insufficient to ensure the realization of a gender-equal society. The council proposed the concept of *danjo kyodo sankaku* according to which men and women could ensure their respective rights by joint participation on the basis of individual character rather than socially and culturally formed gender distinctions.[18] In an address delivered on June 16, 1997, to the council, then prime minister and president of the LDP Hashimoto Ryutaro stated, "It is my belief that building a gender-equal society can be considered a form of social reform and that gender equality will be one of the pillars of 'reform and creation' in every field of society."[19] Did this public statement signal the breakdown of the LDP's conservative view of women, family, and gender roles? Was Japan really heading toward such a participatory society?

Top-Down Affairs of State-Led Feminism: Institutional and Legal Changes

The year 1999 was a watershed year in the history of women in Japanese politics. The public policy paper drafted by the Council for Gender Equality became the blueprint for the newly introduced Basic Law for a Gender-Equal Society that came into effect in June 1999. This law marked a radical departure from the stance of earlier policy concerning women in Japan. Article 3 of this law states:

> Formation of a Gender-Equal Society shall be promoted based on respect for the human rights of women and men, including: respect for the dignity of men and women as individuals; no gender-based discriminatory treatment of women or men; and the securing of opportunities for men and women to exercise their abilities as individuals.[20]

This opening article of the law proposed a "gender-free"' society that would not reflect the stereotyped division of gender roles but instead would have as neutral an impact as possible on the selection of social activities by men and women working as equal partners. The law was also the first state-led attempt in

Japan to incorporate gender feminism (prominent second-wave movements) into social policy and to seek a model for the development of a gender-equal society. This required the state to implement measures promoting equal gender participation and gender equality. Mainstream women's groups in Japan had been demanding state intervention for some time, as attested by their campaigns for laws mandating equal pay, for taxpayer-financed day care, for sexual harassment prevention, for a domestic violence prevention bill, for legalization of the oral contraceptive pill, and for legislation against child pornography and sexual abuse. As a result, the Japanese government, in recent years, is dealing with new political issues such as domestic violence and sexual harassment that had been previously viewed as personal matters outside the reach of the state. It seems that the Japanese government had begun to acknowledge that "the personal is political," that personal lives are also ruled by political forces, and that state intervention into the personal realm was and is necessary to eliminate the obstacles that prevent women from achieving freedom and equal rights.[21]

After decades of campaigning by Japanese reproductive rights advocates, the Japanese government finally legalized the oral contraceptive pill in June 1999.[22] That same year, the Equal Employment Opportunities Law, which was revised especially to prevent sexual harassment at work, took effect.[23] Employers were now legally obligated to prevent sexual harassment in the workplace. In November 1999 the Anti-Child Sexual Abuse Law (Law for Punishing Acts Related to Child Prostitution and Child Pornography, and for Protecting Children) also became effective.[24] It is important to note that this legislation reversed the responsibility of prostitution by targeting the illegality of the consumer rather than the provider in order to deter the sexual exploitation of women and children. Perhaps one of the most publicized changes in gender policy was the government initiative of public, mandatory Long-Term Care Insurance (LTCI), which started in April 2000.[25] This new program was quite a surprising initiative and a major departure from the patriarchal style of government policy in which the family, particularly women, were viewed as the primary providers for the care of the elderly. Under this expensive program, everyone aged 65 or over was deemed eligible for benefits of both institutional and community-based caregiving based on physical and mental disability spread over six categories (re-classified into seven categories in April 2006) of need.[26] The Japanese government had decisively shifted towards the "socialization of care" for bedridden or frail older persons by transferring responsibility from women to the state. In the view of the Japanese government, the personal realm, in this particular respect, is no longer deemed separate from the state; the need to intervene—rather than to expediently remain apart—is now regarded as appropriate when promoting and protecting the rights of women. State reinforcement of gender equality was embraced and strengthened by the 2000 enactment of the Law on Proscribing Stalking Behavior and Assisting Victims together with Japan's first comprehensive law against spousal violence, the Law for the Prevention of Spousal Violence and the Protection of Victims passed in the National Diet (national legislature) in April 2001. Over one hundred Spousal Violence

Counseling and Support Centers are now operating across the nation. In December 2000 the Law on the Promotion of Human Rights Education was introduced for the elimination of violence against women, which became a national goal in the Japanese educational system. These institutional and legal changes of 1999–2000 represented a fundamental shift in Japanese government policy toward women's issues, and were incorporated under the slogan of *josei no jinken* (women's human rights). These changes, in their entirety, amounted to an astonishingly rapid expansion of state-led gender policies. This was a significant change from the early 1980s, when the Japanese government was tacitly endorsing traditional gender roles by avoiding the promotion of equal gender participation.[27] It is now clear that the Japanese government has made sudden changes in relation to gender policy at the national level. At a more general level, this policy expansion reflected the government's response to the increased needs of the Japanese economy. Japan's population was expected to peak at 128 million in 2006 and then face a period of decline. The population is aging much faster than in other major OECD countries; the fertility rate is continuing to drop (recording 1.29 in 2004) and it is expected that 25 percent will be above 65 years of age in 2014.[28] As a result, the work-capable population is declining. The key task is to increase both the birth rate and women's participation in the labor market to sustain Japan's healthy economy.

These figures and concerns indicate the increasing need for a new gender policy; however, gender norms and practices have been changing at a constant pace over the long term while institutional and legal changes in gender policy have been quite abrupt. Although demographic changes and other shifts often set the parameters for a change in the stance of the government, and subsequent government actions in relation to policy formation, they are not the direct determinants of more immediate changes within policy. Thus, it is important to look at factors within the political system and the political environment including demographic shifts and attitudinal shifts of leaders and policymakers, to explain these sudden changes in policy.[29] By the late 1990s, some senior LDP politicians began to argue that the old patriarchal ideal of the full-time housewife and mother would no longer be a viable option for Japan's future. LDP labor minister Okano Yutaka stated, "The so-called *shoshika* [low birth rate phenomenon] will lead to a decline in the working population, and will be one of the biggest problems we will ever have to deal with."[30] He further argued that "in *shoshika's* progress, it is a very important task to allow working women to fully realize their abilities."[31] Perhaps because there was also a rhetorical element to these statements, other LDP conservatives did not recognize the need for substantial change within gender policy as a whole. Former prime minister Mori Yoshiro, for example, reportedly said that women who grow old without having children did not deserve state aid; and another senior LDP lawmaker, Ota Seiichi, remarked that men who participated in gang rapes were closer to normal than those who put off marriage.[32] Firmly entrenched sexism, as demonstrated by these statements, indicates that the basic beliefs and values of leaders are not likely to change dramatically in a short period. While there is no relevant survey data available, it is unlikely that a significant change of attitude within national leaders' perception of gender issues would be the ultimate cause of 1999 institutional and legal changes in state-led gender policy. It is more likely that it is party politics—often working in favor of specific constituencies, ideologies, declared policies, and programs—that has led to specific policy outputs. One dimension of party politics relevant to this study is that the leading government party may take over the platform of their coalition partner in order to remain the dominant force in power. The House of Representative election, held in the fall of 1996, allowed the conservative LDP to restore some of its lost popularity but did not regain the majority of seats. To maintain power, the LDP gave priority to the LDP-SDP (Social Democratic Party)-Shinto Sakigake (New Party Harbinger) coalition.[33] In October 1996 Prime Minister Hashimoto managed a three-party accord with both the SDP and the Sakigake, under which it was decided that the two junior partners would not contribute cabinet members to the administration but would, instead, provide out-of-cabinet support. Both the SDP and the Sakigake were headed by female leaders, Doi Takako and Domoto Akiko respectively, who, in return for cooperation from outside the cabinet, successfully included the passage of major legislation on gender equality into the accord.[34] Chairperson Domoto confirmed this course of events by saying, "If Ms. Doi and I had not been party leaders, not one of these legislations would have been carried through."[35]

Analysis at an international level, including the influence of international norms and foreign pressures on domestic forces in Japan,[36] is of equal importance to an explanation of institutional and legal changes in 1999. The World Conference of the International Year of the Woman in 1975 proved to be a turning point for the status of women to be brought into the public agenda in Japan.[37] In responding to the World Plan of Action recommended by the UN, the Miki Takeo cabinet established the first "national machinery" in Japan: the Headquarters for the Planning and Promotion of Policies Relating to Women (headed by the prime minister), the Office for Women's Affairs in the Prime Minister's Office, and the Advisory Council to the Prime Minister on Planning and Promotion of Women's Affairs. The Japanese government was concerned about its international reputation and, in 1980, signed the 1979 Convention on the Elimination of All Forms of Discrimination against Women. It was then implemented into domestic law including the 1985 Equal Employment Opportunity Law and the 1984 revision of the Nationality Law; and it also led to the introduction of compulsory home economics education for both girls and boys in 1989.[38] The compliance of states to international norms is never immediate or automatic.[39] The Japanese government has been highly sensitive to accusations that Japan is not sufficiently internationalized to be regarded as an advanced nation, and is therefore more vulnerable to pressures invoking international standards.[40] Since the ratification of the 1985 convention, Japan has dutifully submitted its periodic reports to the UN, in a bid to demonstrate its ability to implement international standards at a domestic level. It is through this mechanism of required reporting that the UN Committee on the Elimination

All Form of Discrimination against Women has continued to hold the Japanese government accountable for discrimination-related reforms. Japan responded to foreign observers with a series of proposed reforms that laid the foundation for the first Basic Law for a Gender-Equal Society.

It is female leaders in party politics and their support groups that have been more successful in their compliance to international norms for national agendas and policymaking processes.[41] In September 1996 the Council for Gender Equality submitted to Prime Minister Hashimoto the "Vision of Gender Equality," a radical policy paper that was heavily influenced by the Beijing Conference, and that set the tone for the passage of the Basic Law for a Gender-Equal Society.[42] The Japanese government submitted its report to the UN in April 1999 as part of its response to the Beijing Platform for Action while financially backing the UN initiative for the Elimination of Violence against Women. Perhaps the Japanese government was motivated more by the need to preserve its international reputation than the pursuit of a gender-equal society when it extended unexpected rights to women by implementing the international standards into domestic law within such a short period of time.

Building a Gender Equal Society from the Ground Up: Eliminating Barriers to Women's Participation in Political Processes

The principle of gender equality was established with the legislative enactment of the Basic Law for a Gender-Equal Society and other associated laws. This swift, formal development was accompanied by a gradual but steady evolution of gender norms and expectations among the general public. Traditional beliefs and expectations surrounding gender roles, which are deeply rooted in Japanese society, have been gradually changing in recent years. Government surveys indicate a steady decline in the ratio of those interviewed who "fully" or "partially" supported the premise that "the man should work outside and the woman should remain at home" from 73 percent in 1979, to 58 percent in 1997, and 45 percent in 2004.[43] Changes in the attitudes of the community were also evident in 1991 when 64.3 percent of female respondents and 68.1 percent of male respondents supported need to increase the numbers of female elected-representatives.[44] While discrimination against women in general and women as electoral candidates in Japan has clearly decreased, this seems to have had little bearing on women's share of seats, which constituted just 9.2 percent in 2005 for national assemblies and 7.9 percent in 2003 for local assemblies.[45] Such weak relationships are also found in other countries such as Australia, Britain, and the United States.[46]

The structural constraints embedded in Japan's electoral system have a direct relationship to the low rate of women holding office. Some scholars have demonstrated that larger electoral district systems better accommodate the efforts of female candidates to win seats,[47] while others argue that a proportional representation system is more supportive of women in this respect than a single-member district system.[48] In the first post-WWII election of 1946, when Japanese women were first given the right to vote, 39 women were elected under a large constituency system[49] to the House of Representatives. In the following year, Japan introduced a new system for the lower house, made up of medium-sized multimember districts (three to five seats in each district) with single nontransferable votes; under this system, women's seats declined immediately to 15 in the 1947 election and, by the 1986 election, had dropped further to a low of 7 seats. By 1993, the 38-year rule of the LDP ended, and Japan reformed its electoral system to small-sized single-member districts combined with a proportional representation system. In the subsequent 1996 election, women's seats increased to 23, with 16 of these seats being proportionally elected. Proportional representation seemed to have presented the most favorable environment for female candidates.[50] While Japan's experience at national elections seems to support the links and observations in the above-mentioned literature, local elections in Japan suggest a different story. Elections for local assemblies have been organized under a large constituency system with 1 to 18 seats in each district for prefectural and designated city assemblies, and a large number of seats in single districts covering the whole area for city/ward/town/ village assemblies.[51] Contrary to the claimed link between women representatives and a larger constituency, women's share of seats in larger constituency-based local assemblies remained extremely low, arguably stagnant, until the 1983 unified local election. From this point there were small incremental changes at local assembly elections with women gaining 1.7 percent of seats in 1986.[52] It is interesting though that women holding public office at the local level rapidly increased during the late 1990s.[53] It is highly unlikely that the highly structured electoral system was a primary factor enabling the sudden rise of female representatives. Other critical factors may include women's awareness of, and willingness to, incorporate their voices within policy formulation and decision-making processes.

In this respect, women's campaigns in local elections in recent years have illustrated the capacity of Japanese women to form networks, to help raise the awareness of women in general, and to successfully increase the number of female representatives. Figure 7.1 illustrates that 1999 was a turning point for women at the grassroots level. In simultaneously held local elections in April 1999, a total of 2,381 women were elected to local assemblies (in prefectures, cities, towns, and villages), with the percentage of women elected increasing to 6.2 percent, an increase of 1.3 percent from the previous election. In the 1999 unified local elections, for the first time ever, nearly 20 percent (cf. 14.3 percent in 1998) of the 972 representatives in 23 special ward assemblies of Tokyo were female; equally significant, the number of women elected to prefectural assemblies soared by a stunning 70 percent from the previous 1995 elections. The 1999 unified local elections were also something of a political milestone, for women were elected to local assemblies in *all* the ten prefectures (Akita, Ehime, Iwate, Nagasaki, Niigata, Oita, Shimane, Tokushima, Tottori, and Toyama) which, till that point in time, had been represented only by men.[54] As will be discussed later in this chapter, the campaigns of female candidates and their support

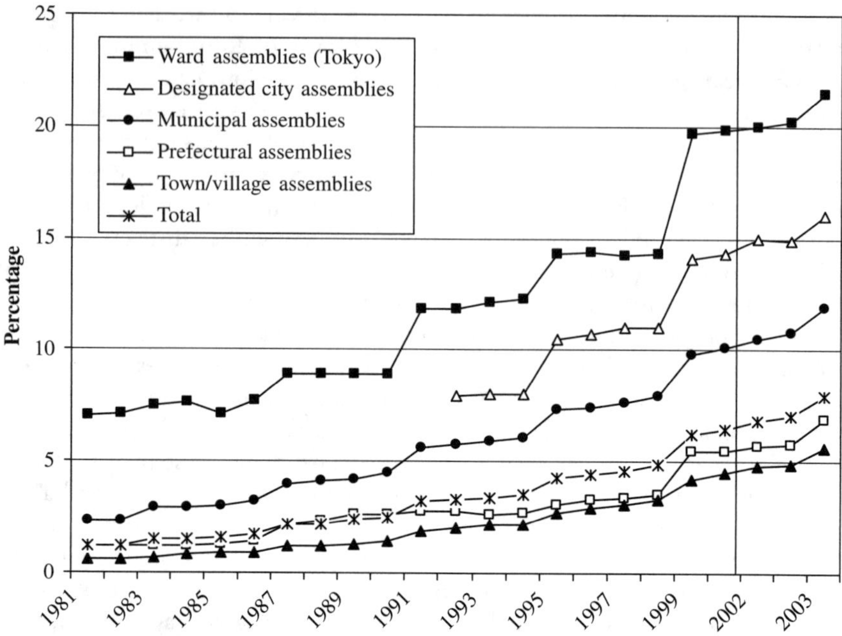

Source: Compiled from data provided by Japan, Ministry of Internal Affairs and Communications (MIAC), Bureau of Local Administration, and the National Association of Municipal Assembly Chairpersons.

Figure 7.1   Women's share of seats in local assemblies, 1981–2003.

groups and networks gained considerable attention in the media and helped raise awareness of the need for gender equality among the general public.

In 1992 a women's group, the Alliance of Feminist Representatives, was formed by nonpartisan elected representatives and those endeavoring to elect more women to local and national assemblies. Together, they launched a campaign urging an increase in the ratio of female representatives in the quota system to at least 30 percent. Mitsui Mariko, a Tokyo Metropolitan assembly-woman, and other founder members who were familiar with similar proposals at UN women's conferences, argued that a ratio of 30 percent would provide the minimal threshold for forming a critical mass whose voices could not be ignored in assemblies.[55] In 1994 the alliance investigated the numbers of female representatives and found that women were not included as representatives in 58 percent of some 3,300 local assemblies.[56] To rectify the position, they launched a project known as "Eliminate Zero-Women Representatives Assemblies!" in 1997 demanding that political groups and parties include female candidates in targeted electoral districts across the nation. Three years earlier, in 1994, the Ichikawa Fusae Memorial Association had established the Promotion Center for Women's Political Participation, which was a training program to help women stand for local elections. It offered two courses, one providing practical knowledge for running local elections and the other providing political education.[57] The majority of participants were aged between 40 and 55 who lacked *sanban* (the three foundations) of family support, organized support groups, and financial resources.[58] There were eight to ten two-day sessions over the space of one year in the first course, five two-day sessions over one year in the second course.[59] In 1994, 93 women from 19 prefectures across Japan participated in the training program[60] with a further 709 women completing the program during the following nine years.[61] Training for the program was almost freely provided by enthusiastic academics, government officials, politicians, journalists, and accountants. This was fortuitous as the program was not financially supported by any government body but operated through membership fees and private charitable contributions. It neither recommended nor supported specific political ideologies and parties, nor did it endorse or recommend any specific candidate for election campaigns. It provided an independent place for networking among participants from all parts of Japan. In the 1995 unified local elections, 36 of 93 inaugural program participants ran for election and 24 of these participants won a seat.[62] This concept of providing training for prospective candidates spread throughout grassroots groups across the nation, and such training programs were called *bakku-appu sukuru* (backup schools). In 1996 the Women and Politics Information Center in Kansai initiated a Women to Assemblies backup school. By 1998 grassroots groups in 17 of 47 prefectures had organized similar backup schools and, in 2003 these groups were active in 24 prefectures.[63] Although there was some variation in their activities, they all shared common features: no affiliation with any political party, a commitment to women's political participation, and financing through internal funds (for example, membership fees).

Local governments also developed a scheme called *josei kaigi* (women's simulation assembly), which was designed to promote activities for women to participate in local decision making and to send more women to assemblies. Despite the value of the local government's scheme, it was women's groups that had initially requested the local administration to hold simulation assemblies on a regular basis, and it was the existing assembly-women who had proposed inclusion of simulation assembly as part of local gender-equality policy.[64] In 1996 there were just 10 local governments running simulation assemblies, a figure that rose to 48 in 1999, and 116 in 2002.[65] For example, the Yamanashi prefecture implemented a simulation assembly program in 1988 as part of its gender-equality policy called Yamanashi Human Plan 21. In 1999, 6 of the 22 simulation assembly participants ran for unified local elections, and were elected to Yamanashi's local assemblies that had never had female representatives.[66] The participants were openly recruited or recommended by women's organizations (such as housewives' and consumers' associations), with the number of participants mirroring the total number of seats in the real assembly. Simulation assemblies were typically held as one-day or half-day events, although participants would be invited to attend several preparatory meetings and training sessions, which, in the Toyama prefecture for example, ran for 100 days.[67] Actual assembly halls were then made available for simulation in which participants took the floor to question chief executives from the community or government officials in charge of policy issues in line with practices at actual assembly sessions. Simulation plays allowed participating women to experience what it would be like to be an assembly-member and to learn how to transform their involvement at a community level into political strategies and solutions. The local government–sponsored *josei kaigi* received much publicity, notably in photographs of women chairpersons at simulation assemblies, which helped to increase public awareness in conservative rural communities. As a result, the usually empty public seats were packed with women and their spouses and the relatives of women participating in simulation assemblies.[68] These facilitated assemblies also assisted participants by offering family support such as child care, which had been one of the key barriers (*sanban*) to their participation in political processes.[69]

Networks were also organized to support backup schools and simulation assemblies. In 1996, for example, Higuchi Keiko, Domoto Akiko, and others (National Diet women, local assembly-women, scholars, journalists, activists, and housewives) acknowledged that information available in the existing mass media on women's issues was limited and launched a nationwide, information exchange network known as JJ-Net.[70] In addition to issuing a regular newsletter called *JJ-Net News,* the network provided and shared information through fax and e-mails. By 1998 JJ-Net had grown into an ICT-based instantaneous information provider that members increasingly utilized for electoral campaigns and policymaking processes.[71] As of 2005, JJ-Net had over 1,000 registered members. In 1999 former education minister Akamatsu Yoshiko, journalist Shimomura Mitsuko, and four other female leaders established the organization WIN WIN as a membership network of support and fund raising to increase women's presence in political processes. This network was modeled after EMILY's List, an organization founded in the United States to further the number of female representatives in the Democratic Party. As of 2000, WIN WIN had 861 members.[72] Each member was designated a specific candidate of her own choice from the WIN WIN's recommendation list, and supported the chosen candidate with a donation of ¥10,000 or more. The female candidates that the WIN WIN committee unanimously recommended were included in the recommendation lists at major local and national elections.[73] The first recommended candidate, Ota Fusae, won a seat in the 2000 Osaka gubernatorial election and became Japan's first woman governor. It is important to note here that these networks operated on a nonpartisan basis but with a strong sense of mission to promote gender equality policy.

In the 1999 unified local elections, the support groups and networks outlined above developed an impressive electoral campaign known as the Women and Politics Campaign 1999. This was the brainchild of the Eliminate Zero-Women Representatives Assembly campaign, which was initiated by the Alliance of Feminist Representatives. In September 1998 the alliance designated a person (in principle, an independent representative) in charge of this campaign in all of the 47 prefectures. Campaign participants then took simultaneous actions throughout the nation by holding press conferences calling for "more women to assemblies" and participating in public demonstrations in front of each prefectural office for this purpose.[74] This nationwide campaign highlighted the public profile of female politicians, attracted the interest of the mass media, and raised public awareness of the necessity of increasing the number of female representatives, while urging accomplished women to run for election.[75] Some scholars argue that in the 1999 elections, campaigners kept the focus of the media on the single issue of "more women to assemblies" and, in the process, effectively sustained the visibility of this nationwide campaign throughout the entire campaign period.[76] As a result of these 1999 elections, women were successfully elected to prefectural assemblies in all of the ten prefectures, which was exceptional as women had never been represented in these prefectures prior to this time.

Even more impressive, in the 1999 unified local elections, 45 female candidates within the Tokyo Citizens' Network were elected in 32 cities/wards of Tokyo; and a member of the Tokyo Citizens' Network, Uehara Kimiko, won the mayoral election in Tokyo's Kunitachi city, to become Tokyo's first female mayor. In the 2001 election for the Tokyo Metropolitan assembly, six female candidates from the same network were all successfully elected. In the 2003 unified local elections, 52 female candidates of the network ran for office and 47 were elected in cities/wards of Tokyo. The Citizens' Network spurred the growth of local groups throughout Japan; it formed the basis of 109 local networks (most of which existed in Hokkaido, Iwate, Tochigi, Saitama, Chiba, Tokyo, Kanagawa, Nagano, and Fukuoka) across the nation. In the 2003 unified elections, 164 female Citizens' Network candidates stood for local assemblies of Tokyo and 107 of those candidates won seats (accounting for 45 percent of the successfully elected female Citizens' Network candidates across the nation), Kanagawa (28 percent), Chiba (15 percent), and three other prefectures (12 percent).[77]

The Case of the Tokyo Citizens' Network: Alternative Political Participation

In town/village assemblies, as illustrated in figure 7.1, female representatives accounted for less than one percent of all seats until 1986. Female representatives in those assemblies increased from 2.7 percent in the 1995 simultaneous local elections to 4.2 percent in the 1999 elections. Nonetheless, nearly 60 percent of 1,702 town/village assembly-women were conservative independents who were elected primarily by both blood-tie relations and a shared territorial bond of neighborhood organizations, while about 40 percent of the assembly-women were affiliated with a progressive political party.[78] Less than one percent of the assembly-women were Citizens' Network activists or progressive independents elected by citizens' networks and coalitions of support whose goal was to incorporate citizens' voices into policy formulation and decision-making processes.[79]

Not surprisingly, 85 percent of Citizens' Network assembly-women concentrated on municipal assemblies in urban areas as opposed to towns and villages.[80]

It is interesting to consider what stimulated the emergence and subsequent success of the Citizens' Network in urban areas. The origin of the Tokyo Citizens' Network dates back to the creation of the consumers' cooperative organization, the Life Club Cooperative Society, which began operation in Setagaya ward, Tokyo, in 1968.[81] Originally, this organization sought to ensure the safety and quality of consumer goods and services at reasonable prices while protecting consumer interests by directly connecting consumers with producers. By 1989 it had grown into the Federation of the Life Club Cooperative Society, based in 13 prefectures across the nation.

Throughout the 1970s, producer-oriented government policies were causing a wide and escalating range of social problems arising from industrial pollution and food safety issues. Citizens participating in co-op activities deemed themselves to be responsible consumers and found it difficult to accept the established order of political priorities geared toward the interests of the producers. Members of the Life Club Cooperative Society began to feel powerless and vulnerable as the society only acted as a service provider to its members. Realizing the necessity of advocacy,[82] one of the society founders, Iwane Kunio, proposed the "Representative Authorization Campaign" by proclaiming that "the Life Club is not only an organization for purchasing goods, but also a place where we further the independence and participation of citizen in a democratic community."[83] This proposal in March 1977, led to the establishment of a political organization called the Group Citizens, which was the predecessor of the Citizens' Network. It was not long before this service provider of mutual support based on self-help was promoting the political involvement of women. By July 1977 women participating in the Life Club Cooperative Society were, for the first time, recruiting their own female candidates to challenge incumbents in the Nerima district for a Tokyo Metropolitan assembly election. While this challenge was unsuccessful, it paved the way for the Representative Authorization Campaign that recruited women to represent the voices of citizens in assemblies. In 1979, for the first time, the Group Citizens—renamed as the Tokyo Citizens' Network in 1988—successfully sent a female representative to the Nerima Ward Assembly.[84]

The Rotation System

The larger goal of the rotation system, over and above the production of women representatives, is to create citizens for political change. Citizens' Network members served as representatives in local assemblies on a rotation basis. The network also established limited terms for assembly-women specifying a maximum number of three terms or 12 years in office. In the 2003 unified local elections, Tokyo Citizens' Network members came to share the view that a limit of three terms or 12 years was acceptable, but that a limit of two terms or 8 years would be more desirable.[85] This rotation system, which was set up in 1990, was implemented to avoid the professionalization of representatives (that lends itself to the creation of vested individual interests over time), and to facilitate the passage of as many members as possible into local assemblies.[86] As described in more detail below, the Citizens' Network acted as a support mechanism for assembly-women, helping inexperienced and less qualified citizens to act as representatives. According to the Citizens' Network, the ultimate objective of the rotation system is to empower individual citizens through their representative experience.[87] It is their view that this system provides an alternative pathway into political engagement while helping to eliminate the distance between citizens and policymaking processes.[88] The traditional and salient features of Japanese politics at a local level are personal networks based upon voters as clients and elected representatives as patrons. In short, voters trade electoral support for personal favors—a traditional engagement that diminishes citizen's participation in decision-making processes. The value of the rotation system is that it incorporates a large number of citizens in policy formulation and decision-making processes. It was through this system, for example, that 21 Tokyo Citizens' Network assembly-women retired, an action that enabled 30 new assembly-women to be elected as part of the local elections of April 2003.[89] Network members also acknowledged that they needed to assume responsibility for ensuring the quality and continuity of the representatives' work. To this end, former –assembly-women handed down their accumulation of trust and experience to the next generation, and set up the Citizen Thinktank-People Town Institute in 1998.[90] The primary members of the institute are former assembly-women who have been undertaking investigations and conducting research to help solve community problems and to help incumbents draft alternative policy proposals. Among its major activities, the institute has organized training workshops for increasing assembly-member-initiated policies and ordinances; a wide range of surveys on the implementation of a new social welfare system for the elderly (the LTCI discussed earlier in this chapter); and has acted as a third party evaluator, authorized by the Tokyo Metropolitan government, holding welfare providers accountable to users.[91]

The rotation system has done much to foster the inclusion of citizens in political processes, yet Citizens' Network assembly-women recognize a number of serious barriers to the further development of the system. Under the compulsory government-operated pension membership of local assemblies, assembly-members who stay in office for just two terms or under are required to surrender the full benefits of their assembly-member pension. In fact, some Citizens' Network assembly-women, such as Fukushi Keiko, withdrew their membership from Tokyo Citizens' Network after serving the maximum term and continued to run for office beyond the three-term limit. Through this course of action, they became eligible for their full pension benefits. Another difficulty is that career women serving on the rotation system as assembly-women find it difficult to return to their place of employment at the end of their term as their jobs are not held open for them. Some critics argue that the majority of Citizens' Network members are housewives and therefore have no need for remuneration as assembly representatives.[92] The Citizens' Network has been successful in raising the awareness of women and their participation in political processes, but in order to increase the numbers of assembly-women, the network needs to revise its strategies for continued success.[93]

Intermediary Roles in Participatory Policymaking

Citizens' Network assembly-women play a role in coordinating a meeting of policy consultation between citizens and the metropolitan administration. The voting group of Citizens' Network assembly-women has organized and coordinated a series of conferences to help facilitate negotiations between the Tokyo Metropolitan administration and citizens. As part of this process, the assembly-women have provided citizens a standing forum to present to the administration their choice of policies through utilizing assembly members' right of investigation and policy proposal. Then, at the conclusion of the conference, Citizens' Network representatives take action to initiate citizen's preferences and wishes.

The first Citizens-Administration Conference was held in October 1994, and has since continued on a yearly or twice a year basis. A citizens' working party was formed to prepare documents and strategies for each conference, while Citizens' Network assembly-women contacted the relevant metropolitan departments and provided their expertise and knowledge to interested citizens. The assembly-women have admitted that it has not been easy for a wide range of social groups to make a concerted effort toward a policy proposal, yet argue that the process is worthwhile given its contribution to agenda setting and to the articulation of community interests in political processes.[94] The general public has also recognized these efforts as useful in building a livable community, particularly given the number of achievements arising from the conferences. The 2001 conference, for example, led to the establishment of two Tokyo Metropolitan government guidelines: the 2003 Chemical Material Guidelines Applied to Children (Indoor Air Quality) and the 2004 Chemical Material Guidelines Applied to Children (Food Safety).[95] Although relevant guidelines existed for adults, this was the first time that the needs of children had been considered. Furthermore, when the issue of domestic violence was placed on the agenda of the 2004 conference, the Tokyo Citizens' Network successfully persuaded six relevant metropolitan departments and three political parties to participate. As a result, the combating of domestic violence has been incorporated as a large program within the Tokyo Metropolitan government's welfare section and there is now a consulting hotline for victims, financial support for the provision of shelters for victims, and education for abusive men.[96]

Intermediary Roles in Local Government's Cooperation with Community Groups

The Tokyo Citizens' Network has also helped to establish, and to facilitate, collaboration between nonprofit organizations (NPOs) and the Tokyo Metropolitan government at the 2002 conference where government officials, for the first time, directly exchanged information with citizens participating in NPO activities.[97]

Two intermediary organizations, the Community Fund-Town Future and the Tokyo Community Power Bank (Tokyo CPB), were established by the Citizens' Network in 2003, to improve social equity in the community and to help revitalize the local economy.[98] The mission of the Community Fund-Town Future is to provide citizens with the appropriate knowledge and expertise—such as fund-raising, marketing, management skills, and partnership with the public sector—to open a community enterprise. The Tokyo CPB has provided loans raised from the investments of individuals and organizations whose goal is to support citizen enterprises that make a contribution to local communities. One of the successful NPOs supported by the network is Ecomesse, which has been promoting a recycling system that helps to preserve the local environment. It channels the proceeds from membership fees and donations and from the nine secondhand shops it runs in Tokyo to a number of schemes including a variety of tree-planting drives and providing solar panels and batteries in public facilities.[99]

Grassroots Election Campaigns

The election campaigns that the Tokyo Citizens' Network proposes are carried out only by the donations of individual citizens and/or the work of volunteers. Corruption occurs in Japan, as in other democracies, when politicians exchange personal favors for monetary rewards. In the early 1990s, the ruling LDP faced a political crisis over a series of scandals involving questionable "donations" to politicians' election funds. In contrast to many mainstream political parties, the Tokyo Citizens' Network has shown a commitment to a high standard of transparency and accountability by regularly and publicly stating its revenue and expenditure flows.[100] In its view, assembly-members are ordinary citizens who donate to the network according to their income and their participation in political activities.[101] To this end, the network has negotiated an agreement known as the "Representative Authorization Contract" with assembly-members to donate a contracted portion of their income to the network. These donations, together with membership fees and voluntary donations from the community, support the activities of the network.

Conclusion

In post-WWII Japan, the state authority strategically concentrated key resources, including legal authority, political legitimacy, fiscal resources, organizations, information, and expertise, at the national level. The local community was linked to these state resources through local power brokers. These influential politicians used their access to state benefits as a means of assisting their personal supporters. They would promote the special interests of their supporters and, in return, gain the votes of supporters for their reelection. The allocation of state resources was devoted to creating rivalries among local power brokers as this was deemed to be part of a political system shaped by hierarchies of power and influence. Thus, special or sectional interests prevailed, with little incentive to make decisions for the common good.

When a phase of post-WWII state expansion ended in 1975, the Japanese government increasingly resorted to deficit financing as stagnant tax revenues combined with political pressure to increase the number and quality of public services. Concentration of resources at the national level was no longer an effective strategy for meeting the political demands of the electorate or for solving social problems, and scarce resources were increasingly directed toward those most in need rather than toward the special interests of individuals or groups. Japanese women's groups challenged the male-dominated allocation of resources and worked toward a more equitable allocation of resources. They welcomed state interventions on gender issues for creating a gender-equal society, while understanding that the real solution of gender issues was beyond the top-down reach of the state. In the early 1990s, Japanese women's networks and coalitions became better informed and were more active in sending greater numbers of women to assemblies and parliament. By the late 1990s, they began to form nationwide partnerships and to mobilize resources at all levels of society.

There have been significant changes in the inclusion of women as representatives at the local level, especially in urban areas. Female representatives have increasingly held chief executives and city departments accountable for their performance, and have facilitated direct exchanges between the administration and individual citizens in agenda setting, policy formation, implementation, and evaluation processes. Furthermore, women's networks have developed an alternative form of equitable political participation for stakeholders that contrasts with traditional vertical patron-client relationships. Women's organizations, such as the Citizens' Network, are spreading a socially centered form of governance that draws upon, and coordinates, government and voluntary sector participation, effectively providing an alternative to the traditional system of local government. This has enabled a better delivery of services through the exchanges of resources—including information, expertise, and funding—among government and societal stakeholders. The full impact of women's horizontal partnership initiatives on Japanese politics at the nationwide systemic level has yet to be seen; however, the visible successes of these partnerships in urban areas remain encouraging.

Economic rationalism or neoliberalism in recent years has sustained structural economic inequality, in which gender difference plays a significant role. Yet economic equality still matters.[102] Underpinning the task of building a gender-equal society is the need to reconnect political equality with economic equality, which entails significant political reforms. Equally important to reform is the promotion of gender equality that calls for the inclusion and influence of women in political and in decision-making processes over and above an increase in the numbers of women in political institutions.[103] Building a gender-equal society demands that equal participation of women in public life remains on the political agenda and in public debate. The study in this chapter strongly argues that women's mobilization "from the ground up" will ensure that the impetus toward a gender-equal society will remain on the political agenda, and that public debate on this issue will be preserved and strengthened throughout the country.

CHAPTER 8

Foreigners in Local Communities: Beneficiaries to Participants

"If Japan wishes to keep the size of its population at the 2005 level, the country would need 17 million net immigrants up to the year 2050, or an average of 381,000 immigrants per year between 2005 and 2050."[1] Perhaps even more alarming is the fact that in order to keep its working-age population constant at the mid-1990s level, Japan would need to more than double the intake of foreign workers.

"I found through my own experiences that my efforts to hide my Korean family background meant accepting the prejudices [of the majority in Japanese society] and yet I faced crises of personal guilt. I have now decided to let my kids use our real surname at school. They may be distressed with this, but I'm sure that they'll understand my concerns as they grow. As a permanent resident, I pay my taxes and carry out my civic duties. So why don't I have the right to vote?"[2]

The thoughts of this second-generation Korean highlight a critical contemporary issue that has its roots in Japan's colonial rule over Korea from 1910 to 1945. Korean residents in Japan are generally referred to as the "old-comers" and other foreign residents as the "new-comers."[3] Many of the newcomers were part the influx of immigrants as Japan sought to cope with a severe labor shortage during the economic boom of the late 1980s. As predicted in the United Nations' (UN's) report cited above, the newcomers were the beginning of a very necessary migration flow yet their presence has sparked a strong debate throughout the country. There are a number of elements underpinning this debate including Japan's recognition of historical relationships with its previous colonies, its moral obligation toward Korean residents, combined with an uneasiness about the numbers of "foreigners" entering the country. At the same time, the steady immigration flows that have clearly influenced the balance of ethnic and cultural diversity have brought about an ongoing reevaluation of the understandings and practices that constitute social cohesion within Japanese society. There is no doubt that Japan can expect to benefit greatly from the overall growth in the immigrant working-age population, yet the Japanese national government is still striving to maintain its policy of racial homogeneity. It is also unfortunate that most members of the Japanese community are unaware of the positive net contributions and long-term benefits of immigrants to the host community.

Throughout this chapter, I will be examining whether Japan's immigration policy is moving in a desirable direction and evaluating the capacity of Japanese communities to adapt their collective understandings of international migration impacts and integration. I will also identify the entrepreneurs actively shaping the direction of policies toward foreign residents living in Japan.

Policy on immigration is normally decided at the national level, yet the concrete consequences of international migration are mostly felt at the local level, which is the meeting place, the point of integration, between citizens and new arrivals. While the national government has responded to the increased flow and diversity of labor migration to Japan, the impact of rapid demographic changes in a number of urban areas has outpaced changes in national policy. As a result, Japanese local governments have worked hard to meet the particular needs of changing circumstances that, in themselves, are an outcome of swiftly changing global forces. Stated differently, international migration is linked to multilayered processes and relationships: immigration policies are primarily national policies, while the impacts of international migration are directly handled by cities that continue to attract migrant workers within globalized labor markets. Furthermore, local governments depend on the links between the global, the national, and the local for the successful integration of international migration into a local community. While they are working to turn the impacts of international migration into tangible benefits, local governments still need to promote policy cohesion between levels of government and to advance social cohesion among various communities whose groups and networks maintain contact across national borders. For this reason, this chapter will also examine the impact of Japanese local government initiatives for promoting the protection of foreigners' rights and thus facilitating the integration of foreign residents into the host community. Central to this chapter is the premise that local government is the driving force behind the determination of new pathways for immigrant integration and the single most important factor for promoting foreigners' rights.

Integration of Foreigners in the Local Community

Japan has always maintained strong ethnic homogeneity. As it is far less ethnically and racially diverse than major Organisation for Economic Cooperation and Development (OECD) countries,[4] it would be reasonable to expect that Japan would be less concerned about the need to integrate its ethnic noncitizens. However, by 1986, the country had dramatically extended a wide range of social benefits to registered foreigners under 13 different national laws, with direct relief to the poor being the *only* social service not available to foreign residents.[5] There was considerable momentum underlying this policy expansion, including close scrutiny of the exclusive voting rights of Japanese nationals, and a nation-wide debate surrounding the political participation of foreigners. In 1998 law-makers set foreigners' voting rights on the National Diet (national legislature) agenda for the first time, but only in regard to voting rights at the local level.

The impact of international migration brings a new dimension to civil society. While the original concept of transnational relations is defined as physical inter-actions across state boundaries,[6] my research on the voting rights of foreigners suggests that this definition is no longer adequate to highlight the transnational phenomenon of international migration. National identities and a sense of com-munity may cross national borders, yet the voting rights of foreigners do not. Traditional concepts underpinning voting rights are much too wedded to a one-dimensional understanding of actors living inside or outside of territorial bound-aries. In this respect, this inside/outside distinction relates more to the rights and obligations, and less to the physical location, of the individuals in question. What remains to be seen is that the political participation of foreigners, which would indicate a transcendence of sociopolitical boundaries typically imposed on nonnationals by host countries, has the potential to help build a transnational civil society within Japan.

The status of foreigners' residence in Japan is stipulated by the 1951 Immi-gration Control and Refugee Recognition Act (last amended in 2006) and is classified into 27 distinct categories. The act stipulates the following:

- Foreigners residing in Japan may engage in the scope of activity specified by their status of residence.
- Their period of stay is to be determined by their status as foreigners.
- Those intending to reside in Japan must register as foreign residents within 90 days of entering the country as well as submit a Foreign Resident Regis-tration application form at their local ward or municipal office to obtain a Foreign Resident Registration Card.

These are the key procedures for the eligibility of foreigners to access social services. One of the largest categories of registered foreigners is the "special permanent resident" status typically granted to immigrants and their descendants from the former Japanese colonies of Taiwan and Korea. These residents hold a status that places no restrictions upon their employment. Another major status is migrant workers, the numbers of which category rose rapidly in the 1990s. These workers are increasingly staying longer in Japan, with many remaining illegally beyond the expiration of their authorized term. One of the greatest con-cerns for foreigners living and working in Japan is access to appropriate health care. There are two major types of state-operated medical insurance: the Health Insurance System for company employees and the National Health Insurance System for the self-employed, the latter being the insurance plan mostly used by foreigners. There are, however, some short-term registered foreigners who are not covered by either insurance plan and who often find themselves unable to pay medical costs. If successfully employed, they have the option to join the

Mutual Aid Associations plan that covers most public service employees. There are also many local governments, as will be discussed later in this chapter, that employ foreign workers and extend their subsidies to include medical treatment. Illegal foreign residents, however, are excluded from all social benefits. Some medical practices will take care of foreign patients—whether legal or not, or solvent or not. There are also a number of local authorities that offer direct relief to foreigners in immediate need of medical help but who have overstayed their visas. This variance within attitudes and practices reflects the diversity of state activity, and the different functions and priorities at each level of government. For the most part, local government is responsible for the provision of social services and social consumption policies,[7] despite the fact that they have almost no control over the costs and the conditions that migration flows and settlement create.

Overall, the current practice of social benefits to foreigners is far removed from Japan's traditionally perceived ideal of racial homogeneity and nonintegration. Even in 1979, when the Japanese government finally ratified the UN's international covenants on political, economic, and social rights, Japan's traditional exclusionary culture against foreigners seemed firmly entrenched. Japan was clearly expressing its zeal to obtain a permanent seat on the Security Council, yet the Japanese government had a poor record of human rights' activities and was known for its extreme reluctance to implement international norms into its domestic human rights' policies. Before 1982, for example, Korean residents, who had been recognized as Japanese nationals during Japan's colonial period, were excluded from the state-operated pension fund. Given Japan's small non-citizen population and exclusionary political culture of the past, it is both necessary and illuminating to ascertain why the country is now doing so much to protect the rights of foreign residents.

There is no single factor that will fully explain the scope of any policy change. Each policy area is distinctive in terms of its participants, the actions taken, and the results achieved. In the system of national government, most policy expansions in relation to existing programs occur in an incremental fashion, with little public awareness of the process.[8] In contrast, decision making in relation to the rights of foreigners in Japan, involves not only a new commitment of national resources, but also an alteration of the relationships between the state and citizens. A variety of social groups and organizations participate in the process, and this attracts much public attention.

It is the combination of international agreements, foreign pressure, and domestic factors associated with increasing foreign migration to Japan that has contributed to growing calls for foreigners' rights.[9] International treaties relating to refugees, pressure from the South Korean government, domestic court decisions, noncitizens' social movements, and electoral politics can all be considered as contributory factors in policy expansion and the growth of new initiatives. But even if accepted as major contributing factors to extending rights to foreigners, they still do not clearly answer the question of what was the major underlying condition for the promotion of foreigners' rights during the 1980s and the 1990s.

The central claim of this chapter is that the extension of rights to foreign residents is a distinctive process, and that the primary source feeding this process is found in the very particular role of local government. At the national policy level, foreigners' rights were very often expanded when Japan ratified treaties such as the 1965 Korea-Japan Legal Status Agreement and the Convention Relating to the Status of Refugees, which were accordingly implemented into domestic law. No doubt, this was an immediate and necessary condition for the nationwide extension of foreigners' social benefits. But the policy area of foreigners' rights also involved a redistribution of power and resources between the state and its citizens. Indeed, the policy innovation and initiatives taken by Japanese local governments for the protection of foreigners' rights have made this redistribution more visible and have helped shape public opinion on reform. It is interesting that the Japanese national government has been extremely reluctant to fully engage in international norms, yet Japanese local governments have been assiduously cultivating new categories of norms and standards in relation to foreigners' rights. Japanese local authorities and residents have taken issues arising from the increasing numbers of foreigners into their hands and are working together at the grassroots level. This has certainly provided a sufficient condition for the extension of rights to foreigners, insofar as local authorities are free to engage in such activities without intervention by the national government. In the main, it is Japanese local governments that have helped to legitimize the extension of foreigners' rights at the national level and continue, at a local level, to extend the rights of foreigners beyond the reach of the state.

There are two fundamental reasons for this. First, local government occupies a strategic position, straddling the division between the state and citizens. State authority, as already noted, tends to preserve the fixity of nationality by closing the public "space" in which foreign residents can exercise the rights and obligations accorded to Japanese citizens. Local governments, however, are in a position to develop a number of safeguards to meet pressing needs that exist beyond the reach of the state. They are able to monitor encounters between associations dominated by those of Japanese nationality and the newly emerging multiethnic political climate in Japan. Second, local governments act as an intermediary, a safety zone, through the provision of social services and social consumption policies, which can be accessed by foreigners and native Japanese alike. The state has been unable to manage the exigencies of international migration, and has left it to local communities to deal with the increasing presence of foreigners' needs. Thus, it is primarily because the state has stood back that local communities have been at the forefront of coping with these issues.

Growth in Foreign Population: Demography

It is important, in this part of the chapter, to trace the course of events relating to the extension of rights to foreigners in order to give due prominence to the specific role of local government, and to examine how this role interrelates with other contributing factors. The discussion is thus organized according to

Table 8.1 Registered foreigners as percentage of total population, 1980–2004

	1980	1985	1990	1995	2000	2001	2002	2003	2004
Registered foreigners	0.67	0.70	0.87	1.08	1.33	1.40	1.45	1.50	1.55

Source: Calculated from figures provided by the Immigration Bureau of Japan.

general factors relevant to any policy area, and to a number of distinct factors pertaining to policies relating to the expansion of foreigners' rights. Broadly speaking, policy expansion is the government's response to increased needs of its citizens. In 2005 there were 1.97 million registered alien residents in Japan and, with 1 person in 65 classified as a foreigner,[10] newspapers were reporting the dramatically increased number of foreigners in Japan as the single most important factor for promoting their rights.[11] But the media rationale does not hold up under close examination. It is true that Japan has become more diverse in terms of the growth rate of registered foreigners (see table 8.1). Yet the proportion of registered foreigners to total population remained unchanged from 1975 to 1980, increased steadily by 29.8 percent from 1980 to 1990, and then rose rapidly by 52.9 percent from 1990 to 2000.[12] This trend would seem to indicate the increasing needs of registered foreigners living and working in Japan to receive social services; however, the current national system of social benefits for foreigners was established in 1986, prior to the major influx from 1990 to 2000 and there have only been marginal modifications since then. As far as political rights are concerned, it was only in 1998 that politicians in the National Diet *began* to deliberate about foreigners' local suffrage. Taking all these factors into account, the increased presence of foreigners in Japan did not directly determine the course of national policy expansion, although this is not to say that the increased needs did not set parameters for policy expansion in the long term. In contrast, the impact of the increasing numbers of foreigners on policy priorities at the local level was distinct from that at the national level. As examined later in the chapter, local government was constantly responsive to a range of foreigners' interests that often did not find a voice at the national level.

The Bubble Economy: Economic Growth

Another general explanation for policy expansion is the increase in government revenue. For the most part, high economic growth creates a larger income-tax base that, in turn, gives the government more freedom in operating services as its revenue expands. While such high economic growth may enable a large and new commitment of national resources, the extension of social benefits such as health care and child allowances to foreigners would involve a significant redistribution of resources that average taxpayers would prefer to avoid. Thus, such a redistributive initiative appears to be taken only when the nation is immersed in periods of high economic growth. Between 1987 and 1990, Japan's gross national product (GNP) increased by an average of 5.1 percent each year in real terms. This boom was known as the "bubble economy." Fiscal years (FYs) 1988 to 1991 accordingly saw a large government budget expansion, with an average annual growth rate of 6.8 percent. Nonetheless, the 1982–1986 extension of foreigners' benefits ran far ahead of the high budget growth. During the first half of the 1980s, when the policy expansion occurred, alliances of leading conservative politicians, led by Prime Minister Nakasone Yasuhiro, joined forces with big business leaders to attack the national bureaucracy for an alleged "mindless" growth in government spending. In 1982 the Ministry of Finance began to impose the principle of zero growth on budget requests and, in 1983, that of minus growth. Thus, the relationship between resource increases and policy expansion is far from significant.[13]

Weight of Popular Pressure: Public Opinion

In any democratic nation, it is expected that the weight of popular pressure and opinion will, to some extent, influence the decision-making process in favor or disfavor of policy expansion. Probably the most fundamental condition for the promotion of foreigners' rights is change in basic social values—in particular, views on foreign residents and workers. But such social value structures are not likely to abruptly change in favor of foreigners' rights in a short time frame. Stated differently, popular pressure is a more indirect mode of influence, and thus an inadequate explanation of the policy surge. As a matter of fact, between 1990 and 2000, according to nationwide government surveys, Japanese people's concerns with the issues of foreign workers remained almost unchanged.[14] It is also interesting that this study found there to be no correlation between the trend of public opinion about foreign workers and that about local suffrage for foreigners. Nationwide opinion polls did show a significant change during the 1990s in eligible voters' attitudes toward foreigners' political participation. From the mid-1990s to 2000, voter support for foreigners' local suffrage increased by nearly 40 percent.[15] In sum, public concern about foreigners' political participation did change significantly in the second half of the 1990s, although the level of general public concern for foreign workers remained essentially unchanged. The continuously increasing number of foreigners in Japan explains neither the significantly changed opinion about foreigners' political participation nor the unchanged opinion toward foreigner workers. It is most likely that voters' increased support for foreigners' local suffrage was due in significant part to frequent public exposure via local government actions promoting foreigners' political participation, and to the resulting media coverage of foreigners' local suffrage. The upward trend of pro-local suffrage among voters coincided with increasing calls of the local government, and related newspaper articles, to grant foreigners voting rights. In 1993, for the first time in Japan, 16 local governments passed resolutions calling for foreigners to be allowed to vote in local elections, and in the following year, another 172 local governments passed similar resolutions. By 2001, 1,439 local governments had passed such resolutions, representing 73 percent of Japan's total population.[16] The number of articles devoted to foreigners' local suffrage in two major national newspapers, the *Asahi Shinbun* and the *Nihon Keizai Shinbun,* dramatically increased from 9 articles in 1987–1993 to 104 articles in 1994–2000.[17]

Noncitizens' Rights: Historical Legacies

Historically, the notion of foreigners' rights can be traced to the Roman *jus gentium* (law of nations), the principles of which are believed to have been universally applicable—but especially to non-Romans. Medieval writers, drawing on Marcus Tullius Cicero who argued that the law of nature applied to all men equally,[18] imported these principles into their notion of "natural rights," drawing upon the universalistic terms of Christendom. In order to protect the relevancy of such universal norms, modern political thinkers such as Thomas Hobbes, John Locke, and Jean-Jacques Rousseau developed the modern concept of citizenship. Ironically, the concept of citizenship became relevant only to the practices of the sovereign state in a particularistic rather than universalistic way.[19] The source of the so-called natural rights did not exist outside of the nation-state in the universalistic way envisaged, but rather was a part and parcel of the jurisdiction of the modern states in positivist terms.[20] In other words, the jurisdiction of territorial sovereign states decides whether such rights exist or not. The nation-state essentially claimed to be exclusive of all the outsiders on its territory, thereby alienating a larger number of people from theoretically universal natural rights. In the West, from the seventeenth century to the end of the nineteenth century, national citizenship was central to the state building that sought uniform people speaking uniform languages. In this respect, a citizen became identical with a national; citizenship rights belonged exclusively to nationals.

The relationship between citizenship and nationality is tightly linked along a well-traveled historical pathway—but is now problematic as it is no longer relevant to contemporary globalizing trends and tends to ignore the greater prominence of foreign residents in local communities. Over the last two decades especially, the growth of international migration has been propelled by a number of factors including economic differentials, domestic political disorganization, and transnational networks of communication and transportation. These factors have also generated conflicts and tensions within states and among states and contributed to an upsurge of right-wing antimigrant movements throughout Western Europe. At the same time, these countries in Western Europe have increasingly extended rights to noncitizens. But why did states extend foreigners' rights when they did? The historical relationship between citizenship rights and nationality described above does not directly explain why, but it explains under what circumstances it occurred. The following sections will identify and examine the primary source of the extension of rights to foreigners in Japan.

Japan's Colonial Path: Legal and Moral Obligations

In Japan, the incongruency between the status accorded to nationality and to citizenship grew out of specific historical paths. After its victory in the Russo-Japanese War in 1910, Japan annexed Korea and Koreans were forced to become Japanese citizens. This was to lead to an influx of Korean laborers to Japan, with many Koreans forcibly brought to the country from 1939 to 1945 and mobilized into the war effort. This led to the formation of Korean communities in Japan, with Korean male residents eligible to vote and to stand for public office. By the end of World War II (WWII) in August 1945, there were nearly 2.3 million Korean residents in Japan of whom 500,000 to 600,000 decided to remain in Japan.[21]

Shortly after Japan's surrender in the Pacific War in August 1945, conservative forces, including Kiyose Ichiro as speaker of the House of Representatives, were attempting to keep existing imperial ties between the throne and the Japanese people intact, and strongly insisted that Korean residents be excluded from political participation, in anticipation of the opening of a new National Diet under a new constitution.[22] In December 1945 the National Diet stripped Koreans residing in Japan of their suffrage by revising the Election Law. Then, as the San Francisco Peace Treaty came into effect in April 1952, the Japanese government unilaterally argued that Korea would no longer be part of the Japanese state and stripped Korean residents of their Japanese nationality.[23]

In 1945 the League of Korean Residents was established in Japan to facilitate the migration of Koreans to their home country. Yet, the movement the league embodied was destined to reflect the geopolitical and ideological divide in the Asia-Pacific region. Following the partitioning of the Korean Peninsula, the league split up into two organizations: the pro-Seoul Korean Residents Union and the pro-Pyongyang General Association of Korean Residents. As soon as the Republic of Korea was formed in 1948, it recognized the Korean Residents Union of Japan as the official organization. In 1955, after the Korean War, the General Association of Korean Residents, whose leaders saw South Korea as a U.S.-controlled puppet state, was created in contradistinction to the Korean Residents Union. One-quarter of Korean residents in Japan, loyal to Pyongyang, retained North Korean nationality. Social movements by Korean residents in early post–WWII Japan focused predominantly on their desire to rebuild and return to a unified home country. These were predominantly first-generation Koreans in Japan who only intended to be temporary residents, assuming that they would eventually return to Korea. With this backdrop, their major concerns were focused on asserting their ethnicity's rights of free assembly and free association in the face of Japanese government obstructions, rather than on their rights as residents to seek improved infrastructure for daily life and local political participation.[24] Meanwhile, the municipal government continued to provide public services based on the Residents' Basic Register, from which foreign residents, including Koreans, were excluded in accordance with the nationally imposed Article 39 of the Residents' Basic Register Law.[25]

In 1964 South Korea and Japan signed a treaty normalizing their relations, which made Korean residents eligible for permanent resident status. This shift was widely considered a practical instrument in the ideological divide of the Cold War with North Koreans who refused to acquire South Korean nationality even in the face of being refused a permanent resident status in Japan. In the early 1970s, however, the driving force of the Korean residents' movement shifted from the first to the second generation, many of whom decided to reside permanently in Japan. The new generation of Korean residents increasingly felt an attachment to Japan, and spoke Korean less frequently in their day-to-day life.[26] The political climate consequently led Korean residents' movements to focus on grassroots politics rather than ideological and interstate politics.

Turning to the Law

The use of litigation as a conflict-solving mechanism became more prominent among Korean activists without electoral resources. Although recourse to lawsuits is unlikely to transcend the confines of the existing legal system, litigation can have a considerable impact on the climate of public opinion. A new policy or a policy revision is also an unlikely outcome; at most, such actions might generate a constitutional "reinterpretation" in the judicial process that could legally force the government to change the scope of policy. The lawsuit against Hitachi, brought in 1970 by Korean resident Park Jong Suck, was the first to call for the elimination of job discrimination. It was followed by a variety of litigations filed by Korean residents against the government and business sectors, seeking judicial remedies for social problems such as public housing discrimination, mandatory fingerprinting, ineligibility for government jobs, discriminatory access to higher education, and so forth. The course of these events led to a key 1990 lawsuit filed by 11 Koreans in Osaka regarding foreigners' suffrage, which was eventually brought to the Supreme Court. In 1995 the Supreme Court issued a landmark decision designed to clarify or "reinterpret" the constitution by stating that the political participation of foreign residents was not to be forbidden at the local level, yet should be left to the National Diet to legislate.[27]

Although this decision found foreigners' local suffrage to be constitutional, it precluded a judicial solution for resolving the voting rights of foreign residents. What it did was to open up national legislation as a possibility for a political solution. In the aftermath of the ruling, major Korean organizations preferred not to exercise the option of recourse by calling for such national legislation.[28] The Korean Residents Union had passed a pro-suffrage resolution in 1986, yet it took no steps until 1989 toward a plan to petition local authorities across Japan for voting rights. The implementation of this plan was then further delayed by internal divisions within the union. It was not until 1994, when Shin Yong Sang was elected head of the Korean Residents Union after campaigning on a promise to realize local suffrage, that the organization's campaign for local voting rights finally got under way. In contrast, the pro-Pyongyang General Association of Korean Residents was not in favor of local suffrage. Official statements by the association viewed such suffrage as a policy of assimilation, designed to deny ethnic Koreans their rights to establish a unified home country.[29] In April 1996 the association urged the Social Democratic Party of Japan to take a stand against foreigners' suffrage.

International Agreements and Norms: External Factors

Article 1-1 of the 1965 Korea-Japan Legal Status Agreement stipulated that Korean residents in Japan who applied for permanent resident status *within* five years of the accord being implemented would be successful in their application. They would then be eligible, like Japanese nationals, to receive medical benefits under National Health Insurance. This is just a means through which the implementation of international agreements directly impacted on the extension of rights to foreign residents.

Once such an international agreement is made, the state is not only obligated to integrate it into domestic law but may also need to amend a wide range of existing laws so that it will be in accord with domestic interests. One such example is the case of the Convention Relating to the Status of Refugees and the Protocol Relating to the Status of Refugees. Ironically, when Japan ratified these treaties in 1982, the Japanese government was forced to remove the *kokuseki-joko* (nationality clauses, which restricted the benefits of public services to Japanese nationals exclusively) in four welfare laws. Had these nationality clauses not been removed, political refugees would have been entitled to more and better public services than long-term foreign residents. Although there had been external pressure for the national government in Japan to work toward a coherent system of social benefits for foreign residents, in the view of Japanese local governments, the enforcement of the international agreement validated and legitimized many of the practices already implemented by local authorities.

While some scholars argue that international norms play a key role in extending rights to foreigners, others argue that their implementation is not automatic but it is put into practice through the intervention of a number of agents.[30] For example, it is through nongovernmental organizations (NGOs) and the efforts of immigrant activists that international norms promoting noncitizens' rights and benefits are effectively implemented throughout the country.[31] In fact, academics such as the Korean scholar Suh Yong-Dal; local governments, notably Kawasaki city; and pro-immigration groups including the Tokyo Bar Association, have all been promoting the extension of foreigners' rights, citing international norms. Norms are thus one of the resources mobilized to achieve and to legitimize advocacy objectives and thus become a benchmark for extending rights to foreign residents. However, I return to my earlier argument that the implementation of norms alone cannot explain the considerable scope within the policy surge of the 1980s.

International norms can be defined as a shared expectation of state behavior that is common or usual in accordance with a given value system. They are technically nonbinding as a matter of international law, but a high level of compliance among states sets standards for states to promote. This then encourages states to codify the norms in the form of an international agreement. There are norms directed toward the protection of economic and social rights extended to noncitizens; these are, to a large extent, embodied and codified in international agreements such as the Convention Relating to the Status of Refugees and the Council of Europe Convention on Migrant Workers. As of 2007 the extension of political rights to noncitizens has yet to become common practice among states, and international standards for noncitizens' suffrage have yet to be established.

Although foreign residents living in Ireland have been able to vote and stand for local public office since 1964, and in the Netherlands since 1984,[32] it is the Scandinavian countries that have made significant advances in this area. In 1975 Sweden extended local voting rights and the right to stand for local public office to *all* foreign residents—a policy adopted by Norway (1978), Denmark (1981), and Finland (1992). The establishment of the European Union (EU) has also influenced voting right practices. According to Article 8 of the 1992 Maastricht Treaty, nationals in any member state are deemed citizens of the EU and are granted local voting rights on the basis of residence, a provision that is implemented by EU members.

While this chapter has been focusing upon the extension of local voting rights to foreign residents, it is important to note that the extension of voting rights to foreigners for *national* elections is a far more controversial issue. Currently, only New Zealand and Chile have granted such rights to foreign residents and even the Scandinavian countries, which have done so much to extend the political rights of foreigners in recent years, have not been willing to allow them to vote at the national level. Conservative republican views prevail throughout most countries[33] given an apprehension that foreigners might lack national loyalty and might not participate in civic duties such as jury and military service. There is an imperative for responsible citizenship, in which political theorist David Miller articulates the concern that foreigners who do not share widely held perceptions of the common good could undermine the interests and security of both community and country.[34]

In the absence of solid international norms regarding the political participation of foreign residents, there has been highly politicized, yet unsuccessful, external pressure for Japan to extend to suffrage to this group of people. The 1991 Korea-Japan Memorandum urged the Japanese government to allow South Korean residents in Japan to vote in local elections.[35] Japanese politicians lingered over their response until the visit of the South Korean president Kim Dae Jung in 1998. Carefully matching their timing to his visit, the Democratic Party of Japan and the parliamentary group Heiwa-Kaikaku (Peace-Reform), jointly submitted a legislative proposal in October 1998 at the 143rd National Diet to give permanent residents of foreign nationality voting rights at the local government level. During his visit, Kim publicly stated that he wished to see the bill passed during the then current National Diet session, pointing out that Korean residents had contributed greatly to Japanese society, paid their taxes, and were thereby entitled to local suffrage.[36] Despite his intervention, the bill was carried over to National Diet sessions in the following year.

Surprisingly, in September 1999, South Korea's Ministry of Home Affairs announced a plan to grant local suffrage to foreign residents before the 2002 nationwide local elections. This action brought pressure on those Japanese conservative politicians who had argued for local suffrage yet would not move ahead with legislation until home countries agreed to reciprocate the same rights for Japanese nationals living in their territory. When the conservatives realized that the principle of reciprocity would not serve as a *de facto* denial of local suffrage for permanent foreign residents living in Japan, the argument against local suffrage then shifted to the conception of the exclusive right of the state to articulate rights and obligations within its sovereign territories.[37] When at the Korea-Japan Summit meeting held in Manila in November 1999, Kim Dae Jung attempted to hold the antisuffrage moves in check by urging Japanese prime minister Obuchi Keizo to reach an agreement on Koreans' voting rights by the end of the following year, the prime minister failed to do so.

Local Government Initiatives: Strategic Position

Local policy innovation in Japan has actively cultivated the establishment of international norms for the economic and social rights of foreign residents by attempting to influence the stances of various states participating in international forums. As stated earlier, it is common practice among states that provide the Japanese government with a critical source of, and imperative for, international standards for extending rights to foreigners. In practice, however, the major pressures for protecting the rights of foreigners have come directly from local governments working to solve urgent community problems related to the rapidly growing number of foreign residents.

By the early 1970s, temporary direct relief to insolvent foreigners proved to be an unavoidable practice of local authorities, particularly given the decision of Japanese-born Koreans to reside permanently in Japan. Local governments were confronted with the issue and, in dealing with it head-on, they spearheaded the expansion of social benefits to foreigners throughout the country. In 1971 a number of cities such as Kawasaki, Sapporo, and Yokohama worked against the wishes of the national government in providing the National Health Insurance for all foreigners, including North Korean residents who were registered at the local level.[38]

Another local practice was aimed at countering the 1954 directive from the Ministry of Health and Welfare to prefectural governors stating that applications for direct relief from unregistered foreigners were to be rejected unless deemed urgent and consequential.[39] Local governments strategically reinterpreted and extended this directive to include the provision of direct relief for short-stay and overstay foreigners in immediate need. In the 1960s and 1970s, the numbers of such foreigners residing in Japan were statistically negligible and, as such, the ministry neither condoned nor condemned this local practice. With the numbers increasing in the late 1980s and 1990s, the overstaying of foreigners became a major policy concern of the ministry, which, in February 1990, instructed welfare specialists in local welfare offices to exclude short-stay and overstay foreigners from direct relief applications. However, most local governments continued to assist foreign residents irrespective of national directives. This proved to be an embarrassment to the ministry, which then indicated this to be a misappropriation of public funds. In response, in September 1991, 12 government-designated cities formally called for the withdrawal of the ministry's 1990 instructions.[40]

The ratio of Korean residents to all registered foreigners was 86.4 percent in 1976 and 48.9 percent in 1995. This change over 19 years was due to the continual arrival of newcomers from various countries from the late 1980s seeking to escape the widening gap between wages paid in their home countries and wages paid in Japan, and to benefit from the strong state of the yen and an acute labor shortage faced by small manufacturers throughout Japan. Accordingly, the Japanese government decided to relax immigration policies in 1989 and amended the Immigration Control and Refugee Recognition Act to permit foreigners of Japanese descent to enter and work in Japan as unskilled workers. The number of workers of Japanese descent entering the country, especially from Brazil and Peru, rose rapidly from 7,200 in 1990 to 342,000 in 2004. The massive influx of foreigners into local communities was to result in a wide range of discriminatory practices relating to labor, medical care, housing, and education.[41]

The Japanese government eventually integrated the Convention Relating to the Status of Refugees into domestic law. However, the protection of foreigners' rights remained far from adequate. In 1990, when the national government refused to apply the 1950 Livelihood Protection Law—which provides direct relief to the poor—to foreign residents, Kobe city made the decision to carry the medical expenses for a critically ill overseas student. A grassroots community group in Kobe then sued the national government for failing to apply the Livelihood Protection Law to the student and for refusing to cover its legally defined three-fourth share of medical expenses. While the suit was rejected on procedural grounds by the Kobe District Court, the national government's lack of action in the matter attracted prominent media exposure. The lawsuit also highlighted the inability of local governments to solve community issues and conflicts involving foreign residents if they had to strictly adhere to prevailing legal procedures. The most urgent issue involved medical expenses that foreigners were unable to pay. In 1993 the Gunma prefectural government adopted a policy of providing subsidies for foreigners' medical treatment, and the practice quickly spread to other prefectures including Kanagawa in 1993; Hyogo in 1994; and Chiba, Saitama, and Tokyo in 1996.

The Ministry of Health and Welfare began to apply the National Health Insurance Law to registered foreigners in 1986; yet, by 1992, their eligibility was conditioned on the proof of a minimum twelve-month residency. As a result, a number of short-term registered foreigners who had lived in the country for less than a year found themselves unable to access health insurance cover, and illegal foreign residents and those who had overstayed their visas were completely excluded from the process. The refusal of the Ministry of Justice to extend the National Health Insurance Law to illegal foreign residents was based on the argument that such an extension would only encourage foreigners to overstay in Japan.[42] To redress the situation, local governments joined forces with local grassroots groups to help protect these *de facto* residents and to acknowledge the realities they faced within their day-to-day life. A relevant example involves the medical expenses of overstay foreigners who were victims of the 1995 Kobe earthquake. According to a provisional national law, a gift of money was to be handed to all victims irrespective of their nationality. However, the health and welfare minister, Ide Shoichi, denied this benefit to overstay foreigners by arguing that they were illegal residents who had no right to be in the country.[43] The actions of the Hanshin Earthquake Local NGO Rescue Liaison Conference contrasted strongly with the resistance of the national government when they organized a rescue network for foreigners and formally requested the Hyogo prefectural government to support noncitizen victims. The prefectural government immediately affirmed that it would apply the Natural Disaster Rescue Law and cover some of the medical expenses without discrimination on the basis of nationality and legality.[44] Hyogo prefecture, Kobe city, the Japanese Red Cross, and other nonprofit organizations also extended some direct financial relief to foreigners affected by the earthquake.

There were also a number of local government officials who publicly argued that local governments should make available the Employees' Insurance, the National Health Insurance System, and the Livelihood Protection Law to foreign workers who had overstayed their visas. They drew attention to a vacuum in the state administration of such public services, at the same time making it clear that national laws did not explicitly deny local government the legal power for service delivery.[45]

From the mid-1980s to the mid-1990s, it was predominantly Japanese citizens who organized and operated grassroots support groups to act as service providers to foreign residents. One such example is the large number of study support groups for foreigners' school-aged children. In 1998 there were 146 study support groups in Kanagawa prefecture alone.[46] Their founding members were company workers, housewives, university students, teachers, and retired elderly who helped improve the capacity of the learning environment beyond the scope of public education and, in doing so, offered a practical contribution toward a viable multiethnic society.[47] By the mid-1990s, as foreigners' need for assistance invariably exceeded the resources offered by grassroots community groups, compatriotic foreigner residents began to establish their own networks for mutual aid, such as the Association for Liaising with Resident Foreigners (Kawasaki), the Latin America Friendship Association (Kawasaki), the Kanagawa City Union (Kawasaki), and the Asian People's Friendship Society (Tokyo). Portuguese- and Spanish-language newspapers, such as the *International Press,* began to develop a comprehensive system for the distribution of information for foreigners of Japanese descent.[48] As of 2007, there are estimated to be over 100 ethnic newspapers and magazines in 15 different languages circulated in Japan. Furthermore, progressive local governments such as Kawasaki city have been striving to provide local and foreign residents with a common social base by bringing them together as participants in community development. This coincided with the 1993–1994 shift of policy debate from an acknowledgment of foreign residents as members of a local community to include their direct participation in a number of undertakings.

To this point, support groups in Kawasaki had mostly viewed foreign residents, including long-time Korean residents, as beneficiaries of help rather than as participants in local decision-making processes.[49] In 1993 the Kawasaki municipal government, together with citizens' groups acting as coinvestigators, conducted an extensive survey that was to be followed, two years later, with interviews with foreign residents to ascertain their needs and problems. This type of coordination between municipal government and citizens' groups played a key role in bridging the gap between local and foreign residents. This is clearly illustrated in Kawasaki in the mid-1990s, when a number of citizens' groups began to emphasize equal partnerships between foreign residents and Japanese citizens. These citizen-based support groups directly encouraged foreign residents to participate in the process of community development. As part of this process, the support groups promoted the need for Japanese literacy among foreign residents, with the acquisition of such language skills not perceived as forced assimilation but as a viable means for foreigners to represent their own interests.[50] Kawasaki's experience highlights an international dimension within understandings and practices of citizenship, arguably weakening the identification of political rights with exclusive nationality. In the past, as discussed earlier, there have been considerable advances made in the enhancement and protection of the economic and social rights of foreign residents, yet issues surrounding their political rights—particularly in relation to their entitlement to vote or their eligibility to run for public office—have remained virtually untouched. In short, notions of political rights have remained territorially grounded on the basis of nationality. Although the right of equal participation in political processes in Japan was extended to include women and other minority groups after WWII, such changes were premised on national domestic concerns that excluded immigrants and foreigners. However, now that foreign residents are remaining longer in Japan and pay taxes, their political rights can no longer be ignored.

Kawasaki city did attempt to include foreigners within some of the city's administrative programs as the number of registered foreigners steadily doubled in the five years following the 1989 change in immigration policy. The city enabled foreign residents to participate in a system that monitored city services, in city consultation meetings, and in councils attached to city departments. Yet this presented a token gesture. In the same manner that voting rights had been restricted to Japanese nationals, national law continued to exclude foreign residents from positions such as the civil liberties commissioner, the social welfare commissioner, and from membership on the Board of Education. It was in 1994 that the municipal assembly of Kawasaki passed a resolution demanding that the national government take immediate measures to grant foreign residents the right to vote and to run in local elections. In the same year, the city established the Investigation Committee on the Establishment of a Kawasaki City Representative Assembly for Foreign Residents.[51] Their proposal for a foreigners' assembly in October 1996 led the Kawasaki municipal assembly to unanimously pass an ordinance for the implementation of a public forum for foreign residents—the Kawasaki City Representative Assembly for Foreign Residents. It consisted of 26 foreign residents who had been recommended by ethnic groups and chosen by a selection committee. While this assembly's decisions have no legal binding force,[52] it has proposed a wide range of measures to solve foreigners' integration problems. These include initial adjustments such as the immediate need for material goods, employment, and housing; social and economic adjustments including language training, information services, public health, access and equity in service provision, social support networks, and career advancement opportunities; and later adjustments, such as reestablishing family, socialization for migrant families, and migrant school education. Similar assemblies were established by the Tokyo Metropolitan government in 1997 (known as the Assembly for "Foreigner-Citizens" of Tokyo, with 25 foreign residents on its committee); by Kyoto city in 1998 (named the Forum of Kyoto City's Policy for Foreign Residents, with membership consisting of seven foreigners and five local academics); by Kanagawa prefecture in 1998 (known as the Kanagawa Assembly for Foreign Prefectural Residents, comprising 20 foreigners); and by Mitaka city in 1999 (called the Mitaka Internationalization Roundtable, comprising seven foreigners and seven municipal government officials or leaders of citizens' groups). As Okayama city followed suit in 2005, this type of institutionalization for the civic participation of foreign residents was incorporated in 14 other local governments across the nation. Civic participation (or participatory accountability) became the means through which foreign residents were acknowledged and valued in Japan, and through which they were further encouraged to participate in community decision-making processes and to run for local elections. Social cohesion between local and foreign residents has yet to be tested by the inclusive participation of foreign residents.

In 1985 Mayor Ito Saburo of Kawasaki city stunned national authorities by declaring that the municipal government would not prosecute those who refused to be fingerprinted under the Alien Registration Law.[53] In 1986 the city assembly, working in partnership with the Seikyusha (an ethnic Korean social welfare foundation), adopted a Basic Policy for Foreign Residents Education and, two years later, established and jointly managed a public venue known as the Fureaikan for the exchange of information and contacts between Japanese and foreign residents. This venue facilitated introductions between otherwise unconnected residents in different parts of the local community. At the participatory loci, for example, Japanese voluntary groups began to assist first-generation Korean residents—who were largely forced to migrate to Japan in the pre–WWII period—by improving their knowledge of the Japanese language. News of such training quickly spread to other foreign residents, who then joined this gathering.[54]

Cultural understandings became a two-way process as residents of Southeast Asian background began to participate with Japanese residents in ethnic Koreans' festivals and parades that had been founded as a means of informing the local community of their culture.[55] The multiethnic relationships are likely to promote the formation of a bridging social capital, which reaches beyond their own ethnic groups and pursues inclusive networks with diverse groups in a local community. By the same token, after retiring from the Kawasaki City Representative Assembly for Foreign Residents, most former members continued to be engaged in multiethnic community development beyond the exclusive nature of their compatriot groups.[56]

When Kawasaki became the first government-designated city to eliminate the nationality clause for hiring city employees in May 1996, the national Ministry of Home Affairs immediately questioned the legality of the action. In early post–WWII Japan, there were no specific legal provisions for hiring foreigners as local civil servants. In 1953 the Cabinet Legislation Bureau had clearly stated that Japanese nationality would be required for any work entailing "the exercise of public authority or the formation of nation's will." Twenty years later, in 1973, the Ministry of Home Affairs reinterpreted and extended this requirement to local government employees by substituting the "will" of the nation with the "will" of local public entities. Nevertheless, though the ministry continued to instruct local authorities not to hire foreigners, the Cabinet Legislation Bureau issued a notice in 1986 stating that Japanese nationality would not be required for such technical and specialized jobs as public health workers, midwives, and nurses (regulated under the Law for Public Health Workers, Midwives, and Nurses).[57] A 1990 nationwide survey conducted on 722 local governments by the major newspaper *Mainichi Shinbun* showed that one-third were implementing a policy that completely excluded foreigners from employment.[58] By 1996, however, a follow-up survey showed that 45 percent favored the elimination of the requirement for Japanese nationals only, with less than 20 percent of respondents supporting the discriminatory policy.[59] Kawasaki city then openly defied the Ministry of Home Affairs by making all city job categories (with the exception of firefighting) available to foreigners. The ministry then warned local chief executives against the elimination of the nationality requirement in June 1996, yet by this time the practice of foreigners' participation in the public sector had diffused among other local governments with astonishing speed. Within just five months of his warning, Home Affairs Minister Shirakawa Katsuhiko was forced to acknowledge this informal support for foreign residents among local governments, and to concede that decisions to eliminate or retain the nationality requirement should be left to local discretion.[60] By January 2002, elimination of the nationality requirement was adopted by all government-designated cities (with the exception of Chiba and Tokyo), and by 11 of 47 prefectural governments.[61]

As Kawasaki's proactive policies progressed toward protection of foreigners' rights, a new pattern of relationships among residents and the city authority began to emerge in the mid-1990s.[62] Ethnic groups, especially long-term Korean residents, old-comers, were increasingly trusted as partners in Kawasaki ventures. Newcomers were not sufficiently organized to represent their own interests, yet Korean ethnic groups took full advantage of changing attitudes and structures and began participating in municipal decision-making efforts such as the revitalization of the multiethnic Oohin district and the organization of "Korea Town" in Hama-cho.[63] The mutual trust generated in these ventures added to the reserves of social capital that would open the door to further cooperation in the future.

As of March 2005, nearly half (47.6 percent) of local governments in Japan had officially called for local suffrage for foreign residents, effectively challenging statists' claims that only states can specify individual rights within their sovereign territories, and that citizenship cannot exist apart from exclusive nationality. The expectation underlying this proposed extension of rights was that the considerable publicity surrounding municipal assemblies for foreigners would help facilitate comprehensive national legislation. Mayor Takahashi Kiyoshi of Kawasaki city, for example, stated in 1994 that the creation of the municipal assembly for foreigners was part of an attempt to eventually persuade the national government and National Diet to embrace and expand this practice of foreigners' voting rights through national legislation.[64]

In January 2002 Maihara town in Shiga prefecture passed a public referendum ordinance for a merger with neighboring communities, which would recognize voting rights for permanent foreign residents. This local ordinance allowed eligible Japanese residents as well as permanent foreign residents aged 20 or older who had lived in the town for more than three months to vote at the referendum. After the ballot was cast in March 2002, voting rights were granted for the first time to permanent resident foreigners living in Japan. Muranishi Toshio, mayor of Maihara, explained, "Our society will not develop further unless we give thought to such issues as living together with foreigners and promoting exchanges between different cultures."[65] As of March 2005, 184 municipalities had passed similar local referendum ordinances that gave foreign residents the chance to vote, 100 of these municipalities holding referenda under the ordinances.[66]

Arguments supporting foreigners' local suffrage in Japan primarily derive from three sources: the principle of "no taxation without representation," the close association of foreign residents within their local communities, and specific historical paths of Korean-Japanese relations. First, Ooita prefecture governor Hiramatsu Morihiko applied the principle of no taxation without representation when he argued that foreign residents who pay the same taxes as Japanese nationals should have the right to vote at the local level.[67] Second, foreigners who have a close relationship with local communities should be granted local voting rights. This can be seen in *ikensho* (opinions on the matter) that were submitted by local governments to the cabinet and subsequently adopted through the 1995 Supreme Court decision. The court decision stated that the provision of livelihood-related public services should be secured in accordance with the will of local residents. It further argued that it was not constitutionally forbidden to grant local suffrage to foreign residents, especially to permanent residents, who are closely associated with a local community's daily life and local government.[68] Third, local governments, in partnership with the Korean Residents Union, have continued to assert the voting rights of Korean residents on the basis of Japan's specific colonial background. As discussed previously, it is Kawasaki city that is leading such partnerships in an exploration of new forms of multiethnic communities.

Non-Decision Making: Electoral Interests

Some political parties saw foreigners' suffrage as a means of enhancing their support base. In 1994 the Shimane branch of the Shinto Sakigake (New Party Harbinger), for the first time among Japanese political parties, decided to allow foreign residents to become party members. Two months later, the central committee of the Clean Government Party also adopted this practice. Other parties, such as the Social Democratic Party and the New Frontier Party, quickly followed suit. After the 1995 Supreme Court decision to leave the matter of foreigners' local suffrage to the National Diet to legislate, the debate heated up among political parties. A survey of all National Diet members conducted by the Federation of Korean Resident Youths of Commerce and Industry in 1995 indicated that over 88 percent of respondents were in favor of foreigners' local suffrage, with only 3 percent opposed.[69] This led lawmakers to set a National Diet agenda on foreigners' voting rights in 1998. However, conservative politicians such as Okuno Seisuke and Murakami Ichiro of the Liberal Democratic Party (LDP) argued that foreigners should be naturalized as Japanese citizens if they wanted the right to vote.[70] Advocates of local suffrage for foreign residents have had a tough battle with powerful conservative forces.

The 1998 legislative proposal to extend local voting rights to permanent residents was carried over to the 1999 National Diet sessions. In October 1999 a new ruling coalition of the LDP, the Liberal Party, and the New Komeito began efforts with an accord calling for all three parties to work toward passing the bill. In January 2000 the Liberal Party and the New Komeito, in a bid to persuade the reluctant LDP, submitted a compromise bill to grant voting rights to permanent residents from countries with which Japan had diplomatic relations. Those affiliated with North Korea, to which Japan would not extend diplomatic recognition, would be barred from voting, under the proposed legislation. Many pro-suffrage grassroots groups were outraged by this exclusive proposal, saying that it would deny voting rights to North Koreans who were equally resident in Japan.[71] In April 2000 the Liberal Party, led by Ozawa Ichiro, left the three-party coalition. His departure split the Liberal Party into two parts, one of which became the Conservative Party, which then joined the ruling coalition. The coalition of the LDP, the New Komeito, and the Conservative Party inherited the three-party accord. In July 2000 the New Komeito and the Conservative Party, influenced by the weight of popular pressure, decided to remove the stipulation that excluded North Koreans and jointly submitted a bill of local suffrage for all permanent residents.

As the New Komeito publicly pressed the LDP to follow through on the accord, a group of conservative legislators led by the LDP argued for conditional local suffrage, to be reciprocated by home countries. In the author's view, countries in the Third World, from which most newcomers had come, were less likely to take similar steps toward foreigners' political participation. Despite the tactics of Japan's conservative forces, South Korea's announcement of its plan for granting local voting rights to foreign residents was unexpected, and a blow to the conservative forces. Some conservative LDP politicians, such as Eto Takami, thus began to argue directly against foreigners' political participation. In their view, extended suffrage would work against the interests of Japanese citizens in areas such as national security and education. They warned that local suffrage for foreigners could eventually lead to the extension of such a right at the national level.[72] In December 2000 the National Diet session ended, carrying the bill, once again, over to the next session.

The Koizumi Jun'ichiro Cabinet took office in April 2001 and won popularity among voters. Nonetheless, Prime Minister Koizumi was very reluctant to extend voting rights to foreign residents, and instead suggested the possibility of easing legal requirements to be naturalized in Japan.[73] This suggestion began to be seen as an alternative to the local suffrage bill, and anti-suffrage LDP politicians, seizing the opportunity, argued that time had come to discard this proposed bill once and for all. In 2002 the National Assembly of South Korea decided not to include the proposed stipulation of granting local voting rights to foreign residents in the revision of election laws.[74] This decision to delay the introduction of foreigners' local suffrage worked in favor of the ongoing opposition from those LDP lawmakers.

In August 2004, to halt the rising momentum of Japan's anti-suffrage forces, South Korean president Roh Moo-hyun strongly urged LDP/New Komeito secretary generals to grant local voting rights to Korean residents in Japan.[75] The New Komeito secretary general Fuyushiba Tetsuzo then told Roh Moo-hyun that this would be realized as soon as possible.[76] In the same year, the South Korean government passed national legislation for a referendum on the introduction of voting rights for permanent residents. This move was seen as a formal recognition of foreigners' suffrage in its early stages.

The New Komeito was frustrated by the LDP's inaction in Japan and, on its own, proposed a new bill for foreigners' local suffrage in February 2004. Local suffrage for all permanent residents had been under deliberation since the submission of the first bill in 1998, and had gone through a total 13 hours of debates in the National Diet. This 2004 attempt was carried over to the following National Diet session yet again, due to the ongoing opposition from the anti-suffrage LDP group. In early 2007 legislation for foreigners' rights to vote at the local level had yet to be passed in the National Diet.

While national politicians brought the issue of foreigners' political participation to a standstill, local government initiatives continued to evolve and to transform politics at the grassroots level. "To help ensure the future progress of this region," as Mayor Muranishi Toshio of Maihara town in Shiga prefecture explained, "it is vital that residents of other nationalities also have a sense of fruitful participation in community development."[77] This statement was made in January 2002, when the town passed a public referendum ordinance that granted voting rights for permanent foreign residents. Never before had there been such direct recognition of foreigners' political participation in Japan.

Conclusion

Increasingly, Japan is an important destination for international migration as it is still regarded as a significant economic power that provides a great volume of job opportunities despite its decade of economic woes. As Japanese society ages, at a rate faster than any other Western country, and with the numbers of work-capable young people proportionately declining, the country will increasingly depend on the participation of both foreigners and Japanese women in the workplace. Migrant workers, both legal and illegal, continue to come to Japan. National policy needs to focus on foreign residents' membership and participation in Japanese society in view of their future role in sustaining an aging Japanese society. Yet, the national government's approach continues in a piecemeal fashion, with a reiterated traditional notion of homogeneity. *Ad hoc* decisions such as the 1989 relaxation of immigration policy, which permitted only foreigners of Japanese descent to migrate to Japan, confirmed the central authority's intention to exclude foreigners whenever possible and to maintain the "homogeneous" nation.

In contrast, political forces at the grassroots level have presented as the most important factor in the promotion and protection of the rights and participation of foreigners in Japanese society. Well-organized policy coalitions and networks among foreign and local residents and local authorities have developed, beyond the reach of the national administration. Local forces, by coping with problems at the grassroots level, have simultaneously applied pressure on National Diet members and the national government to be accountable and responsive to their needs. As seen in this study, local government occupies a position that straddles the division between the absolutes of territorial governance at the national level and the pressing need of solving nonterritorial problems, such as international migration, at the grassroots level. Holding such a strategic position allows local government to help create a diverse political space toward transnational citizenship. Japanese local government is the most regulated in the world, yet it has been shaping a collective life beyond the confined political space premised on nationality alone.

This chapter has sought to explore the various factors contributing to the extension of rights to foreigners living in Japan. It has suggested a list of plausible factors that created the necessary conditions for change including the increasing numbers of foreigners, rising public support, legal and moral obligations arising from the historical relationship between Japan and its former colonies, the obligation of the state to implement international agreements within domestic law, and electoral interests for expanding politicians' support base. Although necessary, these conditions were not sufficiently powerful to create the initiatives, and the extensions of these initiatives, alone. Rather, they provided political actors with opportunities for policy initiatives and expansion. On the one hand, national bureaucrats from home affairs and justice tended to minimize, where possible, the extension of rights to foreigners, while National Diet members tended to handle the matter in an opportunistic manner, often acting indecisively. On the other hand, local chief executives and assemblies strongly exploited the possibilities inherent within this politicized environment to present reforms as part of an effort to cope with encounters between Japanese nationality-dominated citizenship and newly emerging inclusive citizenship for foreign residents in local communities. The actions of local officials were not simply a reactive response to the necessary conditions outlined earlier in the chapter, but rather, the involvement of local authorities making strategic choices about what needed to be done, thus providing a source of cohesion amid all the divisions between the Japanese state and its citizens (including nonnationals). In this sense, local governments acted as the ultimate factor for political transformation.

Conclusion: In Search of
New Directions for Japan

The twentieth century was a period of great success for Japan. It was a century of unprecedented history in which the small, resource-poor, island nation successfully made its emergence onto the world stage. In order to "catch up or overtake" the Western powers, Japan prioritized the needs of the state, the national bureaucracy, and big business. During the Meiji period (1868–1912), a centralized, top-down government-business sector style of administration was established to help modernize the country. Japan caught up with Western industrial powers when it adopted a readymade model of the West, premised on mass industrial production and mass commodity consumption, in the post–World War II (WWII) era and proved to be more successful in its adaptation of this Ford-style mass production model than its Western counterparts. By the late 1980s, Japan was simultaneously the world's largest creditor nation and the largest foreign aid donor and seemed to have achieved its goal of catching up with Western nations. But Japan also faced a new dilemma as at this particular point in time there was a dearth of readymade models in the West and the country needed to forge its own pathways to achieve new national goals. Japan could no longer afford to maintain its one-size-fits-all policy of developmentalism that had dominated Japanese ways of strategic thinking during the 1960s and 1970s. Various communities in Japan began to emphasize the importance of meeting diverse social needs and argued that Japan needed to be open to, and to be accepted and respected by, the rest of the world.

At present, the world economy is in the midst of a profound structural transition. It is evolving as a global knowledge-based economy in which new information and telecommunication technologies are reorganizing the means of production, distribution, and consumption. The changing global economy is also forcing a restructuring of state-society relations, with more emphasis being placed on an equitable partnership between governmental and nongovernmental organizations (NGOs). This is particularly evident in the rising role of NGOs in the solution of key social concerns and issues arising in advanced democracies. There is a clear trend of de-statization, a move away from the national government toward a more decentralized form of governance.

The economy has dominated the governing of member countries of the Organisation for Economic Co-operation and Development (OECD) over the past half century. However, in the next two to three decades, it is anticipated that social issues and concerns, which heavily affect the foundation of the economy, are likely to have a more commanding influence over these countries. Given that the falling birth rate and aging population in Japan is accelerating at a faster rate than in other Western countries, there is also the strong possibility that Japan, in being forced to respond to the innumerable outcomes of changing social demographics, could emerge as the front-runner in the solution of a number of emerging global social issues and concerns.

Patterns of daily life in the local living sphere are shaped, in part, by the social issues and concerns that may cause changes within state-society relations. There is a vital need for a new relationship between the state and citizens, complete with a new set of rules, both formal and informal, to create the necessary public "space" for these problems to be solved. To this end, as discussed in this book, civil society groups and local governments have increasingly joined together to take responsibility for public welfare and safety and, as a result, have helped build up processes of governance and reserves of social capital throughout the country. This study also indicates that participatory institutionalization is a key to establishing such local governance. However, such participation within institutional settings has required far greater receptiveness on the part of local government toward the sharing and disclosure of information, agenda setting, policymaking, *ex post facto* policy assessment and review, administrative evaluation, and ombuds (OMBs) and referenda systems. The decade of the 1990s in Japan was not just a matter of dismal economic performance as perceived by foreign observers, but it marked a fundamental power shift of state-society relations that drew citizens and community groups into a more democratic style of governance. This is partly because the national government tended to stand back, leaving citizens and local governments to deal with unprecedented developments within the local living sphere. First, one of the most important developments is with respect to the dramatically increased demand for personalized/individualized services, such as long-term care for bedridden or frail older persons. Second, the personal realm is increasingly politicized as seen in the prevention of spousal violence, in which the mutual intervention of the public and private spheres has been strongly evident. Third, there are rapidly increasing local needs to deal with the consequences of global issues, particularly the integration of foreign migrant workers into local communities, where the pace of change in many Japanese communities has been exceeding changes within national policy. In recent years, a top-down alliance of conservative politicians, high-ranking bureaucrats, and big business persons has been attempting to solve some of these social issues. However, their attempts have proved to be largely unsuccessful given their primary goal of avoiding adverse effects on the national economy and the intermeshing of vested interests with a centralized, standardized governing system. As argued throughout this book, it is primarily local governance driven by independently elected local governments and civil society groups that is the force behind resolving social issues and the single most important factor for determining Japan's evolution into a civic nation. This finding is consistent with the principle of subsidiarity that sees problems to be best solved at the level in which they arise. In this respect, this is the local living sphere.

National Identity

In the early 1990s, it was very important to Japanese citizens that their country be understood and accepted by the rest of the world. They had worked hard to remake their collective identity and to restructure their society far from the military excesses of WWII. To this end, they identified pacifism as an essential ingredient of democracy and developed their own democratic pathways through an antimilitarist ethic. The widespread affluence of the 1960s then encouraged an inward-looking pacifism, one that pursued peace within Japanese borders in the interests of serving the country's economic prosperity. In post–Cold War Japan, understandings of a pacifist identity entered a new phase as a result of dramatic shocks and crises within the nation and abroad. This led to a more proactive form of pacifism shaped, in part, by changing needs and expectations within civil society and the likely acceptance of international community. The emergence of this proactive variant of pacifism provided a foundation for the participation and voluntarism of civil society groups in socially mobilized activities.

Citizens

Perhaps the most fundamental condition for the strengthening of civil society is changes in basic social values, particularly changing public attitudes toward civic duty and engagement in local governance. Ordinary citizens are very aware that they can no longer depend on public authorities for the safety and welfare of the community and must join together to advance the accountability and responsiveness of community projects and services. This continues to be a challenge for citizens, particularly those needing to understand and acknowledge that sharing social responsibilities in this manner is uncommon and that it can be difficult and arduous for all the actors involved to reach a mutually acceptable agreement. However, the self-reinforcing and cumulative values underpinning the formation of social networks were already in place, instilled within the wider national identity with the cultural evolution of modern Japan. As discussed in chapter 5, these values were adapted and further reconstructed in a short period of time by ordinary citizens who formed grassroots social networks to help share responsibility for community problems, needs, and concerns. This may not have been possible without the effective leadership of local governments, which have been providing incentives for local residents to participate in community affairs, for new social values, and for decision-making processes.

Women

In an era of economic rationalism, the focus on economic efficiency as a panacea for all social ills has tended to overshadow any impetus toward economic equality and the equitable redistribution of resources. Too little is questioned about the injustice of economic inequalities that structure, and are structured by, gender differences. In terms of economic efficiency alone, it is necessary to ensure equal rewards to women as a means of revitalizing the declining workforce and to foster sustainable development and growth in Japan. However, any remedy of current economic inequality will also require policies that engage women as equal participants in political processes. While Japanese women are neither more nor less willing than men to participate in political processes, it is clear that they perceive overwhelming gender-specific barriers to their political participation. At the same time, as discussed in chapter 7, Japanese women are becoming more engaged in political processes and are overcoming gender-specific barriers to stand for election. Japanese women's groups have been seeking a new form of political participation that provides an alternative to the male-dominated pork-barrel politics catering to special interest groups. Women's pioneer groups, such as the Tokyo Citizens' Network, are now developing a local governance form of societal coordination that spans the boundaries of local government and civil society groups. In short, they are sharing responsibility with local authorities to meet local community needs.

It is independent, citizen-based women activists who are neither affiliated with a political party nor supported by neighborhood/kinship-based groups, who occupy a strategic position to deepen awareness of women's rights and who arouse a greater level of political activism among women. Just as important, there are now signs that, irrespective of gender, those alienated from established political process are becoming more receptive to the initiatives of independent female representatives for achieving social equity. On the whole, it is women's activism that seems to be strengthening Japanese civil society, as the broad scope of their activities embraces, yet looks beyond, women's issues in the search for good governance.

Foreigners

International migration to the self-styled "homogeneous" nation of Japan has increased significantly in recent years. Given the aging population, Japan requires millions of additional migrant workers over the next half century to maintain the current size of the working-age population. The national government has acknowledged this social and economic reality, yet has responded to the issue of labor migration in a rather piecemeal fashion. The impact of migration is mostly felt at the local level as it is Japanese cities that are continuing to attract migrant workers in globalized labor markets. Japanese local governments have become increasingly instrumental in dealing with the consequences of international migration and are attempting to turn its impact into tangible benefits. To this end, they have acted as intermediary organizations between national government and local communities to help bridge gaps between national immigration policy and local needs, between traditional neighborhood communities and emerging multiethnic communities, and between citizens and noncitizens to help initiate the process of successful integration into a local community.

Local authorities have attempted to interpret and coordinate national immigration policies geared to their own particular circumstances and have achieved a number of concrete results. Furthermore, both citizens and noncitizens rely on local government for assuring social cohesion and their health and safety as individuals in their day-to-day life. In this respect, local government is well placed for its dual function as part of the state apparatus and as a partner of civil society groups by helping to facilitate the process and goals of integration, social cohesion, and social change among various communities. Japan's immigration policy was formulated from the mid-1980s to the end of the 1990s, to place appropriate controls on migrant workers and to maintain a policy of nonintegration, for homogeneity was considered necessary for national success. In 1990 Japan began to relax its immigration policy to enable descendants of Japanese immigrants from Latin America to live and work in Japan. It is notable that descendants of other migrant groups were not included in this policy decision and that the larger framework of racial homogeneity was virtually left intact. However, the decision did evoke the prospect of considerable migration flows and opened up a nationwide debate on issues arising from the immigration and integration of migrant workers, including the provision of social services. Local authorities were quick to act. By the mid-1990s, they had done much to increase public awareness of the rights of foreigners in a host country and had brought local voting rights for foreign residents in a host country onto the national agenda.

In many local communities, as discussed in chapter 8, foreign residents are now encouraged to participate in community decision-making processes and to gain political representation. It is expected that their increasing civic participation will give additional clarity and weight to local government processes dealing with national government's policies about the demographic, economic, and fiscal impact of international migration as well as to public concerns about the impact of immigration on public safety and employment opportunities. In sum, the active engagement of foreign residents in local processes has two positive outcomes: it helps foreign residents, as individuals, to transcend sociopolitical boundaries imposed by the host country and it also furthers the integration of all migrants into the local community.

In Japan, national policy on migrant workers has often been outpaced by the introduction of innovative local government practices that provide temporary direct relief to insolvent migrants; compensate medical expenses that migrants are unable to pay; extend Employees' Insurance and National Health Insurance to migrants who overstay their visa; intervene in labor disputes of migrant workers; employ foreigners as local civil servants; provide education for children of undocumented migrants; revitalize urban areas such as "Korea Town"; and facilitate community development projects in multiethnic districts.

Independently elected local governments and community-based organizations in migration destination cities have already proven their competence in deciding how they should govern and be financed, and have demonstrated considerable flexibility in working with groups and individuals at the grassroots level.

However, as the national government continues to delegate power to local authorities as part of its decentralization drive, the onus will be on local governments and organizations to assist migrants to integrate into the community. How they deal with this is yet to be seen.

The importance placed on public safety in Japan poses a dilemma for policymakers: whether to close national borders for a greater sense of security or whether to promote the open and inclusive participation of all residents irrespective of their cultural background. Local governments are seen as providing a possible solution to this dilemma, given the intermediary role they play in reconnecting the state with citizens and noncitizens who embrace and support widely shared civic values. This intermediary role is regarded as a viable means to social renewal, particularly as it also has the potential to consolidate social capital and thus enhance the security of the nation. Particularly important to the successful implementation of this intermediary role is the creation of inclusive networks, or bridging social capital, that draws together local and foreign residents in the pursuit of common values and interests. The case of Kawasaki has already demonstrated that local authorities that work with support groups to facilitate the integration of migrant workers into the community boost the reserves of social capital that benefit the community as a whole.

An Aging Population

Japan is aging faster than any other country in the world. This poses a critical dilemma for Japan. One in four Japanese citizens will be 65 years or older by 2015, and the ratio of workers to retirees is likely to drop to a little over two to one in 2025. Irrespective of their financial preparedness for retirement, the massive group of these future pensioners will impose a heavy burden on Japanese society, particularly as everything they consume will need to be produced by the working population. However, birthrates are falling and the proportion of work-capable citizens is declining accordingly. To ease this problem, Japan will need to ensure that women can easily enter and reenter the labor force and be granted the same rewards and benefits as male workers. Equally important, Japan will need to further open its labor market to foreign nationals, and to carefully prepare the necessary resources for those immigrants who wish to reside permanently in the country. The Japanese government will need to solve problems generated by the inevitable rapid growth in consumption, particularly the increasing demands placed on the health system, through policies that will incur tax increases and/or cuts in government programs. It is unlikely that the introduction of such policies will be popular with the electorate. Policymakers will also need to face the close scrutiny and organization of the elderly whose electoral power will clearly grow in Japan as it has in many other countries. In the United States, for example, organized senior citizens' groups, such as the American Association of Retired Persons (AARP), continue to lobby for elderly entitlements, while the Pensioner Party in the Netherlands has already made a successful debut at the voting booth. My recent field research indicates that the elderly in Japan have yet to systematically organize themselves into groups and associations, which they will need to do to have their voice heard within political processes.

There are specific reasons why the Japanese elderly are not as well organized as they should be. The organization of senior citizens requires active members from 60 to 70 years of age who are mentally and physically fit. The difficulty is that Japanese men tend to work beyond the age of 60, which is the official retirement age for those working in medium and large companies. Approximately one-half of all Japanese men from 60 to 70 years of age, and one-quarter of those from 70 to 75 years of age, have remained in the workforce. Furthermore, self-employed individuals, such as farmers and shopkeepers, who have no mandatory retirement age imposed on them, are encouraging the interests of the producer rather than the consumer through their support of the pro-business Liberal Democratic Party (LDP). Most elderly people living in rural areas belong to senior clubs for recreation and leisure and are heavily dependent on agricultural associations, which are the strongest lobbying groups in Japan, to voice their concerns in political processes. In 2007 some 2.7 million Japanese workers born between 1947 and 1949 will start retiring. These are the eldest of the first-wave baby boomers who are politically influential, have done much to bolster Japan's high economic growth, and are the most likely to emerge as the spearhead of socially mobilized senior citizens groups. It appears that retired baby boomers are already in the process of organizing and institutionalizing themselves as a social movement in major urban areas such as Tokyo and Osaka. In October 2005 Kan Naoto, a representative of the major opposition Democratic Party of Japan (DPJ), identified himself as a baby boomer when he proposed the formation of a new political party known as the *Dankai* (baby boomer) Party.

It is possible that the growing political power of elderly voters may prove counterproductive to a sustainable Japan, particularly if they should adopt a traditional pressure group focus in the pursuit of entitlements for individuals or narrowly focused interests at the expense of collective needs and interests. The relatively high numbers of senior citizens with political and social clout could also hamper much needed reform in Japan. It is a finding of this study that socially mobilized senior citizens would further social capital and prosperity in Japan by joining civil society groups, or by forming coalitions and networks, that could provide the necessary incentives to make decisions for the common good rather than for special or sectional interests alone. Such coalitions and networks may help refine understandings of the empirical link between consumption and production, perhaps balancing the needs and entitlements of senior citizens' with those of the existing workforce (as the future recipients of retirement benefits) including the unpaid and largely unrecognized female workforce based at home who are providing care for the elderly under the patriarchal framework.

It is best that the network of relationships that senior citizens are seeking to build with the government be in the form of horizontal partnerships rather than vertical patron-client relationships. Furthermore, it would be advantageous for senior citizens groups to connect with independently elected local governments to engage with other citizen-based groups in community-driven initiatives rather than to focus solely on retirees' entitlements to additional national subsidies. By taking into account the needs of the community as a whole, senior citizens are more likely to address the problems inherent in an aging population including the consumption of public goods that the shrinking working population needs to continue to produce.

Regionalization

In February 2006 the Study Commission for Local Government System submitted a report to Prime Minister Koizumi Jun'ichiro on the *doushusei* (a regional government system to be established by the merger of several prefectures). There was a secondary and arguably more immediate agenda underlying the *doushusei* reform, which reflected national government concerns over the accumulative increase in government debt. The government's immediate goal for the *doushusei* initiative was to improve financial conditions by increasing the efficiency of local governments. However, the *doushusei* reform also needs to be based on a long-term perspective that encourages the principle of regional autonomy. Should regional government continue to function as the arm of national government, the nature and scope of the very capable networks that are emerging in civil society would be constrained and inhibited. It is clear that government must be reorganized, yet more power needs to be designated to local and regional levels. In this premise, it can be seen that a larger region has the ability to provide its different localities with opportunities to utilize locally available resources in a coordinated fashion. This is already evident in a number of multiple prefectures that have been liaising with each other to promote a number of larger-sphere policy issues such as environmental regulations, transportation infrastructure, and tourism promotion. The coordination of policies among prefectures also furthers the flexibility of community-based organizations to meet specific regionwide needs. This then paves the way for network members, such as community groups, local business, and universities active beyond prefectural borders, to turn the potential of regionwide initiatives into tangible benefits.

The mass movement of migrant workers and capital at the global level seems to converge on specific region-based areas. As a result, many of these regions have proven to be more aware of, and responsive to, global issues directly affecting them, and have worked across national borders to achieve solutions. For example, the Kyushu region in Japan has worked with a number of coastal areas in China to control pollution, and the Japan Sea coastal region has cooperated with the Russian Far East to establish open economic ties in Northeast Asia. These initiatives and programs were autonomous of the national government in Japan and took the stress off the capital city of Tokyo.

Information and Communication Technologies

Information and communication technologies (ICTs) have a number of potential roles in the development of social relations and social capital. Two major patterns of development in ICT application are currently emerging. The first pattern is found in ICT-driven social developments that emphasize civic values and solidarity and are grounded in the expectation of democratic outcomes and benefits. In this manner, ICTs help serve public interests and purposes through the engagement of citizens in political processes that also helps to reduce social inequalities and exclusion. Second, the ICT-driven economic development is based on the principles of neoliberalism that gives priority to commercial benefits and efficiency and requires civil society to adapt to the logic of the ICT-based economy. In the first pattern of development that works to advance public interests, personalized ICT access is more likely to ensure the engagement of a relatively small network of citizens who are already familiar with this form of communication. Their engagement is evident at the local level in Japan, which has been actively constructing this new form of participatory democracy through ICT-based technological mediation. Despite barriers to e-participation, such as the digital divide and weak privacy protection, the use of ICTs is clearly presenting a new potential tool for creating social cohesion in the local living sphere.

Finally, I hope that the material presented in this book will offer a means to understand changes in state-society relations across a wide range of nations, including those in Asia, that have taken an interventionist stance toward civic life. As the experience of Japan demonstrates, patterns of state intervention in associational life that were largely bound to the pursuit of rapid economic development, have changed over time in response to the impact of globalization, the financial limits of state expansion, environmental degradation, the expansion of ICT-based resources, demographic changes, and a range of other factors.

All these contributory factors are allowing a realignment of central-local and state-society power relations with some welcome effects of democratizing Japan. State intervention can not only restrict civil liberties, but also has the capacity to promote civil activism by guaranteeing citizens' rights and by extending tax benefits and subsidies to voluntary associations. Indeed, civil society groups and independently elected local governments in Japan are forming partnerships for local governance and taking steps to increase political participation and activism. At the same time, local governments increasingly exist apart from the central state to the extent that they are now seen as an alternative to the national government. Societal steering of local governments with civil society groups in the local living sphere merits inclusion within the realm of civil society.

Notes

Introduction

1. Personal conversation with the author on April 15, 2006. (Note that all participants in this conversation have been given pseudonyms.)
2. John W. Hall, "The Castle Town and Japan's Modern Urbanization," in *Studies in the Institutional History of Early Modern Japan,* eds. John W. Hall and Marius B. Jansen (Princeton: Princeton University Press, 1968), pp. 169–88.
3. Thomas. C. Smith, *The Agrarian Origins of Modern Japan* (Stanford: Stanford University Press, 1959), pp. 50–64.
4. Hirasawa Kiyohito, "Edo Jidai no Noson no 'Mujin'" (The *Mujin* of Villages in Edo Japan), *Ina* 88 (December 1961): 42–68; Kaneko Ikuyo et al., *Borantari Keizai no Tanjo* (The Birth of the Voluntary Economy) (Tokyo: Jitsugyo no Nihonsha, 1998); Ishikawa Eisuke and Tanaka Yuko, *Oo-Edo Borantia Jijo* (The State of Volunteers in Greater Edo) (Tokyo: Kodansha, 1999).
5. Kyogoku Jun'ichi, *Nihon no Seiji* (Politics in Japan) (Tokyo: University of Tokyo Press, 1983), pp. 150–62; Hirano Ken'ichiro, "Ajia ni okeru Chuo to Chiho" (The Center and the Periphery in Asia), *Ajia Kenkyu* 33 (March 1987): 1–17.
6. Oshima Taro, *Nihon Chiho Gyozaisei Shi Josetsu* (Introduction to a History of Local Administration and Finance in Japan) (Tokyo: Miraisha, 1968).
7. Tokyo Shisei Chosakai, ed., *Jichi Gojunenshi: Seido Hen* (A Fifty-Year History of Local Autonomy: The Volume of Institutions) (Tokyo: Ryosho Fukkyukai, 1940), pp. 28–40; Kikegawa Hiroshi, *Meiji Chiho Jichiseido no Seiritsu Katei* (The Formation Process of the Meiji Local Autonomy System) (Tokyo: Tokyo Shisei Chosakai, 1955), pp. 17–31.
8. Iokibe Makoto, "Japan's Civil Society: An Historical Overview," in *Deciding the Public Good: Governance and Civil Society in Japan,* ed. Yamamoto Tadashi (Tokyo: Japan Center for International Exchange, 1999), pp. 67–68.
9. Sato Masanori, "Meiji Chiho Jichi to Mura" (Meiji Local Autonomy and Villages), in *Kindai Nihon no Togo to Teiko* (Integration and Resistance in Modern Japan), vol. 1, eds. Kano Masanao and Yui Masaomi (Tokyo: Nihon Hyoronsha, 1982), pp. 215–47; Irokawa Daikichi, *The Culture of the Meiji Period* (Princeton: Princeton University Press, 1985), pp. 19–50.
10. Maruyama Masao, *Thought and Behaviour in Modern Japanese Politics* (London: Oxford University Press, 1963), p. 6.

11. Sheldon Garon, *Molding Japanese Minds: The State in Everyday Life* (Princeton: Princeton University Press, 1997).

12. Tsujinaka Yutaka, "From Developmentalism to Maturity: Japan's Civil Society Organizations in Comparative Perspective," in *The State of Civil Society in Japan,* eds. Frank Schwartz and Susan Pharr (Cambridge: Cambridge University Press, 2003), pp. 83–115.

13. Muramatsu Michio, "The Impact of Economic Growth Policies in Local Politics in Japan," *Asian Survey* 15, no. 9 (September 1975): 799–816; Ronald Aqua, "Political Choice and Policy Change in Medium-Sized Japanese Cities, 1962–1974," in *Political Opposition and Local Politics in Japan,* eds. Kurt Steiner, Ellis S. Krauss, and Scott C. Flanagan (Princeton: Princeton University Press, 1980), pp. 354–61.

14. Kent E. Calder, *Crisis and Compensation: Public Policy and Political Stability in Japan* (Princeton: Princeton University Press, 1988).

15. It is true that some local governments initiated new, independent policies of their own, such as a policy of free medical care for the elderly, and the national government followed. Yet the local independent activism appeared as episodic and perhaps even ad hoc; it did not move into the mainstream of decision-making patterns in the local sphere. For local innovation in the 1960s and 1970s, see Muramatsu, "The Impact of Economic Growth Policies in Local Politics in Japan," pp. 813–15; John C. Campbell, "The Old People Boom and Japanese Policy Making," *Journal of Japanese Studies* 5, no. 2 (Summer 1979): 321–57.

16. Campbell, "The Old People Boom and Japanese Policy Making"; John C. Campbell, "Problem, Solution, Non-Solutions and Free Medical Care for the Elderly in Japan," *Pacific Affairs* 57, no. 1 (Spring 1984): 53–64.

17. Noguchi Yukio, "Public Finance," in *The Political Economy of Japan: The Domestic Transformation,* vol. 1, eds. Yamamura Kozo and Yasuba Yasukichi (Stanford: Stanford University Press, 1987), pp. 186–222.

18. Paul Pierson, "The New Politics of the Welfare State," *World Politics* 48, no. 2 (January 1996): 143–79; Lester M. Salamon, "The Rise of the Nonprofit Sector," *Foreign Affairs* 73, no. 4 (July/August 1994): 115–16.

19. Takao Yasuo, "The Rise of the 'Third Sector' in Japan," *Asian Survey* 41, no. 2 (March/April 2001): 290–309.

20. Susan Pharr and Robert Putnam, eds., *Disaffected Democracies: What's Troubling the Trilateral Countries* (Princeton: Princeton University Press, 2000).

21. Japan National Council of Social Welfare, *Heisei Jyuichi-nendo Shakai Fukushi Kyogikai Kihon Chosa* (The 1999 Basic Investigation by the Japan National Council of Social Welfare) (Tokyo: Japan National Council of Social Welfare, 1999); Japan National Council of Social Welfare, *Heisei Jyuichi-nendo Todofuken Shiteitoshi Shakai Fukushi Kyogikai Borantiasenta Kankei Chosa* (The 1999 Social Welfare Council Investigation on Volunteer Activities in Prefectures and Designated Municipalities) (Tokyo: Japan National Council of Social Welfare, 1999).

22. Takao Yasuo, "Participatory Democracy in Japan's Decentralization Drive," *Asian Survey* 38, no. 10 (October 1998): 950–67.

23. For a similar vein of arguments in the French case, see Jonah D. Levy, *Tocqueville's Revenge: State, Society, and Economy in Contemporary France* (Cambridge, MA: Harvard University Press, 1999), pp. 329–30.

24. Manuel Castells, *The Information Society: Information Technology, Economic Restructuring, and the Urban-Regional Process* (Oxford: B. Blackwell, 1989).

25. Daniel Bell, *The Coming of Post-Industrial Society: A Venture in Social Forecasting* (London: Heinemann Educational, 1974).

26. Salamon, "The Rise of the Nonprofit Sector," pp. 109–22.

27. See, for example, Guillermo O'Donnell and Philippe C. Schmitter, *Transition from Authoritarian Rule: Tentative Conclusions about Uncertain Democracies* (Baltimore: Johns Hopkins University Press, 1998); Philip C. Schmitter, "Civil Society East and West," in *Consolidating the Third Wave Democracies: Themes and Perspectives,* eds. Larry Diamond, Marc F. Plattner, Yun-han Chu, and Hung-mao Tien (Baltimore: Johns Hopkins University Press, 1997), pp. 239–62.

28. Frank Schwartz, "What Is Civil Society?" in *The State of Civil Society in Japan,* eds. Frank Schwartz and Susan Pharr (Cambridge: Cambridge University Press, 2003), p. 23.

29. Victor Pérez-Díaz, "The Possibility of Civil Society: Traditions, Character and Challenges," in *Civil Society: Theory, History, Comparison,* ed. John Hall (Cambridge: Polity Press, 1995), pp. 80–109.

30. See, for example, André Gorz, *Farewell to the Working Class: An Eassy on Post-Industrial Socialism* (Boston: South End Press, 1982); Claus Offe, *Contradictions of the Welfare State* (Cambridge, MA: MIT Press, 1984).

31. Susan Pharr, "Preface," in *The State of Civil Society in Japan,* eds. Frank Schwartz and Susan Pharr (Cambridge: Cambridge University Press, 2003), xiii.

32. Jean L. Cohen and Andrew Arato, *Civil Society and Political Theory* (Cambridge: MA: MIT Press, 1992), x.

33. Alexis de Tocqueville, *Democracy in America,* trans. Harvey C. Mansfield and Delba Winthrop (Chicago: University of Chicago Press, 2000), I 2.1–2.6, II 2.1–2.8.

34. By contrast, Hannah Arendt criticized the pluralist versions of mass society by regarding social movements as proto-totalitarian. In Arendt's view, social movements would invade private domains of life, destroying the social realm of the public and the private. See Hannah Arendt, *The Origin of Totalitarianism* (New York: Meridian Books, 1958) and *On Revolution* (New York: Penguin Books, 1977).

35. Throughout *Democracy in America,* Tocqueville utilized a relatively narrow concept of "civil society." He saw it as a very particular, inward-looking sphere, in which citizens engaged in mundane, day-to-day economic activities. In contrast, he viewed citizens' involvement in public affairs as part of a wider "political society."

36. Larry Diamond, *Developing Democracy: Toward Consolidation* (Baltimore: Johns Hopkins University Press, 1999), pp. 224, cited in Schwartz, "What Is Civil Society?" p. 32.

37. Gary J. Miller, *Managerial Dilemma: The Political Economy of Hierarchy* (New York: Cambridge University Press, 1992).

38. Levy, *Tocqueville's Revenge,* pp. 329–30.

39. Max Weber, *Economy and Society,* trans. Talcott Parsons et al. (New York: Bedminster, 1968), p. 314.

40. Peter Saunders, *Social Theory and the Urban Questions,* 2nd ed. (New York: Homes & Meier, 1986), p. 265; Stephen Bailey, *Local Government Economics: Principles and Practice* (Basingstoke: Macmillan, 1999), p. 262.

41. Arendt, *The Origin of Totalitarianism*; Arendt, *On Revolution.*

42. Cohen and Arato, *Civil Society and Political Theory,* p. 201.

43. Jürgen Habermas, *The Structural Transformation of the Public Sphere* (Cambridge: MIT Press, 1989).

Chapter 1

1. *Asahi Shinbun,* Editorial, August 15, 1954.

2. *Asahi Shinbun,* Editorial, August 15, 1990.

3. Sakamoto Yoshikazu, "Heiwashugi no Gyakusetsu to Koso" (The Antithesis and Conception of Pacifism), *Sekai,* 597 (July 1994): 30.

4. *Mainichi Shinbun,* Editorial, August 15, 1991.

5. *Yomiuri Shinbun,* Editorial, August 15, 1953, and August 15, 1965; Thomas Berger, "From Sword to Chrysanthemum: Japan's Culture of Anti-militarism," *International Security* 17, no. 4 (Spring 1993): 135.

6. The Cabinet Office, Cabinet Public Relations Office (the former Ministry of Public Management), Japan, has been conducting a public opinion survey on national security every three years since 1969. The office administers a lengthy questionnaire to 3,000 men and women in their 20s and over (except the 2000 survey that was conducted over the sample size of 5,000).

7. *Mainichi Shinbun,* May 27, 1946.

8. Toshitani Nobuyoshi, "Kenpo Dai-Kyujo to Kokumin no Hoishiki" (Article 9 and the Legal Consciousness of the Public), *Shiso,* 457 (June 1962): 19.

9. This opinion poll was conducted by *Mainichi Shinbun.* Also cited in Morishita, "Sengo Nihon Kokumin no Heiwa Ishiki no Tenkai," p. 35.

10. The first opinion poll was conducted by *Asahi Shinbun;* and the second one by *Mainichi Shinbun.* Cited in Morishita Toru, "Sengo Nihon Kokumin no Heiwa Ishiki no Tenkai" (Developments in the Peace Consciousness of the Japanese Public in Postwar Japan), *Rekishi Hyoron,* 553 (May 1995): 35.

11. For this general trend indicated by the public opinion polls of *Asahi Shinbun, Mainichi Shinbun,* and the Cabinet Office, see NHK Yoron Chosa Kenkyujo (NHK Research Center for Public Opinion), ed., *Zusetsu Sengo Yoron Shi* (Illustrated History of Postwar Public Opinion) (Tokyo: Nihon Hoso Shuppan Kyokai, 1975), pp. 124–29.

12. In 1950, immediately after the outbreak of the Korean War, the Occupation authority under American influence directed Japan to form a National Police Reserve of 75,000. John Dulles, the U.S. presidential adviser, repeatedly urged Yoshida to build a force of 300,000 men, but he refused. In 1952 this reserve became the National Safety Force; in 1954, with the passage of the Defense Agency Establishment Law, it was transformed into the SDF. The SDF was built up slowly from a 120,000-man military. The results of the opinion polls are from those conducted by *Yomiuri Shinbun* in January 1954 and those by the Cabinet Office in 1956 and 1959.

13. See, for example, *Asahi Shinbun,* Editorial, August 15, 1954; *Mainichi Shinbun,* Editorial, August 15, 1955, and Editorial, August 15, 1956. These editorials were written for the memorial day for the end of the war.

14. The Institute of Statistical Mathematics in Tokyo conducted an opinion survey on constitutional revision 17 times from 1954 to 1962. Until 1959 about 30 percent favored "should revise it sooner," and another 30 percent preferred "should not revise it at all." During the same period, only 10 percent were for "unadvisable now (to revise it)." But this ratio rose sharply to nearly 35 percent by 1962.

15. In the Sunagawa case of 1959, the Supreme Court ruled that Japan's constitutional ban on rearmament did not prohibit the stationing of U.S. troops on Japanese soil. Following the popular acceptance of the existing SDF, LDP politicians also began to argue that a sovereign nation has the right of self-defense, and thus that any armed

forces for self-defense do not violate Article 9. Therefore, Prime Minister Ikeda stated, "The existing self-defense capability is within the limits of the constitution." See Japan, Diet, House of Representative, Minutes of the Committee on the Cabinet, April 13, 1961.

16. See, for example, *Asahi Shinbun,* Editorial, August 15, 1963,and Editorial, August 15, 1964; *Yomiuri Shinbun,* Editorial, August 15, 1965, and Editorial, August 15, 1966.

17. For a clear argument of this point, see *Asahi Shinbun,* Editorial, August 15, 1972.

18. The Cabinet Office, Cabinet Public Relations Office, Japan, conducted a public opinion survey on this question in 1963, 1965, 1970, and every three years since 1978.

19. Herbert Asher, *Polling and the Public: What Every Citizen Should Know* (Washington, D.C.: Congressional Quarterly Press, 1998).

20. Thomas Risse-Kappen, "Structure, and Foreign Policy in Liberal Democracies," *World Politics* 43, no. 4 (July 1991): 494–99.

21. See, for example, Elizabeth Hastings and Philip Hastings, eds. *Index to International Public Opinion,* annuals (Westport: Greenwood Press, 1978/79–1998/99). There are some exceptions between 1969 and 1990; in 1969 Americans favoring reduction in defense spending rose to over 50 percent and in 1981 those supporting increases also had a majority.

22. Richard Eichenberg, *Public Opinion and National Security in Western Europe: Consensus Lost?* (Ithaca: Cornell University Press, 1989); Christopher Wlezien, "The Public as Thermostat: Dynamics of Preferences for Spending," *American Journal of Political Science* 39, no. 4 (November 1995): 981–1000.

23. Sources from *National Accounts of OECD Countries,* various issues. The figure in 1969 calculated from sources produced by Japan, Economic Planning Agency (EPA).

24. *Asahi Shinbun,* Editorial, August 15, 1991; *Yomiuri Shinbun,* Editorial, August 15, 1992.

25. *Mainichi Shinbun,* Editorial, August 15, 1991, and Editorial, August 15, 1995.

26. See, for example, *Asahi Shinbun,* Editorial, August 15, 1990, and Editorial, August 15, 1995; *Mainichi Shinbun,* Editorial, August 15, 1992, and Editorial, August 15, 1997.

27. *Yomiuri Shinbun,* April 6, 1995; *Nihon Keizai Shinbun,* August 15, 1995; *Mainichi Shinbun,* January 5, 1996.

28. The question content of pro-/anti-revision in all the surveys is almost identical, but the sequence of the question and other related questions differs with each survey. This may explain some differences in the survey results; however, it is evident that the overall trend has been revision-oriented.

29. See, for example, a public opinion survey conducted by the Japan Broadcasting Corporation (NHK) from March 2 to 4, 2002; another by *Yomiuri Shinbun* from March 20 to 21, 2004.

30. *Asahi Shinbun,* May 3, 2005.

31. See, for example, a public opinion survey conducted by the NHK from March 2 to 4, 2002.

32. Tsujinaka Yutaka, "NPO/NGO no Jidai to Chikyu Nettowaku Gata Seiji Katei no Tojo" (The Emergence of Global Network-Oriented Political Processes in the Era of NPOs and NGOs), *NIRA Policy Research* 12, no. 3 (March 1999): 39–42; JapanNGO Center for International Cooperation (JANIC), ed., *Data Book on Japanese NGOs '98* (Tokyo: JANIC, 1998), p. 3.

33. JANIC, *Data Book on Japanese NGOs '98,* pp. 8–16.

34. Japan, Economic Planning Agency, "The National Survey on Lifestyle Preferences" (1977 and 2000), available at http://www5.cao.go.jp/j-j/wp-pl/wp-p100/hakusho-00-1-13.html (accessed December 2006).

35. In August 2005, the Cabinet Office, Cabinet Public Relations Office, Japan, conducted a public opinion survey on nonprofit organizations. The office has administered a lengthy questionnaire to 3,000 men and women in their 20s and over.

36. Japan, Diet, House of Representatives, Minutes of the Constitution Research Council, December 6, 2001.

37. Japan, Diet, House of Representatives, Minutes of the Special Committee on Emergency Contingency Bills, May 20, 2003.

38. Ibid.

39. In February and March 2004, *Yomiuri Shinbun* administered an opinion survey of 476 Lower House members on the constitutional issue. Of the 297 usable responses, LDP members represented 47 percent and Democratic Party members accounted for 39 percent. See *Yomiuri Shinbun*, March 17, 2004. The Japanese government claims that Japan has the "inherent right" of collective self-defense as a sovereign nation, including collective security activities under UN peace enforcement operations and joint military operations with U.S. forces, but it has been interpreting Article 9 as a prohibition of collective self-defense.

40. In April 2004, *Mainichi Shinbun* conducted an opinion survey of 722 Lower and Upper House members on constitutional revision. The party-based breakdown figures are available for the 545 respondents. See *Mainichi Shinbun*, May 3, 2004.

41. *Mainichi Shinbun*, May 3, 2004.

42. Institute for National Strategies Studies, "The United States and Japan: Advancing toward a Mature Partnership," *INSS Special Report* (Washington, D.C.: Institute for National Strategies Studies, October 11, 2000), p. 5.

43. Japan, Diet, House of Representatives, Minutes of Plenary Session, June 5, 2003.

44. This legislation involves three bills: a new bill to set out procedural guidelines for a response to armed attacks on Japan; revisions of the Self-Defense Forces Law for providing troops easier access to land in an emergency; and revisions to the law on the establishment of Japan's Security Council to strengthen its role.

45. See the 1997 new Guidelines for U.S.-Japan Security Cooperation; Institute for National Strategies Studies, "The United States and Japan: Advancing toward a Mature Partnership."

46. Japan, Diet, House of Representatives, Minutes of the Special Committee on an Emergency Contingency Bill, July 3, 2002.

47. Japan, Cabinet Office, Cabinet Public Relations Office, a public opinion survey on national security, 1991, 1994, 1997, and 2000.

48. *Asahi Shinbun*, May 2, 2001; NHK, a public opinion survey, conducted from March 2 to 4, 2002.

49. For example, see *Yomiuri Shinbun*, April 2, 2004.

50. JANIC, ed., *Data Book on Japanese NGOs '98*, pp. 8–16.

Chapter 2

1. Torigoe Hiroyuki, "Borantari-na Koi to Shakai Chitsujo" (Voluntary Action and Social Order), paper presented at the First Conference for the Integrate Study of Future Generations, Kyoto, February 3–4, 2001.

2. Peter Saunders, "Rethinking Local Politics," in *Local Socialism? Labour Councils and New Left Alternatives,* eds. Martin Boddy and Colin Fudge (London: Macmillan, 1984), p. 28.

3. Japan, Economic Planning Agency (EPA), ed., *Keizai Hakusho* (Economic White Paper) (Tokyo: Okurasho Insatsukyoku, 1995), p. 417; Noguchi Yukio, "Public Finance," in *The Political Economy of Japan: The Domestic Transformation,* vol. 1, eds. Yamamura Kozo and Yasuba Yasukichi (Stanford: Stanford University Press, 1987), pp. 204–9; Organisation for Economic Co-operation and Development (OECD), *Economic Outlook,* vol. 41 (Paris: OECD, 1987), p. 162.

4. In the early 1990s, to stimulate its ailing economy, Japan launched an economic stimulus policy that scaled up the ratio of general government expenditure to GDP again to over 30 percent (33 percent in 1993 and 1994, 34 percent in 1995, and 35 percent in 1996). While amending the 1997 Fiscal Structural Reform Law, which initially required the Japanese government to reduce government deficits to no more than 3 percent of GDP by fiscal year (FY) 2003, Japan actually increased the ratio to 8.6 percent in 1998 and to 10 percent in 1999. Accordingly, the ratio of general government expenditure to GDP increased to 36 percent in 1999 and further to 38 percent in 2004.

5. Japan, Ministry of Internal Affairs and Communications (MIAC) *Chiho Zaisei Hakusho* (White Paper on Local Public Finance) (2003), http://www.soumu.go.jp/menu_05/hakusyo/chihou/17data/17cz.html (accessed February 2006).

6. In Japan, as in other advanced democratic societies, government seeks not only to promote allocative efficiency, but also social equity. However, direct relief (i.e., public aid) as a percentage of the total cost of social security dropped continuously from 8.1 percent in 1960 to 2.5 percent in 1990, while the ratio of health and pension insurance rose from 55.6 percent in 1960 to 78.2 percent in 1990. In Japan, per capita welfare state expenditure on universal social insurance for all citizens (e.g., ¥0.4 million in 1990) has grown to a comparable level with that of the United States (e.g., ¥0.62 million in 1990) and the UK (e.g., ¥0.55 million in 1990), yet direct relief has failed to keep pace with this growth rate.

7. The figures in the late 1990s, provided by Japan, Ministry of Posts and Telecommunications, for example, showed that Japanese workers were saving more of their salaries as they faced wage cuts and job losses. While Japan's unemployment rate remained at a postwar record high of over 4 per cent, postal savings, the world's largest reservoir of deposit, increased by 6.9 percent from November 1997 to November 1998.

8. Geoffrey Garrett, *Partisan Politics in the Global Economy* (New York: Cambridge University Press, 1998); Evelyn Huber and Leonard Ray, "The Welfare State in Hard Times," in *Continuity and Change in Contemporary Capitalism,* eds. Herbert Kitschelt et al. (New York: Cambridge University Press, 1999); Duane Swank, "Social Democratic Welfare States in a Global Economy: Scandinavia in Comparative Perspective," in *Globalization, Europeanization and the End of Scandinavian Social Democracy?* eds. Robert Geyer, Christine Ingebritsen, and Jonathon Moses (London: Macmillan, 1999).

9. Kent R. Weaver, "The Politics of Blame Avoidance," *Journal of Public Policy* 6, no. 4 (1986): 371–98; Paul Pierson, "The New Politics of the Welfare State," *World Politics* 48, no. 2 (January 1996): 143–79.

10. See, for example, Alan T. Peacock and Jack Wiseman, *The Growth of Public Expenditure in the United Kingdom* (Princeton: Princeton University Press, 1961).

11. Paul Pierson, *Dismantling the Welfare State? Reagan, Thatcher, and the Politics of Retrenchment* (New York: Cambridge University Press, 1994), p. 15.

12. John C. Campbell, "Problems, Solutions, Non-Solutions, and Free Medical Care for the Elderly in Japan," *Pacific Affairs* 57, no. 1 (1984): 53–64.

13. Martin Collick, "Social Policy Pressures and Responses," in *Dynamic and Immobilist Politics in Japan,* eds. J. A. A. Stockwin et al. (London: Macmillan, 1988).

14. The scandal involving the Recruit Co. first broke in 1988, dominating the newspaper headlines for more than a year. The Recruit executive provided most LDP faction leaders and at least 13 high-ranking bureaucrats with low-priced stocks. The story disclosed a breeding ground for political corruption.

15. Ito Motoshige, "Shoddy Taxes, Shady Politics," *Japan Echo* 16 (1989): 52–57.

16. The Social Democratic Party of Japan (SDPJ) was formerly known as the Japan Socialist Party (JSP). The Shinto Sakigake (New Party Harbinger) was a new independent party that a former LDP National Diet member, Takemura Masyoshi, established in 1993.

17. Kato Junko, "Tax Policy in Japan after the Demise of Conservative Dominance," in *Japanese Politics Today: Beyond Karaoke Democracy?* eds. Purnendra Jain and Inoguchi Takashi (South Melbourne: Macmillan, 1997).

18. Hirose Michisada, *Hojokin to Seikento* (Grants and Party in Power) (Tokyo: Asahi Shinbunsha, 1981); Imamura Naraomi, *Nogyo Noson to Hojokin* (Agriculture, Villages and Subsidies) (Tokyo: Ie no Hikari Kyokai, 1978).

19. Japan, Second Provisional Commission for Administrative Reform (SPCAR), *Basic Report,* July 30, 1982; Japan, Financial System Council (FSC), *Council Report,* December 21, 1994.

20. When the Collective Decentralization Law went into effect in 2000, local governments were no longer required to obtain approval from the Ministry of Home Affairs before introducing special-purpose local taxes. About 40 percent of local governments wished to introduce special-purpose local taxes, such those on expressway use by large diesel vehicles to support environmental policies and on the industrial waste to cut the amount of waste discharged. See *Yomiuri Shinbun* November 25, 2000.

21. Takao Yasuo, "Welfare State Retrenchment: The Case of Japan," *Journal of Public Policy* 19, no. 3 (September–December 1999): 274–75.

22. Hirose Michisada, "Gyosei Kaikau to Jiminto" (Administrative Reform and the Liberal Democratic Party), *Sekai* 429 (1981): 245–57; Shindo Mumeyuki, "Yawarakana Shuken Taisei no Kiro" (Soft Centralization at Crossroads), *Sekai* 476 (1985): 22–34.

23. Maki Taro "Rincho no Naibu Rikigaku" (Internal Dynamics of the Provisional Commission for Administrative Reform), *Sekai* 435 (1982): 42–48; Hirose Michisada, "Hojokin Sakugen no Tadashii Shuho to Ayamatta Shuho" (Right and Wrong Ways of Grant Cutbacks), *Gekkan Jichiken,* 26 (1984): 14–19; Ogita Tamotsu "Hojokin Ichiritsu Sakugen Mondai ni tsuite Omou" (Some Consideration for the Problem of Uniform Grant Share Ratio Cuts), *Chiho Zaisei* 24 (1985): 4–14.

24. Takao Yasuo, *National Integration and Local Power in Japan* (Aldershot: Ashgate, 1999), pp. 109–14.

25. Takao Yasuo, "The Welfare State and Its Effect on Municipal Government in Japan: A Case Study," *Modern Asian Studies* 32, no. 4 (October 1998): 985–1016.

26. See, for example, Terry Clark and Lorna Ferguson, *City Money: Political Processes, Fiscal Strain, and Retrenchment* (New York: Columbia University Press, 1983).

27. See, for example, Hugh Helco and Aaron Widavsky, *The Private Government of Public Money* (Berkeley and Los Angeles: University of California, 1974).

28. Hirose, *Hojokin to Seikento.*

29. Cited in Hirose, "Hojokin Sakugen no Tadashii Shuho to Ayamatta Shuho," p. 15.

30. *Sankei Shinbun,* January 8, 1996.

31. Muramastu Michio, "Hojokin Seido no Seiji Gyoseijo no Igi" (Political and Administrative Significance of the Grants-in-aid System), *Jichi Kenkyu* 57 (September 1981): 3–32.

32. In 2001, with the reorganization of the national bureaucracy, the Ministry of Internal Affairs and Communications (MIAC) was established by integrating the Ministry of Home Affairs with the Ministry of Posts and Telecommunications and the Management and Coordination Agency.

33. Japan, Local Decentralization Promotion Committee, Minutes of the Committee in the 50th Session (Hearings from Budget Bureau, Ministry of Finance), September 19, 1996.

34. Yokota Shozo, "Kyujuni-nendo Chiho Zaisei Keikaku no Naiyo to Mondaiten" (Contents and Problems of FY 1992 Local Fiscal Plan), *Chiho Seiji,* 386 (March 1992): 34–36; Yamaguchi Tetsuo, "Kyujusan-nendo Kokka Yosan no Bunseki to Mondaiten" (Analysis and Problems of FY 1993 National Budget), *Chiho Seiji* 400 (April 1993): 11–13.

35. *Mainichi Shinbun,* January 9, 1996; *Nihon Keizai Shinbun,* May 3, 1999.

36. Takahashi Makoto and Yorimoto Katsumi, "Chiho Kofuzei no Yakuwari to Kadai o Kiku" (Inquiries about the Role and Task of the Local Allocation Tax), *Gekkan Jichiken* 27 (1985): 28–37.

37. Endo Saburo, "Chiho Zaisei Kiki to Chiho Kofuzei" (Local Fiscal Crisis and the Local Allocation Tax), *Toshi Mondai* 75, no. 5 (May 1984): 18–34; Takahashi and Yorimoto, "Chiho Kofuzei no Yakuwari to Kadai o Kiku," p. 36.

38. Pierson, "The New Politics of the Welfare State," p. 177.

Chapter 3

1. The term *chien-ketsuen* refers to ties of both neighborhood and kinship. Within neighborhood-based or kinship-based groups, members feel secure through tightly knit activities but their security is often maintained at the expense of their individual autonomy. These ties tend to function externally to preclude their relationships with persons "outside" their community.

2. Robert Putnam, "Bowling Alone: America's Declining Social Capital," *Journal of Democracy* 6, no.1 (January 1995): 65–78.

3. Yamaoka Yoshinori, interview by the author at the NPO Center on June 26, 2000.

4. Interview with a volunteer worker for the organization LET'S, Kawasaki City, June 12, 2004.

5. Lester M. Salamon, "The Rise of the Nonprofit Sector," *Foreign Affairs* 73, no. 4 (July–August 1994): 109.

6. Helmut K. Anheier, and Wolfgang Seibel, eds. *The Third Sector: Comparative Studies of Nonprofit Organizations* (Berlin/New York: DeGruyter, 1990); Benjamin Gidron, Ralph M. Kramer, and Lester M. Salamon, eds. *Government and the Third Sector: Emerging Relationships in Welfare States* (San Francisco: Jossey-Bass, 1992); Estelle James, ed., *The Nonprofit Sector in International Perspective: Studies in Comparative Culture and Policy* (Oxford: Oxford University Press, 1989); Katheen D. McCarthy, Virginia Hodgkinson, and Russy Sumariwalla, *The Nonprofit Sector in the Global Community* (San Francisco: Jossey-Bass, 1992).

7. Paul J. DiMaggio, and Helmut K. Anheier, "The Sociology of Nonprofit Organizations and Sectors," *Annual Review of Sociology,* no. 16 (1990): 137–59.

8. See, for example, Marilyn Taylor, Joan Langan, and Paul Hoggett, *Encouraging Diversity: Voluntary and Private Organizations in Community Care* (Gower House, England: Arena, 1995).

9. Adopted from Yamamoto Tadashi, "Nihon no Shibiru Sosaete no Hatten to Gabanansu e no Eikyo" (Developments in Japan's Civil Society and Its Impact on Governance), in *Kan kara Min e no Pawa Shifuto* (Power Shifts from "Public" to "Private"), eds. Yamamoto Tadashi et al. (Tokyo: TBS Britannica, 1998), p. 135. See, for example, feature articles, "Afurero Minryoku" (Overflow, Civil Power!), *Asahi Shinbun,* January 1–9, 1999.

10. Tsujinaka Yutaka, "NPO/NGO no Jidai to Chikyu Nettowaku Gata Seiji Katei no Tojo" (The Emergence of Global Network-Oriented Political Processes in the Era of NPOs and NGOs), *NIRA Policy Research* 12, no. 3 (March 1999): 42. For public benefit organizations, see Japan, Prime Minister's Office (PMO), ed., *Koeki Hojin Hakusho: Koeki Hojin ni kansuru Nenji Hokoku* (White Paper on Public Benefit Organizations: Annual Report on Nonprofit Organizations) (Tokyo: Okurasho Insatsukyoku, 1999). For citizens' voluntary organizations, see Japan, Economic Planning Agency (EPA), ed., *Shimin Katsudo Repoto: Shimin Katsudo Dantai Kihon Chosa Hokoku* (Report on Citizens' Activities: Basic Research Report on Citizens' Action Groups) (Tokyo: Okurasho Insatsukyoku, 1997).

11. Japan, Economic Planning Agency (EPA), ed., *Open the NPO: Kokateki na Joho Hasshin no tame ni* (Open the NPO: For Effective Information Disclosure) (Tokyo: Okurasho Insatsukyoku, 1998), p. 84.

12. Japan, PMO, *Koeki Hojin Hakusho,* pp. 145, 575–76.

13. See Japan, Economic Planning Agency (EPA), ed., *Nihon no NPO Keizai Kibo: Minkan Hieiri Katsudo Dantai ni kansuru Keizai Bunseki Chosa Hokoku* (The Economic Scale of NPOs in Japan: Economic Analysis Report on Private Nonprofit Activity Organizations) (Tokyo: Okurasho Insatsukyoku, 1998), pp. 2–4, 25.

14. Lester M. Salamon, and Helmut K. Anheier, *The Emerging Nonprofit Sector: An Overview,* (Manchester, UK: Manchester University Press, 1996): 38–44. The project's data showed that the United States has the largest nonprofit sector, employing an exceptionally high of 6.9 percent of total employment, and an operational spending that is again a high of 6.3 percent of GDP.

15. Figures from Japan, Economic Planning Agency (EPA), *Kokumin Keizai Keisan Nenpo* (Annual Report on National Economic Statistics), 1979 and 1999 eds. (Tokyo: EPA, 1979 and 1999). In these reports, the production output is calculated as "nonprofit institution serving household."

16. Figures from Japan, Ministry of Health, Labor and Welfare (former Ministry of Labor), *Rodo Kumiai Kiso Chosa Hokoku* (Basic Investigation Report on Labor Unions), annuals, 1998 and 2005 (Tokyo: MHLW); Japan, Ministry of Education, Culture, Sports, Science and Technology (former Ministry of Education), *Gakko Kihon Chosa Hokokusho* (Fundamental Investigation Report on Schools), annuals, 1997 and 2005 (Tokyo: MECSST); Japan, Agency for Cultural Affairs, *Shukyo Nenkan* (Annual of Religion), 1999 and 2004 (Tokyo: ACA).

17. Japan, EPA, *Shimin Katsudo Repoto,* p. 6.

18. Ibid., pp. 3–5.

19. See Tsujinaka, "NPO/NGO no Jidai to Chikyu Nettowaku Gata Seiji Katei no Tojo," pp. 39–42, for data on global NGOs. For data on environmental associations, see Japan

Environment Association, *Kankyo NGO Soran* (Environmental NGO Survey) (2004), http://www.erca.go.jp (accessed June 2005).

20. See, for example, Norman Uphoff, "Why NGOs Are Not a Third Sector: A Sectoral Analysis with Some Thoughts on Accountability, Sustainability and Evaluation," in *Beyond the Magic Bullet: NGO Performance and Accountability in the Post-Cold War World*, eds Michael Edwards and David Hume (West Hartford, CT: Kumarian Press, 1996), pp. 23–39.

21. Calculated from materials provided by Japan, PMO, *Koeki Hojin Hakusho;* Japan, Ministry of Internal Affairs and Communications (MIAC), *Koeki Hojin ni kansuru Nenji Hokoku* (2004), http://www.soumu.go.jp/daijinkanbou/kanri/h16koueki/mokuji.html (accessed June 2005).

22. Japan, MIAC, *Koeki Hojin ni kansuru Nenji Hokoku.*

23. See, for example, Shizen Hogo Nenkan Henshuiinkai, ed., *Shizen Hogo Nenkan* (Natural Environment Protection Yearbook), 1992 and 1996 (Tokyo: Nishosha, 1992 and 1996); Fukushimaken Shizen Hogo Kyokai, ed., *Oze: Shizen Hogo Undo no Genten* (Oze: The Origin of Nature Protection Movements) (Tokyo: Tokyo Shinbun Shuppankyoku, 1993).

24. Japan, EPA, *Shimin Katsudo Repoto,* p. 6; Kansai Sogo Kenkyujo, ed., *1996 NIRA Research Report: Chiiki Fukushi ni okeru NPO Shien Ikusei Hosaku no Teigen* (Proposals for the Ways to Support and Promote Local Welfare NGOs) (Tokyo: National Institute for Research Advancement, 1996).

25. Japan, EPA, ed., *Shimin Katsudo Repoto,* p. 45.

26. Oshima Taro, *Nihon Chiho Gyozaisei Shi Josetsu* (Introduction to the History of Local Administration and Finance in Japan) (Tokyo: Miraisha, 1968), pp. 10, 302, 306, 328; Oshima Mitsuko, *Meiji no Mura* (Villages in Meiji Japan) (Tokyo: Kyoiku Sha, 1977), pp. 170–84.

27. Kato Koichi, speech delivered to the Committee on the Budget, House of Representatives, January 27, 1995.

28. Okawara Yoshio, "The Future of International Exchange and Cooperation," keynote address delivered at the Local Government International Exchange Seminar, Tokyo, November 1996.

29. Yamamoto, "Nihon no Shibiru Sosaete no Hatten to Gabanansu e no Eikyo," pp. 127–29, 150; Murata Tetsuo, "Kankyo Mondai to NGO/NPO no Yakuwari" (Environmental Problems and the Role of NGO and NPO), *Toshi Mondai* 88, no. 4 (April 1997), p. 64.

30. Japan, MIAC, *Koeki Hojin ni kansuru Nenji Hokoku.*

31. Ibid.

32. Ibid.

33. Inoguchi Takashi, "Japanese Bureaucracy: Coping with New Challenges," in *Japanese Politics Today: Beyond Karaoke Democracy?* eds. Purnendra Jain and Inoguchi Takashi (South Melbourne: Macmillan, 1997), pp. 92–107.

34. *Mainichi Shinbun,* January 23, 1997.

35. Hatoyama Yukio, "Minshuto to Watashi no Seiken Koso" (The Democratic Party and My Political Views), *Bungei Shunjyu* (November 1996): 122; Sumizawa Hiroki, "Minshushugi no Yukue" (Pathways to Democracy), *NIRA Policy Research* 11, no. 9 (September 1998): 10–15.

36. From August 3–18, 1999, C's conducted a survey of prefectural officials in charge of NPO applications from all 47 prefectures.

37. *Mainich Shinbun,* February 4, 1999.

38. Japan, EPA, *Shimin Katsudo Repoto*, p. 8; Japan, Cabinet Office, "Jittai Chosa Hokokusho" (Investigation Reports) (2001), http://www.npo-homepage.go.jp/index.html (accessed December 2006).
39. Yamauchi Naoto, ed., *Nonprofit Organization Data Book* (Tokyo: Yuhikaku, 1999), p. 68.
40. Japan NGO Center for International Cooperation (JANIC), ed., *Data Book on Japanese NGOs '98* (Tokyo: JANIC, 1998), p. 43.
41. *Civil Society Monitor* 6 (July 2001): 3.
42. *Civil Society Monitor* 8 (December 2003): 2.
43. In June 1999, C's, Japan NPO Center, and the organization Sawayaka Fukushi conducted a joint survey called "Hojin Shinsei Dantai Ankeito" (Survey on Applicant Groups for Authorization). It was sent to all 669 NPO applicants of whom 402 responded.
44. Materials provided by Japan, EPA.
45. The June 1999 Survey conducted by C's et al.
46. The data in this paragraph were compiled from the June 1999 Survey conducted by C's et al.; Japan, EPA, *Shimin Katsudo Repoto*, p. 10; a 1996 survey of 1,507 voluntary organizations conducted by Policy Information Investigation Department, Tokyo Metropolitan Government.
47. See, for example, Kansai Sogo Kenkyujo, *1996 NIRA Research Report*.
48. See, for example, Edwards and Hume, *Beyond the Magic Bullet*.
49. Japan, EPA, *Open the NPO*, pp. 16, 24, 34–35, and 91.
50. Japan, Economic Planning Agency (EPA), "Kojin kara Mita Shimin Katsudo ni Kansuru Chosa" (Survey on Citizens' Activities in the Eyes of Private Individuals) (1998), http://www.epa.go.jp/98/c/19980707c-kojin.html (accessed January 2001).

Chapter 4

1. Nisho Masaru, *Mikan no Bunken Kaikaku: Kasumigasei Kanryo to Kakutoshita Sensanbyaku-nichi* (Incomplete Decentralization Reforms: 1300 days Dealing with Kasumigasei Bureaucrats) (Tokyo: Iwanami Shoten, 1999), p. 3.
2. In post-WWII Japan, local government responsibilities increased by way of functional delegation, not by decision-making delegation. The number of functions assigned by the national government to each prefecture climbed from 128 in 1952 to a peak of 328 in 1975. Those assigned to municipalities also rose from 74 in 1952 to 139 in 1975. By 1999, when the law was passed in the National Diet, prefectural governments spent about 80 percent of their time on the agency-assigned functions; and municipal governments over 50 percent. See Takao Yasuo, *National Integration and Local Power in Japan* (Aldershot, UK: Ashgate, 1999), p. 73.
3. In the 1990s, Japanese local governments collectively spent three-quarters of all tax revenue collected by both central and local governments. The unusual position of Japanese local governments largely resulted from the massive agency-assigned functions. Nonetheless, the national government collected over 60 percent of the total tax revenue and spent less than 30 percent, transferring the remainder to local government. See Takao, *National Integration and Local Power in Japan,* pp. 225–26.
4. *Sankei Shinbun,* January 8, 1996, carried a report on the survey of 1,905 chief executives (57.7 percent of all local chief executives) in Japan. The same survey found further inconsistencies at the two territorial levels of local government. Nearly 70 percent of the prefectural governors surveyed responded that the two-layer system

should be maintained without a territorial reorganization, while more than 70 percent of municipal mayors called for various forms of reorganization.

5. See Amakawa Akira, "Henkaku no Koso: Doshu Seiron no Bunmyaku" (Reformation Ideas: The Context of *Doshu* Debates), in *Nihon no Chiho Seifu* (Local Government in Japan), eds. Omori Wataru and Sato Seizaburo (Tokyo: Tokyo Daigaku Shuppankai, 1986), pp. 118–31.

6. Ozawa Ichiro, *Blueprint for a New Japan: The Rethinking of a Nation* (Tokyo: Kodansha International, 1994), pp. 76–82.

7. *Asahi Shinbun,* December 21, 1996.

8. *Sankei Shinbun,* March 30, 1996.

9. *Mainichi Shinbun,* April 22, 1996.

10. Japan, Diet, House of Councilors, Minutes of Committee on Local Administration, December 9, 1997. The committee also proposed that only 11 agency-assigned tasks should be abolished without replacement and 21 agency-assigned tasks should be carried out directly by the national government.

11. *Mainichi Shinbun,* March 9, 1982.

12. Japan, Ministry of Internal Affairs and Communications (MIAC), *Hodo Shiryo* (News Releases), August 27, 2004.

13. For the infected blood products scandal, the *jusen* bailout, and the nuclear cover-up, see Inoguchi Takashi, "Japanese Bureaucracy: Coping with New Challenges," in *Japanese Politics Today: Beyond Karaoke Democracy?* eds. Purnendra Jain and Inoguchi Takashi (South Melbourne: Macmillan, 1997), pp. 92–107.

14. Japan, Diet, House of Representatives, Minutes of the Committee on the Cabinet, April 13, 1982; and Japan, Diet, House of Representatives, Minutes of the Committee on the Audit, April 23, 1982.

15. Nishio Masaru et al., "Joho Kokai o Meguru Shomondai" (Some Problems of Information Disclosure), *Chiho Jichi,* no. 413 (April 1982): 37.

16. Aoyama Nizo, "Kawasaki-shi Joho Kokai Jorei no Shikkogo no Mondaiten" (Post-enforcement Problems of Kawasaki City's Information Disclosure Ordinance), *Chiho Seiji,* no. 357 (December 1989): 16.

17. Adapted from data provided by MOHA.

18. Cited in *Sankei Shinbun,* December 17, 1995.

19. Ibid.

20. *Sankei Shinbun,* January 8, 1996.

21. Ibid., December 17, 1995.

22. Interview with Kato Tomiko, *Sankei Shinbun,* January 21, 1996.

23. See, for example, *Sankei Shinbun,* January 28, 1996; *Asahi Shinbun,* May 26, 1996; and *Yomiuri Shinbun,* April 9, 1996.

24. Materials provided at the Council for Decentralization Reform (former Committee for the Promotion of Decentralization), February 4, 2004.

25. Ibid. Ordinances regarding information disclosure, personal information protection, quorum, assembly members' remuneration, and local elections are excluded in the figures.

26. Materials provided at the Council for Decentralization Reform (former Committee for the Promotion of Decentralization), February 4, 2004.

27. The survey on the background of auditors conducted by House of Councilors' Third Special Inquiry went to all 47 prefectures. Figures from two prefectures are not available.

28. *Mainichi Shinbun,* April 17, 1996, and *Asahi Shinbun,* April 26, 1996.

29. *Sankei Shinbun,* February 18, 1996.

30. Japan, MOHA, *Gyosei Jitsurei* (Administrative Practical Examples), January 26, 1949. This old directive was still seen as the authoritative interpretation by auditors. See *Sankei Shinbun,* February 18, 1996.

31. Cited in Japan, Diet, House of Councilors, Third Special Inquiry Section, ed., *Onbuzuman Seido Kankei Shiryoshu III* (Materials on Ombuds Systems III) (Tokyo: Third Special Inquiry Section, 1995), p. 6.

32. Cited in Japan, Diet, House of Councilors, Third Special Inquiry Section, ed., *Onbuzuman Seido Kankei Shiryoshu I* (Materials on Ombuds Systems I) (Tokyo: Third Special Inquiry Section, 1995), p. 157.

33. *Sankei Shinbun,* February 25, 1996.

34. Chino Torao, "Onbuzuman Seido ni tsuite no Ikkosatsu" (Some Considerations of Ombuds Systems), *Chiho Jichi,* no. 411 (February 1982): 2–8.

35. Kikuchi Hidefumi, "Kawasaki-shi Shimin Onbuzuman Seido no Jissai" (The Kawasaki City Ombuds System in Practice), *Toyo Hogaku* 39, no. 1 (September 1995): 171–75.

36. Kikuchi, "Kawasaki-shi Shimin Onbuzuman Seido no Jissai," pp. 174–75.

37. Third Special Inquiry Section, ed., *Onbuzuman Seido Kankei Shiryoshu I,* pp. 143–235.

38. Japan, Diet, House of Councilors, Minutes of Committee on the Budget, June 3, 1994.

39. Japan, Prime Minister's Office, Local System Investigation Council, *Report on Measures Promoting the Consciousness of Residents for Local Autonomy* (Tokyo: Local System Investigation Council, 1976).

40. Study Group for Long-Term Strategies on the Vitalization of Local Administration, *Local Autonomy in the Twenty-First Century* (Tokyo: Study Group for Long-Term Strategies on the Vitalization of Local Administration, 1987).

41. See "Jumin Tohyo: Tokushu" (Local Referenda: Special Issue), *Toshi Mondai* 87, no.1 (January 1996); and cf. Kurt Steiner, *Local Government in Japan* (Stanford: Stanford University Press, 1965), pp. 451–66.

42. Cited in Yorimoto Katsumi "Jichitai no Ishiki Keisei to Jumin Tohyo" (The Formation of Local Entities' Intention and Referendum), *Gekkan Jichiken* 36, no. 416 (May 1994): 31–32.

43. *Niigata Nippo,* July 29, 1996.

44. Ibid., August 5, 1996.

45. Ibid., August 8, 1996.

46. Ibid., November 22, 1996.

47. See Shiohira Yoshikazu, "Okinawa, Kenmin Tohyo, Sonogo" (Okinawa, the Prefectural Referendum, and thereafter), *Toshi Mondai* 88, no. 2 (February 1997): 67–78.

48. *Yomiuri Shinbun,* June 21, 1996.

49. Japan, Ministry of Internal Affairs and Communications (MIAC), *Hodo Shiryo,* April 14, 2005. The law was designed to create larger municipalities so that more decision making and financial power could be transferred to the local level. Accordingly, the number of municipalities in Japan declined from 3,232 in 1999 to 2,521 in 2005.

50. See, for example, Takeda Shin'ichiro, "Jumin Tohyo o Meguru Hoteki Mondai" (Legal Problems Surrounding the Local Referendum), *Horitsu no Hiroba* 46, no. 6 (June 1993): 29.

Chapter 5

1. Personal communication with Norman Nakamura, former chairperson of the Kawasaki City Representative Assembly for Foreign Residents, July 12, 2004.

2. Personal communication with Yamada Takao, municipal government official of Kawasaki, July 15, 2004.

3. Nippon Research Center, *The Asia-Europe Survey of 2000* (Tokyo: Nippon Research Center, 2000); Edelman, *Edelman Trust Barometer: The Seventh Global Opinion Leaders Study*, January 2006.

4. Japan, Ministry of Internal Affairs and Communications (MIAC), *White Paper on Local Public Finance* (2003)http://www.soumu.go.jp/english/whitepaper/index.html (accessed May 2006).

5. Robert Putnam, *Making Democracy Work: Civic Traditions in Modern Italy* (Princeton: Princeton University Press, 1993).

6. Putnam, *Making Democracy Work*, p. 36. Also see Kawachi Ichiro, Bruce Kennedy, and Roberta Glass, "Social Capital and Self-Rated Health: A Contextual Analysis," *American Journal of Public Health* 89, no. 8 (August 1999): 1187–93; Stephen Aldridge, David Halpern, and Sarah Fitzpatrick, *Social Capital: A Discussion Paper* (London: Performance and Innovation Unit, 2002).

7. Putnam, *Making Democracy Work*; Francis Fukuyama, *Trust: The Social Virtues and the Creation of Prosperity* (London: Hamish Hamilton, 1995).

8. Jonathan Fox, "The Difficult Transition from Clientelism to Citizenship: Lessons from Mexico," *World Politics* 46, no. 2 (January 1994): 151–84; David Brown and Darcy Ashman, "Participation, Social Capital, and Intersectoral Problem Solving: African and Asian Cases," *World Development* 24, no. 9 (September 1996): 1467–79; Vivien Lowndes, Gerry Stoker, Lawrence Pratchett, Steve Leach, and Melvin Wingfield, *Enhancing Public Participation in Local Government*, (London: Department of the Environment, 1998).

9. Peter Hall, "Social Capital in Britain," *British Journal of Political Science* 29, no. 3 (June 1999): 417–61; Peter Hall "Great Britain: The Role of Government and the Distribution of Social Capital," in *Democracies in Flux: The Evolution of Social Capital in Contemporary Society*, ed. Robert Putnam (New York: Oxford University Press, 2002), pp. 21–57.

10. Kim Kiseong, "Social Capital and the Role of Local Government: A Virtuous Cycle between Institution and Culture," *Journal of Public Policy Studies* 5 (2005): 130–40.

11. Lindon Robinson, Allan Schmid, and Marcelo Siles, "Is Social Capital Really Capital?" *Review of Social Economy* 60, no.1 (March 2002): 1–24.

12. Michael Woolcock, "Social Capital and Economic Development: Towards a Theoretical Synthesis and Policy Framework," *Theory and Society* 27 (1998): 153; Paul Dekker and Eric Uslaner, "Introduction," in *Social Capital and Participation in Everyday Life*, ed. Eric Uslaner (London: Routledge, 2001), pp. 1–8.

13. Robert Putnam, *Bowling Alone: The Collapse and Revival of American Community* (New York: Simon & Schuster, 2000), pp. 22–23.

14. Dekker and Uslaner, "Introduction," pp. 1–8.

15. Pierre Bourdieu, "The Forms of Capital," in *Handbook of Theory and Research for the Sociology of Education*, ed. John Richardson (New York: Greenwood Press, 1986), pp. 241–58; Paul Adler and Seok-Woo Kwon, "Social Capital: Prospects for a New Concept," *Academy of Management Review* 27, no. 1 (January–February 2002): 17–40;

John Gant, Casey Ichniowski, and Kathryn Shaw, "Social Capital and Organizational Change in High-Involvement and Traditional Work Organizations," *Journal of Economics and Management Strategy* 11, no. 2 (Summer 2002): 289–328.

16. Carles Boix and Daniel Posner, "Social Capital: Explaining its Origins and Effects on Government Performance," *British Journal of Political Science* 28, no. 4 (October 1998): 688.

17. The proposed fiscal decentralization measures included: elimination or reduction of national subsidies, review of the Local Allocation Tax (block grants to local governments) and transfer of tax revenue resources to local governments.

18. See, for example, Nikkei Human Resources, *Nikkei Navi* (2006), http://job.nikkei.co.jp (accessed June 2006).

19. Figures are calculated from Japan, Ministry of Internal Affairs and Communications (MIAC), *Chiho Zaisei Hakusho* (White Paper on Local Government Finance), 2000 ed (Tokyo: Okurasho Insatsukyoku); Organisation for Economic Co-operation and Development (OECD), *National Accounts 1989–2000* and *Revenue Statistics 1965–2000* (Paris: OECD). Transfer payments from national to subnational government are excluded from national government expenditures.

20. In August 2001 NTT Data conducted this survey on 1,000 people aged 20 and over who resided in ten cities in the capital region, and collected 755 usable responses. See NTT Data, "Denshi Seifu to Minshushugi ni kansuru Shutoken Shimin Chosa" (Investigation Report on Citizens in the Capital Region for e-Government and Democracy), December 2001, p. 11.

21. Figures from OECD, *Economic Outlook,* vol. 78, December 2005.

22. Material provided by Japan, MIAC. In these figures, government employment consists of military employees, local government employees, national government employees, and public enterprise employees.

23. Figures from OECD, *Economic Outlook,* vol. 78.

24. Figures provided by Japan, MIAC, Local Public Finance Bureau.

25. Ibid.

26. Japan, MIAC, *Chiho Bunken* (Local Decentralization) (2006), http://www.soumu.go.jp/indexb4.html (accessed June 2006).

27. Japan, Prime Minister of Japan and His Cabinet, *Sanmi Ittai Kaikau nit tsuite* (Regarding the Trinity Reform) (November 30, 2005), http://www.kantei.go.jp/jp/singi/kunitotihon/dai14/14gijisidai.html (accessed June 2006).

28. Muramatsu Michio, *Nihon no Gyosei: Katsudogata Kanryosei no Henbo* (Japanese Public Administration: Changes in Patterns of Active Bureaucracy) (Tokyo: Chuokoron, 1994); Muramatsu Michio, *Gendai Gyosei no Seiji Bunseki* (Political Analysis of Contemporary Public Administration) (Tokyo, Yuhikaku, 1999).

29. For the relevant argument, see World Bank, *World Bank Development Report 1997: The State in a Changing World* (Oxford: Oxford University Press, 1997).

30. Peter Saunders, *Social Theory and the Urban Questions,* 2nd ed. (New York: Homes & Meier, 1986), p. 265; Stephen Bailey, *Local Government Economics: Principles and Practice* (Basingstoke: Macmillan, 1999), p. 262.

31. Jan van Ours, "An International Comparative Study on Job Mobility," *Labour* 4, no. 3 (1990): 33–55; Masahiro Abe et al., "Worker Displacement in Japan and Canada," in *Losing Work, Moving on: Work Displacement in International Perspective,* ed. Peter Kuhn (Kalamazoo, MI: W. E. Upjohn Institute for Employment Research, 2002), pp. 195–300.

32. *Nihon Keizai Shinbun,* January 28, 2002.

33. Material provided by Japan, MIAC.

34. In Britain, it is not a common practice for local authorities to improve public infrastructure by issuing bonds, which must be approved by the national government. Above all, local government's activities are clearly specified under the doctrine of *ultra vires*. Probably, PFI approaches are one of the ways to ease the statutory rigidity for the efficient delivery of services.

35. Japan, Prime Minister and His Cabinet, *Major Policy Reports* (2006), http://www.kantei.go.jp/foreign/policyindex_e.html (accessed January 2006).

36. In February 2004, the Cabinet Office conducted a nationwide survey on 3,246 local governments.

37. Japan, Cabinet Office, PFI Promotion Office, *PFI Promotion Committee* (2006), http://www8.cao.go.jp/pfi/shiryo_a_12.html (accessed June 2006).

38. Data presented at the PFI Promotion Committee, December 11, 2003.

39. Muto Hiromi, *Jichitai Keiei Kaikau* (Local Public Management Reforms) (Tokyo: Gyosei, 2004), p. 240.

40. See, for example, Japan, Cabinet Office, PFI Promotion Office, *Guidelines* (2001), http://www8.cao.go.jp/pfi/guideline.html (accessed June 2006).

41. See, for example, Christopher Pollitt, *Managerialism and the Public Services: Cuts or Cultural Change in the 1990s?* (Oxford: Blackwell, 1993); Owen Hughes, *Public Management and Administration: An Introduction* (South Melbourne: Macmillan Education, 1998); Owen Hughes and Deirdre O'Neill, *Public Management Reform: Some Lessons from the Antipodes* (Caulfield East, Victoria, Australia: Monash University, 2000); Brendan Nolan, ed., *Public Sector Reform: An International Perspective* (Armidal: Palgrave Macmillan, 2001).

42. Takao Yasuo, "Democratic Renewal by 'Digital' Local Government in Japan," *Pacific Affairs* 77, no. 2 (Summer 2004): 255–56.

43. Kitagawa Yoichi, "Chiho Bunken ga Motarasu Gyosei no Manejimentoka to Patonashippuka" (Managerialism and Partnership Trends of Administration Driven by Local Decentralization), in *Hokatsuteki Chiho Jichi Gabanansu Kaikau* (Comprehensive Reform of Local Governance), eds. Muramatsu Michio and Inatsugu Hiroaki (Tokyo: Toyo Keizai Shinposha, 2003), pp. 217–28. The measurement indexes were based on key words, such as managerialism-oriented "outsourcing" and "PFI," and partnership-oriented "partnership" and "cooperation." To identify patterns of local government reform, the measurement was carried out by the frequency or density of those key words, which were collected from a government-run search engine, the *Chiiki Hakken* (Regional Discovery), with 567 municipalities registered at the time of data collection in September 2000.

44. Kitagawa, "Chiho Bunken ga Motarasu Gyosei no Manejimentoka to Patonashippuka," pp. 221–23.

45. Japan, Ministry of Health, Labor and Welfare (MHLW), *Zenkoku Shakai Fukushi Kyogikai no Chosa* (National Social Welfare Council Survey), 2002, p. 449.

46. Ikeda Ken'ichi, "Nisen-nen Shugiin Senkyo ni okeru Shakai Shihon to Komunikeshon" (Social Capital and Communication in the 2000 Lower House Election), *Japanese Journal of Electoral Studies* 17 (2002): 5–18; Hirano Hiroshi, "Shakai Shihon to Seijisanka" (Social Capital and Political Participation), *Japanese Journal of Electoral Studies* 17 (2002): 19–21; Ra Ilkyung, "Nihon ni okeru Soshiarukyapitaru to Jyumin Ishiki" (Social Capital and Residents' Consciousness in Japan), in *Chiho Jichitai ni okeru Shimin Ishiki no Dotai* (Dynamics of Citizens' Consciousness in Local Governments), ed. Kobayashi Yoshiaki (Tokyo: Keio

University Press, 2005), pp. 107–31; Ikeda Ken'ichi, "Seijiteki Hiseijiteki Nettowaku wa Shakaikankei Shihon o Umi Seiji no Riariti o Kiteisuruka" (The Creation of Social Capital and Political Reality from Political and Non-political Social Networks), *JGSS Kenkyu Ronbunshu* (JGSS Research Articles Collection), vol. 4 (March 2005), pp. 169–203.

47. Ra, "Nihon ni okeru Soshiarukyapitaru to Jyumin Ishiki," pp. 119–26. Also see Japan, Cabinet Office, *Soshiaru Kyapitaru: Yutakana Ningen Kankei to Shimin Katsudo no Kojunkan o Motomete* (Social Capital: Search for Positive Feedback from Rich Human Relationships to Citizens' Activities) (Tokyo: Quality-of-Life Policy Bureau, Cabinet Office, 2003), p. 5.

48. Ikeda, "Nisen-nen Shugiin Senkyo ni okeru Shakai Shihon to Komunikeshon," p. 15.

49. Japan, Economic Planning Agency (EPA), ed. *Shimin Katsudo Repoto: Shimin Katsudo Dantai Kihon Chosa Hokoku* (Report on Citizens' Activities: Basic Research Report on Citizens' Action Groups) (Tokyo: Okurasho Insatsukyoku, 1997).

50. In 2001 the national government began to allow eligible NPOs to receive tax-deductible donations, but the requirements to qualify for tax-deducible status were so strict that only 10 of the 9,000 NPO Legal Persons had met the criteria. In 2003 these requirements were loosened, but the changes were minor (only 24 of the 16,000 NPO Legal Persons qualified for the status). See *Civil Society Monitor* 6 (July 2001): 3 and *Civil Society Monitor* 8 (December 2003): 2.

51. Kobayashi Hiroshi (Planning Department, Mitaka City), "Mitaka-shi ni okeru Patonashippu ni yoru Tenkai to Kongo no Hoko" (Developments and Future Directions of Partnership in Mitaka City), *Chiiki Seisaku Kenkyu* 25 (December 2003): 48–49.

52. Kiyohara Keiko, *Mitaka ga Tsukuru Jichitai Shinjidai* (A New Age of Local Government that Mitaka Creates) (Mitaka: Mitaka City, 2000).

53. *Nihon Keizai Shinbun,* September 6, 1998.

54. Kobayashi, "Mitaka-shi ni okeru Patonashippu ni yoru Tenkai to Kongo no Hoko," p. 52.

55. Interview with Ozaki Seiichi, Planning Department, Shiki City, cited in "Gyosei Patona Seido" (Administrative Partnership), *Chiiki Seisaku Kenkyu* 25 (December 2003): 53.

56. Ibid.

57. Ibid.

58. Boix and Posner, "Social Capital," p. 690.

59. This survey was based on two sources: 2,000 respondents on Web and 1,878 respondents via mailing. The first data were collected in January/February 2003, and the second in February/May 2003. See Japan, Cabinet Office, *Soshiaru Kyapitaru: Yutakana Ningen Kankei to Shimin Katsudo no Kojunkan o Motomete,* pp. 38–39.

60. Hasegawa Koichi, *Kankyo Mondai to Atarashii Kokyoken* (Environmental Problems and a New Public Sphere) (Tokyo: Yuhikaku, 2003); Bernd Kasemire et al., eds. *Public Participation in Sustainable Science: A Handbook* (Cambridge: Cambridge University Press, 2003).

61. Mifune Tsuyoshi, "Nihon ni okeru Shakai Sanka to Jumin Ishiki" (Social Participation in Japan and Residents' Consciousness) in *Chiho Jichitai ni okeru Shimin Ishiki no Dotai* (Dynamics of Citizens' Consciousness in Local Governments), ed. Kobayashi Yoshiaki (Tokyo: Keio University Press, 2005), pp. 71–106.

62. From November 2002 to January 2003, Mifune Tsuyoshi conducted an Aichi prefecture-wide survey on 491 local residents. Mifune, "Nihon ni okeru Shakai Sanka to Jumin Ishiki," pp. 81–82.

63. The NTT Data administered a questionnaire to 3,000 people, aged 20 and over across the nation, and collected 2,036 usable responses. *NTT Data News Releases,* "eDemokurashi ni kansuru Zenkoku Kojin Ankeito" (National Survey of Individuals concerning e-Democracy), April 10, 2002.

64. In 1978 the Center conducted a survey on the perception of local government officials in planning departments of seven municipalities such as Narashino, Musashino, Fuchu, Sagamihara, and Kobe.

65. Matsushita Keiichi, *Jichitai no NPO Seisaku* (Local Government NPO Policy) (Tokyo: Gyosei, 1998), pp. 87–88.

66. Putnam suggests that citizen-initiated contacts with public officials in the more trusting, more civic communities tend to involve larger issues with implications for the welfare of the community as a whole, rather than issues of narrowly personal concerns. See Putnam, *Making Democracy Work,* chs. 2 and 4.

67. Japan, Cabinet Office, *Soshiaru Kyapitaru: Yutakana Ningen Kankei to Shimin Katsudo no Kojunkan o Motomete,* p. 47.

68. Ibid., p. 53.

69. Ibid., p. 52.

70. This section is based on Tokyo Bureau of Citizens and Cultural Affairs, *Tokyo-to no Jiho Kokai* (Information Disclosure by Tokyo Metropolitan Government), 2004 ed; Osaka Public Relations Office, *Osaka-fu no Joho Kokai* (Information Disclosure by Osaka Prefectural Government), various years; Kanagawa Prefectural Residents Bureau, *Joho Kokai Seido Unyo Jokyo* (Implementation of the Information Disclosure System), various years; Hyogo Planning and Management Department, *Hyogo-ken no Jiho Kokai/Kojin Joho Hogo* (Information Disclosure and Personal Information Protection by Hyogo Prefectural Government), 2004 ed.

71. *JILG: Information Service* 51 (May 2005): 4.

72. Ibid., p. 3.

73. Japan, MIAC, Local Administration Bureau, *Gappei Dejitaru Akaibu* (Merger Digital Archive) (2006), http://www.soumu.go.jp/gapei/index.html (accessed June 2006).

74. Horii Ken'ichi, "Jumin Tohyo Joreian no Doki ni Kansuru Kenkyu: Kantoken ni okeru Gikai Gijiroku no Bunseiki ni yoru" (Studies on the Motives of Proposals for Local Referendum Ordinances: Analysis of Minutes of Assembly Meetings in the Kanto Region) (postgraduate thesis, Department of Social Engineering, Tokyo Institute of Technology, 2005).

75. Putnam, *Making Democracy Work,* pp. 20–22.

76. Japan, Cabinet *Office, Soshiaru Kyapitaru: Yutakana Ningen Kankei to Shimin Katsudo no Kojunkan o Motomete,* p. 74.

77. Nihei Norihiro, "Borantia towa Dareka: Sanka ni kansuru Shimin Shakairon-teki Zentei Saikento" (Who Are Volunteers? Re-examination of the Theoretical Premise of Civil Society Regarding Participation) *Soshioroji* 48, no. 1 (May 2003): 102.

78. Data used in this finding is based on Tanioka Ichiro, et al., *Japanese General Social Survey (JGSS), 2000 and 2001* [Computer file] (Osaka: Osaka University of Commerce, Office of Japanese General Social Surveys, 2002 and 2003).

79. Takao Yasuo, "Welfare State Retrenchment: The Case of Japan," *Journal of Public Policy* 19, no. 3 (September–December 1999): 265–92.

Chapter 6

1. Local resident in Yamato City of Kanagawa prefecture, personal conversation with the author on December 7, 2002.

2. Japan, Ministry of Internal Affairs and Communications (MIAC), *Information and Communications in Japan: Building a New Japan-Inspired IT Society* (2003 White Paper), http://www.soumu.go.jp/english/whitepaper/index.html (accessed July 2, 2003).

3. W. B. H. J. van de Donk et al., "Digitalizing Decision Making in a Democracy: For the Better or for the Worse," in *Orwell in Athens: A Perspective on Information and Democracy*, eds. W. B. H. J. van de Donk, I. Th. M. Shellen, and P. W. Tops (Amsterdam: IOS Press, 1995); Graeme Browning, *Electronic Democracy: Using the Internet to Transform American Politics* (Wilton, CT: Pemberton Press, 1996); Andrew Korac-Kakabadse and Nada Korac-Kakabadse, "Information Technology's Impact on the Quality of Democracy," in *Reinventing Government in the Information Age*, ed. Richard Heeks (London: Routledge, 1999); Richard Moore, "Democracy and Cyberspace," in *Digital Democracy: Discourse and Decision Making in the Information Age*, eds., Barry Hague and Brian Loader (London: Routledge, 1999).

4. Peter deLeon, "Reinventing the Policy Science: Three Steps Back to the Future," *Policy Sciences* 27, no. 1 (March 1994): 77–95; Michael R. Ogden, "Politics in Parallel Universe: Is There a Future for Cyber-Democracy?" *Futures* 26, no. 7 (September 1994): 713–29; European Commission, High Level Expert Group of the Information Society, *Building the European Information Society for Us All: First Reflections of the High Level Group of Experts*, Interim Report, European Commission, Brussels, January 1996, pp. 77–78.

5. Garry Rodan, "The Internet and Political Control in Singapore," *Political Science Quarterly* 113, no. 1 (Spring 1998): 63–89; Wing Man Shea, "Electronic Government: Government Utilisation of Internet Technologies in Hong Kong and Singapore" (master's dissertation, August 2000, London School of Economics and Political Science); Shanthi Kalathil, "Dot.com for Dictators," *Foreign Policy*, no. 135 (March–April 2003): 42–49.

6. Donna L. Hoffman, Thomas P. Novak, and Ann E. Schlosser, "The Evolution of the Digital Divide," in *The Digital Divide: Facing a Crisis or Creating a Myth?* ed. Benjamin M. Compaine (Cambridge, MA: MIT Press, 2001); J. W. McConnaughey, W. Lader, R. Chin, and D. Everette, *Falling through the Net II: New Data on the Digital Divide* (Washington, D.C.: NTIA, Department of Commerce, 2002); Organisation for Economic Co-operation and Development (OECD), *Understanding the Digital Divide* (2001), http://www.oecd.org/dataoecd/38/57/1888451.pdf (accessed July 2003).

7. United States, General Services Administration, *US Government's Official Web Portal* (2000), http://www.first.gov/ (accessed July 2003). It is important to note that Scandinavian countries, especially Sweden, call their administrative reforms "Public Modernization" rather than the NPM, but they may still be accounted for by the NPM-oriented pattern. Sweden's public administration traditionally does not emphasize the use of market mechanisms but rather the improvement of democratic participation and equity in corporatist arrangements. It is decentralized with the introduction of agency systems. Since the late 1980s, however, a more results-oriented public management has been implemented through expenditure ceilings in Sweden and is moving toward administrative efficiency and centralization.

Since 2000 a national strategy for e-government has been the use of ICTs for better service and efficiency. Sweden's administrative reform appears to be converging with NPM-oriented reforms. See Per Loegreid, "Administrative Reforms in Scandinavia—Testing the Cooperative Model," in *Public Sector Reform,* ed. Brendan C. Nolan (New York: Palgrave, 2001).

8. Singapore, Infocomm Development Agency, *Connected Singapore—A New Blueprint for Infocomm Development* (2003), http://www.ida.gov.sg/ (accessed July 2003).

9. In terms of functional allocation, while national government tends to devote its attention to national matters, such as economic policy, foreign affairs, and national security, local government is given responsibility for fulfilling a wide range of the mundane functions, such as services related to living conditions, problem solving of residential issues, and other basic public services.

10. IT policy is a new issue that tends to cut across traditional lines of cleavage. In traditional policy areas, such as agriculture, education, and social services, each government department tends to have clear jurisdiction. But the use of ICTs affects every department that participates in e-government programs.

11. United Nations Online Network in Public Administration, "United Nations Global E-Government Readiness Report 2004" (2004), http://www.unpan.org/egovernment4.asp (accessed August 2005).

12. Government Readiness Index is defined by variables, that is, government prioritization of ICTs, government procurement of ICTs, and government online presence. See World Economic Forum, *Global Information Technology Report 2003–2004* (New York: Oxford University Press, 2004), p. 22.

13. World Economic Forum, *Global Information Technology Report 2003–2004*, p. 22. The Government Usage Index is calculated by variables, that is, government success in ICT promotion and government online services.

14. *Asahi Shinbun,* September 19 and 20, 2000; *Yomiuri Shinbun,* September 23, 2000.

15. Japan, Ministry of Internal Affairs and Communications (MIAC), *Joho Tsushin Hakusho* (White Paper on Information and Telecommunications), 2001 edition (Tokyo: Gyosei, 2001), ch. 1.

16. Christopher Hood, "Exploring Variations in Public Management Reform," in *Civil Service Systems in Comparative Perspective,* eds. Hans A. G. M. Bekke, James L. Perry, and Theo A. J. Toonen (Bloomington and Indianapolis: Indiana University Press, 1996); Oliver James, "Varieties of New Public Management" (paper presented at the annual meeting of the American Political Science Association, Atlanta, Georgia, September 2–5, 1999); Hori Masaharu, "Japanese Public Administration and Its Adaptation to New Public Management" (paper presented at the Fifteenth Annual Conference of the Public Administration Theory Network, Cleveland, Ohio, May 29–31, 2002).

17. *Nikkei Konputa,* September 25, 2000.

18. Japan, Ministry of Internal Affairs and Communications (MIAC), *Joho Tsushin Gijutsu Kakumei ni taio shita Chiho Kokyodantai ni okeru Johoka Shisakuto no Suishin ni kansuru Shishin* (Guidelines for the Promotion of Local Government IT Policies in Response to IT Revolution) (2000), http://www.soumu.go.jp/news/000828.html (accessed June 2004).

19. The Ministry of Internal Affairs and Communications (MIAC) was set up in 2001 following the merger of three bodies: the Management and Coordination Agency, the Ministry of Home Affairs, and the Ministry of Posts and Telecommunications.

20. *Nihon Keizai Shinbun,* October 23, 2001.

21. *UNISYS e-Japan News,* March 31, 2004.

22. Japan, Ministry of Internal Affairs and Communications (MIAC), *Paburikkukomento* (Public Comments) (2004), http://search.e-gov.go.jp/servlet/Public (accessed February 2004).

23. Ibid.

24. Nakasone Yasuhiro, "Politicians, Bureaucrats, and Policymaking in Japan," in *Unlocking the Bureaucrat's Kingdom: Deregulation and the Japanese Economy,* ed. Frank Gibney (Washington, D.C.: Brookings Institution Press, 1998); Nakasone Yasuhiro, *The Making of the New Japan: Reclaiming the Political Mainstream* (New York: Curzon Press, 1999).

25. The Koizumi cabinet's approval rating was about 80 percent when he took office in April 2001 and hit a record high of over 85 percent in June 2001. Over 2 million people registered to receive the prime minister's online magazine, *Koizumi Naikaku Meru Magajin,* after its launch in June 2001, meaning that they would receive information by e-mail before it showed up on the prime minister's website. See, for example, *Asahi Shinbun,* May 29, 2001; *Mainichi Shinbun* May 29, 2001.

26. *Mainichi Shinbun,* June 15, 2001.

27. Japan, Diet, House of Councilors, a full session minute, 155th session, October 22, 2002.

28. *Asahi Shinbun,* October 29, 2002.

29. The figures are calculated from sources available at Yahoo! JAPAN, http://dir.yahoo.co.jp/Government/Legislative_Branch/Members/ (accessed June 2004). Also, see the Google Directory, http://directory.google.com/Top/World/Japanese/ (accessed June 2004).

30. *Asahi Shinbun,* July 18, 2001; *Yomiuri Shinbun,* August 8, 2002.

31. *Yomiuri Shinbun,* August 8, 2002.

32. For the survey of National Diet members regarding their use of home pages and e-mail for electoral purposes, see Za Giin, "Giin Ankeito Kekka Vol. 4" (Results of Diet Members Survey) (2004), http://www.giin-net.com/genq_vo14.html (accessed February 2004).

33. Robert D. Putnam, "Bowling Alone: America's Declining Social Capital," *Journal of Democracy* 6, no. 1 (January 1995): 65–78.

34. Japan, Association for Promoting Fair Elections, *Toitsu Chiho Senkyo ni okeru Tohyoritsu no Suii* (Trends of Voter Turnouts in the Unified Local Elections), May 2003, http://www.akaruisenkyo.or.jp/tohyo/top.html (accessed June 2004).

35. *Sankei Shinbun,* January 8, 1996.

36. Ibid., December 17, 1995.

37. Terry MacDougall, "Political Opposition and Local Government in Japan" (PhD dissertation, 1975, Yale University); Steven R. Reed, "Local Policy Making in an Urban State: The Case of Japanese Prefectures" (PhD dissertation, 1979, University of Michigan).

38. For example, see Muramatsu Michio, "Central-Local Political Relations in Japan: A Lateral Competition Model," *Journal of Japanese Studies* 12 (Summer 1986): 303–27.

39. For example, see Richard J. Samuels, *The Politics of Regional Policy in Japan: Localities Incorporated?* (Princeton: Princeton University Press, 1983).

40. Takao Yasuo, "Participatory Democracy in Japan's Decentralization Drive," *Asian Survey* 38, no. 10 (October 1998): 950–67.

41. Japan, IT Strategic Headquarters, *e-Japan Strategy* (2001), http://www.kantei.go.jp/jp/singi/it2/kettei/010122honbun.html (accessed June 2004).

42. The NTT Data administered a questionnaire to 3,000 people, aged 20 and over across the nation, and collected 2,036 usable responses. Nippon Telegraph and Telephone (NTT) Data, *NTT Data News Releases,* "eDemokurashi ni kansuru Zenkoku Kojin Ankeito" (National Survey of Individuals concerning e-Democracy), April 10, 2002.

43. Japan, Ministry of Internal Affairs and Communications (MIAC), *Hodo Shiryo* (News Releases), July 31, 2002.

44. Ibid., September 3, 2002.

45. Ibid., October 17, 2002.

46. Ibid.

47. Ibid.

48. NTT Data mailed a questionnaire to 1,000 people aged 20 and over who resided in ten cities in the capital region, and collected 755 usable responses. See Nippon Telegraph and Telephone (NTT) Data, "Denshi Seifu to Minshushugi ni kansuru Shutoken Shimin Chosa Hokokusho" (Investigation Report on Citizens in the Capital Region for e-Government and Democracy), December 2001, p. 11.

49. NTT Data, "Denshi Seifu to Minshushugi ni kansuru Shutoken Shimin Chosa Hokokusho," p. 28.

50. Ibid., p. 21.

51. *Sanyo Shinbun,* June 28, 2002.

52. Nippon Telegraph and Telephone (NTT) Data, *Research & Development* (2002), http://www.nttdata.co.jp/rd/riss/e-demo/report02.html (accessed June 2004).

53. Tezuka Naoki, "Dejitaru Demokurashi" (Digital Democracy), *Chiiki Seisaku Kenkyu* 15 (June 2001): 21–24.

54. Chiba Mitsuyuki, "Chiba Mitsuyuki Shicho ni Kiku" (Interviews with Mayor Mitsuyuki Chiba), *Gabanansu* 38 (June 2002): 37.

55. Enami Toshihiro, *Denshi Jichitai* (e-Local Government) (Tokyo: Toyo Keizai Shinposha, 2002), pp. 183–84.

56. *Asahi Shinbun,* March 13, 2003.

57. Ibid., January 30, 2003.

58. Enami, *Denshi Jichitai,* pp. 193–94.

59. Kanashiro Yuichi, "Paburiku Manejimento" (Public Management), *Chiiki Seisaku Kenkyu* 15 (June 2001): 14.

60. Japan, MIAC, *Hodo Shiryo,* November 28, 2002.

61. Ibid., October 23, 2001.

62. Enami, *Denshi Jichitai,* p. 184.

63. For a list of public comments solicited by Japanese local governments, see Deta Besu/Paburikku Komento(Database—Public Comments) (2004), http://www.geocities. co.jp/WallStreet/3993/note/pcdb.html (accessed February 2004).

64. Iwate prefecture, "Koucho no Homupeiji" (Home Page for Public Hearings) (2004), http://www.pref.iwate.jp/~koucho/index.html (accessed February 2004).

65. Japan, e-Local Government Conference, *Denshi Jichitai ni kansuru Ankeito Chousa* (Survey on e-Local Government) (2003), http://e-lg.jp/ga/ma-tyosa03.html (accessed April 2003); Japan, Digitalization Consortium of Local Governments, *Denshi Seifu Jichitai Gaido* (Guides to e-Government /Local Government) (Tokyo: JMA Management Center, 2002).

66. Japan, Ministry of Internal Affairs and Communications (MIAC), *Digital Opportunity Site* (2001), http://www.dosite.jp/e/do/j-state_net.html (accessed July 2004).

67. *Asahi Shinbun,* June 16, 2002.

68. *Asahi Shinbun,* April 15, 2003.

69. Japan, MIAC, *Hodo Shiryo,* October 17, 2002.

70. *Asahi Shinbun,* January 14, 1999, and November 22, 1999.

71. In general, bigger Japanese cities tend to have more advanced infrastructures for e-government than smaller ones. But the gap is minimal; nearly 80 percent of municipalities have achieved "one PC for each person" for their employees and over 90 percent have been developing their LAN. See Japan, e-Local Government Conference, *Denshi Jichitai ni kansuru Ankeito Chousa;* Japan, Digitalization Consortium of Local Governments, *Denshi Seifu Jichitai Gaido.*

Chapter 7

1. A passage from Ichikawa Fusae's note, "The Flower of Radish," cited in Ichikawa Fusae Memorial Association (IFMA), ed., *Ichikawa Fusae Seiji Sanga Senta de Manabu 47-nin no Chosen* (47 Challengers Who Studied at the Promotion Center for Women's Political Participation) (Tokyo: Ichikawa Fusae Memorial Association, 2002), p. 98.

2. Teramachi Midori, "Shiminha Seiji to Josei Giin" (Citizen-based Politics and Women Representatives), *Toshi Mondai* 97, no. 1 (January 2006): 17.

3. Ichikawa Fusae Memorial Association (IFMA), ed., *Local Assemblies, Handbook of Data on Japanese Women in Political Life, 2003* (Tokyo: Ichikawa Fusae Memorial Association, 2003), pp. 123–25.

4. Gerald L. Curtis, *The Logic of Japanese Politics: Leaders, Institutions, and the Limits of Change* (New York: Columbia University Press, 1999); J. A. A. Stockwin, *Governing Japan: Divided Politics in a Major Economy,* 3rd edition (Oxford: Blackwell, 1999).

5. Watanuki Joji, "Patterns of Politics in Present-Day Japan," in *Party Systems and Voter Alignments: Cross-National Perspectives,* eds. Seymour M. Lipset and Stein Rokkan (New York: Free Press, 1967), pp. 447–66; Miyake Ichiro, "Types of Partisanship, Partisan Attitudes, and Voting Choices," in *The Japanese Voter,* eds. Scott C. Flanagan et al. (New Haven: Yale University, 1991); Kabashima Ikuo, *Hokaku Ideorogi no Henyo: Seiken Koutai to Yukensha no Taido Henyo* (Transformation in Conservative/Progressive Ideologies: Regime Change and the Transformation of Voter Attitudes) (Tokyo: Bokutakusha, 1998).

6. Susan Pharr, *Political Women in Japan: The Search for a Place in Political Life* (Berkeley: University of California Press, 1981).

7. Anne Imamura, "The Japanese Urban Housewife: Tradition and Modern Social Participation," *Social Science Journal* 24, no. 2 (1987): 139–56; Anne Imamura, *Urban Japanese Housewives: At Home in the Community* (Honolulu: University of Hawaii Press, 1987).

8. Iwao Sumiko, *The Japanese Women: Traditional Image and Changing Reality* (New York: Free Press, 1993).

9. Dennis Patterson and Misa Nishikawa, "Political Interest or Interest in Politics? Gender and Party Support in Postwar Japan," *Women and Politics* 24, no. 2 (Summer 2002): 1–34.

10. Susan Pharr, "Public Trust and Democracy in Japan," in *Why People Don't Trust Government,* eds. Joseph S. Nye, Jr., Philip D. Zelikow, and David C. King (Cambridge, MA: Harvard University Press, 1997), pp. 237–52.

11. Robin M. LeBlanc, *Bicycle Citizens: The Political World of the Japanese Housewife* (Berkeley and Los Angeles: University of California Press, 1999).

12. Sherry L. Martin, "Alienated, Independent and Female: Lessons from the Japanese Electorate," *Social Science Japan Journal* 7, no. 1 (April 2004): 1–19.

13. LeBlanc, *Bicycle Citizens*; IFMA, *Ichikawa Fusae Seiji Sanga Senta de Manabu 47-nin no Chosen*; Ogai Tokuko, "Josei Mogi Kaigi to Iu Josei Seisaku" (Women's Simulation Assembly as Women's Policy), *The Annual of Japanese Political Science Association*, December 2003, pp. 113–37; Tokyo Citizens' Network (TCN), ed., *Roteshon Giin ga Machi o Tsukuru* (Rotation Representatives Build the Town) (Tokyo: Tokyo Citizens' Network, 2003).

14. Kasuga Masashi, "Local Councillors in Modern Japan: Considerations on Some Sociological Differences between Men and Women Councillors," in *Identity Politics and Critiques in Contemporary Japan,* eds. Vera Mackie et al. (Clayton: Monash Asia Institute, 2000), pp. 165–78.

15. Adopted from a nationwide survey of 17,062 assembly-members' respondents conducted during February–April 2002 by Kasuga Masashi and Takeyasu Hideko.

16. United Nations Development Programme (UNDP), ed., *Human Development Report 2005* (New York: UNDP, 2005). The UNDP developed these indices: the HDI is a composite index that measures the degree of human capabilities with the three basic criteria of "healthy lifestyle allowing longevity," "knowledge," and "average living standard"; the GDI also indicates the degree of human capabilities but deducts disparities between men and women as a penalty; and the GEM evaluates the degree of women's capabilities to participate in economic and political activities, with specific measurements including the ratio of income earned by women, the ratio of women specialists and managers, and the ratio of women parliamentarians.

17. Inter-Parliamentary Union (IPU), *Women in National Parliaments* (2006), http://www.ipu.org/wmn-e/classif.htm (accessed March 2006).

18. Japan, Cabinet Office, Gender Equality Bureau (GEB), *Danjo Kyodo Sankaku Bijon: Nijuisseiki no Arata na Kachi no Sozo* (A Vision of Gender Equality: Creation of New Values for the Twenty-first Century) (1996), http://www.gender.go.jp/english_contents/index.html (accessed April 2006). The Council for Gender Equality was established in June 1994 by a government ordinance; it investigates and deliberates subjects in relation to the establishment of a gender-equal society according to the prime minister's request for advice and submits its opinion to the prime minister.

19. Japan, Cabinet Office, Gender Equality Bureau (GEB), *Gender Information Site* (2000), http://www.gender.go.jp/shimon_toushin_ronten.html (accessed December 2000).

20. Ibid.

21. Nannerl O. Keohane, "Speaking from Silence: Women and the Science of Politics," in *A Feminist Perspective in the Academy: The Difference It Makes,* eds. Elizabeth Langland and Walter Gove (Chicago: University of Chicago Press, 1981), pp. 91–96.

22. Goto Aya, Michael R. Reich, and Iain Aitken, "Oral Contraceptives and Women's Health in Japan," *Journal of the American Medical Association* 282, no. 22 (December 1999): 2173–177.

23. Kobayashi Yoshie, *A Path toward Gender Equality: State Feminism in Japan* (New York: Routledge, 2004).

24. End Child Prostitution in Asian Tourism (ECPAT), "The Summary of Activity 1992–1999 of ECPAT, Japan" (2002), http://www.ecpatstop.org/newkatsudo_ecpatstop_1994_2002/katsudou_houkaku_1999_stop.html (accessed March 2006).

25. John C. Campbell and Ikegami Naoki, "Long-Term Care Insurance Comes to Japan," *Health Affairs* 19, no. 3 (May–June 2000): 26–39.

26. Half of its financing is covered by mandatory insurance premiums paid by those aged 40 or over. The LTCI provides universal coverage for all the elderly in need of care, regardless of income or family situation.

27. In the early 1980s, LDP's policy guidelines, for example, still stated, "Children shall be brought up at home. The elderly shall be looked after at home." See Ichikawa Fusae, "Kokusai Fujinnen no Kodo Keikaku to Katei" (Action Plans for International Women's Year and the Family) *Jujin Tenpo,* April 1980, pp. 5–9.

28. Japan, Ministry of Internal Affairs and Communications (MIAC), *Statistical Handbook of Japan* (2006), http://www.stat.go.jp/English/data/handbook/c02cont. htm#cha2_2 (accessed April 2006).

29. See Hugh Helco, *Modern Social Politics in Britain and Sweden* (New Haven: Yale University Press, 1974).

30. Japan, Diet, House of Councilors (HOC), Minutes of the Committee on Labor, May 29, 1997.

31. Japan, Diet, House of Representatives (HOR), Minutes of Plenary Session, January 23, 1997.

32. *Japan Times,* July 2, 2003.

33. See, for example, *Yomiuri Shinbun,* May 17, 1998. The LDP-SDP-Sakigake coalition government began in June 1994 under the leadership of then SDP prime minister Murayama Tomiichi. The Murayama government lasted until January 1996, when a new cabinet was formed under LDP president Hashimoto. In June 1998 both the SDP and Sakigake decided to withdraw from the ruling alliance.

34. Shindo Kumiko, *Jenda de Yomu Nihon Seiji* (Gendering Japanese Politics) (Tokyo: Yuhikaku, 2004), pp. 252–53; Osawa Mari, "Japanese Government Approaches to Gender Equality since the Mid-1990s," *Asian Perspective* 29, no. 1 (Spring 2005): 159.

35. "Josei Toshu Intabyu: Henkakuki no Josei Seijika" (Interviews with Female Party Leaders: Women Politicians in a Transitional Period), *Fujin Tenbo* (April 1998), p. 5.

36. Amy Gurowitz, "Mobilizing International Norms: Domestic Actors, Immigrants, and the Japanese State," *World Politics* 51, no. 3 (April 1999): 413–45; Jennifer Chan-Tiberghien, *Gender and Human Rights in Japan: Global Norms and Domestic Networks* (Stanford: Stanford University Press, 2004).

37. Yamashita Yasuko "The International Movements toward Gender Equality and Its Impact on Japan." *US-Japan Women's Journal,* English Supplement, no. 5 (July 1993): 35–51; Shindo, *Jenda de Yomu Nihon Seiji,* pp. 212–13.

38. In 1984 the Nationality Law was revised to grant Japanese nationality on birth when the father or mother has Japanese nationality while abolishing the principle of "paternal blood" only.

39. Margaret E. Keck and Kathryn Sikkink, *Activists beyond Borders: Advocacy Networks in International Politics* (Ithaca: Cornell University Press, 1998); Thomas Risse-Kappen and Kathryn Sikkink, "The Socialization of International Human Rights Norms into Domestic Practices: Introduction," in *The Power of Human Rights: International Norms and Domestic Change,* eds. Thomas Risse-Kappen, Stephen C. Ropp and Kathryn Sikkink (Cambridge: Cambridge University Press, 1999), pp. 1–38.

40. Gurowitz, "Mobilizing International Norms."

41. Chan-Tiberghien, *Gender and Human Rights in Japan,* ch. 8; Shindo, *Jenda de Yomu Nihon Seiji,* pp. 200–264.

42. See, for example, part II, 4(1), which defines violence against women as a human right violation.

43. Adopted from surveys conducted by the Cabinet Office of Japan in May 1979 (8,239 respondents), September 1997 (3,574 respondents), and November 2004 (3,502 respondents).

44. Japan, Prime Minister's Office (PMO), Public Relations, *Josei ni kansuru Yoron Chosa* (Opinion Survey on Women), September 1991.

45. Japan, Cabinet Office, Gender Equality Bureau (GEB), *Josei no Seisaku Hoshin Kettei Sankaku Jokyo Shirabe* (Report on the State of Gender Equality Policies and Measures to Promote the Formation of a Gender Equal Society) (2006), http://www.gender.go.jp/ (accessed October 2006).

46. Robert Darcy and Sarah S. Schramm "When Women Run against Men," *Public Opinion Quarterly* 41, no. 1 (Spring 1977): 1–12; Elizabeth Vallance, *Women in the House: A Study of Women Members of Parliament* (London: Athlone Press, 1979); Jonathan Kelley and Ian McAllister "The Electoral Consequences of Gender in Australia," *British Journal of Political Science* 13, no. 3 (July 1983): 365–77.

47. See, for example, Robert Darcy, Susan Welch, and Janet Clark, *Women, Election, and Representation* (New York: Longman, 1987).

48. See, for example, Pippa Norris, "Women's Legislative Participation in Western Europe," in *Women and Politics in Western Europe,* ed. Sylvia Bashevkin (London: Frank Cass, 1985), pp. 95–99; Joyce Gelb, *Feminism and Politics: A Comparative Perspective* (Berkeley: University of California Press, 1989). A single-member district tends to produce the phenomenon of "incumbency advantage"; facilitate a standard candidate, that is, a middle-aged man from a middle-income family, and cause a direct confrontation among candidates for winning a single seat. See Susan Welch and Donley Studlar, "Multi-Member Districts and the Representation of Women: Evidence from Britain and the United States," *Journal of Politics* 52, no. 2 (May 1990): 391–412; Elizabeth Vallance, "Women Candidates in the 1983 General Election," *Parliamentary Affairs* 37, no. 3 (1984): 301–9.

49. Comprising 2–14 seats in each district.

50. Ray Christensen, "The Impact of Electoral Rules in Japan," in *Democracy and the Status of Women in East Asia,* eds. Rose J. Lee and Cal Clark (Boulder, CO: Lynne Rienner, 2000), pp. 25–46.

51. It was characteristic of local assemblies in post-WWII Japan that independents accounted for 30 to 40 percent of the seats. It is thus unrealistic to introduce a party-based proportional representation system at the local level.

52. It is important to note that the single nontransferable vote is used in the large-sized multimember districts in Japan's local elections and thus the findings in Britain and the Unites States cannot be directly applied to those in Japan.

53. The figures in this section are provided by Local Administration Bureau; Ministry of Internal Affairs and Communications; and Secretariat, House of Representatives.

54. The figures in this section are provided by Ministry of Internal Affairs and Communications, and Local Administration Bureau.

55. Mitsui Mariko et al., "Josei no Seiji Sanga to Dairinin Undo" (Women'sPolitical Participation and Representative Authorization Campaign), *Shakai Undo,* no. 233 (1999): 2–26.

56. Ibid., p. 7.

57. The Ichikawa Fusae Memorial Foundation was established in 1962 to "provide political education for women, propagate ideal and fine elections, and build the foundation of Japan's democracy."

58. Kubo Kimiko, Secretary-General, Ichikawa Fusae Memorial Association, Interview by the author on April 20, 2006; Yamaguchi Mitsuko, Executive Director, Ichikawa Fusae Memorial Association, Interview by the author on April 21, 2006.

59. Kubo, Interview.

60. IFMA, *Ichikawa Fusae Seiji Sanga Senta de Manabu 47-nin no Chosen*, p. 11.

61. Ibid., p. 6.

62. Ibid., p. 11. It is also important to mention that in 1993 then Japan New Party Diet Woman En Yoriko launched a series of lectures called "Politics School for Women" given by nonpartisan and well-known politicians.

63. *Fujin Tenbo*, "Josei no Gikai Shinshitsu Shien Kusanone Gurupu" (Grassroots Groups for Promoting Women to Assemblies), March 1998, pp. 4–6; Kubo, Interview; Yamaguchi, Interview.

64. Ogai, "Josei Mogi Kaigi to Iu Josei Seisaku," p. 117.

65. Ibid., p. 116.

66. Ibid., p. 118.

67. Ibid., p. 116.

68. Yamaguchi, Interview.

69. Ibid.

70. *JJ-Net News,* August 10, 1996.

71. Domoto Akiko, "JJ Junen no Ayumi" (Developments in the Decade of JJ) in the Introduction of the compiled issue of *JJ-Net News,* vol. 301 (January 12, 2001)–vol. 404 (June 29, 2004).

72. *JJ-Net News,* March 2, 2001.

73. Ibid.

74. Mitsui et al., "Josei no Seiji Sanga to Dairinin Undo," p. 7; Women and Politics Campaign Office (WPCO), *Women and Politics Campaign 1999 Report* (Tokyo: Women and Politics Campaign Office, 1999).

75. WPCO, *Women and Politics Campaign 1999 Report.*

76. Iwamoto Misako, "1999-nen Chiho Senkyo ni okeru Josei no Yakushin" (Women's Advances in the 1999 Local Elections), *Seisaku Kagaku* 8, no. 3 (February 2001): 21–38.

77. IFMA, *Local Assemblies, Handbook of Data on Japanese Women in Political Life, 2003;* Tokyo Citizens' Network (TCN), *Tosei o Kaeru Seikatsusha Netowaku no Shigoto* (Citizens' Networking for Changing the Metropolitan Governance) (Tokyo: Tokyo Citizens' Network, 2004).

78. IFMA, *Local Assemblies, Handbook of Data on Japanese Women in Political Life, 1999.*

79. Ibid.

80. Ibid.

81. LeBlanc, *Bicycle Citizens,* pp. 127–30.

82. Nakamura Eiko, Secretary-General, Tokyo Citizens' Network, Interview by the author on April 26, 2006.

83. TCN, *Roteshon Giin ga Machi o Tsukuru,* p. 5.

84. This section is largely based on the author's interview with Tokyo Citizens' Network Secretary-General, Nakamura Eiko, April 26, 2006.

85. TCN, *Tosei o Kaeru Seikatsusha Netowaku no Shigoto,* p. 53.

86. TCN, *Roteshon Giin ga Machi o Tsukuru*, p. 1; TCN, *Tosei o Kaeru Seikatsusha Netowaku no Shigoto*, p. 46.

87. TCN, *Roteshon Giin ga Machi o Tsukuru*, p. 1.

88. Nakamura, Interview.

89. TCN, *Tosei o Kaeru Seikatsusha Netowaku no Shigoto*, p. 45.

90. Nakamura, Interview.

91. TCN, *Tosei o Kaeru Seikatsusha Netowaku no Shigoto*, p. 44. In 2003 only 139 ordinance bills were proposed by assembly-members in all the 47 prefectural assemblies; by contrast, 3,235 ordinance bills were initiated by prefectural governors. In March 2004, after attending the training workshops, TCN assembly-women along with residents were able to draft and pass an Underground Water Preservation Ordinance at the Koganei City Assembly.

92. Iwamoto, "1999-nen Chiho Senkyo ni okeru Josei no Yakushin," p. 27.

93. This section is largely based on the author's interview with the Ichikawa Fusae Memorial Association Secretary-General, Kubo Kimiko, April 20, 2006 and with Ichikawa Fusae Memorial Association Executive Director, Yamaguchi Mitsuko, April 21, 2006.

94. TCN, *Tosei o Kaeru Seikatsusha Netowaku no Shigoto*, p. 12; Nakamura, Interview.

95. TCN, *Tosei o Kaeru Seikatsusha Netowaku no Shigoto*, p. 13.

96. Ibid., pp. 12–13.

97. Ibid., p. 13; Tokyo Citizens' Network (TCN), *Tokyo Seikastusha Netowaku no Yobikake: Kihon Seisaku* (Appeal by Tokyo Citizens' Network: Basic Policies) (Tokyo: Tokyo Citizens' Network, 2003), p. 19.

98. Community Fund, "Machi ga Genki ni Naru Shikumi" (Mechanisms for Revitalizing the Town) (2003), http://www.h7.dion.ne.jp/~fund/ (accessed April 2006).

99. Ecomesse, "Kankyo Machizukuri Ekomesse" (Environmental Town-Making, the Ecomesse) (2006), http://www.npo-ecomesse.org/ (accessed April 2006).

100. Nakamura, Interview.

101. TCN, *Tosei o Kaeru Seikatsusha Netowaku no Shigoto*, p. 53.

102. Anne Phillips, *Which Equality Matter?* (Cambridge, UK: Polity Press, 1999).

103. Joni Lovenduski, *Feminizing Politics* (Cambridge, UK: Polity Press, 2005).

Chapter 8

1. United Nations, Population Division, *Replacement Migration: Is It a Solution to Declining and Ageing Populations?* January 6, 2000, pp. 49–50.

2. Kawasaki City, Investigation Committee for Foreign Residents' Perception, *Kawasakishi Gaikokuseki Shimin Ishiki Jittai Chosa Hokokusho: Jirei Mensetsu Hen* (Report on Investigation into the Actual Condition of Foreign Residents' Perception: Case Studies and Interviews) (Kawasaki: Kawasaki City, 1995), p. 112. During the period of Japanese rule of Korea (1910–1945), Koreans were legally encouraged, but in practice forced, to adopt Japanese names. This *doka seisaku* (assimilation policy) created registered Japanese family names that represented more than three-quarters of the population by the end of World War II. In post–WWII Japan, most Korean residents decided to keep using their Japanese names, primarily to avoid being discriminated against in Japanese society.

3. The term "newcomer" is used to differentiate those foreign residents from "oldcomers" who were born (or the direct descendants of those born) in former Japanese colonies and once held Japanese nationality.

4. According to sources provided from OECD, including the *OECD Factbook 2005* (Paris: Organisation for Economic Co-operation and Development, 2005), as of 2002, registered foreign population as a percentage of total population was 1.5 percent for Japan, 8.9 percent for Germany, 5.6 percent for France (1999), 5.3 percent for Sweden, 11.8 percent for the United States (foreign-born immigrants), 4.5 percent for the United Kingdom, and 2.6 percent for Italy.

5. In the 1980s, to extend social services to foreigners, the Japanese government removed the so-called *kokuseki-joko* (nationality clauses) included in a wide range of national welfare laws that had exclusively confined the recipients of public services to Japanese nationals. Perhaps the most significant change was the 1982 removal of a nationality clause in the National Pension Law that excluded all foreigners, including Korean residents. This was followed in the same year by the removal of nationalty clauses in three child-allowance laws. By 1986, when registered foreigners became eligible for the National Health Insurance, the Japanese government had taken measures to apply all national laws relating to social welfare to all legal foreign workers, with the exception of the Livelihood Protection Law (direct relief to the poor).

6. Joseph Nye and Robert Keohane, eds. *Transnational Relations and World Politics* (Cambridge, MA: Harvard University Press, 1970), pp. x–xi.

7. Peter Saunders, *Social Theory and the Urban Questions,* 2nd ed. (New York: Homes & Meier, 1986), p. 265.

8. See Hugh Heclo and Aaron Wildavsky, *The Private Government of Public Money* (Berkeley and Los Angeles: University of California Press, 1974); Aaron Wildavsky, *Budgeting: A Comparative Theory of Budgeting Processes* (Boston: Little, Brown, 1975).

9. Some scholars argue that it is increasingly important for the state to extend citizenship rights to noncitizens for the protection of immigrants. See Yasemin Nuhoglu Soysal, *Limits of Citizenship: Migrants and Postnational Membership in Europe* (Chicago: Chicago University Press, 1994); David Jacobson, *Rights across Borders: Immigration and the Decline of Citizenship* (Baltimore: Johns Hopkins University Press, 1996). Other studies have attempted to provide empirical evidence of why states allow unwanted migration and even extend rights to noncitizens. See Gary P. Freeman, "Modes of Immigration Politics in Liberal Democratic States," *International Migration Review* 24, no. 4 (Winter 1995): 881–902; Christian Joppke, "Why Liberal States Accept Unwanted Immigration," *World Politics* 50, no. 2 (January 1998): 266–93.

10. Calculated from Japan, Immigration Bureau, *Hodo Shiryō* (Press Releases), June 2005.

11. See, for example, *Asahi Shinbun,* September 22, 1993, November 3, 1994; *Sankei Shinbun,* November 4, 1998.

12. Calculated from materials provided by Japan, Immigration Bureau. Also, see table 8.1.

13. Figures in this section are based on Japan, Economic Planning Agency (EPA), ed. *Kokumin Keizai Keisan Hokoku* (Report of Statistics on National Economy, 1955–94) (Tokyo: Zaimusho Insatsukyoku, 1996).

14. The Cabinet Office of the Japanese government conducted two nationwide surveys on foreign workers (one administered in 1990 with a response from 3,681 of 5,000 respondents; the other administered in 2000 with a response from 2,070 of 3,000 respondents). Both the surveys asked the question, "Are you interested in the issues of foreign workers in Japan?" The results were as follows: interested, 48.6 percent (9.5 percent with great interest, 39.1 percent with fair interest) in 1990; 48.8 percent (8.2 percent with great interest, 40.6 percent with fair interest) in 2000; not interested, 49.9 percent (18.1 percent with the least interest, 31.8 percent with not much interest) in 1990; and 50.9 percent (18.1 percent with the least interest, 32.8 percent with not much interest) in 2000.

15. The *Asahi Shinbun,* for example, conducted two nationwide opinion polls of 3,000 eligible voters (one administered in 1994 to 2,318 respondents and the other administered in 2000 to 2,147 respondents). The 1994 nationwide opinion poll, which had surveyed attitudes toward foreign residents' right to vote in local elections, showed that nearly 47 percent of all respondents favored the idea, while over 41 percent did not, but the 2000 poll indicated more than 64 percent for the idea and only 28 percent against it.

16. Calculated from materials provided by International Bureau, Korean Residents Union in Japan.

17. Figures from *Asahi Shinbun,* Digital News Archives, 1984–2002 and *Nihon Keizai Shinbun,* Nikkei Telecom 21.

18. Marcus Tullius Cicero, *De Legibus,* Book 1, trans. and ed. C. W. Keyes (London: Loeb Classical Library, 1928), pp. 1, 10, 28–29.

19. There is a distinction between concepts of national citizenship and the Kantian concept of world citizenship. However, the historical experience of citizenship has predominantly been that of national citizenship; world citizenship so far not been grounded in empirical reality but is significant in a normative sense. See Immanuel Kant, "Idea for a Universal History from a Cosmo-political Point of View," in *The Theory of International Relations: Selected Texts from Gentili to Treitschke,* eds. M. Forsyth, H. M. A. Keens-Soper, and P. Savigear (London: Allen & Unwin, 1970), p. 206.

20. According to Locke, the legitimacy of state power does not exist if natural rights are violated, and thus citizens have the right to reconstitute sovereign power. In this sense, he regarded the shift (from a condition of universal norms to the territorial authority of the modern state) as a natural transformation. See John Locke, *Two Treatises of Government,* ed. Peter Laslett (New York: Cambridge University Press, 1988), pp. 412–18.

21. Figures provided by International Bureau, Korean Residents Union in Japan.

22. Suh Yong-Dal, "Naze Ima Teijyugaikokujin ka" (Why Now Permanent Alien Residents?), *Ushio,* no. 503 (January 2001), p. 149.

23. This argument derives from the legal criteria of *jus sanguinis* for obtaining nationality through naturalization. According to the criteria, children automatically obtain their nationality from the country to which their parents belong as nationals.

24. For the historical development of social movements by Korean residents in postwar Japan, see Suh Yong-Dal, ed., *Kankoku/Chosenjin no Genjo to Mirai* (The Situation and Future of South and North Koreans) (Tokyo: Hyoronsha, 1987).

25. Article 10 of the Local Autonomy Law, regarding foreigners as "residents," stipulates foreign residents' taxation liability. Yet, Article 39 of the Residents' Basic Register Law identifies residents with Japanese nationality only, excluding foreign residents from the Register, which provides the basis for delivering public services.

26. According to a survey conducted by the Japanese government, 42.4 percent of the marriages of Koreans registered in 1970 were intermarriages with Japanese; the ratio rose to 82.5 percent in 1991. Cited in Fukuoka Yasunori, "Koreans in Japan: Past and Present," *Saitama University Review* 31, no. 1 (1996): 12.

27. Japan, Supreme Court, Third Petty Bench, February 28, 1995, no. 163.

28. From 1975 to 1978, Rev. Choi Chang Hwa and his group called for Koreans' voting rights in Kitakyushu city, Fukuoka prefecture, and the national government. Yet, his initiative did not spread to other Korean organizations.

29. Lee Jin-Kyu, *Zainichi Chosenjin Sorengokai Chuo Iinkai Dai-jyurokki Dai-sanji Kaigi Kakudai Kaigi Bunkenshu* (Central Committee, General Association of Korean

Residents, Documents of the Third Conference of the Sixteenth Term) (Tokyo: Kugatsu Shobo, 1993), pp. 26–27; *Chosen Shoko Shinbun* (Korean Commerce and Industry Newspaper), December 6 and 20, 1994. Nonetheless, a 1984 survey conducted on responses from 866 North/South Korean and 161 Chinese residents by Kanagawa prefecture found that both North and South Korean nationals in the prefecture equally acknowledged the necessity of local suffrage, with a support ratio of 79.0 percent and 82.4 percent respectively.

30. For the direct relationship between international norms and state behavior, see Soysal, *Limits of Citizenship,* pp. 42, 131–32. For the necessity of norm diffusion mechanisms, see Joppke, "Why Liberal States Accept Unwanted Immigration," p. 269.

31. Jacobson, *Rights across Borders,* p. 9; Amy Gurowitz, "Mobilizing International Norms: Domestic Actors, Immigrants and the Japanese State," *World Politics* 51, no. 3 (April 1999): 413–45.

32. In some cases, voting rights of foreigners are only granted at local elections. In 1991 Tacoma Park, a town in Maryland, United States, decided to allow foreign residents to vote, but not to stand for public office, in municipal elections. Estonia has granted such rights since 1993.

33. See John Rawls, *Political Liberalism* (New York: Columbia University Press, 1993); David Miller, "Bounded Citizenship," in *Cosmopolitan Citizenship,* eds. Kimberly Hutchings and Roland Dannreuther (London: Macmillan, 1999), pp. 60–80.

34. Miller, "Bounded Citizenship," pp. 60–80.

35. The South Korean government has been a strong source of pressure on the Japanese government to improve the individual welfare of Korean residents in Japan. The January 1991 Korea-Japan Memorandum between South Korea and Japan, which resulted from this effort, also urged Japanese local government to allow Korean residents to take the Teacher Entrance Examination and to employ them on a full-time basis.

36. *Asahi Shinbun,* October 9, 1998.

37. *Yomiuri Shinbun,* September 9, 1999.

38. Yamada Takao, "Zainichi Gaikokujin to Fukushi" (Foreign Residents in Japan and Welfare), *Toshi Mondai* 87, no. 2 (February 1996): 36–37; Takafuji Akira, "Gaikokujin to Shakai Hosho" (Foreigners and the Social Security), *Toshi Mondai* 87, no. 2 (February 1996): 3–13.

39. *Sha-hatsu* (Ministerial Notice), no. 382, May 8, 1954. Interestingly enough, the 1946 Livelihood Protection Law actually applied to foreigners, but the Livelihood Protection Law current in 2007, which was enacted in 1950, excludes foreigners from its direct-relief scheme. As the government explained it, the amended law was based on Article 25 (of the 1947 Constitution), which stated the right to maintain the minimum standards of living. It argued that foreigners did not have the right to claim such a right from the government. See Tokyo District Court, March 31, 1978, in "Tokyo Metropolitan Adachi Welfare Office Director Case," in *Gyosai Shu* (Collection of Administrative Court Cases) 29, no. 3, p. 473.

40. This section is based on materials provided by the Japanese Federation of Bar Associations.

41. The figures in this section are calculated from materials provided by Japan, Immigration Bureau.

42. Japan, Diet, House of Councilors, Minutes of Committee on Judicial Affairs, May 6, 1999.

43. Japan, Diet, House of Councilors, Minutes of Committee on the Budget, February 8, 1995.
44. *Mukuge Tsushin* (Mukuge Correspondence), nos. 148/149 (March 1995).
45. See Yamada, "Zainichi Gaikokujin to Fukushi," pp. 45–46.
46. Figures provided by the Kanagawa Prefecture International Exchange Association.
47. According to a nationwide survey on primary and junior high schools conducted by the Ministry of Education in September 1991, 1,973 schools that responded required a program of Japanese language as a second language, yet 18 percent of those schools had no teachers in their employ for this task, and 27 percent did not pay specific attention to language education.
48. The *International Press* distributes about 30,000 copies of each issue in Portuguese and about 15,000 copies in Spanish across metropolitan areas in Japan.
49. Kawasaki City, *Kawasakishi Gaikokuseki Shimin Ishiki Jittai Chosa Hokokusho*, p. 15.
50. See Kawasaki City, Promotion Committee on Regional Japanese Language Education, *Kyosei Machizukuri o Mezasu Nihongo Gakushu no Arikata* (The Ideal of Japanese Language Learning for Making One Community) (Kawasaki: Promotion Committee, 1997).
51. In this proposal, the Committee developed the concept of "foreigners' citizenship." See Kawasaki City, Investigation Committee on the Establishment of a Kawasaki City Representative Assembly for Foreign Residents, *Kawasakishi Gaikokujin Shimin Daihyosha Kaigi Chosa Kenkyu Hokokusho* (Investigation Report on a Kawasaki City Representative Assembly for Foreign Residents) (Kawasaki: Kawasaki City, International Office, 1996), p. 1.
52. There are some critical problems in operating the foreigners' forum. First, with the exception of some "oldcomers" groups, foreigners' networks are not well organized enough to articulate and aggregate their interests at the foreigners' forum. Second, although having no legal binding force, proposals by the foreigners' forum are to be "respected" by the mayor; this moral obligation leaves the forum's relations with the mayor and the municipal assembly ambiguous.
53. *Asahi Shinbun*, February 23, 1985. By May 1985, 691 municipalities had called for the immediate elimination of compulsory fingerprinting and carrying of Alien Registration Cards, with 43 municipalities declaring that they would not report those refusing to be fingerprinted to the Ministry of Justice. The National Bar Association also took part in this campaign by defending the cases relating to such refusals in court. Fingerprinting was finally eliminated for permanent residents in 1993. The figures are provided by the Japanese Federation of Bar Associations.
54. *Tokyo Shinbun* (Yokohama edition), January 9, 1990.
55. Yamada Takao, municipal government official of Kawasaki, interview by the author on July 15, 2004.
56. Norman Nakamura, former chairperson of the Kawasaki City Representative Assembly for Foreign Residents, interview by the author on July 12, 2004.
57. This section is based on materials provided by the Japanese Federation of Bar Associations.
58. *Mainichi Shinbun*, May 18, 1990.
59. Ibid., May 2, 1996 .
60. *Asahi Shinbun*, November 22, 1996.
61. Figures provided by the Korean Resident Union in Japan.

62. Higuchi Naoto, "Taiko to Kyoryoku" (Resistance and Cooperation), in *Gaikokujin Shimin to Seiji Sanka* (Foreign Citizens and Political Participation), ed. Miyajima Takashi (Tokyo: Yushindo, 2000), pp. 26–27.

63. Yamada Takao, "Kawasaki ni okeru Gaikokujin tono Kyosei no Machizukuri no Taido" (Signs of Town-Making Coexistent with Foreigners in Kawasaki), *Toshi Mondai* 89, no. 6 (June 1998): 58–63.

64. Takahashi Kiyoshi, Mayor, speech delivered to the Municipal Assembly of Kawasaki City, March 18, 1994.

65. *Mainichi Shinbun,* March 19, 2002.

66. *Mindan Shinbun,* July 14, 2005.

67. *Asahi Shinbun* (Osaka edition), December 9, 2000.

68. Japan, Supreme Court, Third Petty Bench, February 28, 1995, no. 163. The *ikensho,* submitted to the cabinet by the Tokyo Metropolitan Assembly in 1995, for example, demanded immediate measures to extend local suffrage to foreign residents on the same ground.

69. On March 10, 1995, the Federation of Korean Resident Youths of Commerce and Industry announced the results of a questionnaire it administered to all 749 parliamentary members. Out of the 315 responses, 88.3 percent agreed with allowing foreigners' voting rights at local elections,; 56.2 percent agreed with their rights to both vote and run for local elections,; 5.1 percent agreed with their voting rights yet thought the idea premature,; and 2.9 percent disagreed Considering the number of National Diet members who had participated in anti-foreigners-suffrage groups, the majority were more likely to have decided not to respond to this survey.

70. In November 2000 a super-partisan parliamentary group, headed by Murakami Ichiro, was established to oppose bills granting foreigners a right to vote in local elections.

71. Lee Young Hwa, who had unsuccessfully filed applications to be a candidate in a total of six national and local elections between 1992 and 1998, said, "Most of us Koreans do not act for the benefit of the countries we belong to, but for the benefit of ourselves on a daily basis. Our major concern is, for example, how tax and welfare issues affect our daily lives, just like those of many Japanese." Cited in *Asahi Evening News,* November 3, 1999.

72. *Asahi Evening News,* November 3, 1999; *Kanagawa Mintoren News,* September 26, 2000.

73. *Asahi Shinbun,* April 14, 2001.

74. Republic of Korea, National Assembly, Minutes of Legislation and Judicial Committee, February 28, 2002.

75. *Jijitsushin,* September 12, 2004.

76. Ibid.

77. *Asahi Shinbun,* January 27, 2002.

Bibliography

Abe, Masahiro, Peter Kuhn, Nakamura Masao, Arthur Sweetman, and Higuchi Yoshio (2002). "Worker Displacement in Japan and Canada." In *Losing Work, Moving On: Work Displacement in International Perspective*, ed. Peter Kuhn. Kalamazoo, MI: W. E. Upjohn Institute for Employment Research.

Adler, Paul, and Seok-Woo Kwon (2002). "Social Capital: Prospects for a New Concept." *Academy of Management Review* 27, no. 1 (January–February): 17–40.

Aldridge, Stephen, David Halpern, and Sarah Fitzpatrick (2002). *Social Capital: A Discussion Paper*. London: Performance and Innovation Unit.

Amakawa, Akira (1986). "Henkaku no Koso: Doshu Seiron no Bunmyaku" (Reformation Ideas: The Context of *Doshu* Debates). In *Nihon no Chiho Seifu* (Local Government in Japan), eds. Omori Wataru and Sato Seizaburo. Tokyo: Tokyo Daigaku Shuppankai.

Anheier, Helmut K., and Wolfgang Seibel, eds. (1990). *The Third Sector: Comparative Studies of Nonprofit Organizations*. Berlin/New York: DeGruyter.

Aoyama, Nizo (1989). "Kawasaki-shi Joho Kokai Jorei no Shikkogo no Mondaiten" (Post-enforcement Problems of Kawasaki City's Information Disclosure Ordinance). *Chiho Seiji*, no. 357 (December): 11–18.

Aqua, Ronald (1980). "Political Choice and Policy Change in Medium-Sized Japanese Cities, 1962–1974." In *Political Opposition and Local Politics in Japan*, eds. Kurt Steiner, Ellis S. Krauss, and Scott C. Flanagan. Princeton: Princeton University Press.

Arendt, Hannah (1958). *The Origin of Totalitarianism*. New York: Meridian Books.

——— (1977). *On Revolution*. New York: Penguin Books.

Asahi Evening News. November 3, 1999.

Asahi Shinbun. August 15, 1954; August 15,1963; August 15, 1964; August 15, 1972; February 23, 1985; August 15, 1990; August 15, 1991; September 22, 1993; November 3, 1994; August 15, 1995; April 26, 1996; May 26, 1996; November 22, 1996; December 21, 1996; October 9, 1998; January 1–9, 1999; January 14, 1999; November 22, 1999; September 19, 2000; September 20, 2000; April 14, 2001; May 2, 2001; May 29, 2001; July 18, 2001; January 27, 2002; June 16, 2002; October 29, 2002; January 30, 2003; March 13, 2003; April 15, 2003; May 3, 2005.

Asahi Shinbun (Osaka edition). December 9, 2000.

Asahi Shinbun. Digital News Archives (a full text database of *Asahi Shinbun*). 1984–2002.

Asher, Herbert (1998). *Polling and the Public: What Every Citizen Should Know*. Washington, D.C.: Congressional Quarterly Press.

Bailey, Stephen (1999). *Local Government Economics: Principles and Practice*. Basingstoke: Macmillan.

Bell, Daniel (1974). *The Coming of Post-Industrial Society: A Venture in Social Forecasting.* London: Heinemann Educational.

Berger, Thomas (1993). "From Sword to Chrysanthemum: Japan's Culture of Anti-militarism." *International Security* 17, no. 4 (Spring): 119–50.

Boix, Carles, and Daniel Posner (1998). "Social Capital: Explaining Its Origins and Effects on Government Performance." *British Journal of Political Science* 28, no. 4 (October): 686–94.

Bourdieu, Pierre (1986). "The Forms of Capital." In *Handbook of Theory and Research for the Sociology of Education,* ed. John Richardson. New York: Greenwood Press.

Brown, David, and Darcy Ashman (1996). "Participation, Social Capital, and Intersectoral Problem Solving: African and Asian Cases." *World Development* 24, no. 9 (September): 1467–79.

Browning, Graeme (1996). *Electronic Democracy: Using the Internet to Transform American Politics.* Wilton, CT: Pemberton Press.

Calder, Kent E. (1988). *Crisis and Compensation: Public Policy and Political Stability in Japan,* Princeton: Princeton University Press.

Campbell, John C. (1979). "The Old People Boom and Japanese Policy Making." *Journal of Japanese Studies* 5, no. 2: 321–57.

——— (1984). "Problems, Solution, Non-Solutions and Free Medical Care for the Elderly in Japan." *Pacific Affairs* 57, no. 1: 53–64.

Campbell, John C., and Ikegami Naoki (2000). "Long-Term Care Insurance Comes to Japan." *Health Affairs* 19, no. 3 (May–June): 26–39.

Castells, Manuel (1989). *The Information Society: Information Technology, Economic Restructuring, and the Urban-Regional Process.* Oxford: B. Blackwell.

Chan-Tiberghien, Jennifer (2004). *Gender and Human Rights in Japan: Global Norms and Domestic Networks.* Stanford: Stanford University Press.

Chiba, Mitsuyuki (2002). "Chiba Mitsuyuki Shicho ni Kiku" (Interviews with Mayor Mitsuyuki Chiba). *Gabanansu* 38 (June): 37.

Chino, Torao (1982). "Onbuzuman Seido ni tsuite no Ikkosatsu" (Some Considerations of Ombuds Systems). *Chiho Jichi,* no. 411 (February): 2–8.

Chosen Shoko Shinbun. December 6, 1994; December 20, 1994.

Christensen, Ray (2000). "The Impact of Electoral Rules in Japan." In *Democracy and the Status of Women in East Asia,* eds. Rose J. Lee and Cal Clark. Boulder, CO: Lynne Rienner.

Cicero, Marcus Tullius (1928). *De Legibus.* Book 1. Trans. and ed. C. W. Keyes. London: Loeb Classical Library.

Civil Society Monitor (2001). General Section. no. 6 (July).

——— (2003). General Section. no. 8 (December).

Clark, Terry, and Lorna Ferguson (1983). *City Money: Political Processes, Fiscal Strain, and Retrenchment.* New York: Columbia University Press.

Cohen, Jean L., and Andrew Arato (1992). *Civil Society and Political Theory.* Cambridge: MA: MIT Press.

Collick, Martin (1988). "Social Policy Pressures and Responses." In *Dynamic and Immobilist Politics in Japan,* eds. J. A. A. Stockwin et al. London: Macmillan.

Community Fund (2003). "Machi ga Genki ni Naru Shikumi" (Mechanisms for Revitalizing the Town). http://www.h7.dion.ne.jp/~fund/ (accessed April 2006).

Curtis, Gerald L. (1999). *The Logic of Japanese Politics: Leaders, Institutions, and the Limits of Change.* New York: Columbia University Press.

Darcy, Robert, and Sarah Schramm (1977). "When Women Run against Men." *Public Opinion Quarterly* 41, no. 1 (Spring): 1–12.

Darcy, Robert, Susan Welch, and Janet Clark (1987). *Women, Election, and Representation.* New York: Longman.

Dekker, Paul, and Eric Uslaner (2001). "Introduction." In *Social Capital and Participation in Everyday Life,* ed. Eric Uslaner. London: Routledge.

Deta Besu/Paburikku Komento (Database—Public Comments) (2004). http://www. geocities.co.jp/WallStreet/3993/note/pcdb.html (accessed February 2004).

deLeon, Peter (1994). "Reinventing the Policy Science: Three Steps Back to the Future." *Policy Sciences* 27, no. 1 (March): 77–95.

Diamond, Larry (1999). *Developing Democracy: Toward Consolidation.* Baltimore: Johns Hopkins University Press.

DiMaggio, Paul J., and Helmut K. Anheier (1990). "The Sociology of Nonprofit Organizations and Sectors." *Annual Review of Sociology,* no. 16: 137–59.

Domoto, Akiko (2005). "JJ Junen no Ayumi" (Developments in the Decade of JJ). Compiled issue of *JJ-Net News,* 301–404.

Ecomesse (2006). "Kankyo Machizukuri Ekomesse" (Environmental Town-Making, the Ecomesse). http://www.npo-ecomesse.org (accessed April 2006).

Edelman (2006). *Edelman Trust Barometer: The Seventh Global Opinion Leaders Study.* http://www.edelman.com/image/insights/content/FullSupplement_final.pdf (accessed December 2006).

Edwards, Michael, and David Hume, eds. (1996). *Beyond the Magic Bullet: NGO Performance and Accountability in the Post-Cold War World.* West Hartford, CT: Kumarian Press.

Eichenberg, Richard (1989). *Public Opinion and National Security in Western Europe: Consensus Lost?* Ithaca: Cornell University Press.

Enami, Toshihiro (2002). *Denshi Jichitai* (e-Local Government). Tokyo: Toyo Keizai Shinposha.

End Child Prostitution in Asian Tourism (ECPAT) (2002). "The Summary of Activity 1992–1999 of ECPAT, Japan." http://www.ecpatstop.org/newkatsudo_ecpatstop_ 1994_2002/katsudou_houkaku_1999_stop.html (accessed March 2006).

Endo, Saburo (1984). "Chiho Zaisei Kiki to Chiho Kofuzei" (Local Fiscal Crisis and the Local Allocation Tax). *Toshi Mondai* 75, no. 5 (May): 18–34.

European Commission, High Level Expert Group of the Information Society (1996). *Building the European Information Society for Us All: First Reflections of the High Level Group of Experts.* Interim Report. European Commission, Brussels.

Fox, Jonathan (1994). "The Difficult Transition from Clientelism to Citizenship: Lessons from Mexico." *World Politics* 46, no. 2 (January): 151–84.

Freeman, Gary P. (1995). "Modes of Immigration Politics in Liberal Democratic States." *International Migration Review* 24, no. 4 (Winter): 881–902.

Fujin Tenbo (1998). "Josei no Gikai Shinshitsu Shien Kusanone Gurupu" (Grassroots Groups for Promoting Women to Assemblies). March, pp. 4–6.

——— (1998). "Josei Toshu Intabyu: Henkakuki no Josei Seijika" (Interviews with Female Party Leaders: Women Politicians in a Transitional Period). April, p. 5.

Fukuoka Yasunori (1996). "Koreans in Japan: Past and Present." *Saitama University Review* 31, no. 1: 1–15.

Fukushimaken Shizen Hogo Kyokai, ed. (1993). *Oze: Shizen Hogo Undo no Genten* (Oze: The Origin of Nature Protection Movements). Tokyo: Tokyo Shinbun Shuppankyoku.

Fukuyama, Francis (1995). *Trust: The Social Virtues and the Creation of Prosperity.* London: Hamish Hamilton.

Gant, John, Casey Ichniowski, and Kathryn Shaw (2002). "Social Capital and Organizational Change in High-Involvement and Traditional Work Organizations." *Journal of Economics and Management Strategy* 11, no. 2 (Summer): 289–328.

Garon, Sheldon (1997). *Molding Japanese Minds: The State in Everyday Life.* Princeton: Princeton University Press.

Garrett, Geoffrey (1998). *Partisan Politics in the Global Economy.* New York: Cambridge University Press.

Gelb, Joyce (1989). *Feminism and Politics: A Comparative Perspective.* Berkeley: University of California Press.

Gidron, Benjamin, Ralph M. Kramer, and Lester M. Salamon, eds. (1992). *Government and the Third Sector: Emerging Relationships in Welfare States.* San Francisco: Jossey-Bass.

Google Directory, http://directory.google.com/ Top/World/Japanese/ (accessed June 2004).

Gorz, André (1982). *Farewell to the Working Class: An Essay on Post-Industrial Socialism.* Boston: South End Press.

Goto, Aya, Michael Reich, and Ian Aitken (1999). "Oral Contraceptives and Women's Health in Japan." *Journal of the American Medical Association* 282, no. 22: 2173–77.

Gurowitz, Amy (1999). "Mobilizing International Norms: Domestic Actors, Immigrants, and the Japanese State." *World Politics* 51, no. 3 (April): 413–45.

Habermas, Jürgen (1989). *The Structural Transformation of the Public Sphere.* Cambridge: MIT Press.

Hall, John W. (1968). "The Castle Town and Japan's Modern Urbanization." In *Studies in the Institutional History of Early Modern Japan*, eds. John W. Hall and Marius B. Jansen, Princeton: Princeton University Press.

Hall, Peter (1999). "Social Capital in Britain." *British Journal of Political Science* 29, no. 3 (June): 417–61.

——— (2002). "Great Britain: The Role of Government and the Distribution of Social Capital." In *Democracies in Flux: The Evolution of Social Capital in Contemporary Society*, ed. Robert Putnam. New York: Oxford University Press.

Hasegawa, Koichi (2003). *Kankyo Mondai to Atarashii Kokyoken* (Environmental Problems and a New Public Sphere). Tokyo: Yuhikaku.

Hastings, Elizabeth, and Philip Hastings, eds. (1978/79–1998/99). *Index to International Public Opinion.* Annuals. Westport: Greenwood Press.

Hatoyama, Yukio (1996). "Minshuto to Watashi no Seiken Koso" (The Democratic Party and My Political Views). *Bungei Shunjyu*, November 1996, pp. 113–22.

Helco, Hugh (1974). *Modern Social Politics in Britain and Sweden.* New Haven: Yale University Press.

Helco, Hugh, and Aaron Widavsky (1974). *The Private Government of Public Money.* Berkeley and Los Angeles: University of California Press.

Higuchi, Naoto (2000). "Taiko to Kyoryoku" (Resistance and Cooperation). In *Gaikokujin Shimin to Seiji Sanka* (Foreign Citizens and Political Participation), ed. Miyajima Takashi. Tokyo: Yushindo.

Hirano, Hiroshi (2002). "Shakai Shihon to Seijisanka" (Social Capital and Political Participation). *Japanese Journal of Electoral Studies* 17, pp. 19–21.

Hirano, Ken'ichiro (1987). "Ajia ni okeru Chuo to Chiho" (The Center and the Periphery in Asia). *Ajia Kenkyu* 33 (March): 1–17.

Hirasawa, Kiyohito (1961). "Edo Jidai no Noson no 'Mujin'" (The *Mujin* of Villages in Edo Japan). *Ina* 88 (December): 42–68.

Hirose, Michisada (1981). "Gyosei Kaikau to Jiminto" (Administrative Reform and the Liberal Democratic Party). *Sekai* 429: 245–57.

——— (1981). *Hojokin to Seikento* (Grants and Party in Power). Tokyo: Asahi Shinbunsha.

———— (1984). "Hojokin Sakugen no Tadashii Shuho to Ayamatta Shuho" (Right and Wrong Ways of Grant Cutbacks). *Gekkan Jichiken* 26: 14–19.

Hoffman, Donna L., Thomas P. Novak, and Ann E. Schlosser (2001). "The Evolution of the Digital Divide." In *The Digital Divide: Facing a Crisis or Creating a Myth?* ed. Benjamin M. Compaine. Cambridge, MA: MIT Press.

Hood, Christopher (1996). "Exploring Variations in Public Management Reform." In *Civil Service Systems in Comparative Perspective*, eds. Hans A. G. M. Bekke, James L. Perry, and Theo A. J. Toonen. Bloomington and Indianapolis: Indiana University Press.

Hori, Masaharu (2002). "Japanese Public Administration and its Adaptation to New Public Management." Paper presented at the Fifteenth Annual Conference of the Public Administration Theory Network, Cleveland, Ohio, May 29–31.

Horii, Ken'ichi (2005). "Jumin Tohyo Joreian no Doki ni Kansuru Kenkyu: Kantoken ni okeru Gikai Gijiroku no Bunseiki ni yoru" (Studies on the Motives of Proposals for Local Referendum Ordinances: Analysis of Minutes of Assembly Meetings in the Kanto Region). Postgraduate thesis, Department of Social Engineering, Tokyo Institute of Technology.

Huber, Evelyn, and Leonard Ray (1999). "The Welfare State in Hard Times." In *Continuity and Change in Contemporary Capitalism*, eds. Herbert Kitschelt et al. New York: Cambridge University Press.

Hughes, Owen (1998). *Public Management and Administration: An Introduction.* South Melbourne: Macmillan Education.

Hughes, Owen, and Deirdre O'Neill (2000). *Public Management Reform: Some Lessons from the Antipodes.* Caulfield East, Victoria, Australia: Monash University.

Hyogo, Planning and Management Department (HPMD) (2004). *Hyogo-ken no Jiho Kokai/Kojin Joho Hogo* (Information Disclosure and Personal Information Protection by Hyogo Prefectural Government). 2004 ed. Kobe: Hyogo Prefectural Government.

Ichikawa, Fusae (1980). "Kokusai Fujinnen no Kodo Keikau to Katei" (Action Plans for International Women's Year and the Family). *Jujin Tenpo*, April, pp. 5–9.

Ichikawa Fusae Memorial Association (IFMA) (1999). *Local Assemblies, Handbook of Data on Japanese Women in Political Life, 1999.* Tokyo: Ichikawa Fusae Memorial Association.

———— (2003). *Local Assemblies, Handbook of Data on Japanese Women in Political Life, 2003.* Tokyo: Ichikawa Fusae Memorial Association.

———— ed. (2002). *Ichikawa Fusae Seiji Sanga Senta de Manabu 47-nin no Chosen* (47 Challengers Who Studied at the Promotion Center for Women's Political Participation). Tokyo: Ichikawa Fusae Memorial Foundation.

Ikeda, Ken'ichi (2002). "Nisen-nen Shugiin Senkyo ni okeru Shakai Shihon to Komunikeshon" (Social Capital and Communication in the 2000 Lower House Election). *Japanese Journal of Electoral Studies* 17, pp. 5–18.

———— (2005). "Seijiteki Hiseijiteki Nettowaku wa Shakaikankei Shihon o Umi Seiji no Riariti o Kiteisuruka" (The Creation of Social Capital and Political Reality from Political and Non-political Social Networks). *JGSS Kenkyu Ronbunshu* (JGSS Research Articles Collection). Vol. 4, pp. 169–203.

Imamura, Anne (1987). "The Japanese Urban Housewife: Tradition and Modern Social Participation." *Social Science Journal* 24, no. 2: 139–56.

———— (1987). *Urban Japanese Housewives: At Home in the Community*, Honolulu: University of Hawaii Press.

Imamura, Naraomi (1978). *Nogyo Noson to Hojokin* (Agriculture, Villages and Subsidies). Tokyo: Ie no Hikari Kyokai.

Inoguchi, Takashi (1997). "Japanese Bureaucracy: Coping with New Challenges." In *Japanese Politics Today: Beyond Karaoke Democracy?* eds. Purnendra Jain and Inoguchi Takashi. South Melbourne: Macmillan.

Institute for National Strategies Studies (2000). "The United States and Japan: Advancing toward a Mature Partnership." *INSS Special Report*, October 11. Washington, D.C.: Institute for National Security Studies, pp. 1–7.

Inter-Parliamentary Union (IPU) (2006). *Women in National Parliaments.* http://www. ipu.org/wmn-e/classif.html (accessed March 2006).

Iokibe, Makoto (1999). "Japan's Civil Society: An Historical Overview." In *Deciding the Public Good: Governance and Civil Society in Japan,* ed. Yamamoto Tadashi. Tokyo: Japan Center for International Exchange, 1999.

Irokawa, Daikichi (1985). *The Culture of the Meiji Period.* Princeton: Princeton University Press.

Ishikawa, Eisuke, and Tanaka Yuko (1999). *Oo-Edo Borantia Jijo* (The State of Volunteers in Greater Edo). Tokyo: Kodansha.

Ito, Motoshige (1989). "Shoddy Taxes, Shady Politics." *Japan Echo* 16: 52–57.

Iwamoto, Misako (2001). "1999-nen Chiho Senkyo ni okeru Josei no Yakushin" (Women's Advances in the 1999 Local Elections). *Seisaku Kagaku* 8, no. 3 (February): 21–38.

Iwao, Sumiko (1993). *The Japanese Women: Traditional Image and Changing Reality.* New York: Free Press.

Iwate Prefecture (2004). "Koucho no Homupeiji" (Home Page for Public Hearings). http://www.pref.iwate.jp/~koucho/index.html (accessed February 2004).

Jacobson, David (1996). *Rights across Borders: Immigration and the Decline of Citizenship.* Baltimore: Johns Hopkins University Press.

James, Estelle, ed. (1989). *The Nonprofit Sector in International Perspective: Studies in Comparative Culture and Policy.* Oxford: Oxford University Press.

James, Oliver (1999). "Varieties of New Public Management." Paper presented at the annual meeting of the American Political Science Association, Atlanta, Georgia, September 2–5.

Japan, Agency for Cultural Affairs (ACA) (1999 and 2004). *Shukyo Nenkan* (Annual of Religion). Tokyo: ACA.

Japan, Association for Promoting Fair Elections (2003). *Toitsu Chiho Senkyo ni okeru Tohyoritsu no Suii* (Trends of Voter Turnouts in the Unified Local Elections). http://www.akaruisenkyo.or.jp/tohyo/top.html (accessed June 2004).

Japan, Cabinet Office (2001). "Jittai Chosa Hokokusho" (Investigation Reports). http://www.npo-homepage.go.jp/index.html (accessed December 2006).

———. (2003). *PFI ni kansuru Zenkoku Jichitai Anketo* (Questionnaire on PFI for Local Governments). http://www8.cao.go.jp/pfi/shiryo_sb_5_3.pdf (accessed December 2006).

——— (2003). *Soshiaru Kyapitaru: Yutakana Ningen Kankei to Shimin Katsudo no Kojunkan o Motomete* (Social Capital: Search for Positive Feedback from Rich Human Relationships to Citizens' Activities). Tokyo: Quality-of-Life Policy Bureau, Cabinet Office.

——— (2006). "NPO Hojin no Ruikei Ninsho Dantaisu no Suii" (Trends in Authorized NPO Legal Persons). http://www.npo-homepage.go.jp/data/pref.html (accessed June 2006).

Japan, Cabinet Office, Gender Equality Bureau (GEB) (1996). *Danjo Kyodo Sankaku Bijon: Nijuisseiki no Arata na Kachi no Sozo* (A Vision of Gender Equality: Creation of New Values for the Twenty-first Century). http://www.gender.go.jp/english_contents/index.html (accessed April 2006).

———— (2000). *Gender Information Site.* http://www.gender.go.jp/shimon_toushin_ronten.html (accessed December 2000).

———— (2006). *Josei no Seisaku Hoshin Kettei Sankaku Jokyo Shirabe* (Report on the State of Gender Equality Policies and Measures to Promote the Formation of a Gender Equal Society). http://www.gender.go.jp/ (accessed October 2006).

Japan, Cabinet Office, PFI Promotion Office (2001). *Guidelines.* http://www8.cao.go.jp/pfi/guideline.html (accessed June 2006).

———— (2004). *PFI ni kansuru Zenkoku Jichitai Anketo* (Questionnaire on PFI for Local Governments). http://www8.cao.go.jp/pfi/1601601questionnaire.pdf (accessed December 2006).

———— (2006). *PFI Promotion Committee.* http://www8.cao.go.jp/pfi/shiryo_a_12.html (accessed June 2006).

Japan, Cabinet Office, Public Relations Office (2003). "Jieitai Boei Mondai ni kansuru Yoron Chosa" (Opinion Poll on the Self-Defense Forces and Security Problems). http://www8.cao.go.jp/survey/h14/h14-bouei/index.html (accessed December 2006).

Japan, Diet, House of Councilors (HOC) (1994). Minutes of Committee on the Budget. June 3.

———— (1995). Minutes of Committee on the Budget. February 8.

———— (1997). Minutes of Committee on Labor. May 29.

———— (1997). Minutes of Committee on Local Administration. December 9.

———— (1999). Minutes of Committee on Judicial Affairs. May 6.

———— (2002). Minutes of Plenary Session. October 22.

Japan, Diet, House of Councilors, Third Special Inquiry Section, ed. (1995). *Onbuzuman Seido Kankei Shiryoshu I* and *III* (Materials on Ombuds Systems I and III). Tokyo: Third Special Inquiry Section.

Japan, Diet, House of Representatives (HOR) (1961). Minutes of the Committee on the Cabinet. April 13.

———— (1982). Minutes of the Committee on the Cabinet. April 13.

———— (1982). Minutes of the Committee on the Audit. April 23.

———— (1997). Minutes of Plenary Session. January 23.

———— (2001). Minutes of the Constitution Research Council. December 6.

———— (2002). Minutes of the Special Committee on an Emergency Contingency Bill. July 3.

———— (2003). Minutes of the Special Committee on Emergency Contingency Bills. May 20.

———— (2003). Minutes of Plenary Session. June 5.

Japan, Digitalization Consortium of Local Governments (2002). *Denshi Seifu Jichitai Gaido* (Guides to e-Government /Local Government). Tokyo: JMA Management Center.

Japan, Economic Planning Agency (EPA), ed. (1996). *Kokumin Keizai Keisan Hokoku* (Report of statistics on national economy, 1955–94). Tokyo: Zaimusho Insatsukyoku.

Japan, Economic Planning Agency (EPA) (1977 and 2000). "The National Survey on Lifestyle Preferences" (1977 and 2000). http://www5.cao.go.jp/j-j/wp-pl/wp-p100/hakusho-00–1-13.html (accessed December 2006).

———— (1979 and 1999). *Kokumin Keizai Keisan Nenpo* (Annual Report on National Economic Statistics). 1977 and 1997 eds. Tokyo: EPA.

————, ed. (1995). *Keizai Hakusho* (Economic White Paper). Tokyo: Okurasho Insatsukyoku.

————, ed. (1997). *Shimin Katsudo Repoto: Shimin Katsudo Dantai Kihon Chosa Hokoku* (Report on Citizens' Activities: Basic Research Report on Citizens' Action Groups). Tokyo: Okurasho Insatsukyoku.

———— (1998). "Kojin kara Mita Shimin Katsudo ni Kansuru Chosa" (Survey on Citizens' Activities in the Eyes of Private Individuals). http://www.epa.go.jp/98/c/19980707c-kojin.html (accessed January 2001).

————, ed. (1998). *Nihon no NPO Keizai Kibo: Minkan Hieiri Katsudo Dantai ni kansuru Keizai Bunseki Chosa Hokoku* (The Economic Scale of NPOs in Japan: Economic Analysis Report on Private Nonprofit Activity Organizations). Tokyo: Okurasho Insatsukyoku.

————, ed. (1998). *Open the NPO: Kokateki na Joho Hasshin no tame ni* (Open the NPO: For Effective Information Disclosure). Tokyo: Okurasho Insatsukyoku.

Japan, e-Local Government Conference (2003). *Denshi Jichitai ni kansuru Ankeito Chosa* (Survey on e-Local Government). http://e-lg.jp/ga/ma-tyosa03.html (accessed April 2003).

Japan Environment Association (2004). *Kankyo NGO Soran* (Environmental NGO Survey). http://www.erca.go.jp (accessed June 2005).

Japan, Financial System Council (FSC) (1994). *Council Report.* December 21.

Japan, Immigration Bureau (2005). *Hodo Shiryo* (Press Releases). June.

Japan, IT Strategic Headquarters (2001). *e-Japan Strategy.* http://www.kantei.go.jp/jp/singi/it2/kettei/010122honbun.html (accessed June 2004).

Japan, Local Decentralization Promotion Committee (1996). Minutes of the Committee in the 50th Session (Hearings from Budget Bureau, Ministry of Finance). September 19.

Japan, Ministry of Education, Culture, Sports, Science and Technology (MECSST) (former Ministry of Education) (1997 and 2005). *Gakko Kihon Chosa Hokokusho* (Fundamental Investigation Report on Schools). Annuals. Tokyo: MECSST.

Japan, Ministry of Health, Labor and Welfare (MHLW) (former Ministry of Labor) (1998 and 2005). *Rodo Kumiai Kiso Chosa Hokoku* (Basic Investigation Report on Labor Unions). Annuals. Tokyo: MHLW.

———— (2002). *Zenkoku Shakai Fukushi Kyogikai no Chosa* (National Social Welfare Council Survey). Tokyo: MHLW.

Japan, Ministry of Home Affairs (MOHA) (1949). *Gyosei Jitsurei* (Administrative Practical Examples). January 26.

Japan, Ministry of Internal Affairs and Communications (MIAC) (2000). *Chiho Zaisei Hakusho* (White Paper on Local Public Finance). 2000 ed. Tokyo: Okurasho Insatsukyoku.

———— (2000). *Joho Tsushin Gijutsu Kakumei ni taio shita Chiho Kokyodantai ni okeru Johoka Shisakuto no Suishin ni kansuru Shishin* (Guidelines for the Promotion of Local Government IT Policies in Response to IT Revolution). http://www.soumu.go.jp/news/000828.html (accessed June 2004).

———— (2001). *Digital Opportunity Site.* http://www.dosite.jp/e/do/j-state_net.html (accessed July 2004).

———— (2001). *Hodo Shiryo* (News Releases). October 23, 2001.

———— (2001). *Joho Tsushin Hakusho* (White Paper on Information and Telecommunications). Tokyo: Gyosei.

———— (2002). *Hodo Shiryo* (News Releases). July 31, 2002; September 3, 2002; October 17, 2002; November 28, 2002.

———— (2003). *Chiho Kokyo Dantai no Baransushito-to no Sakusei Jokyo* (Status of Creation of Balance Sheets in Local Government). http://www.soumu.go.jp/s-news/2003/pdf/030805_1.pdf (accessed December 2006).

———— (2003). *Chiho Zaisei Hakusho* (White Paper on Local Public Finance). http://www.soumu.go.jp/menu_05/hakusyo/chihou/17data/17cz.html(accessed February 2006).

———— (2003). *Hodo Shiryo* (News Releases). August 5, 2003.

———— (2003). *Information and Communications in Japan: Building a New Japan-Inspired IT Society.* http://www.soumu.go.jp/english/whitepaper/index.html (accessed July 2003).

———— (2003). *White Paper on Local Public Finance, 2003.* http://www.soumu.go.jp/english/whitepaper/index.html (accessed May 2006).

———— (2004). *Hodo Shiryo* (News Releases). July 30, 2004; August 27, 2004.

———— (2004). *Koeki Hojin ni kansuru Nenji Hokoku.* http://www.soumu.go.jp/daijnkanbou/kanri/h16koueki/mokuji.html (accessed June 2005).

———— (2004). *Paburikkukomento* (Public Comments). http://search.e-gov.go.jp/servlet/Public (accessed February 2004).

———— (2004). *Status of Implementation of Outsourcing of Services in Municipalities.* http://www5.cao.go.jp/zenbun/wp-e/we-je04/04-2-3-06z.html (accessed December 2006).

———— (2005). *Hodo Shiryo* (News Releases). April 1, 2005; April 14, 2005; September 12, 2005.

———— (2006). *Chiho Bunken* (Local Decentralization). http://www.soumu.go.jp/indexb4.html (accessed June 2006).

———— (2006). *Chiho Kokyo Dantai ni okeru Gyosei Hyoka no Torikumi Jokyo* (Status of Implementation of Administrative Evaluation in Local Governments). www.soumu.go.jp/click/pdf/jyokyo_20060101_01.pdf (accessed December 2006).

———— (2006). *Hodo Shiryo* (News Releases). April 7, 2006.

———— (2006). *Statistical Handbook of Japan.* http://www.stat.go.jp/English/data/handbook/c02cont.htm#cha2_2 (accessed April 2006).

Japan, Ministry of Internal Affairs and Communications (MIAC), Local Administration Bureau (2006). *Gappei Dejitaru Akaibu* (Merger Digital Archive). http://www.soumu.go.jp/gapei/index.html (accessed June 2006).

Japan National Council of Social Welfare (1999). *Heisei Jyuichi-nendo Shakai Fukushi Kyogikai Kihon Chosa* (The 1999 Basic Investigation by the Japan National Council of Social Welfare). Tokyo: Japan National Council of Social Welfare.

———— (1999). *Heisei Jyuichi-nendo Todofuken Shiteitoshi Shakai Fukushi Kyogikai Borantiasenta Kankei Chosa* (The 1999 Social Welfare Council Investigation on Volunteer Activities in Prefectures and Designated Municipalities). Tokyo: Japan National Council of Social Welfare.

Japan NGO Center for International Cooperation (JANIC), ed. (1998). *Data Book on Japanese NGOs '98.* Tokyo: JANIC.

Japan, Prime Minister of Japan and His Cabinet (PMJC) (2005). *Sanmi Ittai Kaikau ni tsuite* (Regarding the Trinity Reform). November 30. http://www.kantei.go.jp/jp/singi/kunitotihon/dai14/14gijisidai.html (accessed June 2006).

———— (2006). *Major Policy Reports.* http://www.kantei.go.jp/foreign/policyindex_e.html (accessed January 2006).

Japan, Prime Minister's Office (PMO), ed. (1999). *Koeki Hojin Hakusho: Koeki Hojin ni kansuru Nenji Hokoku* (White Paper on Public Benefit Organizations: Annual Report on Nonprofit Organizations). Tokyo: Okurasho Insatsukyoku.

Japan, Prime Minister's Office (PMO), Local System Investigation Council (1976). *Report on Measures Promoting the Consciousness of Residents for Local Autonomy.* Tokyo: Local System Investigation Council.

Japan, Prime Minister's Office (PMO), Public Relations, (1991). *Josei ni kansuru Yoron Chosa* (Opinion Survey on Women). September.

Japan, Second Provisional Commission for Administrative Reform (SPCAR) (1982). *Basic Report.* July 30.

Japan, Supreme Court, Third Petty Bench (1995). February 28, no. 163.

Japan Times. July 2, 2003.

Japan, Tokyo District Court (1978). March 31. In "Tokyo Metropolitan Adachi Welfare Office Director Case."

Jijitsushin. January 27, 2002; September 12, 2004.

JILG: Information Service 51 (May, 2005): 3–4.

JJ-Net News. August 10, 1996; March 2, 2001.

Joppke, Christian (1998). "Why Liberal States Accept Unwanted Immigration." *World Politics* 50, no. 2 (January): 266–93.

Kabashima, Ikuo (1998). *Hokaku Ideorogi no Henyo: Seiken Koutai to Yukensha no Taido Henyo* (Transformation in Conservative/Progressive Ideologies: Regime Change and the Transformation of Voter Attitudes). Tokyo: Bokutakusha.

Kalathil, Shanthi (2003). "Dot.com for Dictators." *Foreign Policy,* no. 135 (March–April): 42–49.

Kanagawa Mintoren News. September 26, 2000.

Kanagawa Prefectural Residents Bureau (KPRBB) (2000–2005). *Joho Kokai Seido Unyo Jokyo* (Implementation of the Information Disclosure System). Annual reports. Various years.

Kanashiro, Yuichi (2001). "Paburiku Manejimento" (Public Management). *Chiiki Seisaku Kenkyu* 15 (June): 13–16.

Kaneko, Ikuyo et al. (1998). *Borantari Keizai no Tanjo* (The Birth of the Voluntary Economy). Tokyo: Jitsugyo no Nihonsha.

Kansai Sogo Kenkyujo, ed. (1996). *1996 NIRA Research Report: Chiiki Fukushi ni okeru NPO Shien Ikusei Hosaku no Teigen* (Proposals for the Ways to Support and Promote Local Welfare NGOs). Tokyo: National Institute for Research Advancement.

Kant, Immanuel (1970). "Idea for a Universal History from a Cosmo-political Point of View." In *The Theory of International Relations: Selected Texts from Gentili to Treitschke,* eds. M. Forsyth, H. M. A. Keens-Soper, and P. Savigear, London: Allen & Unwin.

Kasemire, Bernd et al., eds. (2003). *Public Participation in Sustainable Science: A Handbook.* Cambridge: Cambridge University Press.

Kasuga, Masashi (2000). "Local Councillors in Modern Japan: Considerations on Some Sociological Differences between Men and Women Councillors." In *Identity Politics and Critiques in Contemporary Japan,* eds. Vera Mackie et al. Clayton, Victoria, Australia: Monash Asia Institute.

Kato, Junko (1997). "Tax Policy in Japan after the Demise of Conservative Dominance." In *Japanese Politics Today: Beyond Karaoke Democracy?* eds. Purnendra Jain and Inoguchi Takashi. South Melbourne: Macmillan.

Kato, Koichi (1995). Speech delivered to the Committee on the Budget, House of Representatives. January 27.

Kawachi, Ichiro, Bruce Kennedy, and Roberta Glass (1999). "Social Capital and Self-Rated Health: A Contextual Analysis." *American Journal of Public Health* 89, no. 8 (August): 1187–93.

Kawasaki City, Investigation Committee for Foreign Residents' Perception (1995). *Kawasakishi Gaikokuseki Shimin Ishiki Jittai Chosa Hokokusho: Jirei Mensetsu Hen* (Report on Investigation into the Actual Condition of Foreign Residents' Perception: Case Studies and Interviews). Kawasaki: Kawasaki City.

Kawasaki City, Investigation Committee on the Establishment of a Kawasaki City Representative Assembly for Foreign Residents (1996). *Kawasakishi Gaikokujin Shimin Daihyosha Kaigi Chosa Kenkyu Hokokusho* (Investigation Report on a Kawasaki City Representative Assembly for Foreign Residents). Kawasaki: Kawasaki City, International Office.

Kawasaki City, Promotion Committee on Regional Japanese Language Education (1997). *Kyosei Machizukuri o Mezasu Nihongo Gakushu no Arikata* (The Ideal of Japanese Language Learning for Making One Community). Kawasaki: Promotion Committee.

Keck, Margaret, and Kathryn Sikkink (1998). *Activists beyond Borders: Advocacy Networks in International Politics.* Ithaca: Cornell University Press.

Kelley, Jonathan, and Ian McAllister (1983). "The Electoral Consequences of Gender in Australia." *British Journal of Political Science* 13, no. 3 (July): 365–77.

Keohane, Nannerl (1981). "Speaking from Silence: Women and the Science of Politics." In *A Feminist Perspective in the Academy: The Difference it Makes,* eds. Elizabeth Langland and Walter Gove. Chicago: University of Chicago Press.

Kikegawa, Hiroshi (1955). *Meiji Chiho Jichiseido no Seiritsu Katei* (The Formation Process of the Meiji Local Autonomy System). Tokyo: Tokyo Shisei Chosakai.

Kikuchi, Hidefumi (1995). "Kawasaki-shi Shimin Onbuzuman Seido no Jissai" (The Kawasaki City Ombuds System in Practice). *Toyo Hogaku* 39, no. 1 (September): 171–75.

Kim, Kiseong (2005). "Social Capital and the Role of Local Government: A Virtuous Cycle between Institution and Culture." *Journal of Public Policy Studies* 5: 130–40.

Kitagawa, Yoichi (2003). "Chiho Bunken ga Motarasu Gyosei no Manejimentoka to Patonashippuka" (Managerialism and Partnership Trends of Administration Driven by Local Decentralization). In *Hokatsuteki Chiho Jichi Gabanansu Kaikau* (Comprehensive Reform of Local Governance), eds. Muramatsu Michio and Inatsugu Hiroaki. Tokyo: Toyo Keizai Shinposha.

Kiyohara, Keiko (2000). *Mitaka ga Tsukuru Jichitai Shinjidai* (A New Age of Local Government that Mitaka Creates). Mitaka: Mitaka City.

Kobayashi, Hiroshi (2003). "Mitaka-shi ni okeru Patonashippu ni yoru Tenkai to Kongo no Hoko" (Developments and Future Directions of Partnership in Mitaka City). *Chiiki Seisaku Kenkyu* 25 (December): 48–49.

Kobayashi, Yoshie (2004). *A Path toward Gender Equality: State Feminism in Japan.* New York: Routledge.

Korac-Kakabadse, Andrew, and Nada Korac-Kakabadse (1999). "Information Technology's Impact on the Quality of Democracy." In *Reinventing Government in the Information Age,* ed. Richard Heeks. London: Routledge.

Kubo, Kimiko (2006). Secretary General, Ichikawa Fusae Memorial Association, Interview by the author on April 20.

Kyogoku, Jun'ichi (1983). *Nihon no Seiji* (Politics in Japan). Tokyo: University of Tokyo Press.

LeBlanc, Robin M. (1999). *Bicycle Citizens: The Political World of the Japanese Housewife.* Berkeley and Los Angeles: University of California Press.

Lee, Jin-Kyu (1993). *Zainichi Chosenjin Sorengokai Chuo Iinkai Dai-jyurokki Dai-sanji Kaigi Kakudai Kaigi Bunkenshu* (Central Committee, General Association of Korean Residents, Documents of the Third Conference of the Sixteenth Term). Tokyo: Kugatsu Shobo.

Levy, Jonah D. (1999). *Tocqueville's Revenge: State, Society, and Economy in Contemporary France*. Cambridge, MA: Harvard University Press.

Locke, John (1988). *Two Treatises of Government*, ed. Peter Laslett. New York: Cambridge University Press.

Loegreid, Per (2001). "Administrative Reforms in Scandinavia—Testing the Cooperative Model." In *Public Sector Reform*, ed. Brendan C. Nolan. New York: Palgrave.

Lovenduski, Joni (2005). *Feminizing Politics*. Cambridge, UK: Polity Press.

Lowndes, Vivien, Gerry Stoker, Lawrence Pratchett, Steve Leach, and Melvin Wingfield (1998). *Enhancing Public Participation in Local Government*. London: Department of the Environment.

MacDougall, Terry (1975). "Political Opposition and Local Government in Japan." PhD dissertation, Yale University.

Mainichi Shinbun. May 27, 1946; August 15, 1955; August 15, 1956; March 9, 1982; May 18, 1990; August 15, 1991; August 15, 1992; August 15, 1995; January 5, 1996; January 9, 1996; April 17, 1996; April 22, 1996; May 2, 1996; January 23, 1997; August 15, 1997; February 4, 1999; May 29, 2001; June 15, 2001; March 19, 2002; May 3, 2004.

Maki, Taro (1982). "Rincho no Naibu Rikigaku" (Internal Dynamics of the Provisional Commission for Administrative Reform). *Sekai* 435: 42–48.

Martin, Sherry L. (2004). "Alienated, Independent and Female: Lessons from the Japanese Electorate." *Social Science Japan Journal* 7, no. 1 (April): 1–19.

Maruyama, Masao (1963). *Thought and Behaviour in Modern Japanese Politics*. London: Oxford University Press.

Matsushita, Keiichi (1998). *Jichitai no NPO Seisaku* (Local Government NPO Policy). Tokyo: Gyosei.

McCarthy, Katheen D., Virginia Hodgkinson, and Russy Sumariwalla (1992). *The Nonprofit Sector in the Global Community*. San Francisco: Jossey-Bass.

McConnaughey, J. W., W. Lader, R. Chin, and D. Everette (2002). *Falling through the Net II: New Data on the Digital Divide*. Washington, D.C.: NTIA, Department of Commerce.

Mifune, Tsuyoshi (2005). "Nihon ni okeru Shakai Sanka to Jumin Ishiki" (Social Participation in Japan and Residents' Consciousness). In *Chiho Jichitai ni okeru Shimin Ishiki no Dotai* (Dynamics of Citizens' Consciousness in Local Governments), ed. Kobayashi Yoshiaki. Tokyo: Keio University Press.

Miller, David (1999). "Bounded Citizenship." In *Cosmopolitan Citizenship*, eds. Kimberly Hutchings and Roland Dannreuther. London: Macmillan.

Miller, Gary J. (1992). *Managerial Dilemma: The Political Economy of Hierarchy*. New York: Cambridge University Press.

Mindan Shinbun. July 14, 2005.

Mitsui, Mariko et al. (1999). "Josei no Seiji Sanga to Dairinin Undo" (Women's Political Participation and Representative Authorization Campaign). *Shakai Undo*, no. 233: 2–26.

Miyake, Ichiro (1991). "Types of Partisanship, Partisan Attitudes, and Voting Choices." In *The Japanese Voter*, eds. Scott C. Flanagan et al. New Haven: Yale University.

Moore, Richard (1999). "Democracy and Cyberspace." In *Digital Democracy: Discourse and Decision Making in the Information Age*, eds. Barry Hague and Brian Loader. London: Routledge.

Morishita, Toru (1995). "Sengo Nihon Kokumin no Heiwa Ishiki no Tenkai" (Developments in the Peace Consciousness of the Japanese Public in Postwar Japan). *Rekishi Hyoron,* no. 553 (May): 32–46.

Mukuge Tsushin (Mukuge Correspondence). Nos. 148/149 (March 1995).

Muramatsu, Michio (1975). "The Impact of Economic Growth Policies in Local Politics in Japan." *Asian Survey* 15, no. 9: 799–816.

——— (1981). "Hojokin Seido no Seiji Gyoseijo no Igi" (Political and Administrative Significance of the Grants-in-aid System). *Jichi Kenkyu* 57 (September): 3–32.

——— (1986). "Central-Local Political Relations in Japan: A Lateral Competition Model." *Journal of Japanese Studies* 12 (Summer): 303–27.

——— (1994). *Nihon no Gyosei: Katsudogata Kanryosei no Henbo* (Japanese Public Administration: Changes in Patterns of Active Bureaucracy). Tokyo: Chuokoron.

——— (1999). *Gendai Gyosei no Seiji Bunseki* (Political Analysis of Contemporary Public Administration). Tokyo, Yuhikaku.

Murata, Tetsuo (1997). "Kankyo Mondai to NGO/NPO no Yakuwari" (Environmental Problems and the Role of NGO and NPO). *Toshi Mondai* 88, no. 4 (April): 57–67.

Muto, Hiromi (2004). *Jichitai Keiei Kaikau* (Local Public Management Reforms). Tokyo: Gyosei.

Nakamura, Eiko (2006). Secretary-General, Tokyo Citizens' Network. Interview by the author on April 26.

Nakamura, Norman (2004). Former chairperson of the Kawasaki City Representative Assembly for Foreign Residents. Interview by the author on July 12.

Nakasone, Yasuhiro (1998). "Politicians, Bureaucrats, and Policymaking in Japan." In *Unlocking the Bureaucrat's Kingdom: Deregulation and the Japanese Economy,* ed. Frank Gibney. Washington, D.C.: Brookings Institution Press.

——— (1999). *The Making of the New Japan: Reclaiming the Political Mainstream.* New York: Curzon Press.

NHK Yoron Chosa Kenkyujo (NHK Research Center for Public Opinion), ed. (1975). *Zusetsu Sengo Yoron Shi* (Illustrated History of Postwar Public Opinion). Tokyo: Nihon Hoso Shuppan Kyokai.

Nihei, Norihiro (2003). "Borantia towa Dareka: Sanka ni kansuru Shimin Shakairon-teki Zentei Saikento" (Who Are Volunteers? Re-examination of the Theoretical Premise of Civil Society Regarding Participation). *Soshioroji* 48, no. 1 (May): 93–109.

Nihon Keizai Shinbun. August 15, 1995; September 6, 1998; May 3, 1999; October 23, 2001; January 28, 2002.

Nihon Keizai Shinbun. Nikkei Telecom 21 (including a full text database of *Nihon Keizai Shinbun*). 1975–date.

Niigata Nippo. July 29, 1996; August 5, 1996; August 8, 1996; November 22, 1996.

Nikkei Human Resources (NHR) (2006). *Nikkei Navi.* http://job.nikkei.co.jp (accessed June 2006).

Nikkei Konputa. September 25, 2000.

Nippon Research Center (2000). *The Asia-Europe Survey of 2000.* Tokyo: Nippon Research Center.

Nippon Telegraph and Telephone (NTT) Data (2001). "Denshi Seifu to Minshushugi ni kansuru Shutoken Shimin Chosa" (Investigation Report on Citizens in the Capital Region for e-Government and Democracy). December.

——— (2002). "eDemokurashi ni kansuru Zenkoku Kojin Ankeito" (National Survey of Individuals concerning e-Democracy). *NTT Data News Releases,* April 10.

————— (2002). *Research & Development.* http://www.nttdata.co.jp/rd/riss/e-demo/report02.html (accessed June 2004).

Nisho, Masaru (1999). *Mikan no Bunken Kaikaku: Kasumigasei Kanryo to Kakutoshita Sen-sanbyaku-nichi* (Incomplete Decentralization Reforms: 1300 days Dealing with Kasumigasei Bureaucrats). Tokyo: Iwanami Shoten.

Nishio, Masaru et al. (1982). "Joho Kokai o Meguru Shomondai" (Some Problems of Information Disclosure). *Chiho Jichi*, no. 413 (April): 24–76.

Noguchi, Yukio (1987). "Public Finance." In *The Political Economy of Japan: The Domestic Transformation.* Vol. 1, eds. Yamamura Kozo and Yasuba Yasukichi. Stanford: Stanford University Press.

Nolan, Bredan, ed. (2001). *Public Sector Reform: An International Perspective.* New York: Palgrave Macmillan.

Norris, Pippa (1985). "Women's Legislative Participation in Western Europe." In *Women and Politics in Western Europe*, ed. Sylvia Bashevkin. London: Frank Cass.

NUA Ltd. (2002). *NUA Internet Survey.* http://www.nua.com/surveys/how_many_online/index.html (accessed July 2004).

Nye, Joseph, and Robert Keohane, eds. (1970). *Transnational Relations and World Politics.* Cambridge, MA: Harvard University Press.

O'Donnell, Guillermo, and Philippe C. Schmitter (1998). *Transition from Authoritarian Rule: Tentative Conclusions about Uncertain Democracies.* Baltimore: Johns Hopkins University Press.

Offe, Claus (1984). *Contradictions of the Welfare State.* Cambridge: MIT Press.

Ogai, Tokuko (2003). "Josei Mogi Kaigi to Iu Josei Seisaku" (Women's Simulation Assembly as Women's Policy). *The Annual of Japanese Political Science Association.* December, pp. 113–37.

Ogden, Michael R. (1994). "Politics in Parallel Universe: Is There a Future for Cyber-Democracy?" *Futures* 26, no. 7 (September): 713–29.

Ogita, Tamotsu (1985). "Hojokin Ichiritsu Sakugen Mondai ni tsuite Omou" (Some Consideration for the Problem of Uniform Grant Share Ratio Cuts). *Chiho Zaisei* 24: 4–14.

Okawara, Yoshio (1996). "The Future of International Exchange and Cooperation." Keynote address delivered at the Local Government International Exchange Seminar, Tokyo, November.

Organisation for Economic Co-operation and Development (OECD) (1987). *Economic Outlook.* Vol. 41. Paris: OECD.

————— (1998). *Economic Outlook.* Vol. 63. Paris: OECD.

————— (2001). *Revenue Statistics 1965–2000.* Paris: OECD.

————— (2001). *Understanding the Digital Divide.* http://www.oecd.org/dataoecd/38/57/1888451.pdf (accessed July 2003).

————— (2002). *National Accounts 1989–2000.* Paris: OECD.

————— (2004). *Revenue Statistics 1965–2003.* Paris: OECD.

————— (2005). *Economic Outlook.* Vol. 78. December. Paris: OECD.

————— (2005). *OECD Factbook 2005.* Paris: OECD.

Osaka Public Relations Office (OPRO) (2000–2005). *Osaka-fu no Joho Kokai* (Information Disclosure by Osaka Prefectural Government). Annual reports. Various years.

Osawa, Mari (2005). "Japanese Government Approaches to Gender Equality since the Mid-1990s." *Asian Perspective* 29, no. 1 (Spring): 157–73.

Oshima, Mitsuko (1997). *Meiji no Mura* (Villages in Meiji Japan). Tokyo: Kyoiku Sha.

Oshima, Taro (1968). *Nihon Chiho Gyozaisei Shi Josetsu* (Introduction to the History of Local Administration and Finance in Japan). Tokyo: Miraisha.

Ozaki, Seiichi (2003). "Gyosei Patona Seido" (Administrative Partnership). *Chiiki Seisaku Kenkyu* 25 (December): 53–56.

Ozawa, Ichiro (1994). *Blueprint for a New Japan: The Rethinking of a Nation.* Tokyo: Kodansha International.

Patterson, Dennis, and Nishikawa Misa (2002). "Political Interest or Interest in Politics? Gender and Party Support in Postwar Japan." *Women and Politics* 24, no. 2 (Summer): 1–34.

Peacock, Alan T., and Jack Wiseman (1961). *The Growth of Public Expenditure in the United Kingdom.* Princeton: Princeton University Press.

Pérez-Díaz, Victor (1995). "The Possibility of Civil Society: Traditions, Character and Challenges." In *Civil Society: Theory, History, Comparison,* ed. John Hall. Cambridge: Polity Press.

Pharr, Susan (1981). *Political Women in Japan: The Search for a Place in Political Life.* Berkeley: University of California Press.

——— (1997). "Public Trust and Democracy in Japan." In *Why People Don't Trust Government,* eds. Joseph S. Nye, Jr., Philip D. Zelikow, and David C. King. Cambridge, MA: Harvard University Press.

——— (2003). "Preface." In *The State of Civil Society in Japan,* eds. Frank Schwartz and Susan Pharr. Cambridge: Cambridge University Press.

Pharr, Susan, and Robert Putnam, eds. (2000). *Disaffected Democracies: What's Troubling the Trilateral Countries.* Princeton: Princeton University Press.

Phillips, Anne (1999). *Which Equality Matter?* Cambridge, UK: Polity Press.

Pierson, Paul (1994). *Dismantling the Welfare State? Reagan, Thatcher, and the Politics of Retrenchment.* New York: Cambridge University Press.

——— (1996). "The New Politics of the Welfare State." *World Politics* 48, no. 2 (January): 143–79.

Pollitt, Christopher (1993). *Managerialism and the Public Services: Cuts or Cultural Change in the 1990s.* Oxford: Blackwell.

Putnam, Robert (1993). *Making Democracy Work: Civic Traditions in Modern Italy.* Princeton: Princeton University Press.

——— (1995). "Bowling Alone: America's Declining Social Capital." *Journal of Democracy* 6, no. 1 (January): 65–78.

——— (2000). *Bowling Alone: The Collapse and Revival of American Community.* New York: Simon & Schuster.

Ra, Ilkyung (2005). "Nihon ni okeru Soshiarukyapitaru to Jyumin Ishiki" (Social Capital and Residents' Consciousness in Japan). In *Chiho Jichitai ni okeru Shimin Ishiki no Dotai* (Dynamics of Citizens' Consciousness in Local Governments), ed. Kobayashi Yoshiaki. Tokyo: Keio University Press.

Rawls, John (1993). *Political Liberalism.* New York: Columbia University Press.

Reed, Steven R. (1979). "Local Policy Making in an Urban State: The Case of Japanese Prefectures." Ph D dissertation, University of Michigan.

Republic of Korea, National Assembly (2002). Minutes of Legislation and Judicial Committee. February 28.

Risse-Kappen, Thomas (1991). "Structure, and Foreign Policy in Liberal Democracies." *World Politics* 43, no. 4 (July): 494–99.

Risse-Kappen, Thomas, and Kathryn Sikkink (1999) "The Socialization of International Human Rights Norms into Domestic Practices: Introduction." In *The Power of Human Rights: International Norms and Domestic Change,* eds. Thomas Risse-Kappen, Stephen C. Ropp, and Kathryn Sikkink. Cambridge: Cambridge University Press.

Robinson, Lindon, Allan Schmid, and Marcelo Siles (2002). "Is Social Capital Really Capital?" *Review of Social Economy* 60, no. 1 (March): 1–24.

Rodan, Garry (1998). "The Internet and Political Control in Singapore." *Political Science Quarterly* 113, no. 1 (Spring): 63–89.

Sakamoto, Yoshikazu (1994). "Heiwashugi no Gyakusetsu to Koso" (The Antithesis and Conception of Pacifism). *Sekai*, no. 597 (July): 22–40.

Salamon, Lester M. (1994). "The Rise of the Nonprofit Sector." *Foreign Affairs* 73, no. 4 (July–August): 109–22.

Salamon, Lester M., and Helmut K. Anheier (1996). *The Emerging Nonprofit Sector: An Overview.* Manchester, UK: Manchester University Press.

Samuels, Richard J. (1983). *The Politics of Regional Policy in Japan: Localities Incorporated?* Princeton: Princeton University Press.

Sankei Shinbun. December 17, 1995; January 8, 1996; January 21,1996; January 28, 1996; February 18, 1996; February 25, 1996; March 30, 1996; November 4, 1998.

Sanyo Shinbun. June 28, 2002.

Sato, Masanori (1982). "Meiji Chiho Jichi to Mura" (Meiji Local Autonomy and Villages). In *Kindai Nihon no Togo to Teiko* (Integration and Resistance in Modern Japan). Vol. 1, eds. Kano Masanao and Yui Masaomi, Tokyo: Nihon Hyoronsha.

Saunders, Peter (1984). "Rethinking Local Politics." In *Local Socialism? Labour Councils and New Left Alternatives,* eds. Martin Boddy and Colin Fudge. London: Macmillan.

——— (1986). *Social Theory and the Urban Questions.* 2nd ed. New York: Homes & Meier.

Schmitter, Philippe C. (1997). "Civil Society East and West." In *Consolidating the Third Wave Democracies: Themes and Perspectives,* eds. Larry Diamond, Marc F. Plattner, Yun-han Chu, and Hung-mao Tien. Baltimore: Johns Hopkins University Press.

Schwartz, Frank (2003). "What Is Civil Society?" In *The State of Civil Society in Japan*, eds. Frank Schwartz and Susan Pharr. Cambridge: Cambridge University Press.

Shea, Wing Man (2000). "Electronic Government: Government Utilisation of Internet Technologies in Hong Kong and Singapore." Postgraduate dissertation, August, London School of Economics and Political Science.

Shindo, Kumiko (2004). *Jenda de Yomu Nihon Seiji* (Gendering Japanese Politics). Tokyo: Yuhikaku.

Shindo, Mumeyuki (1985). "Yawarakana Shuken Taisei no Kiro" (Soft Centralization at Crossroads). *Sekai* 476: 22–34.

Shiohira, Yoshikazu (1997). "Okinawa, Kenmin Tohyo, Sonogo" (Okinawa, the Prefectural Referendum, and Thereafter). *Toshi Mondai* 88, no. 2 (February): 67–78.

Shizen Hogo Nenkan Henshuiinkai, ed. (1992 and 1996). *Shizen Hogo Nenkan* (Natural Environment Protection Yearbook). Tokyo: Nishosha.

Singapore, Infocomm Development Agency (2003). *Connected Singapore—A New Blueprint for Infocomm Development.* http://www.ida.gov.sg/ (accessed July 2003).

Smith, Thomas C. (1959). *The Agrarian Origins of Modern Japan.* Stanford: Stanford University Press.

Soysal, Yasemin Nuhoglu (1994). *Limits of Citizenship: Migrants and Postnational Membership in Europe.* Chicago: Chicago University Press.

Steiner , Kurt (1965). *Local Government in Japan.* Stanford: Stanford University Press.

Stockwin, J. A. A. (1999). *Governing Japan: Divided Politics in a Major Economy.* 3rd ed. Oxford: Blackwell.

Study Group for Long-Term Strategies on the Vitalization of Local Administration (1987). *Local Autonomy in the Twenty-First Century.* Tokyo: Study Group for Long-Term Strategies on the Vitalization of Local Administration.

Suh, Yong-Dal, ed. (1987). *Kankoku/Chosenjin no Genjo to Mirai* (The Situation and Future of South and North Koreans). Tokyo: Hyoronsha.

——— (2001). "Naze Ima Teijyugaikokujin ka" (Why Now Permanent Alien Residents?). *Ushio*, no. 503 (January): 148–53.

Sumizawa, Hiroki (1998). "Minshushugi no Yukue" (Pathways to Democracy). *NIRA Policy Research* 11, no. 9 (September): 8–15.

Swank, Duane (1999). "Social Democratic Welfare States in a Global Economy: Scandinavia in Comparative Perspective." In *Globalization, Europeanization and the End of Scandinavian Social Democracy?* eds. Robert Geyer, Christine Ingebritsen, and Jonathon Moses. London: Macmillan.

Takafuji, Akira (1996). "Gaikokujin to Shakai Hosho" (Foreigners and the Social Security). *Toshi Mondai* 87, no. 2 (February): 3–13.

Takahashi, Makoto, and Yorimoto Katsumi (1985). "Chiho Kofuzei no Yakuwari to Kadai o Kiku" (Inquiries about the Role and Task of the Local Allocation Tax). *Gekkan Jichiken* 27: 28–37.

Takao, Yasuo (1998). "Participatory Democracy in Japan's Decentralization Drive." *Asian Survey* 38, no. 10 (October): 950–67.

——— (1998). "The Welfare State and Its Effect on Municipal Government in Japan: A Case Study." *Modern Asian Studies* 32, no. 4 (October): 985–1016.

——— (1999). *National Integration and Local Power in Japan.* Aldershot: Ashgate.

——— (1999). "Welfare State Retrenchment: The Case of Japan." *Journal of Public Policy* 19, no. 3 (September–December): 274–75.

——— (2001). "The Rise of the 'Third Sector' in Japan." *Asian Survey* 41, no. 2: 290–309.

——— (2004). "Democratic Renewal by 'Digital' Local Government in Japan." *Pacific Affairs* 77, no. 2 (Summer): 255–56.

Takeda, Shin'ichiro (1993). "Jumin Tohyo o Meguru Hoteki Mondai" (Legal Problems Surrounding the Local Referendum). *Horitsu no Hiroba* 46, no. 6 (June): 25–34.

Tanioka, Ichiro et al. (2002 and 2003). *Japanese General Social Survey (JGSS), 2000 and 2001* [Computer file]. Osaka: Osaka University of Commerce, Office of Japanese General Social Surveys.

Taylor, Marilyn, Joan Langan, and Paul Hoggett (1995). *Encouraging Diversity: Voluntary and Private Organizations in Community Care.* Gower House, UK: Arena.

Teramachi, Midori (2006). "Shiminha Seiji to Josei Giin" (Citizen-based Politics and Women Representatives), *Toshi Mondai* 97, no. 1 (January): 14–17.

Tezuka, Naoki (2001). "Dejitaru Demokurashi" (Digital Democracy). *Chiiki Seisaku Kenkyu* 15 (June): 21–24.

Tocqueville, Alexis de (2000). *Democracy in America*, trans. Harvey C. Mansfield and Delba Winthrop. Chicago: University of Chicago Press.

Tokyo Citizens' Network (TCN) (2003). *Roteshon Giin ga Machi o Tsukuru* (Rotation Representatives Build the Town). Tokyo: Tokyo Citizens' Network.

——— (2003). *Tokyo Seikastusha Netowaku no Yobikake: Kihon Seisaku* (Appeal by Tokyo Citizens' Network: Basic Policies). Tokyo: Tokyo Citizens' Network.

——— (2004). *Tosei o Kaeru Seikatsusha Netowaku no Shigoto* (Citizens' Networking for Changing the Metropolitan Governance). Tokyo: Tokyo Citizens' Network.

Tokyo Metropolitan Government, Bureau of Citizens and Cultural Affairs (TBCCA) (2004) *Tokyo-to no Joho Kokai* (Information Disclosure by Tokyo Metropolitan Government). Tokyo: Tokyo Metropolitan Government.

Tokyo Shinbun (Yokohama edition). January 9.

Tokyo Shisei Chosakai, ed. (1940). *Jichi Gojunenshi: Seido Hen* (A Fifty-Year History of Local Autonomy: The Volume of Institutions). Tokyo: Ryosho Fukkyukai.

Torigoe, Hiroyuki (2001). "Borantari-na Koi to Shakai Chitsujo" (Voluntary Action and Social Order). Paper presented at the First Conference for the Integrate Study of Future Generations, Kyoto, February 3–4.

Toshi Mondai (1996). "Jumin Tohyo: Tokushu" (Local Referenda: Special Issue) 87, no. 1 (January).

Toshitani, Nobuyoshi (1962). "Kenpo Dai-Kyujo to Kokumin no Hoishiki" (Article 9 and the Legal Consciousness of the Public). *Shiso*, no. 457 (June): 1–23.

Tsujinaka, Yutaka (1999). "NPO/NGO no Jidai to Chikyu Nettowaku Gata Seiji Katei no Tojo" (The Emergence of Global Network-Oriented Political Processes in the Era of NPOs and NGOs). *NIRA Policy Research* 12, no. 3 (March): 39–42.

———— (2003). "From Developmentalism to Maturity: Japan's Civil Society Organizations in Comparative Perspective." In *The State of Civil Society in Japan*, eds. Frank Schwartz and Susan Pharr. Cambridge: Cambridge University Press.

Ueda, Michiaki (2005). "Jumin Tohyo no Kako Genzai Mirai" (The Past, Present, Future of Local Referenda). *Information Services*, no. 51 http://www.jilg.jp/iservice/info51_1.html (accessed August 2005).

UNISYS e-Japan News. March 31, 2004.

United Nations Development Programme (UNDP) (2005). *Human Development Report 2005*. New York: UNDP.

United Nations, Division for Public Economics and Public Administration (2003). *Benchmarking E-government: A Global Perspective*. http://unpan1.un.org/intradoc/groups/public/documents/un/unpan003984.pdf (accessed July 2004).

United Nations Online Network in Public Administration (2004). "United Nations Global E-Government Readiness Report 2004." http://www.unpan.org/egovernment4.asp (last August 2005).

United Nations, Population Division (2000). *Replacement Migration: Is It a Solution to Declining and Ageing Populations?* http://www.un.org/esa/population/publications/ReplMigED/migration.htm (accessed August 2005).

United States, General Services Administration (2000). *US Government's Official Web Portal*. http://www.first.gov/ (accessed July 2003).

Uphoff, Norman (1996). "Why NGOs Are Not a Third Sector: A Sectoral Analysis with Some Thoughts on Accountability, Sustainability and Evaluation." In *Beyond the Magic Bullet: NGO Performance and Accountability in the Post-Cold War World*, eds. Michael Edwards and David Hume. West Hartford, CT: Kumarian Press.

Vallance, Elizabeth (1979). *Women in the House: A Study of Women Members of Parliament*. London: Athlone Press.

———— (1984). "Women Candidates in the 1983 General Election." *Parliamentary Affairs* 37, no. 3: 301–9.

van de Donk, W. B. H. J. et al. (1995). "Digitalizing Decision Making in a Democracy: For the Better or For the Worse." In *Orwell in Athens: A Perspective on Information and Democracy*, eds. W. B. H. J. van de Donk, I. Th. M. Shellen, and P. W. Tops. Amsterdam: IOS Press.

Van Ours, Jan (1990). "An International Comparative Study on Job Mobility." *Labour* 4, no. 3: 33–55.

Volunteer worker for organization LET'S (2004). Interview by the author on June 12, 2004.

Watanuki, Joji (1967). "Patterns of Politics in Present-Day Japan." In *Party Systems and Voter Alignments: Cross-National Perspectives,* eds. Seymour M. Lipset and Stein Rokkan. New York: Free Press.

Weaver, Kent R. (1986). "The Politics of Blame Avoidance." *Journal of Public Policy* 6, no. 4: 371–98.

Weber, Max (1968). *Economy and Society,* trans. Talcott Parsons et al. New York: Bedminster.

Welch, Susan, and Donley Studlar (1990). "Multi-Member Districts and the Representation of Women: Evidence from Britain and the United States." *Journal of Politics* 52, no. 2 (May): 391–412.

Wildavsky, Aaron (1975). *Budgeting: A Comparative Theory of Budgeting Processes.* Boston: Little, Brown.

Wlezien, Christopher (1995). "The Public as Themostat: Dynamics of Preferences for Spending." *American Journal of Political Science* 39, no. 4 (November): 981–1000.

Women and Politics Campaign Office (WPCO) (1999). *Women and Politics Campaign 1999 Report.* Tokyo: Women and Politics Campaign Office.

Woolcock, Michael (1998). "Social Capital and Economic Development: Towards a Theoretical Synthesis and Policy Framework." *Theory and Society* 27: 151–208.

World Bank (1997). *World Bank Development Report 1997: The State in a Changing World.* Oxford: Oxford University Press.

World Economic Forum (2004). *Global Information Technology Report 2003–2004.* New York: Oxford University Press.

Yamada, Takao (1996). "Zainichi Gaikokujin to Fukushi" (Foreign Residents in Japan and Welfare). *Toshi Mondai* 87, no. 2 (February): 35–47.

——— (1998). "Kawasaki ni okeru Gaikokujin tono Kyosei no Machizukuri no Taido" (Signs of Town-Making Coexistent with Foreigners in Kawasaki). *Toshi Mondai* 89, no. 6 (June): 53–66.

——— (2004). Municipal government official of Kawasaki. Interview by the author on July 15.

Yamaguchi, Mitsuko (2006). Executive Director, Ichikawa Fusae Memorial Association. Interview by the author on April 21.

Yamaguchi, Tetsuo (1993). "Kyujusan-nendo Kokka Yosan no Bunseki to Mondaiten" (Analysis and Problems of FY 1993 National Budget). *Chiho Seiji* 400 (April): 11–13.

Yamamoto, Tadashi (1998). "Nihon no Shibiru Sosaete no Hatten to Gabanansu e no Eikyo" (Developments in Japan's Civil Society and its Impact on Governance). In *Kan kara Min e no Pawa Shifuto* (Power Shifts from "Public" to "Private"), eds. Yamamoto Tadashi et al. Tokyo: TBS Britannica.

Yamaoka, Yoshinori (2000). Interview by the author on June 26.

Yamashita, Yasuko (1993). "The International Movements toward Gender Equality and its Impact on Japan." *US-Japan Women's Journal.* English Supplement no. 5 (July): 35–51.

Yamauchi, Naoto, ed. (1999). *Nonprofit Organization Data Book.* Tokyo: Yuhikaku.

Yokota, Shozo (1992). "Kyujuni-nendo Chiho Zaisei Keikaku no Naiyo to Mondaiten" (Contents and Problems of FY 1992 Local Fiscal Plan). *Chiho Seiji* 386 (March): 34–36.

Yomiuri Shinbun. August 15, 1953; August 15, 1965; August 15, 1966; August 15, 1992; April 6, 1995; April 9, 1996; June 21, 1996; May 17, 1998; September 9, 1999; September 23, 2000; November 25, 2000; August 8, 2002; March 17, 2004; April 2; 2004.

Yorimoto, Katsumi (1994). "Jichitai no Ishiki Keisei to Jumin Tohyo" (The Formation of Local Entities' Intention and Referendum). *Gekkan Jichiken*, 36, no. 416 (May): 31–32.

Za Giin (2004). "Giin Ankeito Kekka Vol. 4" (Results of Diet Members Survey). http://www.giin-net.com/genq_vo14.html (accessed February 2004).

Index